Women and the Autobiographical Impulse

Women and the Autobiographical Impulse

A History

Barbara Caine

BLOOMSBURY ACADEMIC
LONDON • NEW YORK • OXFORD • NEW DELHI • SYDNEY

BLOOMSBURY ACADEMIC
Bloomsbury Publishing Plc
50 Bedford Square, London, WC1B 3DP, UK
1385 Broadway, New York, NY 10018, USA
29 Earlsfort Terrace, Dublin 2, Ireland

BLOOMSBURY, BLOOMSBURY ACADEMIC and the Diana logo are trademarks
of Bloomsbury Publishing Plc

First published in Great Britain 2023

Copyright © Barbara Caine, 2023

Barbara Caine has asserted her right under the Copyright, Designs and Patents Act, 1988, to be identified as Author of this work.

For legal purposes the Acknowledgements on p. vii constitute an extension of this copyright page.

Cover image © Cover images: Laetitia Pilkington (1712–1750), Wikimedia; Harriet Martineau (1802–1876), Spencer Arnold Collection/Hulton Archive/Getty Images. Annie Kenney (1879–1953), Topical Press Agency/Hulton Archive/Getty Images. Margaret Storm Jameson, Culture Club/Getty Images. Buchi Emecheta (1944–2017), Juliet Highet/Art Directors/Alamy Stock Photo.

All rights reserved. No part of this publication may be reproduced or transmitted in any form or by any means, electronic or mechanical, including photocopying, recording, or any information storage or retrieval system, without prior permission in writing from the publishers.

Bloomsbury Publishing Plc does not have any control over, or responsibility for, any third-party websites referred to or in this book. All internet addresses given in this book were correct at the time of going to press. The author and publisher regret any inconvenience caused if addresses have changed or sites have ceased to exist, but can accept no responsibility for any such changes.

A catalogue record for this book is available from the British Library.

Library of Congress Cataloging-in-Publication Data
Names: Caine, Barbara, author.
Title: Women and the autobiographical impulse : a history / Barbara Caine.
Description: London ; New York : Bloomsbury Academic, 2023. | Includes bibliographical references and index. | Summary: "Esteemed historian Barbara Caine skilfully produces an overview of British women's autobiographies over three centuries, showing important changes in motivation, context, style, and life experiences"– Provided by publisher.
Identifiers: LCCN 2023022774 (print) | LCCN 2023022775 (ebook) | ISBN 9781350237612 (hb) | ISBN 9781350237629 (pb) | ISBN 9781350237636 (epdf) | ISBN 9781350237643 (ebook)
Subjects: LCSH: Autobiography–Women authors. | Women–England–Biography–History and criticism. | England–Biography–History and criticism.
Classification: LCC CT25 .C33 2023 (print) | LCC CT25 (ebook) | DDC 941.0099–dc23/eng/20230523
LC record available at https://lccn.loc.gov/2023022774
LC ebook record available at https://lccn.loc.gov/2023022775

ISBN:	HB:	978-1-3502-3761-2
	PB:	978-1-3502-3762-9
	ePDF:	978-1-3502-3763-6
	eBook:	978-1-3502-3764-3

Typeset by RefineCatch Limited, Bungay, Suffolk
Printed and bound in Great Britain

To find out more about our authors and books visit www.bloomsbury.com and sign up for our newsletters.

CONTENTS

List of Illustrations vi
Acknowledgements vii

   Introduction 1
1 Transgressive Women and the Origins of
   Secular Autobiography 19
2 Women's Autobiography Comes of Age 57
3 Autobiography as a Form of History 109
4 The Personal is Political 163
5 Autobiography in the Wider British World 219
   Epilogue 261

Bibliography 267
Index 279

ILLUSTRATIONS

1. Courtesan and adventuress Teresia Constantia Phillips (1709–1765), later Teresia Muilman, 1748. From a mezzotint engraving by John Faber Jr. after Joseph Highmore. (Photo by Hulton Archive/Getty Images.) — 18
2. Engraving after Harriet Martineau by Alonzo Chappel. (Photo by Hulton-Deutsch / Hulton-Deutsch Collection / Corbis via Getty Images.) — 56
3. Circa 1910: Fabian socialist thinker, historian, economist and writer Beatrice Webb (1858–1943). (Photo by Hulton Archive/Getty Images.) — 108
4. British novelist Doris Lessing in her north London flat, March 2003. (Photo by John Downing/Getty Images.) — 162
5. Sindiwe Magona, Festival Atlantide 2021, Nantes. (Courtesy of Wikimedia Commons.) — 218

ACKNOWLEDGEMENTS

Several institutions have been very helpful in the writing of this book. First amongst them is the Australian Research Council and I would like to acknowledge the Professorial Fellowship I was awarded in 2008 while I was still at Monash University, which enabled me to begin work on it. Subsequently, periods of research and study leave at the University of Sydney helped immensely in getting the book written. Sections of the book have been given as papers in too many seminars and conferences to list, but I thank all those who have listened to them and offered comments.

Friends and former colleagues have played a major part in how I framed and wrote this book. Clare Monagle, David Garrioch and Carolyn James are particularly important here. The approach that we developed for our collaborative history of European women's letters provided an invaluable model for how to approach the history of women's autobiography too. Clare Monagle was not only key to that project but has also read several chapters of this book and I thank her for her generous reading and many insightful and imaginative suggestions.

Other friends and family have offered invaluable help and support along the way. My greatest debt is to Pauline Nestor whose careful and critical reading of the whole draft was invaluable. Not only did she point out major problems in each chapter, but always had suggestions for how to resolve them. The generous hospitality that Sophie Watson and Sally Alexander provided in London made all my research trips a great pleasure and I thank them also for their interest in this project and for many wonderful and helpful conversations about it. Moira Gatens, Glenda Sluga and Diana Caine have helped me work through some of the particular problems the book posed. I thank Sally Murray and Hannah Kay for their helpful comments on several chapters. Larry Boyd has lived with this book for a number of years and I thank him for the equanimity with which he has done so and dealt with the lows as well as the highs in the writing process.

Introduction

'I was thinking the other night', Virginia Woolf wrote in a letter to the composer and suffragist Ethel Smyth in 1940, 'that there's never been a woman's autobiography. Nothing to compare with Rousseau. Chastity and modesty, I suppose have been the reason.'[1] Woolf's sweeping dismissal of women's autobiography comes as something of a shock. She had read many women's autobiographies, published essays on several and noted the impact on her of some contemporary ones in her diary. She found it impossible to put down Vera Brittain's *Testament of Youth*, for example, commented more than once on how Beatrice Webb's *My Apprenticeship* 'has made me think a little what I could say of my own life'.[2] Yet somehow, even for one who had written so extensively and insightfully about other women writers and about the many different forms of oppression and marginalization they had experienced, when it came to autobiography, it was Rousseau who set the standard, and no woman had yet measured up to it. What Woolf found particularly lacking in the memoirs and autobiographies that women had published to date and what she hoped to see in Smyth's autobiography, was 'an analysis of your sex life. As Rousseau did his. More introspection. More intimacy'.

In making Rousseau the standard by which to judge a woman's autobiography, Woolf was endorsing the canonical status of Rousseau's *Confessions* within the history of autobiography and at the same time underlining the difficulties that women faced in establishing the alternative approach that many of them had taken in writing their life stories. Then as now, Rousseau's *Confessions* were seen as one of the founding texts, indeed

---

[1] Virginia Woolf to Ethel Smyth, 24 December 1940, in *The Letters of Virginia Woolf*, vol. VI, ed. Nigel Nicolson (London: The Hogarth Press, 1980), p. 453.
[2] Anne Olivier Bell, ed., *The Diary of Virginia Woolf* (London: Penguin Books, 1982). Vol. 3, 22 Feb 1926, p. 60.

for some *the* founding text, of modern secular autobiography.[3] Prior to its publication in the late 18th century, most autobiographical writing had focused on spiritual experience or religious conversion. By contrast, Rousseau was concerned to explore himself, his experiences and his feelings. He was aware of the novelty of his approach and insisted on the uniqueness and importance of his autobiography in his very first sentence. 'I have entered upon a performance which is without example, whose accomplishment will have no imitator,' he wrote.

> I mean to present my fellow-mortals with a man in all the integrity of nature; and this man shall be myself.
>
> I know my heart and have studied mankind; I am not made like anyone I have been acquainted with, perhaps like no one in existence; if not better, I at least claim originality, and whether Nature did wisely in breaking the mould with which she formed me, can only be determined after having read this work.[4]

That Woolf should have regarded the detail Rousseau offered about his sexual experiences and feelings as particularly valuable is not surprising for one enmeshed, as she was, in the Bloomsbury group with its fascination with questions about sexuality in all its forms. Others were rather more critical of this aspect of Rousseau's work, however, and found it extremely discomforting. His openness, even about the perverse aspects of his sexuality, was amongst the things that made British readers question the value and merits of the *Confessions* in the late 18th century and prevented it from being taken as a model when autobiography was becoming established in the 19th.[5] Nonetheless, his importance as a philosopher ensured that the work was widely read, and many aspects of his approach became accepted as the central core of modern autobiography. Amongst the most significant are his division of his life into separate stages, beginning with childhood, his focus on his feelings and subjectivity, his introspection and reflection on his intellectual development and his sense of his own individuality.

Introspection and reflection on the development of an individual's sense of autonomous selfhood were particularly important issues in the history of autobiography. They were seen as its defining characteristics when

---

[3]See for example, Huntington William, *Rousseau and Romantic Autobiography* (Oxford: Oxford University Press, 1983); James Treadwell, 'The Case of Rousseau' in his *Autobiographical Writing and British Literature* (Oxford: Oxford University Press, 2005); Peter Abbs, 'The Full Revelation of the Self: Jean Jacques Rousseau and the Origin of Deep Autobiography', *Philosophy Now* 68 (July/August, 2008).
[4]Jean Jacques Rousseau, *Confessions* (Launette Aux Deux-Ponts, 1782–1789). Although completed in 1769, the work was not published until 1782, four years after his death.
[5]Phyllis Grosskurth, 'Where Was Rousseau?' in *Approaches to Victorian Autobiography*, ed. George P. Landow (Athens, Ohio: Ohio University Press, 1979).

autobiography became the subject of serious scholarly attention in the 1950s and '60s. Georges Gusdorf, one of the pioneering figures in this field, emphasized this point in his essay 'The Conditions and Limits of Autobiography' that served as a foundational text of autobiographical studies. Autobiography, he insisted, is not so much a literary form as a kind of consciousness. It demanded a conscious awareness of the singularity of each individual life as well as a sense of history and of human agency. Above all, it required the capacity for introspection and reflection in order to make a life story into a coherent narrative.[6] Memory was important for autobiography, but it had to be transformed through introspection. An autobiography required not simply the telling of a life story, but its re-examination. It offered a second reading of experience with perspective and self-consciousness added.

For Gusdorf and his followers, as this definition makes clear, autobiography was an exclusively masculine endeavour. It was only men who could combine recognition of the singularity of themselves as individuals with a sense of history and of agency. Until relatively recently, the legal, social and economic dependence of women made it all but impossible for them to see themselves in this light. When one gets down to detail, moreover, Gusdorf's definition excludes women not only as the authors of autobiography but also as significant figures in the autobiographies of men. While he insists that autobiography requires discussion of both public and private or inner life, his definition of 'private life' does not encompass family or home. On the contrary, in his definition 'private life' refers to an individual's reflections on intellectual, religious and moral questions. There is no place in his approach to autobiography for discussion of the intimate, familial or domestic life that is so important for most women. The exclusion of women is made absolutely definitive by the autobiographical canon that Gusdorf and his followers set out, beginning with Augustine's *Confessions*, and including Montaigne's *Essais*, Rousseau's *Confessions* and Newman's *Apologia*.

The importance of individualism and autonomy have been seen as crucial, not only in definitions of autobiography, but also in defining modern identity which has often been linked to the emergence of autobiography.[7] In Britain, where autobiography was firmly established in the 19th century, it is the canonical Victorian autobiographies of Thomas Carlyle, J. H. Newman and John Stuart Mill that are often taken as the best illustrations of the intense struggle that modern individuals underwent to gain and assert this autonomy. The framework for this struggle was provided by the crisis of belief which was so prominent a feature of Victorian intellectual life. Their loss of religious faith and the emotional and spiritual crisis that this involved

---

[6]Georges Gusdorf, 'Conditions and Limits of Autobiography (1956)', in *Autobiography: Essays Theoretical and Critical*, ed. James Olney (Princeton: Princeton University Press, 1980).
[7]See for example Charles Taylor, 'The Politics of Recognition', in *Multiculturalism and 'The Politics of Recognition'*, ed. Amy Gutmann (Princeton: Princeton University Press, 1992).

dominated the adolescent and early adult life of many Victorian intellectuals and writers until it was more or less resolved by finding the new forms of belief and activity that allowed an independent adult life. This religious struggle was articulated powerfully in semi-fictional form in Carlyle's *Sartor Resartus*, but directly and in relation to their own lives by Newman, J. A. Froude and many others. It had a secular counterpart in the autobiography of John Stuart Mill who described eloquently the emotional and intellectual crisis he faced when he ceased being able to accept the utilitarianism of his father.[8] In all of these cases, the struggle is depicted as one that the author underwent alone, sometimes helped by reading particular books, but never with human assistance. On the contrary, one essential part of it is the need to separate from families and communities with whom the author can no longer identify – and to become dependent only on himself.[9]

Gusdorf saw individualism and autonomy as not only important to autobiography but admirable. These qualities have been questioned and looked at much more critically in recent decades, however. Feminist and postcolonial scholars have pointed not only to the gendered assumptions on which they are based but also to their racist and imperialist ones as only Western men seem to have regarded themselves in this way. Gusdorf regarded autobiography as expressing 'a concern peculiar to Western man, a concern that has been of good use in his systematic conquest of the universe', but saw this as unproblematic.[10] He was not concerned that this way of thinking about and representing oneself was not only alien to but impossible for most women and for men of many other cultures for whom a sense of identity is established through relationships with others. Later scholars have questioned whether these qualities are possible even for Western men. John Paul Eakin, for example, insists that this notion of autonomy is a myth. Autobiography, he argues, 'promotes an illusion of self-determination: *I* write my story; *I* say who I am; *I* create myself'. This form enables and even encourages people to forget the extent to which the self is defined by and lived in terms of its relation to others.[11] Approaching the question from a slightly different angle in looking particularly at 19th-century men's autobiographies, Martin Danahay has argued that, in the process of representing their emergence as autonomous individuals, the authors of these works repressed the social

---

[8] See for example Richard Hughes Gibson and Timothy Larsen, 'Nineteenth-Century Spiritual Autobiography: Carlyle, Newman, Mill', in *A History of English Autobiography*, ed. Adam Smyth (Cambridge: Cambridge University Press, 2016).
[9] Deborah Nord has argued that in many cases, these were oedipal struggles centring upon the relationship of the author with his father – something they were reluctant to acknowledge. Deborah Epstein Nord, 'Victorian Autobiography: Sons and Fathers', in *The Cambridge Companion to Autobiography*, eds Maria di Battista and Emily O. Wittman (Cambridge: Cambridge University Press, 2014).
[10] Gusdorf, p. 29.
[11] John Paul Eakin, *How Our Lives Become Stories* (London and Ithaca: Cornell University Press, 1999), p. 44.

context of their lives and silence and ignored the women on whom their lives often depended.[12] Drawing on Bakhtin, Danahay argues that Victorian male autobiographers created monologic rather than dialogic texts which involved 'repressing other voices as the author seeks mastery over the contingent'.

Not only did these autobiographers repress the general social and familial context of their lives and work, but they silenced the particular women on whose labour they have often drawn and depended. Wordsworth's *Prelude*, for example, like much of his writing, drew extensively on the diaries of his sister Dorothy who is never acknowledged. John Stuart Mill is a particular target for Danahay. Mill is notable here because of his support for some aspects of Victorian feminism and his heroic status amongst some 19th-century feminists. His autobiography, however, excludes any reference or even mention of his mother, depicting his father as the dominating figure in his education and in framing his intellectual and professional life. Mill did acknowledge the importance of his wife, Harriet Taylor Mill, in both his intellectual and emotional life. This acknowledgement itself has been subject to harsh criticism, however, because of the way in which he conflated Harriet Taylor's words with his own and, as Danahay sees it, 'effectively erases her as a separate consciousness'. His exaggerated praise of Taylor as his intellectual superior and guide has led to much discussion of whether she actually wrote some of his texts. In Danahay's view, 'Mill's hyperbolic descriptions of Taylor reveal her as the overdetermined site of his own fantasies'.

This erasure of family life and of the women on whom they depended, was not only evident in a few canonical works but widespread in Victorian middle-class male autobiography generally. Donna Loftus sees it as the dominant approach in the fifty autobiographies of businessmen, clergymen, lawyers, doctors and civil servants writing between 1850 and 1914 that she studied. Generally, she found that the narratives began with accounts of ancestral heritage followed by descriptions of the author's birth, childhood, education and introduction to a profession. But women were not part of these lives.

> Overwhelmingly, female relations were silenced and masculinity was defined through relations with other men. These often cliched accounts nevertheless demonstrated an ontology that saw the self emerging out of childhood struggles, to face the challenges and battles that defined early manhood, and the security that rewarded success. This emergent self, however, was plotted through the narrated significance of relationships with family, friends, colleagues and a network of like-minded men.[13]

---

[12]Martin Danahay, *A Community of One: Masculine Autobiography and Autonomy in Nineteenth-Century Britain* (New York: State University of New York Press, 1993).
[13]Donna Loftus, 'The Self in Society: Middle-Class Men and Autobiography', in *Life Writing and Victorian Culture*, ed. David Amigoni (London: Routledge, 2006; reprint, e-book 2017).

Although ignored in the foundational writings of autobiographical studies, women have been writing their own life stories and autobiographies for centuries. They too have a long history of spiritual autobiography, with secular ones first appearing in the mid-18th century, even before Rousseau, and then increasing in number and changing in form until the present. The writing of an autobiography was both difficult and risky for women, especially in the 18th and 19th centuries, when the accepted beliefs about modesty and chastity that Woolf refers to not only prevented women from writing about their intimate lives but indeed prevented them from drawing attention to themselves at all. Ideas of feminine propriety required them to immerse themselves in the world of family and home and not to court publicity. The very notions here of a 'public man', generally meaning one who engaged in political and public causes, and a 'public woman', generally meaning a prostitute, illustrates this point well. Rousseau could write quite openly about his sexual feelings and experience, his many failings and his 'reprehensible conduct' in abandoning his children, without any suggestion that such concessions might stop him from being widely read or considered a major philosopher. By contrast, as Woolf suggests, at least until the mid-20th century, any discussion of sexual behaviour, and particularly of sexual indiscretion or irregularity, by women in an autobiography invited opprobrium and social ostracism. This disapproval of any hint of unconventional behaviour in women helps to explain why some of the great women novelists, like George Eliot, for example, refused to write their life stories. Eliot knew only too well the social and personal cost of her contravening the norms of sexual propriety, and though she considered writing an autobiography from time to time, she always ended up finding the idea repellent.[14]

When women did begin to write their own life stories, they did not take the form expected of a male autobiography. In place of a childhood dominated by education and widening social experiences, an adulthood organized around a profession and public or intellectual and a quest for autonomy throughout, women's autobiographies usually stressed the importance of family life, including relationships with parents, especially mothers. Almost every aspect of their lives, including their education, was often dominated by family as were the gendered social expectations that framed their lives and often circumscribed their activities. In the 19th and 20th centuries, some women described how they struggled for and gained independence, but even then their social and emotional world and their parental and familial ties remained central in their lives.

In part as a consequence of these differences, little attention was paid to women's life writings, until feminist scholars began to read them in the late

---

[14]Valerie Sanders, *The Private Lives of Victorian Women: Autobiography in Nineteenth-Century England* (New York: St Martin's Press, 1989), p. 17.

1970s. Estelle Jelinek, editor of one of the first collections of essays on women's autobiography, explains in her *Preface* how the idea for this collection 'came to me in 1976 when I was writing my dissertation on the tradition of women's autobiography. I found practically no criticism on women's autobiographies, except for that on Gertrude Stein's.'[15] Jelinek began a discussion that continued amongst feminist scholars for some time, focusing not just on how comprehensive the exclusion of women was from the existing scholarship on autobiography, but also on how to establish and clarify the ways in which women's autobiographies differed from those of men. While a man's autobiography is expected to provide 'a mirror of his era', Jelinek argued, women's autobiographies are less likely to do so. They tend to focus more on intimate lives and domestic relationships than on public activities, to say less about the author's own public activity than men do, and to be less introspective. Above all, women's lives tend to lack the clear structure or progression of men's lives. Few had the lengthy formal education that for men preceded a career, and their lives were usually interrupted, or dominated, by marriage, childbearing and a range of other personal and familial demands. This did not mean that women did not write their own life stories, which exist in abundance. The question that needed to be addressed, Jelinek suggested, was rather how women set about writing autobiographies in different ways from those of men.

Just as Jelinek was raising these issues, a different way of thinking about women's autobiography was suggested by Mary Mason who took issue directly with the idea of the autonomous individual as the subject of autobiography. In an influential article titled 'The Other Voice in Women's Autobiography', Mason argued that, in contrast to men, for whom it was usually done in isolation, for women the process of self-discovery was often linked to some 'other' closely connected consciousness. It was this sense of close connection that seemed to enable women to write openly about themselves. The 'other voice' could take different forms: in the early modern period, it was sometimes a transcendent voice, or one belonging to a group or collectivity, such as a small religious community. But it could also be that of a beloved husband or partner. One could still see the importance of this 'other voice', Mason argued, amongst a number of prominent 20th-century women autobiographers, including Beatrice Webb and Simone de Beauvoir.[16] However, not all women's autobiographies conform to this pattern.

The work of Jelinek and Mason was followed by several other attempts to define or establish a distinctive pattern for analysing and understanding women's autobiographies, including suggestions that different terms be used

---

[15] Estelle C. Jelinek, *The Tradition of Women's Autobiography: From Antiquity to the Present* (Boston: Twayne Publishers, 1986), p. iii.
[16] Mary G. Mason, 'The Other Voice: Autobiographies of Women Writers', in *Life/Lines Theorizing Women's Autobiography*, eds Bella Brodzki and Celeste Schenk (Ithaca and London, Cornell University Press, 1988), pp. 19–44.

to describe them such as 'autogynography'.[17] Like Mason's, however, all of these attempts to find a particular way to approach women's autobiography ended up confronting the same problem: the impossibility of finding some essential quality that encompassed all women's experiences and subjectivity and determined the ways in which they wrote their life stories. The 'other voice' might have been important for Beatrice Webb, for example, but it has no place in the autobiographies of Harriet Martineau or Vera Brittain. Indeed, the minute one begins to read different women's autobiographies, it becomes clear that there are considerable differences between them and that no single gendered approach fits them all. While many women do address their intimate and family lives, for example, it is simply not the case that all women prefer to dwell on their personal rather than on their professional or public lives. In a similar way, while the lives of some women are structured around marriage, childcare and family demands, the lives of others share much more of the clear structure of education and employment deployed by men. Rather than seeking a model for women's autobiography, a later generation of feminist scholars argued, what was needed was rather a recognition of its diversity.[18] It was necessary also to critique the narrowness and restrictiveness of prevailing ideas about men's autobiography.[19] The model of Gusdorf and his followers failed to apply not only to the writings of women but to those of many men as well, especially those of different ethnicities. In place of the prescriptive conception that had emerged in some Western scholarship, a broader notion of autobiography was needed that could encompass the many different ways in which women – as well as some men – have written their own life stories. And indeed, as one can see in much recent scholarship on autobiography, broader conceptions of the field that encompass diversity in terms of the nature of the subject and of the form have come increasingly to be accepted.

This broader conception of the nature of autobiographical writing is fundamental to this study, to my own exploration of the history of women's autobiographies and of how they have changed over the past two and a half centuries. These changes include the kinds of women who wrote autobiography, the ways in which they wrote and produced their books, and how their lives were framed and depicted in them. Developments in women's autobiography also reflect wider historical change: the expansion in the

---

[17]Domna C. Stanton, 'Autogynography: Is the Subject Different', in *The Female Autograph*, ed. Domna C. Stanton (Chicago and London: University of Chicago Press, 1984); Susan Stanford Friedman, 'Women's Autobiographical Selves: Theory and Practice', in *The Private Self: Theory and Practice of Women's Autobiographical Writings*, ed. Shari Benstock (Chapel Hill and London: University of North Carolina Press, 1988).

[18]Sidonie Smith, *Subjectivity, Identity, and the Body: Women's Autobiographical Practices in the Twentieth Century* (Bloomington: Indiana University Press, 1993).

[19]James Olney, ed. *Autobiography: Essays Theoretical and Critical* (Princeton University Press, 1980).

educational opportunities available to women and their growing political involvement as well as changing ideas, assumptions and expectations about femininity and 'appropriate' female conduct and expression. Thus, the establishment of a career as a journalist and writer is an important aspect of some 19th-century women's autobiographies, while involvement in the militant suffrage movement or in national and international politics feature prominently in the 20th century. There were also changes in how the different phases of life were depicted in women's autobiographies. The narration of childhood, which was dealt with only briefly in eighteenth-century autobiographies assumed ever greater importance in the 19th and 20th centuries, under the influences of Romanticism, new approaches to pedagogy and then the growing interest in psychology.

Although I am adopting a current practice by using the word 'autobiography' to describe all of these works, there were many women who wrote the story of their life without using this term. The word autobiography only entered the language at the very end of the 18th century and was not widely applied until the 1820s. Even when the term came into common parlance, some women continued to prefer using other terms like memoir, narrative, story, or life in their titles. In some cases, women did this because of a fear of the expectations that the term 'autobiography' carried, and a desire to write more informally. In resisting the term autobiography, some were also reflecting what has been a long-standing debate about the meaning of the term and about whether and how it differs from other terms, especially memoir. This is a debate that continues today, bringing with it considerable changes in how the terms are understood.[20] Memoir has become more popular recently and is seen sometimes as allowing more intimate reflections on an individual's life, in contrast to an earlier meaning that stressed the ways that memoir often focused on the people the author had known.[21] There is, however, no general agreement on the meanings of the terms or the differences between them. While looking at some of the issues surrounding the language of autobiography, I propose to use a fairly simple definition of autobiography to mean a published account of a person's life given by herself. This definition is one used in the *Oxford English Dictionary*, and I intend to follow it also by regarding the terms 'memoir' and 'autobiography' as interchangeable. While encompassing a wide range of women's accounts of their lives, this definition makes it clear that I will not be discussing diaries, journals, fiction or travel writing, all of which, many would argue, have some connection with the lives of their authors. I am interested specifically in published life stories that are clearly autobiographical in form and are presented as in some sense 'true lives'.

---

[20]Julia Rak, 'Are Memoirs Autobiography? A Consideration of Genre and Public Identity', *Genre* XXXVI (2004).
[21]P. Madden, 'The New Memoir', in *The Cambridge Companion to Autobiography*, eds Maria di Battista and Emily O. Whittman (Cambridge: Cambridge University Press, 2014), pp. 222–236.

This book, then, is a history of British women's autobiography since the mid-18th century. As a history, its structure is chronological, beginning with the first secular autobiographies written in the mid- to late 18th century, works often regarded as scandalous because they told the lives of women whose sexual misdemeanours or general conduct meant they were cast out of respectable society. The second chapter explores the 19th century, the period when women's autobiography, like men's, came to be accepted and recognized as a serious literary form, even if Woolf did not recognize it as so. Almost as if in reaction to their 18th-century predecessors, the Victorian women who wrote autobiography emphasized their propriety and conformity to accepted conventions of decorum. The best known of these autobiographies were written by respectable single women of achievement. This emphasis on individual achievement disappeared, to a great extent, in the first half of the 20th century. Involvement in the militant suffrage struggle and in the First World War as nurses and VADs, offered a new framework for women's autobiography which now emphasized their direct engagement in major historical developments and events. Many women thus saw their life stories as a form of history, and one that could only be told from personal experience.

The final decades of the 20th century saw a great boom in autobiography as more and more life stories appeared. It also brought major innovation and change in the conceptualizing and writing of women's autobiography. It is this period that finally saw the end of the model of autobiography that originated with Rousseau, as women began to draw on history, psychoanalysis and questions of gender as they sought to find new ways to tell their stories. Many eschewed chronology and devised new literary forms, as well as drawing on myth, fiction and case studies to explore their lives. The final chapter explores the emergence of women's autobiography in the wider British world in the 1980s and '90s, in Namibia, Kenya, Pakistan and especially in Australia and South Africa. These works too offer a new model of autobiography, one in which in place of the emphasis on psychology and family dynamics so important in the West, colonialism and repressive political structures are seen as dominating individual lives.

One major point that emerges from a chronological structure is precisely how much the understanding of individual lives and the issues that could be discussed in autobiography changed over time. Another is just how much the once very limited group of women able to write autobiographies expanded to include working-class women and many different Black and Indigenous women. Improved educational provision contributed to this expansion as did the assistance of collaborators and editors, and the support provided by a range of different organizations, including feminist publishers, concerned to encourage and support women in their endeavour to write and to produce autobiographies.

As this outline makes clear, I am using the term 'British' broadly to refer to the wider 'British World' established by the British Empire. Most British autobiographies were written and published in the British Isles, mainly in London, although a significant number were produced in Dublin and sometimes Edinburgh. In recent years, increasing attention has been paid to the autobiographical writing of women who came to Britain from different parts of the Empire: as freed slaves or nurses seeking to participate in the Crimean War in the 19th century, as students seeking to further their education and to gain professional admission in the early 20th century, or as part of the move from settler colonies and provincial towns to metropolitan centres, especially London in the mid-20th century. The work of these women was published and read in London and greatly expanded the kinds of lives encompassed in autobiography and the ways in which those lives were written. Some of these women were known only through their autobiographies, while others became major literary figures. I intend to include some of them here. In the final decades of the 20th century, however, the writing of autobiography became something of a global phenomenon. In some British settler colonies, most notably Australia and South Africa, women wrote powerfully of the impact of colonial rule and dispossession on their lives and those of their family and kin. These autobiographies transformed understanding of the impact of colonial rule on native and Indigenous people internationally and especially on women's daily life.

A major challenge in writing this book has been the question of which autobiographies to choose from the hundreds, even thousands, that have been published across this period. Even from the 18th century, when the numbers were relatively small, it is not possible to include all published works and this problem is multiplied as one gets closer to the present time. My selection was necessarily limited in number as I wanted not only to chart changes over time, but also to note the major features of any particular period and to discuss important texts in enough detail to make their salient details evident to readers. It is my concern to delineate what I see as the significant changes in women's autobiography since the mid-18th century that has determined my selection of texts. All the texts I have chosen seem to me either to exemplify the most important qualities of any period or to indicate the significant changes occurring in it that differentiate it from the previous one. I have tried to make sure that I have included all the well-known autobiographies across the period which readers would expect to find in a work of this kind, and that have already been the subject of extensive, detailed discussion by literary scholars and historians and that are generally readily available and hopefully already known to some readers. Each chapter has a separate list of the autobiographies discussed in it.

As the question of what to include is essentially an empirical one, based on my own interpretation and judgement it seems important to state briefly which autobiographies I have chosen and why I did so. The number of women's autobiographies published was quite small in the 18th century and, while mentioning others, I have focused primarily on three: those of

Laetitia Pilkington, Constantia Phillips and Charlotte Charke. Although some contemporary scholarship has demonstrated the importance of many lesser-known texts, as the volume of scholarship on them makes clear, these three are unquestionably the best known and most important 18th-century women's autobiographies. Taken together, they show well the different ways in which women's autobiography was seen by contemporaries as shocking and as scandalous in depicting lives lived beyond accepted social bounds while illustrating also the ways in which their authors sought to explain and justify those lives and to gain more sympathy for themselves. These works also illustrate very well the ways in which 18th-century women shaped their lives, paying little attention to childhood, for example, in order to focus attention on the aspects of adult life they sought to explain. While detailing their actions and the events that affected these lives, these women have little to say about their own personalities or outlooks and very little sense of their own subjectivity.

The changes between 18th-century scandalous autobiography and Victorian women's autobiography of the 19th century could not have been more marked. This was not simply a reflection of changing sexual mores, evident in the exclusion of almost any mention of intimate life or adult relationships, but also of economic and social developments that expanded women's education and made it possible for some to make a living as writers and journalists. Hence, one key aspect of Victorian woman's autobiography was its focus on how its author established herself as a prominent woman, without challenging prevailing ideas of feminine decorum. Harriet Martineau and Frances Power Cobbe, two of the women who exemplify this development seemed to me important to include here. Martineau, widely regarded as the greatest Victorian woman autobiographer is the more important. Her autobiography is the only one by a woman sometimes included alongside Mill and Newman in the male-dominated autobiographical canon, largely because of the clarity with which she depicted her own intellectual development and her religious beliefs and conflicts. But Cobbe too describes her intellectual development, religious difficulties and success in establishing an independent life, and also depicts her public activities and espousal of women's rights.

While wanting to stress the contrast between Victorian autobiography and its 18th-century counterpart, it also seemed important to make clear that the best-known Victorian women's autobiographies only appeared well into the second half of the 19th century and I wanted to make clear that there was not a sudden shift from 18th century 'scandalous autobiography' to its proper Victorian successor, but that the change was really quite a slow one. Victorian approaches were anticipated by some earlier works, like that of the Evangelical novelist, Charlotte Elizabeth Tonna. At the same time, the early decades of the 19th century also saw a continuation of the autobiographies of courtesans. *The Memoirs of Harriette Wilson*, which appeared in the 1820s, was the most successful autobiography of a courtesan ever published. The early decades of the 19th century also saw quite new kinds of work, with the appearance of the slave narrative of Sarah Prince, the first woman's slave narrative ever published, in the 1830s, and the adventures of Mary Seacole, the Jamaican doctoress and adventuress who sought to work alongside Florence Nightingale in the Crimean War, in the 1850s. These works together are important as they show how the notion of 'British autobiography' was beginning to extend outside the confines of the United Kingdom and into the wider 'British world' even in the 19th century.

The contrast between the autobiographies written after the First World War and their Victorian predecessors is not quite as stark as that between the 18th and mid-19th centuries. The changes are nonetheless marked, reflecting women's increasing involvement in major political events and developments. The suffrage struggle which had begun in the mid-19th century and become more and more active in the early 20th, culminating in the militant campaign to which some women devoted their lives completely, was one important issue. This campaign came to an end with the First World War, but the war also drew women into new kinds of activity as nurses, drivers and volunteers. Women who had been involved in the war, like Vera Brittain, shared with the militant suffragettes this sense of participating in significant historical events in a way that was unprecedented for women. Many of these women felt impelled to write their autobiographies at a relatively young age as a way of depicting this historical involvement. It is this sense of writing a life story as a way of writing history that seems to me one of the most significant features of interwar women's autobiography. I have chosen a number of suffragette autobiographies that illustrate this point well, beginning with Annie Kenney who articulates most clearly this sense of seeing her life story as a form of history. I have also included Vera Brittain's *Testament of Youth*, one of the best-known woman's autobiographies of the 20th century, and one in which an individual life story and experiences are seen as a way to offer not only an intimate kind of history but, as she argued, a history of the generation involved in the First World War. This sense that an individual life story could illustrate historical and social developments was evident also in older women's writing at this point. The first volume of Beatrice Webb's *My Apprenticeship* serves in an interesting way to demonstrate both continuity and change: on the one hand, Webb depicts a spiritual and moral crisis not unlike that of John Stuart Mill, while at the same time seeing her own life story as a way to exemplify the lives and values of the social class from which she came.

While there were very marked changes in the understanding and representation of history and political life and of the importance of women being part of them, there were also marked changes in discussions of personal life. Questions about sexual knowledge and sexuality, which were strictly eschewed from Victorian autobiography, returned as women began to write not only about their desire for sexual knowledge and the problem posed by their own sexual ignorance but also about their premarital and marital sexual experiences. Ethel Mannin, one of the most outspoken writers on this question, whose frankness on these questions was the subject of much contemporary comment, seemed to me an important figure here, especially as she also wrote sex education works for children. The other group of women who wrote in detail about their personal lives, including depicting abusive parents, sexual difficulties and marital lives, were popular novelists like Ursula Bloom and Marjorie Bowen. Unlike the 19th century, when few novelists wrote autobiography, in the interwar period they did so in larger numbers, wanting not just to draw on their own lives in novels, as Victorian novelists did, but to describe directly their own often difficult personal lives, as women were to do increasingly as the century developed.

The third chapter deals with the 1970s and '80s: the boom period in autobiography. More women's autobiographies were written than ever before and many by women who had previously not been prominent within the framework of British women's autobiography, including working-class women, on the one hand, and academic women, on the other. These women brought new approaches to the writing of autobiography and new stories that needed to be included. Amongst the innovations that seemed most important were the jettisoning of chronological narrative and the incorporation into autobiography of other kinds of writing: fiction, myth, and psychoanalytic case studies as a way to focus on feelings and identity rather than on relating the major events in a life. One can see these innovations particularly in the work of academic women, most notably Carolyn Steedman and Anne Oakley, whose work offered quite new ways of thinking about and writing autobiography.

Here, as in the previous chapter, in the interest of showing both some continuity as well as change, I have included the autobiographies of a number of older women whose work was also innovative in its form and in its frankness, including Naomi Mitchison and Storm Jameson. Mitchison is important here in the way she sought to link her life with a picture of her social class, choosing to do so in an essay format, however, rather than chronologically. Jameson's importance was different. Her autobiography broke new ground in its detailed discussion of her inner torment and the guilt and anxiety that dominated her life. In some ways she shows the growing importance of psychology and of new ideas about interiority in autobiography. Storm Jameson was also one of a growing number of women whose major work was her autobiography rather than her novels. This period was one in which increasing numbers of people came from the wider British world to live in London and establish themselves there and several wrote autobiographies depicting this journey, contrasting their London and colonial lives. Some of these women became very well known as novelists too. This story is an integral part of the autobiography of the period, and I have included those of Doris Lessing as well as the New Zealander Janet Frame, and the Nigerian Buchi Emecheta.

The final chapter moves outside Britain to encompass much of the wider British world in the last decades of the 20th century. This is a reflection of the way that the boom in autobiography became a global phenomenon as people everywhere began to write life stories, often ones that depicted the impact on their lives of some of the terrible political and historical developments of the time. The issue of decolonization and the struggle for national independence and political rights within many countries that had been part of the British Empire was a major issue here, as was the oppressive racism and discrimination that these women and their families had lived with for generations. There were two countries in particular in which Women's autobiography became important in this period. Australia was one. Indigenous women's autobiographies like Sally Morgan's *My Place* and Ruby Langford's *Don't Take Your Love to Town*, were not only widely read but seen as transforming both how Indigenous lives were understood and Australian literature. South Africa was the other, as Black women's autobiographies, like those of Ellen Kuzwayo and Sindiwe Magona, began to appear in the 1980s, giving voice to their experiences and ideas in a quite new way. In other countries too, Namibia and Kenya, women wrote of their particular experiences – in going into exile to evade South Africa, or as members of the Mau Mau. What links all of these works is the way in which these women saw their lives as dominated by discriminatory colonial laws and policies. At a time when Western women were paying more and more attention to the intimate world of family dynamics and the psychological dimensions of their lives and relationships, these women saw their lives in completely different terms. Family and relationships with parents are shown as playing a small part in their lives, while every aspect of their domestic life, education, employment and adult relationships is seen as dominated by the many forms of discrimination that they faced every day.

As my study includes discussion of how autobiographies were written and published, I have focused on when they were written and published, rather than on the date of birth of the author. As a result, especially in the 20th-century chapters, the work of women of different generations is put together. Beatrice Webb, for example, sits in my interwar chapter alongside much younger women like Vera Brittain and Annie Kenney. Webb was born in 1858 and, as one might expect, there are clearly Victorian elements in *My Apprenticeship*. It was published in 1926, however, and its approach to history and the whole cast of the book, seem to me to fit far more closely with others published in that decade than they do with Victorian autobiography. In a similar way, the autobiographies of Naomi Mitchison, who was born into Edwardian England but published her autobiographies in the 1970s, sit alongside those of younger academic women, like Carolyn Steedman and Ann Oakley, because here too the works were published at a similar time, and all seem to me to illustrate the innovations in autobiographical writing evident in the 1970s and '80s.

In order to emphasize the changing ways in which lives were viewed and understood across this period, I have organized the material in a similar way in each chapter. After an introduction outlining the major features of autobiography as a form in that particular period, each chapter has a section exploring the production of autobiographies, including a discussion of why the authors chose to write their life stories, how they went about doing so and how they managed to get them published. The third section, called 'Shaping a Life', explores the changing ways in which lives were presented. I will track the ways in which childhood grew in importance, in which intimate life shifted from being a major concern to being ignored before resurfacing in the 20th century. I will also look at how women's depiction of public activities and work changed. The final section, called 'A Sense of Self', explores the extent to which these autobiographies reveal a self-conscious interest in the inner life and subjectivity of their authors. This structure is designed to offer a sense of both the core features and the developments of autobiography in each period and the differences between them.

While the detailed study takes the writing of autobiography up to the end of the 20th century, it ends with a brief *Epilogue* that discusses some of the developments evident in the past twenty years. The richness and diversity of these works is extraordinary and suggests that autobiography is in no danger of coming to an end.

FIGURE 1 *Courtesan and adventuress Teresia Constantia Phillips (1709–1765), later Teresia Muilman, 1748. From a mezzotint engraving by John Faber Jr. after Joseph Highmore. (Photo by Hulton Archive/Getty Images.)*

CHAPTER ONE

Transgressive Women and the Origins of Secular Autobiography

The first secular British women's autobiographies were published in the mid-18th century. This is not to say that no women had written memoirs or autobiographies prior to this point. On the contrary, impelled by a sense of religious inspiration, several women had written about their spiritual lives and journeys as a way to articulate their beliefs at least a century before.[1] Others had written family memoirs intended to praise a husband or to tell of family struggles and triumphs.[2] But like Rousseau and for the first time, from the 1740s onwards women began to write directly about themselves, revealing their own experiences and demanding recognition of the challenges and struggles of their lives.[3]

The 18th-century women who wrote memoirs had led unconventional and sometimes scandalous lives, which they depicted and sought to justify. Most of these women had been cast out of respectable family life, and in

---

[1] Patricia Francis Cholakian, *Women and the Politics of Self-Representation in Seventeenth-Century France* (University of Delaware Press, 2000). Amy Culley, *British Women's Life Writing, 1760–1840* (London: Palgrave Macmillan, 2014), p. 3.
[2] See the examples in Devony Looser, *British Women Writers and the Writing of History, 1670–1820* (Baltimore: Johns Hopkins Press, 2000).
[3] Culley, *British Women's Life Writing, 1760–1840*.
The precise number of such works in the 18th century is a matter of dispute amongst historians and literary scholars, partly because of the problem of titles and of definition. Some were very short, certainly not long enough to count as a book, others still were published posthumously and as works edited by a daughter or son. Accepting a rather broad approach to this question of definition, Robert Folkenflik argues that around thirty 18th-century women's autobiographies are actually known. Robert Folkenflik, 'Introduction: The Institution of Autobiography,' in *Culture of Autobiography*, ed. Robert Folkenflik (Stanford: Stanford University Press, 1993).

consequence found themselves in dire financial straits, often needing to exchange sexual favours and intimacy for financial support. The stories are both fascinating and extraordinary as they described their daily lives, various social relationships, financial difficulties, and their sexual indiscretions and the consequences that ensued. These women addressed their own frailties and weaknesses directly, pointing also to the wrongs that had been done to them and providing details of their sufferings and the difficulties they had faced in supporting themselves in an often-hostile world. Their works are sometimes surprising in the frankness with which they depict their exploits and explain the choices that they made. But while happy to accept their weaknesses in a general way they are striking in their lack of self-examination or interest in depicting their inner selves or sense of self. Their concern was often rather to criticize the men who wronged them – and the gender norms and hierarchies that made them outcasts – while the men who had been their seducers or bedfellows maintained their social position.

All of these women wrote in an informal and appealing way, seeking to tell their stories from their own point of view, to justify their actions and to gain a more sympathetic hearing than had been the case to date. Some also hoped that, at the point at which they had ceased to find men to support them, publishing their story would enable them to make a living. The decision to write a memoir as a way both to justify their outrageous or scandalous life course and to support themselves financially was clearly an unusual one for women at the time, but it was not altogether surprising. Writing was one of the few avenues open to these women needing to support themselves and some had written in a variety of ways before writing their memoirs. The expansion of printing and bookselling in the 18th century, accompanied as it was by the emergence of a periodical press, the widespread publication of pamphlets and poetry, and the rise of the novel all indicate the increasing importance of literature and of published writing within British society. Women participated in all of these developments in a variety of ways. For the first time there were now Women of Letters, as well as Men of Letters, who turned to literature as a profession. A Woman of Letters, Norma Clarke has shown, could be 'a poet and a novelist, a historian and a critic; she might busy herself with translation or religious meditations; she might write for the theatre, edit a magazine, be a ferocious polemicist, or a sage and coolly reasoning philosopher'.[4] Some of them were widely celebrated and commercially very successful. Several of these celebrated women writers drew heavily on their own life stories in their fiction and other writings: both Aphra Behn and Delariviere Manley, for example, wrote a number of different versions of their own stories in various fictional forms.

It was not only the successful engagement of women in literary production that might have encouraged these women memoirists, but also the growing

---

[4] Norma Clarke, *The Rise and Fall of the Woman of Letters* (London: Pimlico, 2004), p. 128.

popularity of the seduction of innocent women in popular fiction. Samuel Richardson's *Pamela* (1840), with its depiction of the attempted seduction of a 15-year-old servant by the son of her deceased employer, was particularly important. It was one of the most widely read and discussed novels of the 18th century, indeed, some critics regard it as the first-ever best seller. *Pamela* was, moreover, the first of many seduction novels that both brought new attention to the precariousness and vulnerability of young women seeking to make their own way in the world, and suggested that there was a wide readership for this kind of story.[5] Stories and biographies of women penitents and of well-known prostitutes were also published in the second half of the 18th century, providing a framework for the memoirs that will be discussed here.[6]

The first two women's memoirs to appear, the *Apology of Constantia Phillips* and the *Memoirs of Laetitia Pilkington*, although very different from each other, both owe much to Richardson in the way they created their own personae. Phillips, who depicted herself as forced out of home at the age of thirteen and then raped, suggested that she was left with no alternative but to become a courtesan.[7] Richardson himself, who saw the prostitute as an innocent who had been seduced and abandoned, initially read her memoir very sympathetically and accepted that, if her story was true, the consequence of her ruin should be laid at the door of her rapist, Grimes.[8] He was less sympathetic to Laetitia Pilkington, whose *Memoirs* describe her fall from grace, not as a young innocent, but rather as a married woman who, as we will see, permitted a man other than her husband into her bed-chamber.[9] These were shortly followed by slightly different kinds of memoirs: Lady Frances Vane's *The Memoirs of a Lady of Quality*, published in 1751, depicts a woman who, having made a very successful second marriage to a man she did not love, embarked on a life of sexual pleasure and adventure, secure in the knowledge that she would be supported by her doting, but impotent, husband.[10] A few years later, the *Narrative of Charlotte Charke* appeared in 1755, offering a life that scandalized readers and the general public, not because of sexual indiscretion, but rather because of Charke's love of cross-dressing and her vagabond lifestyle. In the following decades,

---

[5]Katherine Binhammer, *The Seduction Narrative* (Cambridge: Cambridge University Press, 2009).
[6]Julie Peakman (ed.), *Whore Biographies in the Long 18th Century* (London: Pickering & Chatto, 2007).
[7]Constantia Phillips, *An Apology for the Conduct of Mrs Teresia Constantia Phillips*, 3 vols (2nd edition). Printed for the Booksellers of London and Westminster (1847). Accessed through Eighteenth Century Collections Online, Gale Primary Sources, vol. I, pp. 40–42.
[8]Binhammer, *Seduction Narrative*, p. 40.
[9]Ibid., p. 42.
[10]Frances Vane, 'Memoirs of a Lady of Quality', in *T. Smollett, the Adventures of Peregrine Pickle*, ed. J. L. Clifford (Oxford: Oxford University Press, 1983 (first published 1751)), pp. 432–540.

several other women published memoirs accounting for their sexual activities and marital adventures, and sometimes also relating their time on the stage, including Mary Robinson, Fanny Murray, Elizabeth Gooch, George Anne Bellamy and Margaret Leeson.

Whatever the response had been to other women's writing, these memoirs and autobiographies shocked many contemporaries. The cause of the shock was not because they offered salacious sexual details. On the contrary, as Laura Rosenthal points out, many of these memoirs are notable for 'how little space they devote to sexual activity ... and how much they devote to class and economic concerns'.[11] What shocked contemporaries was rather the fact that they were written *by* women about their own lives. What made them scandalous, Felicity Nussbaum argues, was 'the very fact that they are public documents: woman's fall should be a matter of remorse privately confessed to one's God'.[12] Instead of accepting their shame and retreating into silence, these women chose to expose their lives in some detail, promising to tell the 'unvarnished truth' about themselves and to lay bare their own mistakes and misfortunes. By showing, and sometimes almost celebrating, the lives of women lived outside of marriage, their works also served to question the depiction of women in contemporary fiction and undermine the emerging domestic ideology.

The publication of these works and the controversies around them illustrate the growing interest in all forms of life writing evident in the 18th century. There continued to be widespread concern that the desire of readers to know things that should remain secret was morally questionable, however. 'The intimate pleasures of biography', Mark Salber Phillips suggests, has to be seen 'against a background of suspicion of an art whose interest in private life ... seemed all too likely to lead to prurience or scandal mongering'.[13] Concerns about privacy and decency, as Daniel Cook and Amy Culley argue, were more intense in regard to women: 'accusations of egotism, vanity, self-adulation, indecency and treachery, and the unseemly violation of privacy entailed in the representation of lives, might be compounded by an author's sex.'[14] The very writing of memoirs by women transgressed a growing insistence on the family as the centre of women's interest and activity and an ideal of femininity that involved immersion in the domestic world and the rejection of any form of public notoriety.

---

[11]Laura J. Rosenthal, *Infamous Commerce: Prostitution in Eighteenth-Century British Literature and Culture* (Ithaca: Cornell University Press, 2015), pp. 97–98.
[12]Felicity Nussbaum, *The Autobiographical Subject: Gender and Ideology in Eighteenth Century England* (Baltimore: Johns Hopkins University Press, 1989), p. 186.
[13]Mark Salber Phillips, *Society and Sentiment* (Princeton: Princeton University Press, 2000), p. 134.
[14]Daniel Cook and Amy Culley, eds, *Women's Life Writing, 1700–1850: Gender, Genre and Authorship* (London: Palgrave Macmillan, 2012). 'Introduction.' But see also Lynda M. Thompson, *The Scandalous Memoirists: Constantia Phillips, Laetitia Pilkington and the Shame of 'Publick Fame'* (Manchester Manchester University Press, 2000).

Although often still labelled 'scandalous autobiographies', some scholars have suggested alternative ways to name and describe them.[15] The term 'scandalous' emphasizes the extent to which several of these works focus on the sexual behaviour that resulted in these women 'falling' from the norms of respectable womanhood. This designation is problematic, some would argue, because it focuses on only one aspect of the lives of these women, ignoring the many other issues that they raise and the broader scope of their lives that they present.[16] The authors of all of these works sought to show themselves in a range of different relationships, as mothers, for example, or as caring friends with particular skills that added value to their relationships. Phillips, for example, wrote at length about her knowledge of health and healing practices and how she used them to assist ailing friends. Charke offered a great deal of discussion of both London and provincial theatre as well as depicting her love of cross-dressing and somewhat vagabond life.

It is more appropriate, Felicity Nussbaum suggests, to see them as apologies 'in the classical sense of a "defence or justification within admission of guilt"'. They function rhetorically to vindicate the apologist publicly from charges brought against her.[17] The memoirs all narrate peculiarly female forms of distress and appeal to the public for sympathy and aid. What distinguishes appeal memoirs from other 18th-century memoirs or stories of prostitutes, as Caroline Breashears argues, is the fact that they are written by and about 'a woman whose peculiarly female situation has led to loss, displacement and distress'.[18] The issue of loss is a key feature in most of these works. These memoirs describe a broad range of deprivations: reputation, social status, financial stability, home and children. In some cases, they mourn a loss of liberty as many of these women are either exiled or incarcerated for a time in debtors' prisons. The appeals, as many readers recognized, are simultaneously rhetorical and heartfelt, and the distress to which they bear witness felt very real.

Nussbaum herself, like the majority of scholars of these 18th-century memoirs, focuses most of her attention on the work of Phillips, Pilkington and Charke. It is these works that scholars have used to construct the framework for secular women's autobiography and have the closest connection to other forms of contemporary literature. They also offer the model for how women might seek to negotiate the question of reputation. They presented their lives in ways that seek to explain unacceptable conduct,

---

[15]Thompson, *Scandalous Memoirists*, pp. 6–10.
[16]Caroline Breashears, 'Scandalous Categories: Classifying the Memoirs of Unconventional Women', *Philological Quarterly* 82 (2003): 187–202.
[17]Felicity A Nussbaum, 'Eighteenth-Century Women's Autobiographical Commonplaces', in *The Private Self*, ed. Shari Benstock (Chapel Hill: University of North Carolina Press, 1988), pp. 146–171.
[18]Caroline Breashears, 'The Female Appeal Memoir: Genre and Female Literary Tradition in Eighteenth-Century England', *Modern Philology* 107, no. 4 (2010): 610.

while at the same time insisting on the wrongs they had suffered and their entitlement to a public voice. Although reference will be made to some of the later memoirs, this chapter too will focus primarily on these mid-18th-century works.

Producing a Memoir

Although large-scale commercial publishing was beginning in England in the 18th century, it was neither accessible to nor appropriate for the little-known women memoir writers. The introduction of the Copyright Act in 1709 meant that publishers and sometimes printers too sought to purchase the copyright of the work completely, but authors who agreed to this arrangement often earned only a very small amount from their work.[19] Alongside these larger publishers, there were also many small-scale printers who were also booksellers and who entered into various different kinds of relationship with their authors. As most of the women autobiographers sought to make as much as they could from their memoirs they sought means of publishing where they remained in greater control. Some of them insisted on retaining the copyright themselves, merely paying printers to prepare the work – and sometimes also to sell it, so that the authors got the lion's share of the income. Others sought subscriptions from supporters so that they had an upfront payment which often helped subsidize them during the writing time. There was sometimes an element of blackmail involved too: prominent men who had been the lovers of woman writing an autobiography could pay to have their name and the story of their relationship omitted.

Precise information as to how 18th-century women memoirists went about writing, printing and distributing their work is extremely uneven. Constantia Phillips, for example, provided detailed information about the writing process within the text itself, constantly updating it as each new part of the memoir appeared. The practices of others, like Laetitia Pilkington, have been researched and reconstructed by contemporary scholars. But in many cases, little is known. Several of the women who wrote memoirs had written and published other literary works prior to doing so and so had skills and contacts to draw on. Mary Robinson, for example, had been a very popular poet before she turned to her memoirs. Although not as successful as Robinson, Laetitia Pilkington too regarded herself as a poet and had lived by her pen. From the moment her marriage ended, she subsisted on income derived from providing a variety of literary services including letters, pamphlets and poems that were paid for by subscribers.

---

[19]John Feather, 'British Publishing in the Eighteenth Century: A Preliminary Subject Analysis,' *The Library*, s6-VIII, no. 1 (1986).

Charlotte Charke who had extensive experience on the stage, had written three plays and several dramatic preludes. She was employed as a writer and proofreader on the *Bristol Weekly Intelligence* and drafted playbills in the years shortly before beginning to write her autobiography, and she wrote and published four fictional narratives afterwards.[20] Sometimes a wider literary career came after the memoir. After writing various versions of her own life that sold well, Elizabeth Gooch turned equally successfully to the writing of both fiction and poetry.[21]

In addition to the connections provided by their own writing, several of the memoirists had close personal relationships with the 18th-century literary world that were very important to the production of their autobiographies.[22] Laetitia Pilkington, for example, was well aware that her most valuable asset as a writer and memoirist was her friendship with Jonathan Swift and her fund of anecdotes about him.[23] Indeed, she announced on the title page of her memoir that it would offer 'Anecdotes of several eminent persons living and dead. Among others Dean Swift, Alexander Pope Esq'. Almost equally important was the man she described as her mentor and patron, the actor and theatre manager, Colley Cibber. It was Cibber, she insisted, who suggested that she write her life. Cibber had published his own very successful memoir, *An Apology for the Life of Colley Cibber* (1740), shortly before he met Pilkington in London.[24] Hence when, after listening for several hours to Pilkington tell him the story of her life, he said 'Zounds! Write it out, just as you relate it, and, I'll engage it will sell', she decided to do so. Charlotte Charke, who was Colley Cibber's estranged daughter, was also very familiar with many of those involved in the literary and theatrical world and knew Henry Fielding, in whose plays she had appeared. One of the most striking illustrations of the way in which a connection between a woman memoirist and the literary world enabled publication is Lady Frances Vane's *Memoirs of a Lady of Quality*, which first appeared as a chapter in Tobias Smollett's novel, *Peregrine Pickle* – apparently the most popular part of the novel – before being published separately.

Contemporary literary developments more broadly were important for the memoirists, as one can see by the way that several of them modelled their own stories on those of contemporary novels dealing with the attempted

---

[20]Charke, *Narrative of the Life of Mrs Charlotte Charke*, p. xvii.
[21]Elizabeth Gooch, 'The Life of Mrs Gooch', in *Memoirs of Scandalous Women*, ed. Dianne Dugaw (London: Pickering and Chatto, 1792, repr. 2011), pp. 2–3.
[22]Nussbaum, *Autobiographical Subject Gender*, pp. 178–179.
[23]Laetitia Pilkington, *Memoirs of Mrs Laetitia Pilkington, Wife to the Rev. Mr Matthew Pilkington, Written by Herself, Wherein are occasionally Interspersed all her Poems with Anecdotes of Several Eminent Persons, Living and Dead*, 2 vols. Printed for the Author, Dublin, 1748. Accessed through Eighteenth-Century Collections Online, Gale Primary Sources, vol. II p. 88.
[24]Colley Cibber, *An Apology for the Life of Mr Colley Cibber* (London, printed for the author, 1840).

seduction and sometimes the fall of innocent young women. Fielding and Richardson were particularly important in this regard. In the case of Laetitia Pilkington, as Norma Clarke suggests, 'A good deal of *Pamela* and *Shamela* went to the making of the female persona that eventually emerged as narrator and protagonist of the Memoirs'.[25] Another generic framework came from picaresque novels. 'Had the work been published and read posthumously', the ostensible narrator of Constantia Phillips' *Apology* suggested, 'I make no doubt but Mrs Phillips' *Apology* would have been read in the Character of a Romance, as much as *Tom Jones* or any other Novel'.[26]

In addition to novels, women memoirists drew inspiration from other popular literary genres. The most immediate one, Michael Mascuch suggests, was the discourse of the criminal penitent, a form of writing that was becoming increasingly well known.[27] The confessions of criminals apparently made at the very point of execution had become so popular in the early 18th century, Mascuch argues, that they were beginning to replace spiritual autobiographies. These works were designed to show the nature of the crime an individual had committed, and what had led them to the deed. These confessions were usually apologetic in form, but also produced a strong psychological sense of the individual nature of the criminal. They resembled some women's memoirs in that, although rarely written by the criminals themselves, they appeared to offer direct speech. Mascuch sees Constantia Phillips, who chose the title 'Apology' for her work, as the one who most successfully 'appropriated the discourse of the criminal penitent to redeem herself'. Thus while she confessed her sins and failings, she also used her story to show how she had been exploited and victimized.[28]

All of these women were nonetheless very well aware that their writing of an autobiography or memoir was an audacious act, likely to meet a hostile reception. 'As the following History is the Product of a Female Pen, I tremble for the terrible Hazard it must run in venturing into the World,' wrote Charlotte Charke at the start of her *Narrative*, making this point absolutely clear.[29] Others shared Charke's sense of the hazard they would run venturing into the world and often devised ways to try to lessen it. Charke herself insisted that she had 'paid all due regard to Decency' and tried to make all the various subjects of her own story 'so interesting that every Person who reads my story may bear a Part in some Circumstance or other'.[30] Others

---

[25] Norma Clarke, *Queen of the Wits: A Life of Laetitia Pilkington* (London: Faber and Faber, 2008), p. 186.
[26] Constantia Phillips, *An Apology*, vol. III, p. 285.
[27] Michael Mascuch, *Origins of the Individualist Self: Autobiography and Self-Identity in England 1591–1791* (Cambridge: Polity Press, 1997).
[28] Mascuch, *Origins*, p. 190.
[29] Charke, *Narrative*, p. 7.
[30] Charke, *Narrative*, p. 7.

attempted different stratagems. Laetitia Pilkington and Constantia Phillips, both of whom had strayed too far from norms of feminine decorum to avoid the charge of indecency, argued that their stories were nonetheless morally beneficial as their lives offered negative examples that would help virtuous women avoid the pitfalls into which they had fallen. 'Will it not be allowed us, that Example leaves deeper Impressions than Precept?' Phillips asks at the start of her *Apology*.

> And if this is the Case, how must the tender Minds of our fair readers be affected with her melancholy Story? If there could ever possible be found Pleasures in such a Life, must they not have happened to Her?.... But the Fair, we hope, will be warned by her unhappiness, to shun the dangerous paths in which She has trod.[31]

In a similar vein, Pilkington insisted that her story would be useful in demonstrating the incalculable value of maintaining a good reputation. She offered 'a lively Picture of all my Faults, my Follies, and the Misfortunes, which have been consequential to them', because 'I think the Story may be instructive to the Female Part of my Readers, to teach them that Reputation',

> Is the immediate Jewel of their Souls,
> And that the Loss of it
> Will make them poor indeed! (Othello)[32]

Some of these women also included other material in their memoirs, hoping thereby to justify their work and to give it additional interest. Constantia Phillips' *Apology*, for example, includes many legal documents and letters as evidence for her claims to ill treatment on behalf of the man she still insisted was her husband and from whom she was seeking to obtain a regular annuity. Her Apology, as Caroline Breashears shows, was almost overwhelmed by paratexts including two long dedications, six addresses to the reader, and several appendices dealing with legal cases. These paratexts re-enforce Phillips' arguments and helped her avenge herself on her enemies. She also included letters to and from readers all designed to gain the kind of sympathetic reading to which she felt entitled, 'thus leading to a re-evaluation of her character and situation'.[33] Pilkington chose a different course, including in her *Memoir* many of her own poems to show her skill and talent as a poet and to make her work more interesting. Indeed, there are so many poems that they dominate the text, and her life story has to be extracted from them. Ironically, as recent scholars like Catherine Ingrassia

---

[31] Phillips, *Apology*, vol. III, p. 5.
[32] Pilkington, *Memoir*, vol. I, p. 2.
[33] Caroline Breashears, 'Justifying Myself to the World': Paratextual Strategies in Teresia Constantia Phillips's Apology', *Script & Print* 35 no. 1 (2011): 7–22.

have pointed out, for all her efforts, Pilkington never gained enough through subscriptions to publish her poetry – so it was really the memoir that allowed the poems to appear.[34] Even contemporaries felt that the poems were not needed, and indeed detracted from the text. The Oxford scholar who compared Pilkington's work to Phillips' shortly after they were published was strongly of this view. 'The Poetry which seems to please this Lady most, appears to me the least pleasing part of her Book; not that all the Pieces are ill-written, but because there are too many of them, and amongst them very few that do her real honour.'[35]

When it came to the writing process itself, the memoirists adopted a variety of different practices. Literary scholars have recently begun to suggest that the model of an individual and isolated writer sitting down to produce a memoir may be inaccurate for 18th-century women, many of whom collaborated with someone else. Collaboration can be seen both in the writing and in the publication of *The Memoirs of Lady Frances Vane*, for example, still best known in their earliest form as 'The memoirs of a Lady of Quality' that formed chapter VXXXI of Thomas Smollett's *Peregrine Pickle*. Because it celebrated rather than apologizing for the author's infidelity to her husband and extensive sexual conquests, this work has been seen as an outlier within the framework of 18th-century women's memoirs. What has rarely been noticed about Vane's memoir, however, as Caroline Breashears argues, is the extent to which Lady Vane's work was linked to that of a close friend of hers, the contemporary French woman memoirist Madame de La Touche, to whom she frequently referred in her work and who was effectively a collaborator in her writing of it. Unlike Phillips or Pilkington, neither Vane nor La Touche were seeking money from their memoirs. They 'tell their stories to resist their positions as objects of exchange between father and husband. Instead of lamenting their "fall", they glorify their affairs, countering their father's focus on business with an alternative economy of love.'[36] Vane, who continued to be supported by her husband through all her infidelities, underlined her lack of financial interest in her work by giving the memoir to Smollett to include in his novel, apparently without any suggestion that she would receive anything from it.

Collaboration of a rather different kind was important to Laetitia Pilkington too. As her biographer Norma Clarke writes, Pilkington had some difficulty finding the right voice for her memoir. She prided herself on her excellent memory and ability to recall apt quotes or classical references in conversation with ease, but these quotes looked pedantic in a memoir. Her

---

[34]Catherine Ingrassia, 'Elizabeth Thomas, Laetitia Pilkington and Competing Currencies of the Book', *Women's Writing* 23, no. 3 (2016).
[35]*The Parallel; or Pilkington and Phillips Compared, being Remarks upon the Memoirs of those two Celebrated Writers*, by an Oxford Scholar, (London, printed for R. M Copper, 1848), p. 21.
[36]Caroline Breashears, *Eighteenth-Century Women's Writing and the 'Scandalous Memoir'* (London: Palgrave Macmillan, 2016), p. 9.

challenge, Clarke suggests, was 'to link them into a connected narrative that retained the "natural" rhythms of speech. She did this by dictating the memoirs to her son Jack, a process which allowed her to compose aloud as if speaking to friends.'[37] The question of collaboration has also been raised in regard to Constantia Phillips, because her story is told by a male narrator. Most scholars, however, now believe that she wrote it alone, using the male narrator as a device to add weight to her story – and to have an ostensibly male voice to vouch for her integrity and make clear his sympathy.[38]

Having decided to write their life stories, these women faced the question of how to negotiate the publishing world. Several of them rejected the idea of selling the copyright to a printer as they knew this was disadvantageous to authors. Despite her immense popularity as a poet, Mary Robinson, for example, had been paid a pittance by the printer who had made a very handsome sum from her work.[39] As they were counting on their memoirs as something to sustain and support themselves at a time when they were facing poverty, some of these women, notably Phillips and Pilkington, determined to keep control of the publishing process themselves. Finding a printer was not always easy, however.

Theresa Constantia Phillips, the first of the memoirists, was determined to write a memoir in order to expose the wrongs that had been done to her by men who had promised to support her properly in exchange for sexual favours – and then failed to do so. Most of her *Apology* was focused on the Dutch merchant, Henry Muilman, who married her, but then sought to have the marriage annulled. While Muilman seemed devoted to her, after his father heard stories about Phillips' past that made her appear an unsuitable wife for his son, he pressured Muilman into seeking an annulment. Phillips in turn sought to embarrass Muilman to make him pay an annuity she felt he had promised. Muilman seems to have been determined to prevent her from publishing her work. Phillips wrote at some length at the beginning of her *Apology* about the difficulties that she had faced in finding a printer. When she first planned to write the book, she was still engaged in litigation with Muilman and could not get permission from one of the judges concerned in the case to publish the details of her legal battle. She kept all the necessary materials for the book, however. Some years later, she was offered £1,000 for her papers and her story by a bookseller who said they would get some 'proper person' to write it. Rather than accepting this offer, Phillips decided to write the book herself.[40] However, when she actually began writing she could not get anyone to print it. Several printers said they

---

[37]Clarke, *Queen of the Wits*, p. 258.
[38]Patrick Spedding, 'The publication of Constantia Phillips's Apology', *Script & Print* 35, no.1 (2011): 22–38.
[39]Paula Pyrne, *Perdita: The Life of Mary Robinson* (London: Harper Perennial, 2001).
[40]Phillips, vol. 1, p. 261; Patric Spedding, 'The Publication of Constantia Phillips's Apology', p. 24.

were concerned that they would face legal battles with Muilman themselves if they accepted it. Phillips eventually did find a willing printer and published her work in eighteen separate parts, which she decided to sell herself.

Publishing the work in instalments meant Phillips could detail the ongoing difficulties she experienced finding a printer and distributing the work and could emphasize the role of her former husband in creating this situation. She could also make clear each stage in her battle with Muilman and respond to readers' comments. Phillips advertised her *Apology* extensively in magazines including *The General Advertiser, Old England* and *The Gentleman's Magazine*.[41] At the start, she was afraid it might be pirated and insisted on signing each copy herself to guarantee its authenticity. This fear, Patrick Spedding argues, was unnecessary and after a time, Phillips stopped signing all copies. But the process of distribution remained fraught and changed several times as she went from selling the book herself to having particular booksellers do it for her. Phillips' advertising and distribution were clearly effective. She earned around £2,400 from her *Apology*, considerably more than the amount she was originally offered for selling the story.[42] Several of the separate numbers were republished more than once and the work also appeared in three volume octavo form, some of which went through at least two editions. Phillips also continued her plan to embarrass Muilman by having the work translated into Dutch so that it was accessible to his family and colleagues there.[43] However badly she had been treated by Muilman and some of his successors, Phillips did extremely well out of publishing her own account of them. Twenty years after its publication, according to *The Gentleman's Magazine*, Phillips' *Apology* was 'a subject of universal conversation in England'.[44]

Laetitia Pilkington also published her memoir as a means of supporting herself and sought subscriptions in order to do it. From the time she had arrived in London in the early 1740s, after the ending of her marriage, Pilkington had in part supported herself by publishing poems and other prose writings by subscription, often assisted by her friend and mentor, Colley Cibber, who found subscribers and publicized her work. She began planning a memoir almost immediately and worked hard to find subscribers. As her biographer Norma Clarke points out, she enlisted some surprising supporters 'including the Archbishop of Canterbury with whom she took tea at Lambeth Palace'.[45] The project took its final shape only after 1747,

---

[41]Spedding, 'Phillips's Apology', p. 25.
[42]By way of contrast, Charlotte Brontë's best-selling novel, *Jane Eyre*, published almost a century later earned her only 500 pounds.
[43]Spedding, 'Phillip's Apology', loc. cit. p. 37.
[44]*Gentleman's Magazine*, vol. 36, 1766, pp. 83–84 quoted in Cheryl Turner, *Living by the Pen: Women Writers of the Eighteenth Century* (London: Routledge, 2002), p. 221.
[45]Norma Clarke, 'The crowd-funded book: an eighteenth-century revival', in *Histories of the Present, the Practice of History* (History Workshop Online, June 12, 2018).

when Pilkington returned to Dublin, extended her search for subscribers and found a printer to publish her memoirs. The scandal surrounding the failure of her marriage was well known in Dublin and gave her a kind of notoriety that some respectable folk sought to avoid. Her early friendship with Jonathan Swift, however, and the range of stories that she could tell about him, combined with her later friendship with Cibber, who was more than happy to let her publish some of his correspondence with her, lent her story interest. Her success in gaining subscriptions increased markedly, Clarke argues, once she promised not to make the names of her subscribers known! Pilkington easily found a printer willing not only to produce her work but to help her raise subscriptions to finance it. Once published, Pilkington's work was in such high demand in Dublin that a second edition was produced there and then another in London. She made extra money by selling some copies herself, increasing her own revenue. Her income from the book, however, never reached the heights of Constantia Phillips. Pilkington did not survive long after the book began to be published. Her health gave way and she died in 1850, just two years after the publication of her first volume.[46]

Much less is known about the process of publishing another well-known 18th-century woman's memoir, the *Narrative of Charlotte Charke*. Like Phillips and Pilkington, Charke seems to have sought to gain an income from writing the book. Her once successful career on the London stage had come to an end, and, as the narrative itself makes clear, she had been struggling to support herself working in provincial theatre companies and through a variety of other forms of work. The underlying concern of her memoir was not to avenge a husband who had injured her, but rather to attempt to restore herself to the love, favour and financial support of her father, Colley Cibber, from whom she was estranged. The pain of her separation from her father is a recurrent theme that surfaces repeatedly along with comments about those, including her older sister and her first husband, whom she suggests made this estrangement worse. Initially, Charke suggests, she was not planning a full-length memoir, and 'had no design of giving any account of my life, farther than a trifling sketch' which she planned to include as a preface to her novel, *Henry Dumont*. Possibly because of the wealth of detail it offers about 18th-century theatre, however, others urged her to extend the sketch of her life, and so she wrote it at greater length and published it in eight separate parts.[47] Like Phillips, Charke wrote the sections as they were being published and so included comments on them and their reception. As the major purpose of her work was to reconcile herself with her father, she included in the text the attempts she had made to bring about this reconciliation, including the letter she sent

---

[46]Clarke, 'The Crowd-funded Book'.
[47]Charke, *Narrative*, p. 139.

seeking his pardon and begging forgiveness for her youthful follies – and asking to 'know if I may be admitted to throw myself at your feet; and, with sincere and filial transport, endeavour to convince you that I am, Honoured sir, Your truly penitent and dutiful daughter'.[48] The letter was returned unopened.

Public demand for Charke's *Narrative* was sufficient for the combined sections to be published as a book shortly after all the individual parts had appeared. It went through two editions in 1755. Her book was extensively discussed and commented on in the periodical press. Indeed, as Hans Turley has shown, it was given more space and attention in *The Gentleman's Magazine* than any other publication that came out that year. It was attention of a very particular kind, however. In the guise of a long summary extending over more than 10,000 words, Turley argues, her book 'was rewritten completely by taking her first personal narrative and turning it into a third person redaction'.[49] In doing so, the magazine removed any sense of Charke's authorial voice, extravagant language, use of parody, or any of the sense of questioning of gender boundaries that is so important in her own text. What the redaction offers is rather an account of her life that depicts her simply as a woman whose 'masculine turn of mind' and unsuitable (and unfeminine) education led to her thoroughly disreputable life. The ostensibly impartial tone of the article and its emphasis on what it deems to be the facts in her narrative rather than her comments 'reveals the unease it feels towards this woman who refuses to see herself in any normative female role'. Although not scandalous in the sexual ways of Phillips and Pilkington, Charke's autobiography was nonetheless shocking in its absolute rejection of conventional notions of female propriety. From the time she was a child, Charke explains, she enjoyed donning male attire and seeking male work, extending this practice into playing male roles both on and off stage. She lived for much of her life as a cross dresser, enjoying temporary employment as a gentleman servant to a peer in this garb as well as receiving proposals of marriage from infatuated women. Charke's eccentric life of vagabondage was, Turley argues, shocking to her contemporaries. While clearly a cause of considerable interest and comment, it is not clear whether Charke's *Narrative* did provide her with the financial support she sought from it.

This question of remuneration has been widely debated because a lengthy 'Anecdote of Mrs Charke' by Samuel Whyte was published in the 1790s, some decades after her book appeared. Whyte insists that he visited Charke after her *Narrative* appeared, with a friend who was interested in publishing the novel that Charke mentions in the memoir, *Henry Dumont*. He depicts her as living in 'a wretched thatched hovel', in appalling poverty and

---

[48] Charke, *Narrative*, p. 63.
[49] Hans Turley, '"A Masculine Turn of Mind": Charlotte Charke and the Periodical Press', in *Introducing Charlotte Charke*, ed. Philip E. Baruth (Urbana and Chicago: University of Illinois Press, 1998).

disorder. Charke was attended by a friend and was, when they arrived, 'sitting on a maimed chair under the mantelpiece, by a fire merely sufficient to put us in mind of starving'. She had a skeletal dog whose response to them suggested that she had few friends or visitors. As she sat in her chair,

> on her lap was placed a mutilated pair of bellows – the pipe was gone, an advantage in their present office. They served ... for a writing desk, on which were displayed her hopes and treasures, the manuscript of her novel. ... Her inkstand was a broken tea cup, the pen worn to a stump – she had but one.[50]

Whyte's article was published in 1796, the year of Charke's death, and has proved immensely influential in how she is seen and read. His 'harrowing account of her appearance and the squalor of her surroundings' featured in the entry on Charke in the first edition of the *Dictionary of National Biography* in 1887 and is clearly known to all contemporary scholars writing on her and accepted by most. Some, like Sue Churchill, however, point out that it was written some thirty years after the visit Whyte made to her home and question its accuracy.[51] This picture, Churchill argues, seems at odds with the financial success of Charke's *Narrative*, on the one hand, and her expression of delight at being back in London and her plans to write and to open an 'oratorical academy', on the other.

Shaping a Life

One notable feature of 18th-century women's memoirs and autobiographies, especially in contrast to their 19th- and 20th-century counterparts, is the very limited attention devoted to their early lives. If there at all, families of origin are usually described briefly, followed by an equally brief depiction of the author's childhood. There is no concept of adolescence in these works, and they describe a very abrupt transition from childhood to womanhood at the point at which sexual interests and activity begins, often around the age of thirteen, but sometimes extending into the late teens. The ways in which these women 'fell' or become outcast, through desertion or failed marriages, is usually presented in detail and it is here that one sees their greatest sense of wrongs done to them. These accounts of the 'fall' tend to be followed by accounts of how these women managed their lives after this catastrophe. The wrongs these women suffered continue to be discussed, but are contrasted with depictions of the energy, resourcefulness and courage that they showed in managing their subsequent lives.

---

[50]Charke, *Narrative*, pp. vi–viii.
[51]Sue Churchill, '"I Then Was What I Had Made Myself": Representation and Charlotte Charke', *Biography* 20, no. 1 (1997).

Childhood

Although this is not the case in all 18th-century women's autobiographies, the majority pointed to a brief and very unhappy childhood. The cruelty that they suffered in their earliest years is a common feature of several of these works. This ill treatment was most often inflicted by a mother or stepmother. Fathers were rarely perpetrators, but they did not protect their daughters from the cruelties of their wives. Following the line of many fairy tales, Constantia Phillips insisted it was the extreme cruelty of her stepmother that sent her from home while she was still a child and ruined her life. Her natural, and loving mother died when she was still a very young child. Her father then married a former servant who took complete charge of his home and family. 'Such was the influence of that wicked Woman over him', Phillips wrote,

> (a man in all other respects of the utmost good Nature, Humanity and Honour) that he suffered her to treat his children with the greatest cruelty, which was the grand source of all their Misfortunes, for her manner of abusing them was so barbarous it could not be borne with.... She was even detected once endeavouring to poison them.[52]

Under her wicked influence, Phillips' father removed her from the care of their relatives who had treated her well. Subsequently, the abuse she suffered at the hands of her stepmother caused her to leave the paternal roof at the age of thirteen. At this tender age, 'she was launched at once into the wide World, naked, destitute and friendless, without any means of Living but what she could earn by her Needle'.

In the case of Laetitia Pilkington, it was her natural mother whose cruelty ruined her life. Here too, an apparently loving father seemed no match for the savagery of his wife. The love and indulgence she experienced from her father served to,

> qualify my mother's Severity to me; otherwise it must have broken my Heart; for she strictly followed Solomon's Advice in never sparing the Rod; insomuch that I have frequently been whipt for looking blue of a frosty Morning; and whether I deserved it or not, I was sure of Correction every Day of my Life.[53]

Pilkington loved poetry and was keen to read while still a young child, but her eyes were weak after she contracted smallpox and she was not allowed to look at books, 'my mother regarding more the Beauty of my

---

[52] Phillips, *An Apology*, vol. I, p. 48.
[53] Pilkington, *Memoirs*, vol. I, p. 11.

Face, than the improvement of my Mind'. She taught herself to read, however, and demonstrated such proficiency in reciting a poem she had learned that her father encouraged her to read and 'took care to furnish me with the best, and politest Authors'. While Pilkington saw her mother's refusal to let her read as a particular illustration of her mother's cruelty, Christine Gerard points out that her childhood follows the characteristic pattern of many 18th-century women authors whose fathers encouraged their intellectual precocity, while their mothers discouraged any signs of literacy in case they damage the looks and reputation of their daughters.[54]

Similar cases of unhappy childhoods with cruel or neglectful parents or guardians occur in several other 18th-century women's autobiographies, especially where the caring parent died and the child was left at the mercy of someone else. Elizabeth Gooch, for example, lost her loving father when she was three and then lived with a severe mother who paid no attention to her needs or interests and left her prey to the sexual designs of various men.[55] Towards the end of the century, Margaret Leeson described how her happy childhood changed suddenly after the death of her beloved mother and oldest brother. Her father was too distraught by this loss to continue running his farm or home and handed it to her second-oldest brother, Christopher. He became intoxicated by his own pleasures, becoming 'a harsh, unfeeling tyrant', who not only deprived his siblings of what was rightly theirs but also beat them savagely and otherwise abused them.[56]

While unhappy childhoods proved the general rule, there were some exceptions. Frances Vane, for example, albeit briefly, showed herself as loved and indulged in her home. Charlotte Charke also stressed the love and care she received from her parents, especially her mother.[57] Charke provided a more detailed account of family life and childhood than was evident in any other contemporary work, stressing that it was during her childhood that she first manifested the oddness, especially her enthusiasm for wearing masculine dress, that she saw as characterizing her whole life. At the age of four, she explained, 'having, even then, a passionate fondness for a Periwig', she thought 'that, by Dint of a Wig and a waistcoat, I should be the perfect Representative of my Sire', and so paddled downstairs wearing a waistcoat of her brother's and her father's wig and carrying a large-hilted sword. In this 'Grotesque Pygmy-State', she walked up and down along a ditch outside

---

[54]Christine Gerard, 'Laetitia Pilkington and the Mnemonic Self', *The Review of English Studies*, New Series, vol. 70, no. 295 (2018).
[55]Gooch, *Appeal*, pp. 5–7.
[56]Margaret Leeson, *Memoirs of Mrs Margaret Leeson Written by Herself; in Which Are Given Anecdotes, Sketches of the Lifes and Bon Mots of Some of the Most Celebrated Characters in Great Britain and Ireland, Particularly of All the Filles Des Joys and Men of Pleasure and Gallantry Which Have Frequented Her Citherean Temple for These Thirty Years Past*. 3 vols. Dublin: 'Printed and sold by the Principal Booksellers', 1797, vol. 1, p. 13.
[57]Charke, *Narrative*, p. 25.

the house where 'the Oddity of my Appearance soon assembled a Crowd around me'.[58] This was the first of several childhood escapades that Charke recounted, some of which amused her family, while others angered or distressed them, bringing the 'Discipline of the Birch' in their wake. Some of her follies shocked and wounded her father, she suggested, and while they were harmless, her enemies have maliciously aggravated her faults in order to increase his anger.[59]

In depicting her childhood, Charke emphasized her intelligence, her lack of interest in any feminine skills or tasks and her capacity to immerse herself in unusual interests and activities. Her education, comprising two years spent at school where she learnt Latin, Italian and Geography, as well as music and singing, followed by lessons at home, lacked any kind of feminine accomplishment – and led her directly into masculine pursuits. When the family made the rural retreat that her father liked during winter, she found a way to endure her solitude by going shooting on the commons, an activity at which she excelled. A few years later, she became ill and her mother sent her to stay with a Doctor Thorly in Herefordshire in the hopes that she would both be cured and also, possibly through the example of the doctor's wife and family, be taught domestic skills. But this was not to be: 'Though I had the nicest Examples of Housewifely Perfection daily before me, I had no Notion of entertaining the least Thought of these necessary Offices.' She turned her attention rather to the stables and developed a great 'veneration for Cattle and Husbandry'.[60] She also 'grew passionately fond of Physic and was never so truly happy as when the Doctor employed me in some little Office'. She remained with Dr Thorly for two years, attempting to use her experience to provide remedies to neighbours on her return. As a young child, Charke demonstrated her enjoyment of masculine attire and behaviour by dressing up. In her adolescence, she did so rather by attempting to assume masculine roles, first as a doctor and then trying to take on the roles of gardener and of porter at the gate in her own home. In all of these adventures, Charke assured readers, she was indulged by her excessively devoted parents. Her escapades came to an end when she had a serious accident with a horse that she could not control.

The descriptions of childhood in these 18th-century women's autobiographies have been the subject of some discussion by later scholars. Linda Thompson argues that these memoirs foreshadow the development of a culture of childhood that can be seen in the 19th century and after because they 'insisted that their lives were the results of happenings as they accumulate, largely beyond their control and there is clearly a sense in many of these works that had they been better cared for, their lives would have been very different'.[61] However, this sense of the evil consequences that

---

[58]Charke, *Narrative*, pp. 10–11.
[59]Charke *Narrative*, p. 12.
[60]Charke, *Narrative*, pp. 17–18.
[61]Thompson, *Scandalous Memoirists*, p. 12.

follow their ill treatment usually derives from the fact that either they were forced to leave home at a very early age, and hence exposed to predatory men at a point where they were vulnerable, or they entered into an unwise marriage. There is little sense that this ill treatment was psychologically scarring. On the contrary, it is rather parental indulgence that is seen as damaging in the case of Charlotte Charke where it seems to underlie her later life as a vagabond. Frances Vane, who disposed of her childhood in a single sentence, also suggests that it is parental indulgence that set her up for a life of scandal.

> I believe I need not observe, that I was the only child of a man of good fortune, who indulged me in my infancy with all the tenderness of paternal affection; and, when I was six years old, sent me to a private school, where I stayed till my age was doubled, and became such a favourite, that I was, even in those early days, carried to all the places of public diversion, the court itself not excepted, an indulgence that flattered my love of pleasure, to which I was naturally addicted, and encouraged those ideas of vanity and ambition which spring up so early in the human mind.[62]

Vane's suggestion here that the indulgence with which she was treated encouraged the love of pleasure to which she was 'naturally addicted' and led to her later downfall is very clear. But it underlines the extent to which all of these accounts, whether depicting indulgence or cruelty, emphasize the vulnerability and precariousness of the female child endeavouring to make her way in the world.

Becoming a Woman

As they described it, most of the memoirists confronted the demands of maturity while still very young. The end of their childhood and the assumption that they were now women occurred with the commencement of sexual activity, or its anticipation via the social season or marriage. Adolescence as a separate phase of life did not really exist in 18th-century society or culture and there was a widespread acceptance that sexual activity for a girl might begin very early. The age of consent for girls was ten in regard to sexual intercourse and twelve when it came to marriage. Most of the memoirists indicate that they thought of themselves as women – and were seen by men as sexually available and desirable around the age of thirteen. It was at that age that Constantia Phillips left home to support herself by her needle – and experienced the rape that began her first sexual

---

[62] Vane, *Memoirs*, chap. LXXXI.

liaison, Lady Frances Vane 'went to Bath, where I was first introduced into the world as a woman' and Laetitia Pilkington had her first suitors.[63]

While recognizing that they were now women, and therefore in many ways responsible for themselves, all of the memoirists emphasized that they were still extremely young and vulnerable, badly in need of a kind of care and wise counsel that was not available to them. Those who married did so unwisely, lacking adequate guidance from parents. Those women with loving and indulgent parents criticized them for giving way to their daughters and allowing them to marry at the point where they should have shown their young daughters that they were misguided. Others suggested they were pressured into marriage by parents showing no concern for their welfare. Those who entered into sexual relationships without marriage also saw themselves as driven in some way by the loss of familial support. Hence, the coming of womanhood for all the memoirists met none of the normal expectations of an increasingly middle-class world. Instead of marriage, a home and a family, all signifying security, they saw the vulnerability and precariousness of childhood shifting to a new kind of vulnerability as they needed to find their own means of financial support and by whatever means they could.

The most dramatic and violent depiction of one who became a woman very suddenly through a brutal sexual initiation is offered by Constantia Phillips. When she left home at the age of 13, she found herself lodgings and sought to earn a living doing needlework. As she went about her work, she noted, she was seen by a man she calls Mr Grimes. It was impossible for 'a young creature, with all the charms and accomplishments that confessedly adorned Miss Phillips' to escape the eyes of a gentleman 'whose Reason ... was subordinate to his Passions and whose peculiar tastes were for Girls of that Age'. He did his best to seduce her, writing loving letters, some of which she includes in the text, and promising her financial support.[64] When she refused his advances, despite his having bribed her landlady to support his suit, he prevailed on her one evening to come to his rooms. Once she was there, 'he plied me with wine', to which she was unaccustomed, but even so, she refused his advances and he resisted her entreaties and prayers and tears to be allowed to leave. As she sat on a high-backed chair, he came up behind her and,

> catching hold of her Arms, drew her hands behind the Chair, which he held fast with his Feet. In this Position, it was an easy matter for him with one Hand to secure both hers and ... take the advantage of ripping up the lacing of her coat with his Penknife ... he tore away, with very little difficulty, what else she had on.

---

[63]Vane, *Memoirs*, chap LXXXI.
[64]For a long time, 'Mr Grimes' was thought to have been Lord Chesterfield. But recent scholarship suggests that he was actually Lord Scarborough – to whom she wrote an ironic letter of dedication in the first volume of her *Apology*.

Phillips chose to 'pass over in Silence what followed from this Base procedure', sure that readers will be sufficiently shocked and able to imagine what happened after without it needing to be described. 'Let it suffice', she said, 'that her Ruin takes it's Date from that fatal Night; tho' not effected without the greatest Treachery, Force and Cruelty, on the Part of her lover.'[65]

Margaret Leeson too entered womanhood through a sexual relationship outside marriage that made her an outcast. In her case, it was not a rape, however, but a consensual encounter. Nonetheless, she too insisted it was the cruelty she experienced within her family that drove her to it. Hers had been a very happy family in her early years, but the sudden death of her mother and older brother proved too much for her father who handed over his business and control of the family to his second son whom Leeson described as selfish and sadistic, caring for nothing but his own pleasure. 'Had I been treated with the same humanity and tenderness that other like situated girls experienced . . . I might have been honourably married and settled in life.'[66] He beat her and her siblings frequently and brutally, however, and rejected every possible suitor. To escape his brutality, she lived a wandering life moving from Dublin and the pleasant homes of her sisters, where she often met young men and enjoyed herself, to her rural home and a life of deprivation and brutality that sometimes saw her bedridden for weeks. When she was eighteen, the increasingly vicious ill treatment of her brother made her leave home permanently for Dublin. There she met and fell in love with a friend of her brother-in-law and became engaged to him. Regarding him as her husband, she allowed him to visit by night as well as during the day, and their expressions of affection became more fervent until she succumbed to him. For her, as for Phillips, it was the commencement of sexual activity outside marriage that brought the start of womanhood. Her sisters were shocked at her behaviour, however, and refused to help her, leaving no alternative but a life of immorality.

Entering into womanhood was a rather different, if still problematic, process for those who married very young, as one can see in the memoirs of Lady Frances Vane and Charlotte Charke. Frances Vane's doting father agreed after many entreaties, to her early marriage to the young man she loved passionately. The marriage was not untroubled: Vane showed her husband as sometimes unreasonably jealous and then behaving in ways that made her miserable right from its very beginning.[67] However, she insisted, every quarrel or brief parting was followed by a renewal of their unrestrained passion. Her marriage came to an unexpected end after a couple of years, not as a result of jealousy but rather with the sudden illness and death of her husband. Left a grieving widow with no financial provision, she was soon

---

[65]Phillips, *An Apology*, vol. 1, p. 60.
[66]Leeson, *Memoirs of Mrs Margaret Leeson*, p. 47.
[67]Vane, *Memoirs*.

persuaded to accept the hand of Lord Vane (W___ in the text), a man for whom she felt no attraction, simply on the grounds that he was wealthy and could provide for her.

Charlotte Charke too described an early marriage that she later thought should have been postponed or avoided, and that left her needing to support herself, her daughter and often her husband too. Her meeting with the violinist Richard Charke drew her out of a fit of melancholy when she was still very young and led her into a hasty and imprudent marriage to a man whom she thought loved her when in fact what he really wanted was to further his career by being connected with the Cibber family. Her father, seeing her involvement 'out of pure Pity, tenderly consented to a conjugal Union', something Charke later thought might have been handled differently, by sending her for a brief tour into the country, for example, to allow her to get over this infatuation. Both she and her husband were too young for marriage, she insisted.

> We were both so young and indiscreet that we ought rather to have been sent to school than to church, in regard to any qualifications on either side, towards rendering the marriage state comfortable to one another.[68]

While she remained faithful, he was soon enjoying the company and sexual favours of many other women and the marriage soon came to an end.[69] She supported herself and her daughter by returning to the stage as soon as she could.

It was not the fact of marrying young that Laetitia Pilkington regretted: indeed, she insisted that she was quite ready for marriage at the age of thirteen. The problem was the choice of husband. She had several suitors, not because she was beautiful: 'farther than being very fair. But I was well-drest, sprightly, and remarkably well-tempered.' A number of young men offered marriage and she would have been happily settled in adult life, 'but that my Mother's capricious Temper made her reject every advantageous proposal'.[70] Matthew Pilkington, a young clergyman with no fortune or prospects was the most assiduous of her suitors. His lack of prospects meant he was not acceptable to her family. At some point, however, her mother was won over by him and suggested that Laetitia could marry Pilkington but must do it secretly so that her family could appear to disapprove of it! The marriage took place – and in time, the disapproval became real. Not only did her mother genuinely disapprove, but Matthew Pilkington subsequently made matters worse when he fought bitterly with Laetitia's beloved father, causing an estrangement between them.

---

[68] Charke, *Narrative*, p. 27.
[69] Charke, *Narrative*, p. 29.
[70] Pilkington, *Memoir*, vol. I, p. 16.

There was little suggestion that Matthew Pilkington could support his wife. Almost from the start, Pilkington was aware that she needed to take responsibility for their lives and well-being. It was she rather than her husband, she insisted, who worked to establish their social networks, for example, including their friendship with Jonathan Swift. Matthew Pilkington had been introduced to Swift first and Laetitia, feeling left out, persuaded mutual friends to introduce them, composing a poem on the occasion of Swift's birthday to indicate her admiration. The poem ends with these rousing lines:

Behold in Swift reviv'd appears
The virtues of unnumber'd years;
Behold in him with new delight,
The Patriot, Bard and Sage unite;
And know, *Ierne* in that name
Shall rival *Greece* and *Rome* in fame.[71]

The poem elicited the desired invitation from Swift to visit him and thus began the friendship that looms so large in her literary life. Pilkington insisted that she and her husband worked equally hard when it came to writing verse – but that she was the better poet, something that was a factor in the breakdown of her marriage.[72]

The Descent into Infamy – and a Life of Struggle

It is the question of their outcast status, of how they have been seen negatively and judged harshly by the surrounding society, and how they have managed to survive, that these memoirists wanted primarily to address. Hence the major part of each of these works depicts the way the author fell into her life of infamy and how she maintained herself after she was cast out of respectable society. There are different kinds of story here, depending on whether the woman had been married or not, and on whether she saw herself as guilty of sexual transgression or some other kind of indiscretion There is a shift of emphasis too: while the women continue to insist on their vulnerability, on the precariousness of their situation, and on the wrongs they suffer, they also point to their own capacities, and to the qualities that enabled them to make a life for themselves and to survive and manage within a harsh and uncaring world. Several of them show considerable wit

---

[71]Pilkington, *Memoir*, vol. I, p. 52.
[72]Pilkington, *Memoir*, vol. I, p. 74.

and literary skill in their detailed depiction of the men who had wronged them most, relishing their capacity to heap scorn upon them.

Publishing her story as a way to wreak vengeance was something Constantia Phillips had long contemplated. She began planning it when Mr Grimes ceased his payments to her to embarrass him and gain financial support. She was dissuaded from doing so by some of his friends and turned instead to other men for support. Later, however, she told the story in full. It was not so much the question of reputation that bothered her after Grimes deserted her, Phillips insisted, but rather her need for adequate financial support. She ascribed partly to him the taste for pleasure she had developed and explained how, without his support, she was soon in debt and threatened with debtor's prison. As in several 18th-century novels, Phillips pointed to her scheming landlady as one who took advantage of her and led her astray, helping Grimes to further his designs and, after he left, offering new suggestions. One suggestion that Phillips agreed to involved taking advantage of the laws of coverture which meant that a wife's legal identity was subsumed into that of her husband on marriage, and so too was responsibility for her debts. Phillips agreed to marry a man she didn't know and would probably never see again, but who would nonetheless assume all her debts, leaving her free to accumulate new ones!

Phillips now accepted she was on a dissolute pathway. She attracted lovers with ease. A short time after her fictitious marriage, she met the Dutch merchant, Henry Muilman who made great protestations of his affection and desire to make her happy. Although only fifteen, 'she was now too far launched into the world to expect to make her Fortune by an *honourable Marriage*', she wrote.

> She had a clear idea of what he meant, and therefore, listen'd to our Hollander's Proposal, as a Means whereby she might extricate herself from a sad dependence on the World, and be less exposed to the Vicissitudes of a public Life.[73]

To her great surprise, we are told, Muilman wanted to marry rather than to seduce Phillips and she complied willingly. The marriage apparently began well and she got on with his family. At some point, however, Muilman's father was told about her previous life and insisted that his son end the marriage. Dependent as he was on his father's approval and financial support, Muilman began working to this end. Phillips fought bitterly against his attempts to have their marriage annulled, demanding that he provided the life annuity he had once promised. She depicts Muilman as both cowardly and duplicitous: he wrote to her declaring his love, and indeed continued sleeping with her whenever he could, while seeking the

---

[73]Phillips. *Apology*, vol. I, p. 66.

annulment he needed and a more acceptable marriage to pacify his family and secure his fortune.[74]

From this point on, Phillips's story shifts back and forth as she provided lengthy and detailed accounts of her battle with Muilman and the ways in which she tried to make him recognize their marriage and support her, and equally detailed accounts of her encounters and relationships with other lovers. Throughout the text, she insisted on her financial precarity. Several of her lovers apparently lavished jewellery and luxury on her, yet she never succeeded in gaining the regular annuity that would make her life more secure. Hers was a life composed of serial adventures as she travelled back and forth to France and even further afield: to the West Indies on one occasion. Phillips wrote with verve and considerable humour as she sought to obtain her reader's sympathy and support.

Just as Phillips depicted the rape she suffered at the hands of Mr Grimes in terms that could have come from a contemporary novel, so too she depicted some of the men with whom she was involved. The most notable one that also shows both her literary talent and her sense of humour is the story of a man she calls Tartufe. *The Amours of Tartufe* is almost a separate biography within the larger text. Even before we meet Tartufe, we are shown letters illustrating that 'he is sordidly avaricious, his Affability is a mere Grimace, and like his Goodness and sanctity, all Hypocrisy'.[75] Tartufe was the younger son of a Catholic Baronet. His person was agreeable, Phillips noted, his eyes apparently full of meaning, his tongue artful and 'his whole figure altogether graceful: he is clean even to Female Delicacy; and has a dangerous Address'.[76] He was of a 'robust, lascivious Constitution', and 'so artful and selfish that . . . he always preserves an inviolable Adherence to his Interests'. He was not inclined to support children and so preferred to have married women as his mistresses, knowing that their husbands would support any offspring that resulted from his liaisons. Like Phillips, he was a Catholic, but ostensibly more devout, and constantly claimed that he feared damnation. Even in their most intimate moments, 'when it is almost out of Nature to believe the Transport would give Time for Reflection, he would frequently start and cry out, Oh! Heavens! My Girl! We shall both be damned'.[77] Although she spent some years with him, Tartufe gave Phillips nothing. In a way that served both to illustrate the meanness of Tartufe and her own generosity, good nature and possible foolishness, Phillips provided a detailed account of the money that she spent on him. In a section titled 'Mrs Muilman's Folly', she itemized every thing she had spent on him. The total was £4,874.09, to which she added some £100,000 for lodging, so that

---

[74] See also Lawrence Stone, *Uncertain Unions: Marriage in England 1660–1753* (Oxford: Oxford University Press, 1992; repr. Online October 2011).
[75] Phillips, *Apology*, vol. II, p. 90.
[76] Phillips, *Apology*, vol. II, p. 96.
[77] Phillips, *Apology*, vol. II, p. 175.

the 'Balance due to Folly' was £104,874.09. An extraordinary amount for the 18th century. Subsequently, when he was wealthy and Phillips in dire financial straits, she appealed to Tartufe for help, he gave her nothing, suggesting that she go to live in a convent – and offering £10 per year to assist with her board![78] Phillips, who estimated her own needs as £200 per annum, was rendered speechless.

Relationships with several other men followed and were all depicted in some detail. She seems rarely to have seen a man who did not immediately pursue her with great energy and fervour. She was often involved in difficult situations in which she was imprisoned or deprived of money by a jealous lover who feared she was subject to the attention of rivals. All her relationships inevitably came to an end, and after each one she was left in distressed circumstances and returned to her attempt to make Mr Muilman, whom she continued to see as her husband, pay her some form of maintenance. He in turn became more and more irate, having her imprisoned for debt at one point, where she languished for some two years. Phillips, who was capable of black humour, notes that for Muilman, her commitment 'was a Victory to him (as Shakespear (*sic*) says) worth a Jew's Eye'.[79]

Laetitia Pilkington had a very different and rather more complicated story to tell of the events that led to her 'fall' from respectability. It all occurred, she insists, because of her husband's jealousy of her greater poetic capacity and determination to end their marriage, A misstep on her part gave him the opportunity. She was not guilty of any kind of sexual indiscretion, Pilkington insisted, but was brought down by her love of reading and the discovery of a man who owned a book she wanted to read in her bed chamber.

> I own myself to be very indiscreet in permitting any Man to be in my Bed-chamber; but Lovers of learning will, I am sure, pardon me, as I solemnly declare, it was the attractive charms of a new book, which the Gentleman would not lend me, but contented to stay while I read it through, that was the sole Motive of my detaining him. But the Servants, being bribed by their Master, let in twelve Watchmen at the Kitchen Window who, though they might have opened the Chamber-Door, chose rather to break it to pieces, and took the Gentleman and myself prisoner.[80]

Although it was 2 a.m., Matthew Pilkington insisted that she leave the house. He kept her jewellery and gave her very little money, so it was with difficulty she found lodgings, and indeed when she went out the next day, she returned to find her room and the landlady denying her entrance. From the moment her marriage ended, Pilkington was forced onto her own

---

[78] Phillips, *Apology*, vol. II, p. 170.
[79] Phillips, *Apology*, vol. II, p. 273.
[80] Pilkington, *Memoir*, vol. II, p. 231.

resources. She was too well known in Dublin to remain there and so determined to go to London. Her penniless state meant that she was dependent on the generosity of strangers, even for this trip.

From this point on, Pilkington's life was difficult. She took lodgings in St James Street so that she would be close to a genteel clientele and tried to set herself up as a poet and professional writer of letters or pamphlets. Her meeting with Colley Cibber was fortunate as he did his bit to find her subscribers, but it was a hard way to live. Slowly but surely, as Virginia Woolf says in her essay on Pilkington's *Memoir*, she descended the social scale. It was a hard life, Woolf points out.

> To trudge to Chelsea in the snow wearing nothing but a chintz gown and be put off with a beggarly half-crown; next tramp to Ormond Street and extract two guineas from the odious Dr Meader, which, in her glee, she tossed in the air and lost in a crack on the floor; to be insulted by footmen; to sit down to a dish of boiling water because her landlady must not guess that a pinch of tea was beyond her means.[81]

But all the time, Pilkington felt the need to entertain her readers and so made light of her many plights, including being thrown out of her lodgings and incarcerated in a debtor's prison, where she remained, until Colley Cibber raised enough in donations to have her released. The two children she was forced to leave in Ireland joined her in time, both destitute and in need of help and support from her. Like Phillips, Pilkington stressed her lack of practical forethought or capacity to manage money. Whenever she made any money, there were others only too willing to impose on her for it.

> As I paid a Guinea a Week for my Lodgings, kept a Servant, was under a Necessity of being always dressed, and had besides so many distressed Persons of my own Country, who did the Honour to take a Dinner with me, and, in return for my Easiness, said everything of me which they thought could injure, or expose me; that being naturally liberal, till I heartily suffered for my Folly, I rather ran out than saved.[82]

She too insisted repeatedly on the mean and dishonourable behaviour of her husband, and how disproportionately she suffered from the marriage breakdown. She augmented her own story with those of several other women who were seduced and abandoned and suffered terribly at the hands of unscrupulous men. The accounts of her own hardship are interspersed with extended tales of agreeable evenings and encounters in which she shone and was recognized for her wit and talent. There is no suggestion that she

---

[81] Virginia Woolf, 'Laetitia Pilkington', *The Common Reader*, Series I.
[82] Pilkington, *Memoirs*, vol. II, pp. 33–34.

ever bestowed her sexual favours on any of the men who sought them – although, just as it was the indiscretion of allowing a man to sit in her bedchamber while she read a book that brought disgrace on her, there are several other incidents in which she engaged in talk or literary pursuits alone with a man in ways that would not be acceptable in polite society. Pilkington's tales of her own success in gaining subscriptions and recognition for her poems underlined her refusal to see or depict herself as a victim. In one of her many addresses to her readers, she made clear her desire to run away from the treatment of her misfortunes and apologized for needing to deal with something as dismal as her imprisonment.[83] She dealt with her husband and their relationship mockingly.

> I have been a lady of Adventure, and almost every Day of my Life produces some new one: I am sure I ought to thank my loving husband for the Opportunity he has afforded me of seeing the World from Palace to Prison; for had he but permitted me to be what nature certainly intended me for, a harmless household Dove, in all human Probability I should have rested content with my humble Situation, and instead of using a Pen, been employed with a Needle, to work for the little ones we might, by this time, have had.[84]

Although differing from the other two in many ways, Charlotte Charke's story shares with them its deviation from accepted norms of womanly behaviour and any form of respectability. Hers is not a tale of descent into ignominy as a result of sexual indiscretions, but rather a story of one who was never able to conform or meet normal familial or social expectations. She acknowledged this by stressing the 'oddness', evident not only in her frequent cross-dressing, but in her interests and tastes, and escapades. Although written in a comic vein and seeking to amuse by recounting her frequent misadventures, Charke depicted a life of hardship and travail, as she struggled to make a living in a number of different ways, especially after cutting her ties with the established London theatre. It is her depiction of the theatrical world in which she lived and worked in her early years that gives Charke's *Narrative* a particular interest. Her story was written in an episodic way, moving from her first performance in *The Provoke'd Wife* on a benefit night, through a series of other performances in other plays, buoyed up by the approbation of her father and apparently enthusiastic response from the audience. At the start, she was well-connected to the world of London theatre, but Charke broke that connection as a result of several scrapes with theatre managers and with her father. She started working at the Drury Lane Theatre, in which her father was a major shareholder until he sold his shares

---

[83]Pilkington, *Memoirs*, vol. II, pp. 225–226.
[84]Pilkington, *Memoirs*, vol. II, p. 252.

to the theatre manager, Mr Highmore. His son, Theophilus Cibber, who had assumed he would get the shares, then organized a walkout of the actors, which Charlotte joined. She returned, but had a dispute with the new manager, Fleetwood, and walked out again. Her father intervened and Fleetwood took her back. Soon, however, Charke left Drury Lane to join Henry Fielding at the Haymarket Theatre where she played Lord Place in Fielding's play *Pasquin* for four guineas a week over several weeks.

> I cleared sixty guineas and walked with my Purse in my Hand 'till my Stock was exhausted, lest I should forget the Necessity I then labored under, of squandering what might have made many a decay'd family truly happy'.[85]

What she omits to say here is that Fielding, who despised Colley Cibber and satirized him frequently in both fiction and plays, wrote Lord Place as a particularly nasty caricature of him. Although Charke never seemed to recognize that this was the case, it was this act that seems finally to have alienated her from her father and for which he never forgave her. Her work with Fielding, and especially her part in *Pasquin*, damaged Charke in a number of ways that went beyond the familial. The play, which was critical of the government, led Walpole as prime minister to bring in the Stage Licensing Act (1737), which only allowed theatres with royal patents to stage plays. Drury Lane was one of these theatres, but the Haymarket was not. Charke had cut her ties with Drury Lane and the other patented theatres, so from this point on, she found it hard to get parts. For the rest of her life, Charke made do as best she could, alternating various kinds of work outside the theatre with running a puppet theatre and then working with groups of strolling players outside London – earning just enough to live on.

There is no discussion of her exclusion from the licensed theatre in the *Narrative*. In a work that underlines her own oddness, she suggests rather that she was affected by one new whim after another. Without a theatre job, 'I took it into my Head to dive into *Trade*. To that End, I took a Shop in Long Acre, and turned Oil-Woman and Grocer'. Charke knew nothing of trade or shopkeeping, not even how to weigh, measure and charge for her goods – and she provided a comic tale of how she was defrauded and even had her brass weights stolen from under her very eyes. This failure led again to the question of how to support herself and she decided to draw on her theatrical knowledge and talent and set up a puppet show. That too failed, leaving her owing money that led to a brief incarceration in debtor's prison. She was detained suddenly, not able even to tell her daughter where she was until the following day when friends managed to bail her out.[86]

Charke's life was a series of disasters, all depicted in a comic way. She pointed to the facets of her character that explained why things happened

---

[85]Charke, *Narrative*, p. 34.
[86]Charke, *Narrative*, pp. 35–40.

the way they did: her impatience, her lack of judgement, her tendency to spend any money she had immediately. On one occasion when she was in very distressed circumstances in London, she appealed to an uncle for help, and he gave her enough money to set herself up in a public house and wished her to do so immediately. Charke,

> obeyed his commands the next Day, and as I have been in a hurry from the Hour of my Birth, precipitately took the first House where I saw a Bill, and which unfortunately for me, was in Drury-Lane, that had been most irregularly and indecently kept, by the last incumbent, who was a celebrated Dealer in murdered Reputations, Wholesale and retail.[87]

Inevitably, she lost rather than made money, treating people to food who never returned or paid and letting rooms to others who also defaulted on payment and stole all the things she had bought for her kitchen. She was soon seriously in debt and, unable to ask her uncle for more money, 'prudently resolved to throw up my House'.[88] She worked as a strolling player and then entered another hopeless venture as a pigman. Throughout most of her adult life, she was in serious financial straits and had enormous difficulty supporting her daughter. The pain she felt at the loss of the love – and support – of her father is referred to throughout and she blamed a vicious sister for the rift between them. She shared her later years with a close woman friend whom she had occasion to strip of her only good gown in order to raise some money from it. Charke's life was hard, but she depicted it always as a series of comic scenes. Like Pilkington, she insists always on her own capacity to devise new schemes and to meet any challenges. But she also showed herself as lacking in forethought or in basic caution, completely unable to learn from her own experience and throwing herself headlong into one impossible venture after another.

A Sense of Self

While demanding the right to tell their own stories, justify their actions and make their claims against those who wronged them, few of the 18th-century women who wrote memoirs or autobiographies offer a clear or definite statement of how they thought about or understood themselves. Indeed, one of the remarkable features of several of these works is the contrast between the sharpness and clarity with which the authors characterize the men who often wronged them – and their very general and vague descriptions of themselves. They have no difficulty in naming or listing their own weaknesses,

---

[87]Charke, *Narrative*, p. 78.
[88]Charke, *Narrative*, pp. 81–83.

but these are usually described in very general terms, such as a love of luxury or pleasure, and linked to the characteristics thought of as common amongst women of their age. In a similar way, some also depicted their good qualities: their kindness or generosity or concern about the well-being of others, but here too, they often seem to be generic female qualities.

It does seem to be the case here that, while these women saw the men who wronged them as individuals with the agency and power to act as they choose, and hence with moral and ethical responsibility for their actions, they did not see themselves in that way. Hence, while insisting on their right to tell their story, they depicted themselves as people whose physical and moral qualities made them vulnerable to abuse. All of them insisted at some point on their status as victims, *albeit* offering very different depictions of the form their victimization took and the perpetrator responsible for it. In many cases, they saw themselves as victims of designing and unscrupulous men who took advantage of their youth and innocence – or sometimes of their love of ease and luxury. But many also saw themselves as victims of neglectful or cruel parents or siblings. Some even suggested that they are victimized by overindulgent parents who allowed them to follow their own desires when they should have prevented it. At the same time, they all stressed the energy, determination and sometimes ingenuity with which they face their difficult situations and work out how best to pursue their own course of action capacity. Charke, for example, rather relished her many ventures into different kinds of shops and forms of trade, while Pilkington stressed her capacity to turn her hand to any kind of writing.

This contrast between the depiction of herself and those of the men she knew is illustrated particularly vividly by Constantia Phillips. We have seen already her graphic depiction of Tartufe. But there is similar detail in her depiction of Henry Muilman, the chief villain in her story. She showed him as cowardly, but sensual, unable to follow a principled course of action and constantly changing his conduct in the light of his concerns about the good opinion of others, especially his father. This point is well illustrated by the way that, while refusing either to maintain their marriage or to offer her an annuity, he sneaked in to sleep with her as often as he could. His behaviour is 'a complication of villainy, fraud, oppression and folly'. But when it came to describing herself and to why she squandered the money that Muilman did give and got herself into debt, she pointed only to her 'youthful vanity and natural love of pleasure', qualities, as she notes, that are common in young women. Indeed, she suggested that Muilman was largely responsible for her extravagance: he sent her to Paris so that she would not be in London while he pursued the annulment of their marriage there. While there, she developed 'such a relish for pleasure that she had become absolutely enamoured of the *Beau Monde*, an enchantment, I believe, few young people who are their own Governors have the fortune to Escape'.[89] Alas, the

---

[89]Phillips, *Apology*, vol. I, pp. 227–228.

narrator continues, 'when either sex entertain too early a fondness for Pleasure (and Women in particular) they are apt with too little Discretion to pursue the means by which it is to be attained; and seldom are Prudent enough to suffer reason to have the Direction of their Passions'.

Phillips did make claim to some particular capacities and strengths. She noted her kindness and concern for others, for example, especially the wretched people with whom she was incarcerated in the debtor's prison and whom she felt an obligation to write about and to try to help. She also noted her understanding of health and contemporary medical ideas and the ways she sought to apply these things for the help of others. These qualities are certainly part of the appeal she makes to be treated with sympathy by her readers and to stress that she was not all self-indulgence. But they do not add up to any real sense of her personality or indeed of her own sense of herself. It is notable too that, while her *Apology* covers Phillips' life from the time she was thirteen until she was in her forties, there is no sense in it that she learnt anything from experience or developed in any significant way. What is stressed rather is that, despite her many unfortunate experiences and the duplicity of others that she had suffered from, she retained not only her essential goodness, but even her failings, including her extravagance, gullibility, and lack of judgement that led her into scrapes or unfortunate situations. This is illustrated in the final appeal to her readers towards the end of the book. She knew she had taken false steps, but was truly repentant and, as a result of her age, would not fall again.

> Which way can she now offend? This Age produces few who will fall in Love with the Picture she has drawn of her unhappiness; though some, indeed, may be induced to pity: The very Cause of your displeasure is at an End; our Apologist now approaches her fortieth Year; and Time has taken from her the Attractions that theretofore led her into those Mistakes which incurred your Displeasure.[90]

Laetitia Pilkington too gave a very much clearer picture of her cruel and ruthless husband, Matthew, than she did of herself. Pilkington emphasized her love of reading and her skill and talent as a poet. It was the love of reading, evident in her childhood, but continuing into her adult years that was after all the cause of her fall. She was never, as she made clear, a great beauty and when her marriage ended had to rely on her sharpness and conversational and literary capacities to support herself. She clearly saw these capacities as evident in the way she negotiated her way to London and managed her life there as a writer of poems and pamphlets, as differentiating her from other women. Pilkington referred to few other qualities or

---

[90] Phillips, *Apology*, vol. III, p. 56.

characteristics that establish her own sense of identity, however, and falls back on similar qualities to those shown by Phillips in explaining how hard her life was: kindness, gullibility, and a lack of any practical or financial sense. Although she earned a reasonable amount from her poetry in her early years in London, and others might have thought, 'I was in a fair way of growing rich' as we have seen, her extravagance and the demands of other 'distressed Persons of my own country', ensured that this was not to be.

There is little sense in Pilkington's own narrative of the grit and determination that her biographer Norma Clarke describes, in her approach to writing and financing her memoirs.

In the case of Charlotte Charke, this question of the lack of a clear or articulate sense of self in the *Narrative* has been discussed far more extensively than it has in relation to the work of any other 18th-century autobiography. Charke invited it through her emphasis on her own oddness and lack of conformity to the expectations of others in every aspect of her life. 'If Oddity can plead any Right to Surprise and Astonish' she wrote at the beginning of her narrative, 'I may positively claim a Title to be shewn among the Wonders of Ages past, and those to come', and she underlined her oddness or oddities throughout the text.[91] These oddities began in her childhood as she showed in illustrating the many scrapes she got into – and her early love of assuming masculine dress. They continued throughout her adult life and there can be seen to include not only enjoyment in assuming masculine dress and roles, but also the improvidence and lack of forethought and the inclination to undertake new ventures without any sense of the consequences that she suggested one could see in all her actions. But Charke never linked this oddness to a sense of her own personality. Rather than describing herself, she focused on particular incidents or episodes.

One reason that Charke did not discuss her inner life or thoughts, some would argue, is because, as an actor with an extensive repertoire, she drew so heavily on the language of the theatre, often using the character or voices from particular plays to articulate her own life experiences. She cast herself in a number of different roles as she recounted her own life story, including the roles of gentleman's service or pastry cook or beekeeper, rarely saying what she thought or felt about the different kinds of work involved. Her story is always told dramatically and humorously, appealing for laughter – rather than sympathy. Because she played the part of actor throughout, she did not offer her readers a clear or fixed view of herself or of her own sense of identity. This lack of fixity, as Heather Lobban-Viravong, points out 'has

---

[91] Charke, *Narrative*, p. 8.

prompted critics to accuse her of not being fully present in the text, of almost willfully writing herself in absentia'.[92] The point, Robert Rehder argues, however, is not so much that she is absent from the text as that she is present only through her actions so that we learn almost nothing about her inner world.[93] Some critics have argued that Charke is thus an imposter, who, Sidonie Smith argues, 'masquerades in a variety of roles, plots and characters, establishing throughout her autobiography resonances with fictional and dramatic heroines and heroes'.[94] She 'assumes all rhetorical postures, takes on all characters, plays all scenes for the dramatic possibilities inherent in them'.[95]

One of the questions that has been the cause of discussion most recently is that concerning her sexuality. While she clearly enjoyed cross-dressing, often acting as a man off-stage as well as in theatrical performances, Charke would not discuss why she did so or what it meant to her. Charke made it quite clear that she would not discuss why she liked dressing as a man.

> The original Motive proceeded from a particular Cause; and I rather chuse to undergo the worst imputation that can be laid on me on that Account than unravel the Secret, which is an Appendix to one I am bound, as I before hinted, by all the Vows of Truth and honour everlastingly to conceal.[96]

As Felicity Nussbaum notes, Charke 'forever obscures her motivation for masquerading as a man', making it clear that, while she recognizes it as a question a reader might ask, she will not answer it.[97] Overall, one is forced to agree with Robert Rehder's suggestion that her *Narrative*, 'is more a gathering of diverse scattered events than a considered effort of self-fashioning. She wrote before the language of selfhood had been invented. She has no interest in, or sense of psychological processes and is not at all self-analytic.'[98]

Just as developments in fiction and the emergence of the seduction narrative provide an encouragement to these memoirs, so too 18th-century

---

[92]Heather Lobban-Viravong, 'The Theatrics of Self-Sentiment in a Narrative of the Life of Mrs. Charlotte Charke', *a/b: Auto/Biography Studies* 24, no. 2 (2009): 194–195.
[93]Ibid., pp. 194–195.
[94]Sidonie Smith, 'The Transgressive Daughter and the Masquerade of Self-Representation', in *Introducing Charlotte Charke*, ed. Philip E. Baruth (Chicago: University of Chicago Press, 1998), p. 46.
[95]Charke, *Narrative*, p. ix.
[96]Charke, *Narrative*, pp. 114–115.
[97]Felicity Nussbaum, 'Afterword: Charke's Variety of Wretchedness', in *Introducing Charlotte Charke*, ed. Philip E. Baruth (Chicago: University of Chicago Press, 1998), p. 238.
[98]Charke, *Narrative*, p. v.

fiction provides a useful way of thinking about the very minimal sense of self that they contain. In 18th-century fiction, Patricia Meyer Spacks argues, a heroine is characteristically defined by her weakness. That weakness along with her passivity becomes a social resource.[99] Spacks points to the similarities between the heroines of fiction and women's creation of a self in letters, diaries or actual autobiographies. Women writing memoirs, she argues, 'demanded attention, respect, and understanding for their necessary insufficiency. The identities they define derive mainly from their exploration of vulnerabilities: social, sexual, psychic.' In a variety of ways, these women stress what has been done to them rather than what they as protagonists have done. It is their social connections rather than their accomplishments that matter. The fact that, while they might manage to survive, they do not actually succeed in any significant way clearly frames how they can think and write about themselves. Charlotte Charke, as Spacks argues, 'admires her own spirit of constant endeavour but cannot esteem what she does since she inevitably fails', while Pilkington's 'pride in what she has suffered far exceed her pride in authorship'. So, for them too, it is hard to move beyond the weaknesses that link them with other women in writing about themselves.

18th-century fiction provides an explanation for another aspect of the memoirs that is sometimes puzzling to current readers: the lack of any suggestion that the author might learn from her own experiences and avoid falling continually into similar traps or developing as a result of her experience. Here too, as Spacks argues, one sees something helpful in contemporary fiction. Both 18th-century autobiography and 18th-century fiction share their ideas about character. In contrast to the 19th century, when optimism focused on the possibility of change, in the 18th century readers depended 'on the reassurances of stability'. The heroes and heroines of novels did not change substantially. The many things that happen to them, while possibly bringing small change, enabled them to reveal themselves more fully. What is important is that, regardless of what happened, they remained themselves. The triumph of the central character was to remain essentially the same in novels, Spacks argues, and this was true also of the women who wrote memoirs. One of their primary concerns was to insist that, despite their difficult and unfortunate experiences, they retained throughout their adult lives not only their essential goodness but even their failings: their extravagance, their gullibility, the lack of judgement that led them into scrapes or unfortunate situations.

---

[99]Patricia Meyer Spacks, *Imagining a Self: Autobiography and Novel in Eighteenth-Century England* (Cambridge, MA: Harvard University Press, 2013).

Conclusion

The importance of the 18th-century women's secular autobiography in Britain has increasingly come to be recognized and acknowledged by literary scholars and historians. They have recognized not only the intrinsic interest and merit of much of this work but also the complex issues that it raises in terms of how best to classify, label and find an adequate framework for these works and to move outside the pervasive sense of them as scandalous writings. This sense of scandal encompasses both the lives that these women led, many involving a range of sexual indiscretions and the ways in which they contravened prevailing norms and expectations surrounding femininity in the very act of writing and publishing their life stories, an act that drew attention to themselves, rather than remaining in decent obscurity.

This hint of scandal and the different elements of which it is composed suggests both how important it is to recognize the 18th-century origins of women's memoirs and autobiographies and how hard it is for later generations of writers to have any sense of connection with them. As we will see, in the course of the second half of the 19th century, women writing autobiographies sought to avoid any such hint, by stressing the completely moral and worthy lives they led and their achievements, and sometimes also by insisting that their work not be published in their lifetime. This strategy did not always enable them to avoid censure. Of course, although some were sufficiently well known to appear in the first edition of the *Dictionary of National Biography*, there is no suggestion that any of these 18th-century memoir writers were known to the prominent Victorian women who wrote autobiographies a century later. What one has here then is a history without any kind of link. None of these works stands, as the *Confessions of Rousseau* do, for example, as the beginning of a tradition or a way of thinking about autobiography that is significant for both readers and practitioners in subsequent periods.

Autobiographies Discussed in This Chapter

Bellamy, George Anne. *An Apology for the Life of George Anne Bellamy*. London, printed for the authors, 1785.

Charke, Charlotte. *A Narrative of the Life of Mrs Charlotte Charke (1755) Edited and with Introduction and Notes by Robert Rehder*. London: Pickering & Chatto, 2016.

Gooch, Elizabeth. 'The Life of Mrs Gooch (1792)', in *Memoirs of Scandalous Women*, edited by Dianne Dugaw. London: Pickering & Chatto, 2011.

Leeson, Margaret. *Memoirs of Mrs Margaret Leeson Written by Herself; in Which Are Given Anecdotes, Sketches of the Lives and Bon Mots of Some of the Most Celebrated Characters in Great Britain and Ireland, Particularly of All the Filles Des Joys and Men of Pleasure and Gallantry Which Have Frequented Her Citherean Temple for These Thirty Years Past*. 3 vols. Dublin: 'Printed and sold by the Principal Booksellers', 1797.

Murray, Fanny. *Memoirs of the Celebrated Miss Fanny Murray*. 2nd edition London: J. Scott, 1759.

Phillips, Constantia. *An Apology for the Conduct of Mrs Teresia Constantia Phillips*, 3 vols 2nd edition, printed for the Booksellers of London and Westminster, 1847), accessed through Eighteenth Century Collections Online, Gale Primary Sources.

Pilkington, Laetitia. *Memoirs of Mrs Laetitia Pilkington, Wife to the Rev. Mr Matthew Pilkington, Written by Herself, Wherein are occasionally Interspersed all her Poems, with Anecdotes of several eminent Persons, Living and dead*, 20 vols (Dublin, Printed for the Author, 1748), accessed through Eighteenth Century Collections Online, Gale Primary Sources.

Robinson, Mary. *Memoirs of the Late Mrs Robinson Written by Herself* (1801). London: Cobden Sanderson, 1930.

Vane, Frances. 'Memoirs of a Lady of Quality', first published as chapter LXXXI of Tobias Smollett, *The Adventures of Peregrine Pickle* (London, 1751). Edited by J. L. Clifford. Oxford: Oxford University Press, 1969.

FIGURE 2 *Engraving after Harriet Martineau by Alonzo Chappel. (Photo by Hulton-Deutsch / Hulton-Deutsch Collection / Corbis via Getty Images.)*

CHAPTER TWO

Women's Autobiography Comes of Age

Often described as the Golden Age of Autobiography, the 19th century was one in which all forms of life writing flourished. The term 'autobiography' came into common usage early in the century, helped by the publication of popular series like Hunt and Clarke's *Autobiography. A Collection of the Most Instructive and Amusing Lives Ever Published, Written by the Parties Themselves*.[1] The use of the autobiographical form in widely read novels, especially Charlotte Brontë's *Jane Eyre* and Charles Dickens' *David Copperfield*, reflected this growing interest and also offered new ways of telling life stories in which childhood suffering and development became prominent. Publication of the great Victorian male autobiographies of Mill, Newman, Ruskin and Darwin served both to establish a canon and to underline the value of prominent men producing such works. Leslie Stephen, the first editor of the *Dictionary of National Biography*, ventured to suggest that writing an autobiography 'should be considered a duty by all eminent men'.[2] Although some of the 18th-century hesitancy about autobiography remained and many people still felt the need to explain or justify their writing of their own story, interest in individual accounts of personal struggle and development increased. Victorian ideas of decorum also served to establish rules that limited the private revelations and personal issues that might be discussed and governed how others might be described.[3]

---

[1]*Autobiography: A Collection of the Most Instructive and Amusing Lives Ever Published, Written by the Parties Themselves*, 33 volumes (London: Whittaker, Treacher, Arnott, 1920–32).
[2]Leslie Stephen, 'Autobiography', *Cornhill Magazine* LXIII (1881).
[3]There is a good discussion of these rules in Sally Mitchell, 'Frances Power Cobbe's *Life* and the Rules for Women's Autobiography', *English Literature in Transition, 1880–1920* 50, no. 2 (2007).

Although rarely included in general discussions of 19th-century autobiography, women were in many ways beneficiaries of these developments. Stephen's reference to 'eminent men' was not accidental: no women feature in the extensive survey of autobiography that he offered and he would never have extended his injunction to them. Indeed, the notion that it was somehow reprehensible for women to draw attention to themselves by writing about their lives continued until the end of the century. George Eliot disliked the self-importance of Harriet Martineau's autobiography and, as we have seen, found the writing of one herself repellent.[4] Growing numbers of women rejected this view, however. Writing some decades before Leslie Stephen set out his views on autobiography, Harriet Martineau had suggested that prominent women too had an obligation to write their lives. 'From my youth upwards', she declared, 'I have felt that it was one of my duties to write an autobiography. ... When my life became evidently a somewhat remarkable one, the obligation presented itself more strongly to my conscience.'[5]

In referring to her own life as 'somewhat remarkable', Martineau was pointing to her immense success in establishing herself as a successful writer and journalist, able to support herself in considerable comfort and to enjoy her position as a well-known and influential figure in Victorian society. She was not without critics or detractors. Nonetheless, she was able to maintain herself as a single woman as a result of the massive expansion in the daily and periodical press that had accompanied industrialization, urbanization and the expansion in literacy that was so marked in the 19th century. She was able to maintain this position without a hint of impropriety too, something that points to some of the paradoxical aspects of 19th-century developments, especially in relation to women.[6] The expanding size and influence of the middle classes in the 19th century brought a new emphasis on family and home and on the importance of women's domestic confinement and familial role. At the same time, and as Martineau shows, there were new opportunities for women in the professional and public world to live independent lives. One reason for this, as the evidence from the regular census taken of the British population revealed, was that not all women had families or homes. Around ten per cent of women never married and needed to support themselves in whatever way they could. While many lived a precarious and impoverished life, the expanding worlds of education, journalism and philanthropy offered others the opportunity either to become independent professionals or to engage in charitable work or pursue social reforms that interested them. Some became involved in the movement

---

[4] Valerie Sanders, *The Private Lives of Victorian Women: Autobiography in Nineteenth-Century England* (New York: St Martin's Press, 1989), p. 17.
[5] Harriet Martineau, *Autobiography*, 3 vols (London: Virago, 1877, repr. 1983), p. 1.
[6] See Deirdre David, *Intellectual Women and Victorian Patriarchy: Harriet Martineau, Elizabeth Barrett Browning, George Eliot* (London: Macmillan, 1986). R. K. Webb, *Harriet Martineau: A Radical Victorian* (New York: Columbia University Press, 1960).

for women's rights that emerged in the second half of the century, campaigning to improve the educational and employment opportunities of women, to improve their legal status and to give them political rights. For the most part, especially from mid-century onwards, it was these single women who wrote autobiographies and whose work defines 'Victorian women's autobiography'.

Established as they were as public figures, these Victorian women no longer felt the need to offer special apologies and justifications for writing autobiographies. When they offered their reasons for writing autobiographies they often did so in terms that were gender-neutral. Frances Cobbe, for example, insisted at the start of her *Life* that 'the days are past when biographers thought it necessary to apologize for the paucity of adventures they could recall. My life has been an interesting one to live, and I hope this record of it may not be too dull to read.'[7] Annie Besant went even further, using the pronoun 'he' when explaining why she wrote her autobiography. The only excuse for writing a life story, especially if it is an average one, she wrote in the Preface to her autobiography is that it,

> reflects many others, and in troublous (*sic*) times like ours may give the experience of many rather than of one. And so, the autobiographer does his work because he thinks that, at the cost of some unpleasantness to himself, he may throw light on some of the typical problems that are vexing the souls of his contemporaries, and perchance may stretch out a helping hand to some brother who is struggling in the darkness, and so bring him cheer when despair has him in its grip.[8]

And yet, however much they rejected the idea of a specifically feminine justification for writing their lives, all of these women were very much aware of the criticism that women's autobiography continued to attract and of the limitations and restrictions that they and other women faced both in living their lives and in writing about them. Unlike their 18th-century predecessors, these Victorian women autobiographers had no doubt that their lives and stories would be of interest to readers. As prominent women whose achievements were widely recognized, they felt secure in making claims to their own significance. They often included extracts from their own earlier books and articles to expand on their ideas and demonstrate the basis of their renown. Cobbe, Martineau, Besant and many other women autobiographers like Mary Somerville or Louisa Twining had stepped outside the normal bounds of femininity and they generally discussed how they had been educated or educated themselves and developed their interests,

---

[7]Frances Power Cobbe, *The Life of Frances Power Cobbe by Herself* (London: Richard Bentley & Son, 1894), vol. I, p. iii.
[8]Annie Wood Besant, *An Autobiography* (London: T. Fisher Unwin, 1908). Accessed through Nineteenth Century Collections Online, p. 5.

careers and public activities. Sometimes this included discussion of a struggle for their independence. At the same time, almost all of them accepted the prevailing view that a woman should not draw too much attention to herself. It is this belief that explains their acceptance of the convention that the autobiography of a woman should not stand forth by itself, but should rather be formally presented by someone else, either a daughter or a close woman friend whose introduction could provide a demonstration of the modesty of the author. The presenter often insisted that the author had written her autobiography reluctantly, out of a sense of duty or at the behest of friends. The presenter thus showed how closely the author adhered to prevailing norms of feminine propriety and their commitment to an orderly domestic life. The balance between the celebration of public achievement and a deep concern to endorse conventional ideas of feminine modesty and decorum was often a difficult one to establish and maintain. This emphasis on their proper domestic life and adherence to the highest moral standards in terms of conduct, moreover, also made it very clear that Victorian women did not have – and were not claiming – the autobiographical freedom available to men who often ignored the domestic world entirely.[9]

A great deal of the scholarship and discussion of 19th-century women's autobiography has focused attention on women like Martineau and Cobbe, eminent women whose work was published in the 1870s or after and whose writing fits within the broad framework of Victorian women's autobiography in its emphasis on achievement and feminine decorum. But this was not the only form of women's autobiography to appear in the 19th century. Several autobiographies that did not in any way conform to this Victorian approach appeared in the first half of the century. New 'scandalous autobiographies' continued to be published until the 1830s, for example, with the appearance of the *Memoirs* of the very well-known courtesan Harriette Wilson in 1825. They were followed shortly after by the *Confessions* of her one-time friend but later enemy Julia Johnson.[10] Wilson's Memoir, which was published over two years, was the most successful scandalous autobiography ever written. The 1830s also saw the publication of *The History of Mary Prince, a West Indian Slave, Related by Herself*, the first woman's slave narrative to be published in England. Prince's work, describing the life of a woman who was a slave in Antigua, although free once in England, shocked many with its direct treatment of the beatings and the rape and other forms of sexual abuse suffered by women slaves from when they were very young. Another autobiography that came from the wider British world and offered further insight into a very different kind of

---

[9]Linda H. Peterson, *Traditions of Victorian Women's Autobiography: The Poetics and Politics of Life Writing* (Charlottesville: University Press of Virginia, 1999). See also Sanders, *Op. Cit.*
[10]Julia Johnstone, *Confessions of Julia Johnstone Writte by Herself in Contradiction to the Fables of Harriette Wilson* (London: Benbow, Printer and Publisher, 1825).

woman's life was *The Adventures of Mary Seacole* (1857). The Jamaican born Seacole was an entrepreneur and a 'doctoress', and her *Adventures* detailed her activities and experiences first in Panama and then in the Crimea, where she sought unsuccessfully to work alongside Florence Nightingale. Those works in particular brought some new voices from the wider British world that anticipate later global developments in women's autobiography.

What becomes evident when one looks at the full range of 19th-century women's autobiographies, is the extent of the change between the early decades, when continuities with the 18th century are very marked, and the last few decades when one sees something quite different in terms of the kinds of women who wrote autobiographies and the kinds of lives they depicted in them. These changes in autobiography obviously reflect broader economic and social changes and particularly the expanding range of occupations, including paid employment and philanthropic activity, available to women. While Harriette Wilson followed the pattern of 18th-century courtesans in turning to autobiography – and blackmail – as a way to support herself in her later years, just a couple of decades later both Harriet Martineau and then Frances Cobbe made very comfortable livings as journalists writing for a variety of the new periodicals that were appearing in the mid-19th century to meet the interests of an expanding and increasingly literate middle class. At the same time, many women of independent means, like Louisa Twining, made significant names for themselves through their philanthropic activities or interest in social reform. Unlike their 18th-century and some early 19th-century predecessors, these women sought to combine their search for independence and for a voice with the respectability expected of middle-class women. They saw this as essential, if they were to be able to establish themselves and be accepted as professional writers.

This chapter will focus on both the continuities and the changes in women's autobiography across the 19th century. It will begin with a discussion of the different ways in which women's autobiographies were produced as the collaborative practices common in the early part of the century gave way to the single-authored works of prominent women a few decades later. The even more marked changes evident in how the lives depicted in autobiographies were understood and shaped will be dealt with next, looking particularly at childhood, the importance of religion, the establishment of careers and the treatment of personal life. The final section will look at the kind of subjectivity and the new sense of self that emerges in 19th-century women's autobiographies.

Producing a Memoir

While there is marked continuity with 18th-century practices evident in the collaborative ways in which life stories were both written and produced in the early 19th century, one also begins to see new forms of collaboration, some of which served to bring quite new voices into the writing of women's autobiography. While the autobiographies of Harriette Wilson and Julia Johnson involved collaborations between authors and publishers or ghost writers of a familiar kind, *The History of Mary Prince*, for example, offered something new in the way that it was dictated to an amanuensis, even if it was then shaped and edited in a familiar way. The collaborative production of autobiographies continued into the second half of the century: as we will see, Mary Somerville's *Recollections* were put together posthumously by her daughter, her friend Frances Power Cobbe and her publisher, John Murray. But this practice was becoming unusual. From the mid-century on, even if formally presented by someone else after the author's death, women's autobiographies came increasingly to be written solely by their author. Most of these works also began to be published by major commercial publishers. Women like Harriet Martineau, Frances Cobbe and Annie Besant had already published extensively when they turned to writing autobiographies and had a strong sense of how to approach this task. They also knew their way around the publishing world and negotiated agreements from a position of strength.

The continuities between the last autobiographies of courtesans, those of Harriette Wilson and Juliet Johnson, with the work of their 18th-century predecessors are so marked that some scholars link them all together, including their memoirs alongside those of Pilkington, Phillips and others under the general category 'whore biography'.[11] And there are strong similarities in how they came to think about and plan their autobiographies. Like most of her predecessors, Harriette Wilson turned her attention to the writing of memoirs when she had effectively retired and was feeling aggrieved that none of her former protectors would provide her with the ongoing financial support to which she felt entitled. She planned to expose her lovers, as Phillips and Pilkington had done, offering them first the opportunity to pay her to omit them from her work. Her naming of these men was rather more brazen than had been the practice in the 18th century when the identities of particular men were hinted at or given only via initials. Wilson found an enthusiastic partner for this proceeding in the publisher, John Joseph Stockdale, who engaged fully both in her writing and in her effort to blackmail former lovers. Stockdale encouraged her to adopt the 18th-century practice of publishing the memoirs in separate numbers. Serial publication ensured that each issue could advertise the names of the men who would be discussed in the next one, giving them time to pay the £200 Wilson required to leave them out. Stockdale was given a share of Wilson's blackmail money. He also hoped that this approach would avoid the pirating

---

[11] Julie Peakman, 'Blaming & Shaming in Whores' Memoirs: Sex, Scandals and Celebrity', *History Today* 59, no. 8 (2009).

of Wilson's work for longer than would have been possible if the work came out in complete volumes.[12]

Wilson's *Memoirs* were the most successful ever produced by a courtesan. She was extremely well known and her celebrity, Lisa Connell suggests, made their publication a major media event. Queues formed at Stockdale's doors and the *Memoirs* were subject to so much discussion that some newspapers suggested that London was infected with 'Wilson Mania'. Stockdale promoted the work extensively, issuing it in several different formats and marketing-related merchandise, including coloured prints that illustrated Wilson's adventures. The work went through at least 31 editions in the next decade – and was translated into French and German.[13] Stockdale was right to be concerned about it being pirated, however. Some of these editions were cheap versions produced and sold by other publishers just months after it first appeared. Stockdale took one of these publishers to court but, as he had feared, was denied any form of copyright protection. The law, as The Lord Chief Justice made clear, 'cannot recognize as property the history of the low amours of a notorious courtesan'.[14] Hence while the court proceedings and the detailed reports of them in the daily press provided further publicity for the book, neither Wilson nor Stockdale profited from it as much as they would have had Stockdale been the only publisher. As it was, Stockdale got the lion's share of the profit from the *Memoirs* and Wilson seems to have done far better financially from blackmailing former lovers than she did from publishing the work.

Stockdale played a significant role not only in how Wilson's work was promoted and marketed but also in how it was written. She lived in his house part of the time she was writing the book and she describes how he prowled around her room, grabbing what she had written before she had time to revise it. 'My most interesting and valuable memoirs!' she noted,

> might have been better still – but that Stockdale won't let me or anyone else study and correct them. 'The merits of such a light work as this', stupidly says he, 'is, that it is written without study, and naturally, and just as you converse. . . .' So here am I, seated on an easy chair at No. 111, in the Rue de Faubourg St. Honoré à Paris, writing, not for the benefit of my readers, but for my own amusement and profit to boot, and in the full expectation that my work is to pass the twentieth edition![15]

---

[12]Frances Wilson, *The Courtesan's Revenge: Harriette Wilson, the Woman Who Blackmailed the King* (London: Faber and Faber, 2004).
[13]Lisa O'Connell, 'Authorship and Libertine Celebrity: Harriette Wilson's Regency Memoirs', in *Libertine Enlightenment*, ed. Peter Cryle (London: Palgrave Macmillan, 2003), pp. 161–181.
[14]"Court Of King's Bench, Wednesday, Jan, 11". The *Times*, 12 Jan. 1826, p. 3. The Times Digital Archive, Accessed 11 July 2020.
[15]Wilson, Harriette. *Harriette Wilson's Memoirs of Herself and Others*, 3 vols (London: T. Douglas, 1825). Accessed through Nineteenth Century Collections Online, p. 106.

The similarity here between what Stockdale told Wilson about how to write her memoirs and what Colley Cibber had told Pilkington more than half a century earlier is striking. But Wilson was the better writer and contemporaries acknowledged her literary capacity. Sir Walter Scott for one, noted her excellent skills of mimicry and that there was 'good retailing of conversations, in which the style of the speakers, so far as is known to me, is exactly imitated'.[16] And much of the book involves lively and entertaining scenes, dealing with the many men she encountered and citing their conversations apparently verbatim. Even those who objected to what she said about them recognized the merits of her work. Lord Charles Bentinck, for example, one of Wilson's lovers, noted that he and his brother Frederick were 'in the book up to our necks, but we shall only make bad worse by contending against it; for it is not only true, every word of it, but it is excellently written and very entertaining'.[17]

Despite these similarities with her 18th-century predecessors, however, Wilson thought about her life and her writing in very different ways. She had no doubt of the intrinsic interest of her life story, she never apologized for writing it, nor did she see it as necessary to buttress it with any other form of documentation as Phillips and Pilkington had done. She had not only a much stronger sense of her power and identity, but also of her literary capacity and standing. Indeed, when she began writing about her life under the title *Sketches in the Round Room at the Opera House*, she first took them to John Murray, one of the leading publishers of the day. When offered the manuscript, 'Murray looked on me with as much contempt as though Ass had been written in my countenance', Wilson noted, and of course, he refused them.[18] Murray was Byron's publisher and Wilson's choice of him says much about how she saw herself. Wilson also sought a particular connection with Byron. When planning her memoirs, she wrote to Byron 'to solicit the honour of his acquaintance'. After some time, Byron replied, making it clear that while he knew her by reputation, 'I am not the person whom you would like, either as a lover or a friend'. As an admirer of *Childe Harold*, Wilson insisted that she was not seeking anything other than an intellectual engagement with him. Subsequently, Byron occasionally did write to her and also sent money, but he took care to maintain a distance between them. Wilson, however, made a great deal of the few letters she received from him, insisting that she had lost many others. His death in 1824, Sharon Setzer suggests, 'emboldened Wilson to fashion herself as Byron's intimate friend and soul mate as well as his satiric counterpart in the realm of prose'.[19]

---

[16] Wilson, *Courtesan's Revenge*, p. 48.
[17] Wilson, *Courtesan's Revenge*, p. 49.
[18] Wilson, *Memoirs*, vol. I, pp. 212–213.
[19] Sharon M. Setzer, 'The Memoirs of Harriette Wilson: A Courtesan's Byronic Self-Fashioning', in *Women's Life Writing, 1700–1850*, ed. Daniel Cook and Amy Culley (London: Palgrave Macmillan, 2012).

Wilson's sense of both the significance and the nature of her own work is also evident in the contrast she drew between her *Memoirs* and Rousseau's *Confessions*. Her *Memoirs*, she noted, were,

> not a complete confession, like Jean Jacques Rousseau's, but merely a few anecdotes of my life, and some light sketches of the characters of others, with little regard to dates or regularity, written at odd times, in very ill health. The only thing I have particularly attended to in this little work has been, not to put down one single line at all calculated to prejudice any individual, in the opinion of the world, which is not strictly correct.[20]

While the furore around Harriette Wilson's memoirs was at its height, a very different kind of autobiography appeared in London with the publication of *The History of Mary Prince, a West Indian Slave* in 1831. While Wilson fitted into a tradition of scandalous autobiography, as the first woman's slave narrative to be published, Prince, as Henry Louis Gates Jr. points out, was the first female slave to speak for herself.[21] Hence her story added a quite new voice to women's autobiography in Britain. As Gillian Whitlock has argued, some care was taken in the production of this work to ensure that some of the worst episodes were described by the male editor rather than Prince herself through her female amanuensis. Wilson and Johnson dealt openly with their many sexual liaisons, and Wilson in particular named many lovers and protectors, but neither dealt in any explicit way with their sexual encounters. By contrast, Prince's story dealt quite directly with rape and severe sexual abuse, offering details that were not normally found in women's autobiographies and raising a number of questions about how such issues should be dealt with in ways that made them acceptable. This point is emphasized in the Preface to Prince's work written by its editor, Thomas Pringle, the Secretary of the British Anti-Slavery Society. It was Prince herself who suggested the writing of her history, Pringle insisted: 'She wished it to be done, she said, that good people in England might hear from a slave what a slave had felt and suffered.' Mary Prince was illiterate and could not write her story so it was taken down by an amanuensis. Nonetheless, Pringle insisted, it was entirely her own story.

> The narrative was taken down from Mary's own lips by a lady who happened to be at the time residing in my family as a visitor. It was written out fully, with all the narrator's repetitions and prolixities, and afterwards pruned into its present shape; retaining, as far as was practicable, Mary's exact expressions and peculiar phraseology.[22]

---

[20] Wilson, *Memoirs*, vol. I, p. 119.
[21] Henry Louis Gates Jr., (ed.) *The Classic Slave Narratives* (New York: Penguin Books, 1987), p. xv.
[22] Mary Prince, *The History of Mary Prince, a West Indian Slave, Written by Herself* (London: Penguin, 1831, repr. 2001).

Pringle was unquestionably very closely involved in every aspect of the writing and presentation of Prince's narrative and this has led several contemporary scholars to question the extent to which it really is entirely her story. At the time she dictated it, Prince was employed as a domestic servant in Pringle's house. He arranged for her story to be written down by another Anti-Slavery activist, Susan Strickland. When she had finished writing down the story, Pringle interrogated Prince in order to be sure of its truthfulness. 'I went over the whole,' he insists, 'carefully examining her on every fact and circumstance detailed and in all that relates to her residence in Antigua.' Pringle then edited the text and wrote the preface that explained how it came to be written and testified to its truth. He also added a couple of long supplements at the end of Prince's tale, explaining how she came to the attention of the Anti-Slavery Society and the unsuccessful attempts the Society made to get her owner to grant her the freedom she needed in order to return to Antigua as she wished, in order to be reunited with her husband. Pringle's additions are intended to influence the reader and effect how one reads the text. The inclusion in this text of Prince's mention of her own sexual violation and other sexual relationships made it necessary that her story was validated and that she had Pringle's affirmation of her character. Pringle's writings function as paratexts to guide the reader. Indeed, as Sarah Salih argues, with his additions, the whole work 'resembles nothing so much as a lawyer's "bundle" with its witness statements, depositions, and corroborating evidence'.[23] Once it was finished, it was Pringle who arranged for its publication and distribution.

While not as large a seller as Wilson's *Memoirs*, *The History of Mary Prince* attracted considerable attention. It appeared just before the start of a parliamentary session that planned to debate the complete abolition of slavery and it was widely distributed through the provincial anti-slavery network so that it went through three editions in its first year. While interest was greatest amongst those passionately concerned with the question of slavery, Prince's book was also discussed elsewhere: in the *Christian Advocate*, the small circulation *Edinburgh Literary Journal* and the *Weekly Register of Criticism and Belles Lettres*, for example, as well as in much more popular periodicals including *Blackwood's Magazine* and *The Englishman's Magazine*. All of these reviews, as Sue Thomas argues, attest to the power and potential reach of the narrative.[24] Prince's *History* provides a powerful and moving account of the life of a woman slave. Hers was a life of extreme pain and hardship from the moment she was torn from her mother and siblings at an early age and sent away from a fairly benign situation to one involving excessive labour and great cruelty. Her detailed

---

[23]Sara Salih, 'The History of Mary Prince, the Black Subject, and the Black Canon', in *Discourses of Slavery and Abolition: Britain and Its Colonies, 1760–1838*, ed. Brycchan Carey, Markman Ellis, Sara Salih (Basingstoke, Hampshire: Palgrave Macmillan, 2004).
[24]Sue Thomas, '1831 Reviews of the History of Mary Prince', *Notes and Queries* 66, no. 2 (2019).

description of the physical and sexual brutality of slavery, not only in her account of how she was stripped and flogged by both male and female slave owners but of the brutality meted out to other slaves and indeed sometimes to the wives and daughters of slave owners, is graphic and shocking.

Like Wilson's *Memoirs*, Prince's *History* was involved in lawsuits. Its veracity was attacked shortly after its publication by James McQueen, a pro-slavery advocate, who published several articles questioning its truth and pointing to Pringle's involvement in writing and publishing it. Pringle sued one of the publishers of these articles for libel. Pringle in turn was sued for libel by John Adams Wood, the man who owned Prince in Antigua and refused to free her and is described in the Narrative and in Pringle's comments in very critical terms. These legal cases both provided additional publicity for the work – and allowed Pringle a further opportunity to state his case in new supplements.[25] The veracity of Prince's story and questions about her sexual conduct were also raised during the court cases, although no evidence was actually cited of the 'debasement' of which she was accused by her owner, Wood. The truth of Prince's story was of great concern amongst anti-slavery activists too – and she was physically examined at the request of the Birmingham Ladies' Society for Relief of Negro Slaves to see if she in fact had sustained the injuries claimed.

As a dictated story that follows the general pattern of slave narratives and was edited and verified by Pringle, there is a question about the status of Mary Prince's story as an autobiography. James Olney has raised this question regarding whether slave narratives are autobiographies more generally.[26] Working very strictly within the framework of canonical male autobiography and privileging the self-reflection that such works contain, Olney argues that the formulaic nature of slave narratives and their emphasis on a shared story means that they do not 'qualify' as autobiography. And there is no question that Prince's *History* follows a standard pattern of slave narratives in its story of her relatively comfortable childhood in the same house as her mother and siblings, followed by the splitting up of the family and her sale to a series of cruel and brutal owners who demanded excessive labour and beat her and her fellow slaves mercilessly, destroying her health and impairing her physical abilities. However, the pattern of many women's autobiographies in the 18th and early 19th centuries involved a sense of shared stories and vulnerabilities, and many of these stories were edited and presented by others. Indeed, as Linda Peterson argued, 19th-century women's autobiography was 'often a hybrid genre, a combination of first person narrative and editorial amplification or excision'.[27] Different as their actual

---

[25]Sue Thomas, 'Pringle V. Cadell and Wood V. Pringle: The Libel Cases over the History of Mary Prince', *Journal of Commonwealth Literature* 40, no. 1 (2005).
[26]James Olney, '"I Was Born": Slave Narratives, Their Status as Autobiography and as Literature', *Callaloo* no. 20 (1984).
[27]Peterson, *Traditions*, p. x.

stories are, the insistence that this is Prince's voice and the presentation of it by an approved editor links Prince's narrative to the memoirs and letters of 17th- and 18th-century women that were being published as autobiography at the same time – and, as we will see, to the publication of the *Reminiscences of Mary Somerville* in the 1870s.[28]

The Wonderful Adventures of Mary Seacole also raises questions about what constitutes an autobiography. Some 19th-century reviewers thought Seacole's story had been written with the help of another – although this view is not generally held by contemporary scholars. The issue with Seacole is rather her focus on her travel and experiences in Panama and the Crimea. Her book fits within the broad framework of women's travel writings. While some would argue that travel writing is a distinct genre, others insist rather that a number of 19th-century women used the framework of travel as a way 'to authorize themselves and to write autobiographically'.[29] Seacole's work certainly extends beyond travel, as it includes discussions of her childhood and background, her training as a 'doctoress', her general aims and ambitions and the ways that she made her living. Hence her work focuses on the development of her life within travel – rather than having the travel subsume the life story.

While Seacole discussed her struggles and activities as a 'doctoress' and hotelier in Panama where she nursed people through a cholera outbreak, much more of it deals with her life and work in the Crimea in the 1850s, where she sought unsuccessfully to work alongside Florence Nightingale and the group of nurses that she had taken to nurse soldiers injured in the Crimean War. Unable to join the Nightingale nurses, Seacole explained how she followed the same pattern in the Crimea as she had in Panama by combining the running of a hotel with her apparently devoted and skilful nursing. After the Crimean War ended, the company she had established faced immense financial difficulties and she was forced into bankruptcy. Leading British politicians and those who had seen her at work in the Crimea set up a fund to support her because of her selfless devotion to British soldiers in the Crimea. Seacole wrote her book very rapidly to support this fundraising campaign, emphasizing her time in the Crimea as the aspect of her life that would make her work both valuable in Britain and commercially viable.

Seacole's work appeared at a time when there were many other works being published on the Crimean War and stood out because of the unusual nature of her story as a Jamaican woman who had nursed many British soldiers. It was very well received. Most of its reviewers were aware of her straitened circumstances and of the establishment of the Seacole Fund, and

---

[28]Linda H. Peterson 'Institutionalizing Women's Autobiography', in *Culture of Autobiography*, ed. Robert Folkenflik (Stanford: Stanford University Press, 1993).
[29]Gillian Whitlock, *The Intimate Empire: Reading Women's Autobiography* (London: Cassell, 2000), p. 77.

several emphasized how deserving of public support Seacole was rather than engaging with her actual text. The reviewer for the Athenaeum, for example, insists that a sketch of her life was required to complete the literature on the Crimea. He is, moreover,

> persuaded that no reader will lay down this unpretending volume without wishing success to the committee who are endeavoring to raise its heroine above the embarrassed circumstances into which she fell from no fault of her own.[30]

At the time that the autobiographies of Wilson and Prince were published, another set of autobiographical works appeared depicting the lives of 17th- and 18th-century women. The growing interest in history that was evident in Britain in the early 19th century produced a taste for the actual words and writings of individuals from earlier centuries. A number of enterprising antiquarians and editors catered to this interest by publishing the letters, family memoirs and other life-writings of literate 17th- and 18th-century women, under the title 'autobiography'. Most of these letters and family memoirs had been written by women in prominent families as a way to pass genealogical knowledge and family history from one generation to the next. They were kept in manuscript form in family archives and not intended for publication. Now, however, they began to be presented as autobiographies or memoirs. These works include *The Memoirs of Lady Fanshawe* (1820), *The Autobiography of Anne Lady Halkett* (1829) and *The Autobiography of Mary Countess of Warwick* (1848).[31] None of these women referred to their writings as autobiography or thought of publishing them. Indeed, in most cases, the ostensible 'autobiography' was constructed by combining a range of different kinds of records including letters, family memoirs, reminiscences and comments from others into a single narrative. The primary focus was on family life, and the woman narrator usually placed herself in the background as she extolled the virtues and the courageous deeds of husband and menfolk. Initially, their editors were very nervous about publishing women's private documents and justified their publication by stressing the concerns evident in them with familial and domestic life and in a way that provided 'a literary manifestation of the doctrine of separate spheres'. The way these works showed the immersion of women in family and domestic life ensured that their writing did not in any way challenge the masculine autobiographical tradition. Rather, they authorized certain kinds of life writing as legitimately feminine. These works, Linda Peterson argues, came to define and institutionalize a new model of women's autobiography, the model that is now generally termed 'Victorian women's autobiography'.[32] When

---

[30] Mary Seacole, *Wonderful Adventures of Mrs Seacole in Many Lands* (1857), ed. and with an Introduction by Sara Salih (London: Penguin Books, 2005).
[31] Peterson, 'Institutionalizing Women's Autobiography', pp. 85–92.
[32] Peterson, 'Institutionalizing Women's Autobiography'.

Martineau, Cobbe and others came to write their own lives in the second half of the 19th century, they accepted the need to endorse this general ideal of womanliness and of the importance of domesticity, and had to incorporate their personal struggles and professional lives into it.

Harriet Martineau was the first and greatest exponent of Victorian women's autobiography. Her powerful and eloquent depiction of her intellectual development, of the process by which she broke away from her family's religious position to find her own beliefs and the parallel struggle to become independent as a professional and one deeply engaged with many of the dominant issues in her society, meant that her work addressed many of the dominant themes in the canonical Victorian male autobiographies, including those of John Stuart Mill, Charles Darwin and J. H. Newman. At a time when women's education was still very limited, Martineau, as Linda Peterson argues, was one of the few women sufficiently knowledgeable about theological and religious questions to interpret her life and to write about her own dilemmas in the ways it was being done by contemporary male writers. As a consequence, she has long been the one woman autobiographer accepted within this canon. Seeking to reverse this approach, Trev Broughton has recently suggested that instead of praising Martineau's autobiography for its capacity to match the erudition of highly educated men, like Mill and Darwin, one might take it as the model with which to explore how questions of the value, purpose and significance, were dealt with in Victorian autobiography.[33] An immensely successful journalist and writer, well known for her popular essays on political economy, her two-volume *Society in America*, based on her lengthy travels there, her novels and her many articles on contemporary society, Martineau, like her male counterparts, saw it as her duty to write an autobiography. She turned her attention fully to this task in 1855, under the mistaken belief that she had a terminal illness that could bring her death at any time, writing the book rapidly in three months. She had been working on her autobiography for some years and was able to draw on notes and earlier drafts. She now re-wrote everything, however, 'so that the whole might be offered from one point of view, and in a consistent spirit'.[34] But here, as elsewhere, Martineau's path was far from easy. She was immediately confronted by what Linda Peterson calls 'the female autobiographer's dilemma' as she sought to write of her life in general and universal terms – while conscious always of her position as a woman. Martineau was well aware that her work might meet with public disapproval and so refused to publish it in her lifetime. It was printed, bound, illustrated and left with her publisher, Smith Elder & Co., with instructions for them to issue it after her death. It appeared in the early 1870s, with an Introduction

---

[33]T. L. Broughton, 'Life Writing', in *Routledge Companion to Victorian Literature*, ed. Denisof (New York: Routledge, 2019).
[34]Martineau, *Autobiography*, vol. I, pp. 54–55.

and a final volume written by Martineau's friend, the American abolitionist Maria Weston Chapman.

If Martineau had hoped that having her work edited and presented by a surrogate daughter would enable her to avoid criticism, this was not the case. From the start, the work was extremely controversial. This controversy focused less on Martineau's unconventional religious ideas and philosophy than on her often-critical comments on contemporaries and her very clear depiction of her intensely unhappy childhood and painful relationship with her mother. The novelist Margaret Oliphant excoriated it in an anonymous review in *Blackwood's Magazine* as 'a posthumous harangue from the tomb' that offered unkind criticisms of many of those she had met and in a way that allowed of no response. Oliphant was especially critical of her treatment of her childhood and her depiction of her mother as cold, unloving, censorious and the chief cause of her childhood unhappiness. Her dead mother had no chance to speak for herself and in Oliphant's view Martineau's sense of injury was a familiar childhood fantasy that should have been laid to rest.[35] Martineau had written two volumes and Maria Chapman contributed a third which added fuel to the fire. Martineau had left Maria Chapman with a large number of personal documents detailing her life both before and after the autobiography was written. Chapman used them to add an account of Martineau's childhood that underlined her unhappiness in the face of a cold and unloving mother and thoughtless, even brutal, siblings. Chapman also discussed the adult familial conflicts about which Martineau had been silent, including the breach between herself and her favourite brother, the Unitarian minister James, which was highly critical of James and suggested that he resented his sister's popularity.

Responses to Martineau's autobiography were not altogether surprising. From her very first discussion of life writing in 1830, she had insisted on the importance of avoiding either deception or panegyric, insisting on verisimilitude and absolute candour, something she saw as essential if an autobiography was to be a work that could help others. It may not be possible to say everything, but nothing should be said that was not true. Martineau recognized that this approach might cause pain to those connected to the author and the difficulties that might arise from an author's bias but felt it necessary nonetheless that strict truth be adhered to.[36] Hence her careful and critical delineations of her mother and their relationship. As Margaret Oliphant's review suggests, this approach did not accord well with Victorian sensibilities. But one can see here also the problem of how exactly a woman of achievement and intellectual independence could write an

---

[35][Margaret Oliphant], 'Harriet Martineau', *Blackwood's Edinburgh Magazine*, 121 (1877): 472–475.
[36]Mitzi Meyers, 'Harriet Martineau's *Autobiography*: The Making of a Female Philosopher', in *Women's Autobiography: Essays in Criticism*, ed. Estelle C. Jelinek (Bloomington: Indiana University Press, 1980).

autobiography that fitted into the framework demanded by Victorian domestic ideals.

This question of fitting a life that was notable because of how far it extended beyond the normal confines of women into a framework determined by Victorian ideals of femininity was an issue for all Victorian women's autobiographies. It posed a major problem for those seeking to publish the memoirs of the distinguished astronomer Mary Somerville, just a few years before Martineau's work appeared. Somerville had written her reminiscences in the last years of her life. Somerville had published several important scientific works prior to doing this and was well known and widely admired. Writing her recollections, however, meant she had to address the question of how she managed as a woman to be both scientist and a wife and mother. Somerville paid little attention to the demands of Victorian womanliness in her work – and displayed a sense of humour that was quite beyond its bounds.[37] There was much concern amongst her friends and publisher John Murray that allowing the *Recollections* to appear in the form she had left them would diminish Somerville's reputation. So, her work was carefully edited by her daughter Martha, with the active assistance of Somerville's close friend Frances Power Cobbe, and her publisher John Murray. They added an extensive commentary from Martha and passages from letters that underline Somerville's maternal qualities and her warmth and closeness to her friends. As a result, the *Recollections of Mary Somerville* that finally appeared a year or so after her death differ markedly from the original. Sally Mitchell estimates that the original draft was extended by some twenty-five per cent in length as letters and other writings were added to Somerville's original manuscript in order to underline her womanliness.[38] Kathryn Neeley argues that the published version of the *Recollections* omits both examples of Somerville's sense of humour and passages that reveal the complexity of her inner life. Her comments about how she might better have organized her own intellectual life were removed as were others indicating her enthusiasm for new inventions and technology like the railways and for inventors like George Stevenson. These omissions, Neeley argues, 'were apparently designed to protect her identity as an exemplar of Victorian womanhood and as an eminent scientist', but one who was essentially modest. They removed all suggestions of her struggle for self-definition and the extent to which she did or did not achieve it.[39]

The hostile response to Martineau's autobiography had an impact on other women contemplating writing their lives. Sally Mitchell argues that it made Frances Power Cobbe very cautious about how she represented her

---

[37]Mary Somerville, *Personal Recollections from Early Life to Old Age*, ed. Martha Somerville (London: John Murray, 1874).
[38]Mitchell, 'Frances Power Cobbe's *Life*', pp. 135–136.
[39]Kathryn A. Neeley, *Mary Somerville* (Cambridge: Cambridge University Press, 2001), pp. 190–196.

family in her own autobiography, preventing any mention of black sheep, as well as ensuring her complete silence about her long-term and loving relationship with Mary Lloyd.[40] Cobbe, who was not only a very successful journalist and essayist but also a passionate supporter of various causes, most notably those opposing vivisection and supporting women's rights. She made sure that her autobiography discussed the causes that she supported and her reasons for doing so. As a supporter of women's emancipation, she explained to one of her fellow suffragists that one of her reasons for writing her life was that it gave her a way to discuss women's rights and why she supported them. In some ways, hers can be seen as the first outspokenly feminist autobiography to be published. It offered,

> the true and complete history of a woman's existence *as seen from within*; a real LIFE, which he who reads may take as representing fairly the joys, sorrows, and interests, the powers and limitations, of one of my sex and class in the era which is now drawing to a close.[41]

Nonetheless, she wondered whether she might publish the work in her lifetime only in the United States, and sought assurances from her publisher 'that it is really desirable to publish at all. . . . I really *greatly* want experienced advice in taking this step.' Cobbe ultimately agreed to the book being published in the United States and Britain in limited numbers in 1894. It did very well and Cobbe was thrilled both at the enthusiasm of her friends and of reviewers and at the quite substantial sum she earned from it. There is one curious aspect in regard to how Frances Cobbe's autobiography appeared. The 1894 edition of the book about which she had expressed so many qualms appeared quite simply as her work, with a brief preface stressing her sense that the book required no apology and told the story of an interesting and enjoyable life. By contrast, when the book was published posthumously in 1904, it was ostensibly edited and presented by Cobbe's friend Blanche Atkinson, and it contained a long introduction in which Atkinson assured readers that Cobbe had never sought to draw attention to herself and only agreed to write her autobiography when enjoined to do so by Atkinson herself and many friends. Sally Mitchell suggests that Atkinson only came to know Cobbe in 1892–3 when the autobiography was well under way – and so the claims she makes in the introduction seem highly questionable!

One of Cobbe's stated concerns about having her autobiography appear when it was finished in 1894 centred on the fact that it would then be published at the same time as the autobiography of another prominent, even notorious woman Annie Besant. As a woman who had been divorced, proclaimed herself a free thinker, published a work on birth control and been closely involved in industrial action including the 1888 strike of the

---

[40]Mitchell, 'Frances Power Cobbe's *Life*', pp. 139–40.
[41]Cobbe, *Life*, vol. I p. iv.

match-girls, Annie Besant was a scandalous figure who had openly rejected several Victorian norms and conventions. Besant and Cobbe were known to each other – indeed Besant credited Cobbe as one whose writings had helped free her from dogmatic Christianity. But Cobbe disliked Besant's notoriety and feared that her enemies would enjoy bracketing them together in reviews.[42] Ultimately Cobbe overcame these scruples and her autobiography was much more widely reviewed than Besant's and never compared to it. But the publication of these two very different autobiographies in close proximity does offer one an insight into the changing nature of ideas about autobiography at the end of the 19th century.

In what she was prepared to say about her life, as indeed in the way she had lived it, Annie Besant took a very different approach from Martineau and Cobbe: one that openly disregarded many of the Victorian rules to which Cobbe had adhered by addressing her personal life. Besant produced two autobiographies. The first, entitled *Autobiographical Sketches* appeared first in serialized form in *Our Corner*, a small circulation socialist publication that Besant both owned and edited, in 1883–4, coming out as a book in 1885.[43] There is something reminiscent of 18th-century scandalous autobiography in Besant's statement at the start of the sketches that she was planning to pen these sketches 'which may avail to satisfy friendly questioners, and to serve, in some measure, as defence against unfriendly attack'. Despite the title, this first work could well be called simply an autobiography. It provides a chronological account of Besant's life, from her childhood through her marriage and its breakdown – and the loss first of her son in the divorce proceedings and later of her daughter when she espoused free thought and published what was deemed to be an obscene book on birth control. In place of the kind of apology that we saw in 18th-century women's autobiographies, Besant focuses her attention much more strongly on her religious beliefs: her move from devout Evangelical Christianity over several years to a final rejection of Christianity and advocacy of free thought. The organizations and campaigns she became involved with and the people that she became close to are all linked to the shifting nature of her beliefs as she sought new forms of faith after her belief in Christianity came to an end – and with it her marriage.

Almost a decade later, Besant published another autobiography. There are marked similarities between this work and the earlier *Sketches* and whole paragraphs and sections of chapters were moved from the *Sketches* to the *Autobiography*. In the years between these two works, however, Besant had become a Theosophist and a devout believer in the ideal of linking Hindu spiritual wisdom and Western enlightenment promulgated by its leader Madame Blavatsky. As with her other causes, Besant's involvement in Theosophy

---

[42]Carol Hanbery Mackay, 'A Journal of Her Own: The Rise and Fall of Annie Besant's Our Corner', *Victorian Periodicals Review* 42, no. 4 (2009): 324–358.
[43]Annie Besant, *Autobiographical Sketches*, ed. Carol Hanbury (Peterborough, Ontario: Broadview, 1885, repr. 2009).

brought an important and close friendship, this time with Blavatsky. Theosophy was a central issue in Besant's *Autobiography*. It is clear from the start in the way she introduced the book – with a description and chart of the astrological conditions obtaining at her birth in a way that enables her to traverse space and time and connect herself with the wider universe in the way accepted within Theosophy. She used the *Autobiography* as a way to explain her path as she had floundered through Christianity, free thought and socialism until she found in Theosophy her true faith. Her conversion to Theosophy also required that she gave up some of her earlier social beliefs and values, including her advocacy of birth control, and she made it clear in the *Autobiography* that she had done so.

Shaping a Life

How lives were understood and shaped in women's autobiography changed markedly across the 19th century. In the early decades of that century, the similarities with 18th-century ways of shaping a life is very noticeable. By the century's end, however, women's lives were thought about, imagined, and represented in entirely new ways. These changes can be seen in a number of different ways: in the close attention paid to childhood and to education; in the importance of religious beliefs and doubt; in the detailed discussion of careers and activities in the public worlds of philanthropy and politics, all of which are immensely important in later 19th-century women's autobiography, and scarcely even mentioned before. For some women, discussion of their career or public activity involved also paying some attention to the struggle they waged for independence. While all of these issues assume a new importance in late nineteenth-century autobiographies, discussions of sexual behaviour that were so important in the 18th century disappeared, as indeed did almost anything connected to intimate adult life.

Childhood

The continuity between 18th- and early 19th-century women's autobiographies can be seen very clearly in the treatment of childhood. This is particularly notable in courtesan's autobiographies. Julia Johnstone's discussion of childhood in her *Confession* (1825), for example, echoed that of several 18th-century courtesans both in tenor and in brevity. 'I dispose of my family very briefly as they disposed of Julia in her early days', she wrote at the beginning of a few pages outlining her family's relative wealth and its complete neglect of her well-being so that at a quite early age she 'fell victim to my own inexperience, and the passionate solicitations of a man'.[44] Harriette Wilson carried this further, saying nothing at all about her

---

[44]Johnstone, *Confessions*, p. 12.

childhood and beginning her story when she was fifteen. She did indicate that her father was a man of hot temper and that her parents' marriage was so unhappy that it made her foreswear the very idea of marrying herself. But there is not a hint of her own experiences as a child.

Childhood is mentioned only briefly in other early 19th-century women's autobiographies, particularly *The History of Mary Prince* and *The Wonderful Adventures of Mary Seacole*. Like the courtesans, Mary Seacole made clear that it was not her 'intention to dwell at any length upon the recollections of my childhood'. All that she tells us is that her mother kept a boarding house and was a skilled 'doctoress' and that, although she was educated for some years by someone else, she had from her childhood a yearning for medical knowledge and learned her own skills from her mother.[45]

Childhood experience is rarely a feature of slave narratives, and it featured in Mary Prince's story only as a way to contrast between the relatively benign phase of her life and the brutality of her later years. As a very young child, Prince was given to another child her own age whom she calls Miss Betsy. Miss Betsy was the daughter of the man who owned both Prince and her mother – so during these years, she was living in the same house as her mother and siblings.

> I was made quite a pet of by Miss Betsy and loved her very much. She used to lead me about by the hand and call me her little nigger. This was the happiest period of my life; for I was too young to understand rightly my condition as a slave, and too thoughtless and full of spirits to look forward to the days of toil and sorrow.[46]

Prince was separated from Miss Betsy and sold at the age of twelve. But she stayed physically close to her mother and her new mistress, though passionate, did not strike her. This second home only lasted a year or two, however, and then her hard life really began. She was separated from her mother as she and all her siblings were sold separately. She then found herself moved from Bermuda to Turk's Head and consigned to a house where the brutality to slaves was extreme. From her early teens, Prince did the work of an adult and was expected to have the physical strength and stamina of an adult woman. Like the other women in the houses she described, she was subjected to frequent beatings and to various other forms of physical and sexual abuse, as she was stripped naked to be beaten – and required to bathe and presumably have sex with her master.

One does begin to see a change in some works of the 1840s. Charlotte Elizabeth Tonna, for example, described her childhood in some detail, dealing with her early family life, education, religious beliefs – and ill health.[47] This attention to childhood increased in the second half of the

---

[45]Seacole, *Wonderful Adventures*, p. 1.
[46]Prince, *The History of Mary Prince*.
[47]Charlotte Elizabeth, *Personal Recollections* (London: R. E. Seeley and W. Burnside, 1841).

century when whole chapters or indeed several chapters begin to be devoted to describing the author's early and teen years. This new concern to describe childhood experiences reflected the growing interest in the nature of children evident in society more generally. Childhood feelings and experiences had become a subject worthy of attention from the turn of the century, as one can see in some of the work of the Romantic poets. The depiction of childhood innocence and emotion in Wordsworth's 'Prelude', for example, resonated across the 19th century. Concern about the experiences and feelings of children was soon accompanied by new developments in pedagogy, psychology and medicine leading to widespread discussion in the 1840s and '50s about the physical and emotional needs of children and whether they were being adequately understood and managed. Child psychiatry emerged as a new field in the course of the 1840s, emphasizing the significance of a child's feelings and emotions in adult life. These questions were widely discussed in the periodical press. In an essay entitled 'A Revelation of childhood' (1852), for example, the popular writer Anna Jameson argued that there was little recognition of the physical needs of children, so that as a society 'we are perpetually making the grossest mistakes in the physical and personal management of childhood'.[48] In making her argument. Jameson drew on her own intense sufferings and small pleasures as a child between the ages of 5 and 10.

Harriet Martineau too contributed to this general literature, writing a manual on child-rearing entitled *Household Education* (1849). Her recollections of the many fears that she experienced at night and that overshadowed her childhood featured prominently. Charlotte Brontë, who read Martineau's work, commented that it was like meeting her own ghost, so similar were Martineau's recollections to her own. Brontë in turn was one of the major novelists who wrote at length about children and their experiences, underlining the intensity of a child's feelings and also suggesting that childhood experiences had an impact on adult life. This same point was made by Charles Dickens and George Eliot in their novels. The area of child psychiatry was one that showed a close link between the scientific and the imaginative literature. As Sally Shuttleworth has shown, in these early days of child psychiatry, when there was little in the way of case studies, those specialists who wrote about the mental life and health of children drew on novels to illustrate their ideas. Charlotte Brontë's novel *Jane Eyre* was of particular interest as it showed not only the intensity of suffering of a neglected and ill-treated child but also the rage, seen by the household as a form of madness, that was consequent upon it.[49]

---

[48]Anna Jameson, *Commonplace Book of Thoughts. Memories and Fancies* (London: Longman, Brown, Green and Longmans, 1854).
[49]Sally Shuttleworth, 'Victorian Visions of Child Development', *The Lancet* 379, no. 9812 (2012), pp. 212–213.

The autobiography of Harriet Martineau, written in 1855 although not published until the 1870s, marked a very distinctive turning point here, with its detailed depiction of her intense childhood suffering and her strong sense of the impact of this and more generally of the way she was treated by her family in her early years on her personal development. Neither her physical nor emotional needs were met. The severe ill health that afflicted her throughout childhood was ascribed by her mother to her having a wet nurse unable to feed her. It was not until she was an adult that it became clear that milk disagreed with her. 'It was unheard of for children not to be fed on milk; so, till I was old enough to have tea at breakfast, I went on having a horrid lump at my throat for hours of every morning, and the most terrific oppression at night.'[50] Martineau's autobiography depicted her entire childhood as a time of unspeakable misery. She was constantly in fear of certain kinds of light, of unknown people, of unusual sounds, or unexpected terrain. She had terrifying dreams and intermittent spells of panic that completely paralysed her. Her parents knew nothing of the many things that terrified and made her miserable as it never occurred to her to tell them. Looking back as an adult, she felt that 'a little closer observation would have shown them the causes of the bad health and fitful temper which gave them so much anxiety on my account; and I'm sure that a little more of the cheerful tenderness which was in those days thought bad for children, would have saved me from my worst faults and from a world of suffering.'[51] Martineau saw many aspects of her childhood, most particularly the lack of maternal love and tenderness and the boisterousness and sometimes brutality of her siblings, as things that caused acute pain and hampered her development.

> My temper might have been early made a thoroughly good one by the slightest indulgence showed to my natural affections, and any rational dealings with my faults but I was almost the youngest of a large family, and subject, not only to the rule of severity to which all were liable, but also to the rough and contemptuous treatment of the older children who meant no harm but injured me irreparably.[52]

This unhappiness extended into her early education. When she was nine, it was decided that she and her sister Rachel should be taught at home by their older brothers. One of them made their lessons 'his funny time of day', playing practical jokes on them which she found a form of torture. Fortunately, this form of education did not last and at the age of eleven Martineau began her 'delectable schooling' at a small coeducational

---

[50] Martineau, *Autobiography*, vol. I, p. 10.
[51] Martineau, *Autobiography*, vol. I, p. 11.
[52] Martineau, *Autobiography*, vol. I, p. 19.

Unitarian school. For the next few years, she learned Latin, French, composition and arithmetic thoroughly and with immense pleasure under the tuition of a kind and just master. This period of schooling 'was the season of my entrance upon an intellectual life. . . . (where) I found then, as I have found since, refuge from moral suffering, and an always unexhausted spring of moral strength and enjoyment.'[53]

Few other Victorian women's autobiographies depict childhood with the intensity or unhappiness that is evident in Martineau's work. Her deeply unhappy childhood contrasts markedly with those of Frances Power Cobbe and Annie Besant, for example, neither of whom seem to have suffered from the inappropriate diet, the range of fears and anxieties, or the absence of affection that tormented her. Both of these women wrote at some length about their childhoods and about the ways in which their childhood experience affected their adult personalities and tenor of life. But it was generally in a far more positive way. Frances Cobbe, for example, the only daughter and youngest child of her parents, suggests that she was fed only the freshest and healthiest of food and surrounded by love, especially from her mother and older brothers. Hers was a solitary childhood: her mother sustained an injury when Frances was quite young and never recovered, sinking into complete invalidism by the time Frances was in her teens and so could not be a companion to her. But rather than seeing this solitude as a source of suffering, Cobbe insisted that it taught her to rely on her own resources and enjoy her own company: 'From that time to this I have been a rather solitary mortal, enjoying above all things solitary walks and studies; and always finding my spirits rise in hours and days of isolation.'[54] In contrast with Martineau, Cobbe suffered when she had to leave home for her two years at a school which she regarded as appalling and where she was very unhappy. There was no intellectual education: on the contrary, 'everything was taught to us in the inverse ratio of its true importance' and she was forced to spend hours studying music, for which she had no aptitude and dancing and deportment in which she had no interest – while given only a smattering of languages or literature or history. It was only when she got home and had access to the family library that she began to educate herself.[55]

Annie Besant too described a generally very happy childhood, at the centre of which was her adored mother. Besant lost her father early and greatly admired the way her mother, who was left with inadequate means to continue the middle-class life to which they were all accustomed, managed things. Wanting a good school education for her son, Mrs Besant managed by taking a house close to Harrow school where she took in some pupils as boarders and thereby managed to pay for her son to attend Harrow.[56] School

---

[53]Martineau, *Autobiography*, vol. I, p. 61.
[54]Cobbe, *Autobiography*, vol. I, p. 30.
[55]Cobbe, *Autobiography*, vol. I, p. 30.
[56]Besant, *An Autobiography*, pp. 35–37.

was not thought of for Annie, and her biographer suggests that there was no room for her in her mother's house. But Besant describes happy days with her mother and then equally happy ones in the home of a family friend, Miss Marryat, who undertook her education. Miss Marryat, she notes, had a genius for making languages, geography, history and all the subjects that she taught a pleasure to learn. She took her pupils travelling in Europe, enabling them to learn languages in situ. Besant remained grateful to her throughout her life: 'No words of mine can tell how much I owe her, not only of knowledge, but of that love of knowledge which has remained with me ever since as a constant spur to study.'[57] As the novels of Jane Austen suggest, sending children to other people to house and educate was quite a widespread custom in the 19th century and it extended beyond Britain and into the wider British world. Mary Seacole describes being taken from home by an old lady who brought her up alongside her own grandchildren and 'could scarcely have shown me more kindness had I been one of them'.[58] Her life alternated between residing with her kind patroness and returning to her mother where she learned all her mother's skills as a 'doctoress', practising what she had learnt on her dolls. Increasingly in her teen years, she yearned to travel and was able to visit London in the company of relatives.

Discussions of childhood extended into what would now be described as adolescence, but it was not usually depicted as a distinct phase of life in women's autobiography. The term adolescent began to be used in Britain and the United States of America in the 1870s and '80s. It reflected the recognition amongst some psychologists and educators of there being an important developmental stage between childhood and adulthood[59]. Most of this discussion focused on boys and their transition to manhood and independence. Unease with any discussion of the sexuality of girls – and uncertainty about what, if any, independence was appropriate for women, made this a hard concept to apply to them. The teen years, in which 18th-century women autobiographers were already sexually active and considered to be women, were thus ones that involved the continuation of childhood and were usually discussed in women's autobiographies in terms of education and religion. The wonderful school years that Harriet Martineau described began when she was eleven and ended when she was fourteen. At the age of sixteen, she went to live with her Aunt Kentish in Bristol, continuing her education there and becoming deeply and painfully religious. The hateful years that Frances Cobbe spent at school began when she was fourteen and lasted until she was called home to care for her mother and run the house at

---

[57] Besant *Autobiography*, p. 39.
[58] Seacole, *Wonderful Adventures*, p. 1.
[59] John Demos and Virginia Demos, 'Adolescence in Historical Perspective', *Journal of Marriage and Family* 31.4 (1969): 632–638. For an overview of the extensive literature on this subject, see Harry Hendrick, 'Review: The History of Childhood and Youth', *Social History* 9, no. 1 (1984): 87–96.

the age of seventeen. These years were also the ones when Cobbe became a devout Evangelical, further isolating her from her schoolmates.

Religious Conflict

One of the additional issues that gave importance to childhood was the religious feelings that emerged then. Almost all Victorian women's autobiographies describe regular family religious observance including bible reading and church attendance as an integral part of their childhood. Some also suggest that intense religious feelings were evident at a very early age. Charlotte Elizabeth Tonna noted her desire to be a religious martyr at the age of six, by which time she already knew the Bible intimately 'and loved it with all my heart'.[60] Harriet Martineau notes her intensely religious nature at an even earlier age. As a sickly child, she was sent when very young to stay in the country in the hope that it would improve her health. Her hostess and nurse, she notes, was 'a Methodist or melancholy Calvinist of some sort'. On her return, her family said, she was,

> the absurdest little preacher of my years (between two and three) that ever was. I used to nod my head emphatically, and say 'Never ky for tyfles:' (*sic*) 'Dooty fust (*sic*) and pleasure afterwards,' and so forth ... It was probably what I picked up at Carleton that made me so intensely religious as I certainly was from a very early age.[61]

A year or two later she noted that 'religion became her only support and pleasure'. Sundays began to be 'pleasantly marked' days and she pictured heaven as 'a place gay with yellow and lilac crocuses'.[62]

Frances Cobbe too was a very devout Christian from an early age, but in her case, it was closely connected to her sense of being loved and cared for. Her earliest recollections included lessons in religion from both parents.

> I can almost see myself now kneeling at my dear mother's knees repeating the Lord's prayer after her clear, sweet voice. Then came learning the magnificent Collects to be repeated to my father on Sunday mornings in his study; and later the church catechism.[63]

No books were allowed on Sundays in the Cobbe home except the Bible – so there was abundant time for reading it and she remained devout in her beliefs until the age of eleven. This was the same age that Harriet Martineau first experienced the doubts that ultimately led to her loss of religious belief. Martineau's doubt centred on how hard it was to reconcile foreknowledge

---

[60] Charlotte Elizabeth, *Personal Recollections*, Third edition (London: Seeley Burnside & Seeley, Fleet Street, 1847), pp. 13–14.
[61] Elizabeth, *Personal Recollections*, ibid.
[62] Martineau, *Autobiography*, vol. I, pp. 16–17.
[63] Cobbe, *Life*, vol. I, p. 71.

with freewill, or to accept God's absolute power with the idea of people being punished for wrongdoing. In Cobbe's case, doubt arose in connection to the miracle of the Loaves and Fishes and how precisely they were produced.[64] Both women went from this early period of doubt into a period of more intense and devout belief, before their doubts resurfaced and ended their acceptance of their childhood and familial faith.

As one might expect, Martineau's years of intense belief were very painful ones, accompanying one of the periods which otherwise was one of her greatest happiness: the fifteen months she spent at school in Bristol with her beloved and affectionate Aunt Kentish in 1818–19. Her aunt was devoutly religious, but,

> had a remarkable faculty of making her religion suggest and sanction whatever she liked: and as she liked whatever was pure, amiable and unselfish and unspooling, this tendency did her no harm. Matters were otherwise with me. My religion too took the character of my mind; and it was harsh, severe and mournful accordingly.[65]

When she returned home, there was much discussion of her religious position by her family. Her fanaticism was very unlike their Unitarianism and they could not understand it – although Martineau noted that, for the first time, she felt that they had some respect for her and her views alongside the familiar scorn! This discussion had some beneficial results for her: it was one of the few occasions in which her parents offered something slightly better for her and she came later to see great virtue in their religious beliefs that consoled rather than punished, incorporating as they did 'a milder and more beneficent one than the God of the orthodox, inasmuch as he would not doom any of his creatures to eternal torment'.[66] In her early adult as in her late teen years, however, Martineau found herself returning to a problem she had first articulated at the age of eleven: how to reconcile foreknowledge and freewill or how to reconcile God's power with benevolence. Although it was hard to do in the family drawing room, she studied the Bible 'incessantly and immensely', reading chapters daily and getting as many commentaries as she could and turning also to other theological and philosophical writings. One afternoon, her brother James mentioned the doctrine of Necessity and suggested she read about it as offering a possible solution. Martineau found in necessarian philosophy the philosophy she sought. For necessarians, human beings are a product of their circumstances and every event, material or mental, has a causal antecedent. Change is possible, through education and improving the environment, but necessarianism gave Martineau a way of understanding the world and led to her relinquishing her increasingly

---

[64]Cobbe, *Life*, vol. I, p. 12.
[65]Martineau, *Autobiography*, vol. I, p. 95.
[66]Martineau, *Autobiography*, vol. I, pp. 40–41.

unsatisfactory relationship with Unitarianism. Ultimately Martineau was the one for whom this loss of belief seems to have caused least pain, largely because of the non-doctrinal nature of Unitarianism. Unitarianism, Mitzi Myers suggests, 'was less a set of tenets than a model for the virtuous self's interaction with the world'.[67] Martineau slowly moved away from Unitarianism as she came first to believe in the doctrine of necessity and then, as she become increasingly concerned about what was or was not knowable, moved away from any theological beliefs and towards Comtean Positivism.

Frances Cobbe was temperamentally less inclined to extreme anguish than Martineau, but for her too, the years of religious doubt were a very difficult period. The doubts about miracles were temporarily quelled during her unhappy high school years when she came into contact with an Evangelical preacher who had a powerful influence on her. Despite the laughter at her religious devotion by her school-fellows, she continued to pray and underwent a conversion to evangelicalism at the age of seventeen. When she left school these earlier doubts about how the miracles could possibly have occurred or be believed resurfaced more strongly than ever, causing her to question her beliefs. Her mother's illness at that time made her decide she would say nothing that might cause her any pain. But this meant that, although happy to be home from school, she was completely isolated: 'I found myself facing all the dread problems of human existence.' By the summer of her twentieth year, she had entirely ceased to believe in Orthodox Christianity, eventually finding a form of belief that satisfied her in the Theism of Theodore Parker with its rejection of popular Christianity, its belief in the humanity of Christ and its emphasis on the absolute goodness of God. This remained Cobbe's position for the rest of her life.[68]

Both Cobbe and Martineau experienced their most intense and painful doubt in their adolescent years. But neither connect it in any way to puberty. It is only in the more radical and modern autobiography of Annie Besant that any kind of link is made between the intense religious feeling of these mid- and late teen years and sexuality. In her *Autobiographical Sketches*, Besant noted the pain that she experienced at the age of eighteen when for the first time she began to think about some of the contradictions she found in the Bible. There was talk of marriage at the time, but her mother thought her too young and she was not interested: 'Of love-dreams I had absolutely none', she notes, possibly because she read no novels, but also because her inner life was 'absorbed in that passionate love of the "the Saviour" which among emotional Catholics, really is the human passion of love transferred to an ideal'. Besant felt very strongly that the language of love in many devotional exercises was damaging for her, as it was for other young women.

---

[67]Meyers, 'Harriet Martineau's *Autobiography*', p. 65.
[68]Cobbe, *Life*, vol. I, pp. 70–86.

> I was a child awaking into womanhood, with emotions and passions dawning and not understood, emotions and passions which craved satisfaction, and found it in this 'Ideal Man'. Thousands of girls in England are to-day in exactly this mental phase, and it is a phase full of danger. . . ., the perfectly harmless and natural sexual feeling is either dwarfed or forced, and so we have 'prudishness' and 'fastness'. The sweeter and more loving natures become prudes; the more shallow as well as the more high-spirited and merry natures become flirts.[69]

Besant's account of her childhood religion differs in the two versions of her autobiography. Both include descriptions of her father's limited religious beliefs and her mother's very liberal approach to Christianity, noting her preference for attending church services if they were located in beautiful buildings and with good choirs. In the *Sketches* she contrasted this with the devout Evangelical beliefs of Miss Maryatt which influenced her as a child and an adolescent. But in the *Autobiography*, with its concern to stress her lifelong search for spiritual fulfilment, Besant stressed rather the intensity of her own religious feeling and the incompatibility between her religious views and those of her mother from her early years.

> She was of the old *régime*; I of the stuff from which fanatics are made: and I have often thought, in looking back, that she must have had on her lips many a time unspoken a phrase that dropped from them when she lay a-dying: 'My little one, you have never made me sad or sorry except for your own sake; you have always been too religious.'[70]

Just as Besant connected her adolescent religious intensity to the emergence of her sexuality, so too her loss of faith was linked to her unhappy marriage to a very conventional clergyman. She began to question her own belief in God in the face of her intense unhappiness and what seemed to her to be arbitrary and needless suffering, including the near-fatal illness of her young daughter. As she worked through her religious doubts, she was also establishing the points on which she would resist her husband's authority. 'Whatever might be the result', she decided that,

> I would take each dogma of the Christian religion, and carefully and thoroughly examine it, so that I should never again say 'I believe' where I had not proved. So, patiently and steadily, I set to work. Four problems chiefly at this time pressed for solution. I. The eternity of punishment after death. II. The meaning of 'goodness' and 'love' as applied to a God who had made this world with all its evil and its misery. III. The nature of the atonement of Christ, and the 'justice' of God in accepting a vicarious

---

[69]Besant, *Autobiographical Sketches*, p. v.
[70]Besant, *Autobiography*, p. 24.

suffering from Christ, and a vicarious righteousness from the sinner. IV. The meaning of 'inspiration' as applied to the Bible, and the reconciliation of the perfection of the author with the blunders and the immoralities of the work.[71]

Besant sought religious guidance wherever she met a sympathetic cleric. She was particularly influenced by the Rev Charles Voysey, whose Theism, with its emphasis on the humanity of Christ, offered her a way out of her doubts. But her working through of Christian dogma led her to reject entirely the role of a clergyman's wife. She decided for a time to continue to attend church, but not to take communion. This was an impossible compromise that led ultimately to her final breach with her husband.

It is in the discussion of her religious life that the two versions of Besant's autobiography differ most markedly. In part, of course, this is a result of the time that lapsed between them. In her *Autobiographical Sketches*, it is her belief in rationalism and her relationship with Charles Bradlaugh that provided the focus for her life after her marriage ended. But in the years immediately after that, Besant first became interested in socialism, a form of belief that Bradlaugh totally opposed. After that, she became a Theosophist, a new form of belief that required her to renounce earlier beliefs as she took on quite new ones. One of the key reasons for writing the *Autobiography* was to explain her conversion to Theosophy and her devotion to Madame Blavatsky. She did so in part by insisting that, while the outward change appeared sudden, she had been unconsciously marching towards it for years as she sought some more lofty belief than had yet offered.[72] From 1886, she insisted that 'there had been slowly growing up a conviction that my philosophy was not sufficient; that life and mind were other than, more than, I had dreamed'. When she met Mme Blavatsky and heard her views, what she felt was recognition. This was followed by a struggle as she reviewed all her earlier beliefs – and came to feel the need to renounce them, including the advocacy of birth control that had cost her so much, as she adopted the form of Theism that was the basis of Theosophy.

Work, Public Activity and Adult Life

Just as the discussion of religion in the autobiographies of 19th-century women reflect wider social and intellectual changes, so too one can see these wider patterns in relation to the depiction of work and public activity. There was little change at the start of the century from the 18th century, as the autobiographies illustrate. Needlework and the provision of sexual services were amongst some of the only avenues open to women. The decision to undertake sex for commerce was also one that many families either actively supported, as a way to make daughters independent, or at least made no objection to it. The enigmatic start of Harriette Wilson's *Memoirs* certainly

---

[71]Besant, *Autobiography*, p. 112.
[72]Besant, *Autobiography*, pp. 237–243.

suggests that this is the case. 'I shall not say why and how I became, at the age of fifteen, the mistress of the Earl of Craven', she states in her often quoted first sentence.

> Whether it was love, or the severity of my father, the depravity of my own heart, or the winning arts of the noble lord, which induced me to leave my paternal roof and place myself under his protection, does not now much signify; or, if it does, I am not in the humour to gratify curiosity in this matter.[73]

Wilson's autobiography is unique amongst those of courtesans in rejecting the primary scene of the fall that led her into her way of life. As we have seen, Wilson differs from her 18th-century counterparts in the way she rejected any story of bad luck or victimization, emphasizing that she was in control of her life from the time she decided to take a lover at the age of fifteen. She was following her older sister in choosing this life and it was one, as her biographer Frances Wilson argues, that was both expected and accepted in the community in which she lived at the point at which her father wished his daughters to leave him and cease their financial dependence on him. But Wilson was the last of the well-known courtesans. Changing social and sexual mores and a new sense of the importance of family and home amongst both the middle and upper classes ended the social world of the demi-monde in which Wilson had shone.

While still very narrow, the range of options open to women needing or seeking to earn a living and to become financially independent was becoming broader in the second half of the 19th century than had been the case before. Some professions: nursing and teaching, for example, became available while the ways in which women could earn a living as writers expanded considerably. The rise of the popular press was important here as the significant expansion in high-quality and popular journals and magazines offered a number of women the chance to become journalists and essayists. The growing popularity of novels – especially of women's novels – was also important. There were also new opportunities for women to participate directly in public life, particularly in philanthropy, but also in the second half of the century in various campaigns for social and political reform. Accompanying even greater emphasis on the importance of domestic life and of women's role within it in the 19th century, there were social and economic developments that offered new opportunities for middle-class women not only to earn their own livings but also to develop a sense of themselves and a voice.

The fact that there were an increasing number of occupations open to Victorian women did not, however, mean that individual women were free

---

[73] Wilson, *Memoirs*, p. 3.

to choose one. Middle- and upper-class Victorian families were not generally favourably disposed towards their daughters becoming financially or intellectually independent, expecting them to devote their time to family and home, spending their days in the family drawing room and being constantly available to meet familial demands. Careers only became possible – and sometimes necessary – when a change in familial circumstances, usually the death of parents and a consequent loss of income, occurred. This was certainly the case for Mary Seacole in Jamaica. She tells us little about her marriage, except that her husband soon became ill and that she took him back to her mother's home to care for him until his death. Shortly after this sad event, she wrote,

> I had one other great grief to master – the loss of my mother, and then I was left alone to battle with the world as best I might. The struggles which it cost me to succeed in life were sometimes very trying; nor have they ended yet. But I have always turned a bold front to fortune, and taken, and shall continue to take, as my brave friends in the army and navy have shown me how, 'my hurts before'. Although it was no easy thing for a widow to make ends meet, I never allowed myself to know what repining or depression was, and so succeeded in gaining not only my daily bread, but many comforts besides from the beginning.[74]

Seacole worked as a 'doctoress' during a cholera outbreak, combining this role with running a hotel.

For Seacole, there is a clear sense of being forced into a life that she might not otherwise have chosen. In the case of Martineau and Cobbe, by contrast, one has rather a sense of their being liberated from family responsibilities to follow the path they preferred. Both women had begun writing while living in their familial homes. Martineau noted how hard it was to pursue her own interests while forced to spend her days in her mother's drawing room. It was hard even to study the bible as she wished to do in order to deal with her own religious doubts. Her mother was quite sympathetic when Martineau broached with her the possibility of publishing the sketches and studies she was doing on different Bible stories, but one of her sisters mocked her literary pretensions and made her keep all her own work secret. Subsequently, Martineau insists, it was her beloved older and younger brothers, whose word to her was law, who suggested that she take up writing and pursue that as an activity rather than any womanly crafts. She wrote and published secretly, however, until her father died. Shortly after his death, it became clear that the house which had been managing the family fortune had failed and their money was lost. While recognizing that others might describe this event as a calamity, to her it was a gift.

---

[74]Seacole, *Wonderful Adventures*, p. 5.

For there was scope for action whereas in all the long preceding trials, nothing was possible but endurance. In a very short time . . . I began to feel the blessing of a whole new freedom. I, who had been obliged to write before breakfast or in some private way, had henceforth liberty to do my own work in my own way. For we had lost our gentility.[75]

Martineau continued writing for the Unitarian *Monthly Repository*, but soon began publishing the tales of political economy that were so successful and enabled her to set up an independent home in London.

Frances Cobbe too emphasized the way that her becoming a journalist was both enabled and made necessary by the death of her father. Like Martineau, she had begun to write in the family home, in the hours she could steal from her role as housekeeper to her father. Her first book, *The Theory of Intuitive Morals*, was written shortly after she had resolved her own religious crisis and after a severe attack of bronchitis that made her feel called on to help others who might be struggling with faith as she had done. Rather than describing her religious struggles, she decided to write about Kant's *Metaphysics of Ethic*, a work that had transformed her life. In the book, she sought to lay out in a clear and accessible way her belief in and understanding of intuition as the basis of a sense of morality. Cobbe's father disapproved of this activity but agreed to it when she assured him that it would be published anonymously, to avoid any embarrassment to him, while he insisted that she kept it out of sight. On a trip to London, Cobbe prevailed on Longmans to publish her work, subsequently delighted that no reviewer even hinted at the possibility that it might have been written by a woman. She continued to write in her spare hours, never apparently thinking of writing or journalism as a career until her father died, when both the house she had supervised and the family income she had access to passed to her older brother. His wife now assumed all the household tasks that Cobbe had previously undertaken. Rather than remaining as a dependant sister, she decided to leave Newbridge House almost immediately, describing this event as 'the worst wrench of my life. The home of my childhood and youth, of which I had been mistress for nineteen years . . . wherein there was not a room without tender associations.'[76] Within three weeks of her father's death, she cut off her hair, as she would not have been able to manage it without a maid, and set out on a long journey through Europe to the Middle East. She planned a very adventurous trip to Egypt and Jerusalem, relishing the surprise of friends and family that as a 'lone woman' she should even think of doing so. She was also in greatly reduced circumstances having been left an income of £200 a year, wealth to some, but 'for a woman who had always had every service rendered to her by a regiment of well-trained servants, and had had £130-a-year pocket money since she left school. It

---

[75]Martineau, *Autobiography*, vol. I, p. 148.
[76]Cobbe, *Life*, vol. I, p. 213.

must be confessed that this was a narrow provision'.[77] So she turned her mind first to philanthropy and then to journalism, making a very comfortable living writing articles on a range of social and religious questions for many journals and also through the regular column she contributed to a newspaper, *The Echo*.

Annie Besant began to write and publish stories as an activity that helped her endure the unhappiness of her married life. She was shocked to discover that what she earned for her stories belonged legally to her husband. When the marriage ended, this early experience stood her in good stead. She was offered a position as staff, writing for the secularist magazine the *National Reformer*, by Charles Bradlaugh and worked as a journalist for a number of years.

For all of these women, the turn to writing and to journalism was contingent on circumstances that made it possible or necessary for them to engage in activities that lay outside the normal bounds of women of their class. At the same time, all of them emphasized that it was this turn to writing and to a profession that allowed them to become independent, both intellectually and financially. It freed them from burdensome restraints and demands for compliance with the dictates and expectations of others: of her mother and siblings in Martineau's case and her husband in Besant's. While Cobbe insisted on her enjoyment of her domestic and social tasks as her father's housekeeper, she also stressed the limited sympathy they shared and the extent to which her own interests had to be subordinated to his. This sense of their career emerging only as other family ties and demands diminished is one of the many ways in which these women confirmed their adherence to feminine norms. To reject familial demands and duties would have been reprehensible and none dared to do so. Besant came closest, as she resisted the demands made of her as a wife, but she presented herself as being willing to make compromises that her husband would not accept. Once the break into writing and a career had been made, however, they all describe how they became public figures, enjoying the new range of activities that this involved and the expanded social worlds that it enabled them to enter. They gave public lectures which were apparently well received. Besant was apparently an inspired lecturer who drew substantial crowds while Cobbe combined her lectures with sermons in Unitarian churches. Martineau remained aloof from most public causes, but both Cobbe and Besant became prominent in a range of organizations, Cobbe in the campaign for women's suffrage and in that opposing vivisection and Besant in Free Thought and Fabian Socialism before she took a leading role in Theosophy. Their move into becoming public figures and into their particular campaigns is dealt with in detail in all their autobiographies and in a way that makes it the pinnacle of their lives.

---

[77]Cobbe, *Life*, vol. I, p. 195. See also Sally Mitchell, *Frances Power Cobbe: Victorian Feminist, Journalist, Reformer*, English Literature in Transition, 1880–1920 (Charlottesville: University of Virginia Press, 2004).

Personal and Domestic Lives

The detailed attention paid to their public lives and activities by Victorian women contrasts with the very limited discussion they offer of their personal and domestic lives. While most of the changes in women's autobiography across the 19th century involve the discussion of new issues or the paying of more attention to aspects of life that had previously been dealt with sparingly, when it comes to the question of adult life and close or intimate relationships, what one sees rather is its disappearance. As one of the last of the courtesan's autobiographies, Harriette Wilson's *Memoirs* are almost the last to deal not only with her sexual liaisons but with her intimate life. Wilson dealt at length with many of her encounters with male supporters and protectors, often giving conversations apparently verbatim and making very clear who provided financial support and who did not. She also offered a kind of detail reminiscent of a romantic novel about her relationship with Lord Ponsonby, the great love of her life. She described her initial fascination with him and her many visits to his house before he noticed her, their first meetings and how the relationship was established. The three blissful years that it lasted are not described – but its ending including their last meeting, his letter telling her it was over and her desperate letters to him after this are all included in the text. The contrast here with the later autobiographies that scarcely mention intimate relationships could not be more marked.

One begins to see this change in the 1840s, in the *Recollections* of Charlotte Elizabeth Tonna. Tonna mentioned her first marriage to a serving military officer, an event that occurred a few months after the death of her father. We are told nothing about the relationship prior to the wedding or about the wedding itself. It seems clear that it was a difficult relationship: she indicated that when he returned to his regiment in Halifax, he sent her a summons to join him. Tonna described her voyage to Nova Scotia and the challenges of living in such a very different part of the world, especially for one deficient as she was in domestic skills in some detail. But there is no mention of her husband. She spent two years in Nova Scotia – and then suggested she was required to accompany her husband to Ireland where he had a legal issue to resolve. After they had been there a few months, she noted, 'my husband was ordered abroad. I declined to cross the Atlantic a second time, and from this period I became chiefly dependent on my own exertions'. This step apparently brought an end to her marriage. Little more is said about it except that when she published, she did not use her married name, calling herself Charlotte Elizabeth in the hope that her husband would not know it was her or claim her earnings as legally his.[78] His death freed her from this fear of his taking her hard-earned income.

---

[78] Bryan B. Rasmussen, 'From God's Work to Fieldwork: Charlotte Tonna's Evangelical Autoethnography', *ELH* 77, no. 1 (2010).

In Martineau's case, there was no marriage that had to be kept hidden and she was quite prepared to discuss the brief romantic entanglement she was involved in shortly after her father's death. She mentioned, but did not name, the young man who apparently wanted to marry her, and to whom despite some doubts, she became engaged. The engagement was called into question by false rumours that were spread about her family and their finances. This was a source of great strain to the young man who was apparently mentally fragile and then became insane and then died. Martineau said little about what she felt at the time but makes it clear looking back that it was probably better for both of them that the marriage did not take place. Marriage and having children would have been completely incompatible with her literary life or with what she now took as her core concern: 'to think and learn and speak out with absolute freedom what I have thought and learned.' She had had sufficient of the family ties and duties that 'every woman's heart requires', she insisted, and was entirely satisfied with her lot as a single woman, 'probably the happiest single woman in England'.[79]

For Martineau, the question of what to say or not to say in regard to her private life centred on her own family. One key issue here was the continuing difficulties she experienced with her mother throughout much of her adult life and, to the displeasure of some contemporary reviewers, she did show how hard this relationship was. When she was just beginning to make money by undertaking 'literary drudgery' in London in her mid-twenties and feeling that her future lay in London, 'my mother sent me peremptory orders to go home, and to fill the place which my poor young sister was to vacate'. Her mother was acting on the advice of friends who knew nothing of the literary world, and did subsequently encourage Martineau's pursuit of writing, but was always demanding. A few years after this, when Martineau had begun to publish her very successful popular tales of political economy, she returned to London and loved her independent life there. Martineau's life, as depicted in her autobiography, now underwent a transformation. Rather than dwelling on her misery and unhappiness, her account now dealt with the issues and questions that she wrote about and her literary and social relationships. In her years at home, she had hated the social life of balls and other activities forced on her and which her deafness made a torture. 'From the time when I went to London,' she wrote, 'all that was changed.'

> People began with me as with a deaf person; and there was little more awkwardness about my hearing, when they had once reconciled themselves to my trumpet. They came to me in good will, or they would not have come at all. They and I were not jumbled together by mere propinquity; we met purposely; and, if we continued our intercourse, it was through some sort of affinity. I now found what the real pleasures of social intercourse are, and was deeply sensible of its benefits.

[79]Martineau, *Autobiography*, vol. I, p. 133.

Her complete independence lasted only a few months, however, as her mother decided that she would join her. Martineau did not welcome this suggestion but was unable to refuse it. She says nothing in her autobiography of how hard she thought it might be, although the letter she sent her mother at the time makes clear her determination to continue to live as she chose. 'I have no doubt we shall make one another happy,' she wrote,

> if we at once begin with the change of habits which our change of position renders necessary. I fully expect that both you and I shall occasionally feel as if I did not discharge a daughter's duty, but we shall both remind ourselves that I am now as much a citizen of the world as any professional *son* of yours could be.[80]

But it was never easy. Although her mother enjoyed London society when she came to live with Martineau, inevitably 'troubles arose'. One of these, Martineau wrote,

> was, (to pass it over as lightly as possible) that my mother, who loved power and had always been in the habit of exercising it, was hurt at confidence being reposed in me, and distinctions shown, and visits paid to me; and I, with every desire to be passive, and being in fact wholly passive in the matter, was kept in a state of constant agitation at the influx of distinctions which I never sought, and which it was impossible to impart.[81]

One issue here was her mother's desire for a larger and grander home than the one they were currently in and which Martineau did not think they could afford. The troubles continued for the five years that Martineau lived with her mother and were one of the reasons why she decided to visit America. Her close friends recommended that she go away for a long period, insisting that while she was successful and being courted 'my mother's happiness would not . . . be promoted by my presence'. Her siblings agreed. Martineau was profoundly relieved when eventually the family decided it would be better for everyone if her mother ceased living with her and moved closer to some of her other children.

While able to talk about her mother, Martineau is largely silent about the relationship that caused her the greatest pain: that with her youngest brother, the Unitarian minister James, which had reached its height by the time she was eighteen and came to a bitter end in 1851 when James published a savage review of a book of letters in which Harriet was involved. Martineau offered no specific details of the breakdown of this relationship, beyond

---

[80] Harriet Martineau to Elizabeth Martineau, 8 July 1833, in Karen Payne, *Between Ourselves: Letters between Mothers and Daughters 1750–1982* (London: Michael Joseph, 1983), p. 90.
[81] Martineau, *Autobiography*, vol. I, p. 188.

noting that all who know her were aware 'that the strongest passion I ever entertained was in regard to my youngest brother'. In place of specific information, Martineau points to the inherent difficulties in close brother-sister relations, offering a view of them that has recently been supported by contemporary historians.[82] 'Brothers are to sisters what sisters can never be to brothers', she argues, 'as objects of engrossing and devoted affection. The law of their frames is answerable for this: and that other law – of equity – which sisters are bound to obey, requires that they should not render their account of their disappointments where there can be no fair reply.'[83]

Cobbe was the most discreet of all, when it came to private life, making sure that she said nothing about any family black sheep or scandals, insisting on the cordiality that always existed between herself and her brothers and seeming to downplay the difficult relationship she had with her father. There was no question of marriage and Cobbe gloried in her 'single life'. Indeed, demonstrating the possibility for spinsters to live happy and fulfilled lives was one of her primary reasons for writing her life. Although formally single, she did not live alone. But Cobbe said nothing of the close and very loving domestic partnership that she had with Mary Lloyd for over thirty years. Cobbe lets us know that she met Lloyd, a sculptor, when she was in Italy in the late 1850s and visited Lloyd's studio in company with Mary Somerville. Cobbe and Lloyd then went riding on the Campagna together.

> Then began an acquaintance, which was further improved two years later when Miss Lloyd came to meet and help me when I was a cripple, at Aix-les-Bains; and from that time, now more than thirty years ago, she and I have lived together. Of a friendship like this, which has been to my later life what my mother's affection was to my youth, I shall not be expected to say more.[84]

Cobbe wrote poems extolling Lloyd and declaring her love for her and said a great deal about her in letters. Nothing more is said in the autobiography, however, beyond the fact that it was Lloyd who found and bought 'the dear little house in South Kensington which became our home with few interruptions for a quarter of a century'.[85] Cobbe's own sense of the need for discretion about this relationship was re-enforced by Mary Lloyd who insisted that nothing was said about their relationship in Cobbe's autobiography. In a general way, Lloyd wanted everything to be dealt with discreetly and Cobbe wrote much more freely and fulsomely about her

---

[82]See Leonore Davidoff, *Thicker Than Water: Siblings and Their Relations, 1780–1920* (Oxford: Oxford University Press, 2012).
[83]Martineau, *Autobiography*, vol. I, p. 99.
[84]Cobbe, *Life*, vol. II, p. 393.
[85]Cobbe, *Life*, vol. II, p. 396.

feelings for Lloyd in the letters and poems she wrote after her death than she ever had in her lifetime.

The sense of propriety and decorum that demanded silence on intimate matters that was so pronounced from the mid-19th century until the 1880s declined to some extent towards the end of the century. One can see this in the *New Woman* novels of the 1890s that broke with Victorian convention by discussing or at least intimating the devastating impact of the sexual ignorance of young Victorian women on their experience of marriage and in protesting against the sexual double standard. The autobiographies of women whose adult life had occurred in the later part of the century were also inclined to be franker in discussing their lives. Indeed, Annie Besant's *Autobiography*, published when she was in her forties, reads very much like a companion to the *New Woman* novels. Besant's idealized but moving account of herself as an innocent young girl of nineteen, the product of a very protective home and education and filled with impractical dreams and a passionate desire to give herself to a larger cause reads like a sentimental novel. 'Looking back over twenty-five years', she wrote, 'I feel a profound pity for the girl standing at that critical point of life, so utterly, hopelessly ignorant of all that marriage meant, so filled with impossible dreams, so unfitted for the *role* of wife.' She was, at the age of nineteen a dreamy young girl looking for an ideal man with no real judgement and no idea of what marriage involved. She quickly became engaged to a clergyman whom she never loved – but who seemed to assume that the very fact that they had spent a short time walking and conversing together indicated her willingness to marry him. Once he had formally proposed and she had accepted, her mother would not countenance her breaking the engagement. Although she doesn't go into great detail, she makes it very clear that from the start, her marriage was unhappy.

> We were an ill-matched pair, my husband and I, from the very outset; he, with very high ideas of a husband's authority and a wife's submission, holding strongly to the 'master-in-my-own-house theory,' thinking much of the details of home arrangements, precise, methodical, easily angered and with difficulty appeased. I, accustomed to freedom, indifferent to home details, impulsive, very hot-tempered, and proud as Lucifer. I had never had a harsh word spoken to me, never been ordered to do anything, had had my way smoothed for my feet, and never a worry had touched me. Harshness roused first incredulous wonder, then a storm of indignant tears, and after a time a proud, defiant resistance, cold and hard as iron. The easy-going, sunshiny, enthusiastic girl changed – and changed pretty rapidly – into a grave, proud, reticent woman, burying deep in her own heart all her hopes, her fears, and her disillusions.[86]

---

[86] Besant, *Autobiography*, p. 81.

Besant took up writing as a way to fill her days and give herself something new to concentrate on. Throughout the early years of her marriage, her religious doubts increased – something which added to the strain between her and her clergyman husband. Things were not helped when she had children and was often ill. Finally, in 1873 she refused to participate in Holy Communion leading to a final break with her husband and a divorce.

A Sense of a Self

Articulating a sense of self in their autobiographies presented a challenge to 19th-century women. The disapproval that they faced in writing these works and the need to negotiate contemporary ideals of femininity made an assertion of self difficult. In the very act of writing autobiographies, of course, women were rejecting the imperative to silence and insisting on the right to make their life stories known. But as we have seen in the case of 18th-century scandalous women, the writing of this life usually focused on the misfortunes of the author as a vulnerable young woman, rather than representing or reflecting on her own character or sense of herself. This focus on depicting the significant events in a life, rather than reflecting on it, continues in the first half of the 19th century. Even as women seem to apologize less and to state their claims to notice with greater force, they paid little attention to discussing their capacities or thoughts or feelings and provide little sense of the overall meaning of their lives. In the later part of the century, by contrast, women's autobiographies began to trace the intellectual developments, the religious and spiritual crises, the pursuit of an independent life and the public activities that made them who they are. Most of these works reflect a new sense of the importance of history and of the ways in which these women have lived through significant historical change. Hence their lives have a documentary significance that extends beyond their own particular feelings or ideas. They were also buttressed by a strong sense of how their life stories illustrated and connected with a broader struggle for women's rights. Many 18th-century women saw themselves as illustrating the general subordination and victimization of women. Their late 19th-century successors go beyond this in their recognition not only of women's oppression but of the need for this to be challenged and of their own involvement in this challenge. Harriet Martineau, Frances Cobbe and Annie Besant were all involved in or wrote about the various campaigns that made up the 19th-century women's movement. All of them made their feminist commitments clear in their autobiographies and linked them to their demand for recognition as autonomous moral and intellectual beings.

Although it is evident in a number of different ways, the sense of self evident in women's autobiographies in the first half of the 19th century remained limited and fragmentary. This lack of a strong and coherent statement of a sense of self seems in many ways to follow from the lack of personal and financial independence of these women in their daily lives. Harriette Wilson, for example, is both unapologetic and often self-laudatory, depicting her life as a consequence of her own choices in a way that differs markedly from her 18th-century predecessors. Nonetheless, she was a courtesan whose life depended entirely on her capacity to attract and retain the affection and financial support of lovers and protectors. It is on this capacity that her value to herself as well as to others depended and it featured prominently in the way that she represents herself. Wilson underlined her capacity to attract and gain the attention of men by having others make comments about her intelligence and personality rather than saying anything about herself. Hence while she often described the characters and personalities of her lovers in very clear and sometimes critical terms, when it came to herself, she reported conversations which either illustrate how intelligent, witty and sharp on the uptake she was, or had others describe her. 'I remember Lord Petersham', she wrote on one occasion, 'paid me the most flattering compliment.'

> 'You are decidedly a very fine creature, but all that I have known for the last three years, and also that you are the wittiest, cleverest creature in London.'
> Now Lord Petersham knew no more of my wit than that of the man in the moon, only it was the fashion to call me clever and witty, and whoever had said otherwise would have himself passed for a fool.[87]

Wilson lacked either a model or a language for writing directly about herself and her wishes or feelings and refers everything she does to some aspect of her life and role as a courtesan. She always regretted her lack of education, but when she decided to retire from London for a while to educate herself, she insisted that this was something she did not for herself, but as a way to enhance her relationship with the love of her life, Lord Ponsonby.

> 'Ponsonby, being forty already,' thought I, 'will be downright out, while I continue to bloom: therefore, when this idea makes him timider and humbler, I should like to improve my powers of consoling him and charming away all his cares. Let me see! What knowledge will be likely to make me most agreeable to him? Oh! politics. What a pity that he does not like something less dry and livelier! But, no matter!'[88]

Wilson took herself away for two weeks to read seriously, starting with political speeches. But she soon tired of these speeches – and spent her time

---

[87] Wilson, *Memoirs*, vol. III, p. 49.
[88] Wilson, *Memoirs*, vol. I, p. 49.

reading other works more to her taste – regardless of whether or not they were of particular interest to Ponsonby.

> The Greeks employed me for two whole days, and the Romans six more: I took down notes of what I thought most striking. I then read *Charles the Twelfth*, by Voltaire, and liked it less than most people do; and then Rousseau's *Confessions*; then Racine's *Tragedies*, and afterwards, Boswell's *Life of Johnson*. I allowed myself only ten minutes for my dinner.[89]

Regardless of what Ponsonby thought, this reading was of considerable use to Wilson in her own life: as we have seen, she thought about Rousseau's *Confessions* when writing her own memoirs and made clear her sense of the differences between them. This period of intense reading served clearly as a way to demonstrate how much quicker and more intelligent she was than other women, and why she was sometimes referred to as a 'good fellow'. But while she unquestionably valued herself highly and saw herself as unique, she makes this clear to the reader by couching it always in evaluation of others. She makes us very aware that she always generated respect and admiration. As her biographer points out, she always insisted that it was pleasure for people to meet her![90]

Articulating a strong sense of self was also very difficult for women who came from the wider reaches of Empire and had to deal with the marginal position that this produced – and the prejudices that they had to deal with. One can see the problems that this posed in the autobiography of Mary Seacole. At the start of her autobiography, Seacole indicated her recognition of her indeterminate position within the British world, especially in light of her having a Jamaican mother and a Scottish father. She was neither white nor black, describing herself as a Creole and one with 'a fierce allegiance to the British Empire'. Having used the term to describe herself, she immediately differentiated herself from the stereotypes associated with Creoles.

> I have often heard the term 'lazy Creole' applied to my country people; but I am sure I do not know what it is to be indolent. All my life long I have followed the impulse which led me to be up and doing; and so far from resting idle anywhere, I have never wanted inclination to rove, nor will powerful enough to find a way to carry out my wishes.[91]

Seacole was a childless widow dependent on her own quite considerable entrepreneurial capacity. But she worked hard to demonstrate the extent to which, despite this, she accepted and even embodied Victorian norms of

---

[89] Wilson, *Memoirs*, vol. I, p. 150.
[90] Wilson, *Courtesan's Revenge*.
[91] Seacole, *Wonderful Adventures*, p. 1.

womanhood, in her chastity and propriety and in her complete dedication to nursing – especially the nursing of British soldiers.

Seacole told us a little more about herself than Wilson, but she too presented herself hesitantly and in a fragmented way and depended on the words of others as a way to show her qualities and her achievements. She took pride in her love of adventure and her capacity to plan and devise ways of doing things and points out that these qualities were visible from her early days: she managed to get to see England while still in her teens. Her strange and wonderful adventures were so extensive, she insisted that some people 'have called me quite a female Ulysses'. But she was always womanly and concerned about family: when it came to dealing with her time in Panama, she makes it clear that she went there after the death of her husband and her mother in order to be with her only brother. He was in too precarious a position to support her or provide her with a home and so she was forced to rely on her own doctoring and nursing skills, buying up a hotel where she could live and provide others with both accommodation and nursing care. Seacole shows no hesitations in stating her opinion of others, including critical ones about Americans whose racism she saw as connected to the continuation of slavery and deplored. Most of Seacole's clients while she was in Panama were Americans and many were hesitant about letting her treat them. During an Independence Day dinner, she noted, one of her clients drank a toast to her in which he expressed regret that she was a 'yaller woman' and wished that she could be bleached which would make her 'as acceptable in any company as she deserves to be'. Seacole responded tartly, that she did not appreciate their friend's wishes regarding her complexion.

> If it had been as dark as any nigger's, I should have been just as happy and as useful, and as much respected by those whose respect I value; and as to his offer of bleaching me, I should, even if it were practicable, decline it without any thanks. As to the society which the process might gain me admission into, all I can say is, that, judging from the specimens I have met with here and elsewhere, I don't think that I shall lose much by being excluded from it. So, gentlemen, I drink to you and the general reformation of American manners.[92]

Seacole always insisted on her womanliness and adherence to contemporary expectations of feminine conduct. In writing about herself in relation to the Crimea, she combined the adventurousness that took her there with the dedication and heroic service she provided to British soldiers. Her womanliness was underlined in the way she presented herself as 'Mother Seacole', the way in which she was addressed by those she nursed, and a language that underlined her selflessness and the caring and attentive way

---

[92]Seacole, *Wonderful Adventures*, p. 28.

she looked after her men. Seacole describes her travels in the Crimea in a very direct and engaging way, but when it comes to the question of her role as nurse, she hands the narrative voice to others. The chapter entitled 'My Work in the Crimea' was something she discussed reluctantly, but could not omit – as it was the basis of her claim to notice. However, while setting up her positions as 'doctoress, nurse and mother' she says nothing about what she actually did, relying on the written testimony and comments of others to show her resourcefulness, effectiveness and skill. The entire chapter dealing with her work in the Crimea consists of short notes and letters about her, stressing her 'kindness and attention', her generosity and care and the love and devotion she inspired in the soldiers, many of whom believed she saved their lives.

A very different sense of self is evident in the Victorian autobiographies of Martineau, Cobbe and Besant. The key difference here is the way these women reflected on themselves, on their nature and personality and on their development from childhood into adulthood. While all of them dealt at some length with the wider world in which they lived and how it changed over time and with their social worlds and networks, a key aspect of their autobiographies was their concern to delineate their understanding of what *they* were as individuals and how they came to develop that individuality. Martineau articulated this sense most clearly and was most preoccupied with it, but it underlay the ways the others framed their autobiographies too. This new sense of self was not something that was just created by these women. On the contrary, they were using and adapting the language that had become widespread in thinking and writing about the self in the second half of the 19th century, a language that reflected current debates in psychology and was taken up, utilized and indeed modified in contemporary fiction.

As we have seen, the emergence of a new interest in psychology in the mid-19th century is widely recognized. As Sally Shuttleworth has argued, much of this specialist literature, including the medical literature, drew on fiction as a way to provide both evidence and illustrations of the various mental states or pathologies that were of interest.[93] Conversely, many Victorian novelists, including Charlotte Brontë and George Eliot, took a great interest in psychological literature while writing their novels. Both had a particular interest in phrenology but read much else as well. This reading is clearly evident in the characters they constructed. In contrast to the 18th-century novels in which characters do not change, but rather through all that happens reveal themselves as remaining themselves, a key feature of 19th-century novels is the way the character develops through the events they experience and the circumstance in which they live. In many cases, and especially in novels written in the first person, it was not only the author but

---

[93]Sally Shuttleworth, *Charlotte Bronte and Victorian Psychology* (Cambridge: Cambridge University Press, 1996), p. 13.

the character who reflected on this process and on their sense of how they have become who they are.

Charlotte Brontë is particularly significant because her novels, especially *Jane Eyre*, were presented as autobiographies and offered a new way to think about and write autobiography. But she gains particular importance here because of her friendship with Harriet Martineau who read her work with care.[94] Brontë's work is particularly significant in regard to Victorian psychology, Sally Shuttleworth argues, because of 'the way in which she so powerfully condenses and explores in her work the dominant paradigms of her era'.[95] In relation to women's autobiography, it is significant because of her depiction of the self and the sense of selfhood as something that is interior. Rather than being something that becomes known through social acts or exchanges, it was hidden from view, in an inner space. Literary scholars have discussed quite extensively the way that Charlotte Brontë constructed Jane Eyre as a new kind of female subject in fiction. Writing in the first person, Brontë has Jane Eyre report her responses, feelings and behaviour with a quite new kind of intensity and clarity. The adult Jane, as narrator, then analysed them critically in ways that indicate whether or not they were appropriate and what the response to them was. Anna Gibson cites the passage in which Jane Eyre looks back as an adult on the distressing and traumatic incident in her childhood when her outburst to her aunt about how unjust she was, resulted in Jane being locked in the red room for a terrifying afternoon.

> What a consternation of soul was mine that dreary afternoon! How all my brain was in tumult, and all my heart in insurrection! Yet, in what darkness, what dense ignorance, was the mental battle thus fought! I could not answer the ceaseless inward question – *why* I thus suffered: now, at a distance of – I will not say how many years, I see it clearly. I was a discord in Gateshead-hall: I was like nobody there. . . . They were not bound to regard with affection a thing that could not sympathize with one among them; a heterogeneous thing. . . . I know, that had I been a sanguine, brilliant, careless, exacting, handsome, and romping child . . . Mrs. Reed would have endured my presence more complacently.[96]

Jane Eyre, one sympathetic critic suggested, offered a different kind of 'reality' from that usually found in novels, a 'deep, significant reality . . . it [the novel] is soul speaking to soul; it is an utterance from the depths of a struggling, suffering, much-enduring spirit'.[97]

---

[94]Robert B. Martin, 'Charlotte Brontë and Harriet Martineau', *Nineteenth Century Fiction* 7.3 (1952): 198–201.
[95]Shuttleworth, *Charlotte Bronte*, p. 6.
[96]Anna Gibson, 'Charlotte Brontë's First Person', *Narrative* 25, no. 2 (2017): 210–211.
[97]George Henry Lewes, 'Recent Novels: French and English', *Fraser's Magazine* 36 (December 1847): 686–695.

Jane Eyre was very widely read, with interest added by the fact that its author was unknown. It appeared under the name of Currer Bell, but it was widely accepted that this was a pseudonym. As a fictional autobiography, *Jane Eyre* brought a new way of looking at the torments, anger and resentment, fear, loneliness and affections of women. Brontë and several novelists following her provided a new way of thinking about individual life and development and a new language for constructing and describing selfhood.

Harriet Martineau read *Jane Eyre* as well as Brontë's other novels and was, for a period after its publication, on very friendly terms with Brontë. Although Martineau revealed much less about her feelings and inner struggles than Brontë did about her heroine, there is clearly an echo of *Jane Eyre* in the way Martineau depicted her own childhood suffering and in the way that Martineau took, as the central concern of her work, the presentation and explanation of her beliefs, ideas and personality and her constant reflection on the overall framework and pattern of her life. Her concern to depict her character and nature in some detail is underlined in the discussion of her childhood, with its emphasis on her memories, feelings, many fears, sense of shame, inadequacy and anguish when she made a mistake or did something wrong and her continuing and intense unhappiness. Martineau described not only her childhood suffering but also her painful sensitivity, her feeling of being alone and neglected in her family and the personal awkwardness that she thought might have been reduced with more affection and attention. She made an historical point too, deploring the custom of humiliating children and denying them any praise that obtained while she was a child. The one positive thread that runs throughout this painful account is the early sense of her own moral development. At the age of seven, Martineau recalled a trip to Newcastle with her mother and siblings to stay with her grandfather. This was a momentous trip for her in terms of her religious and moral development. It was the moment, she recalled, that she became

> what is commonly called 'a responsible being'. On my return home I began to take moral charge of myself. I had before, and from my earliest recollections, been subject to a haunting, wretched, useless remorse; but from the time of our return from Newcastle, ... I became practically religious with all my strength.[98]

Closely connected to this sense of taking moral charge of herself is the pleasure that Martineau discovered a few years later in learning and in the sense of her own intellectual development. As we have seen, she saw herself as entering an intellectual life while at school and this remained the core of

---

[98]Martineau, *Autobiography*, vol. I, p. 92.

her being. Her pleasure in learning did not outweigh her continuing extreme self-consciousness and fear that she had always done the wrong thing. Nor could it make up for the ongoing pain of her difficult family relationships, or her physical disabilities and frequent ill health. But the very way in which these issues were discussed in her autobiography underlines the ways in which it focuses on the unfolding and development of her own ideas and beliefs. Others play a part, but it is she who is the centre and focus. Her intellectual development remains a key theme of Martineau's autobiography. She dealt at length with the shift away from Unitarianism and the rejection of Christian theology and the acceptance of necessarianism. But these were, in a sense, steps along the way as she continued to seek a broader framework for understanding the world or some kind of belief that was compatible with her desire to focus attention on what was actually knowable rather than on anything that depended merely on faith.

Like a number of other Victorian intellectuals, Martineau found this framework when she read the early work of Auguste Comte. Comte shared her concern with focusing on positive phenomena in a way that linked science with philosophy. Most importantly, Comte postulated one 'great fundamental law': a law of development that states that every race and indeed humankind as a whole passes through three stages of development – 'the theological, or fictitious; the metaphysical, or abstract; and the scientific, or positive'. This schema, which could be applied to individual development as well as to humankind, offered a way of encompassing both long historical sweeps and individual histories so that the adult looking back on her life can see the way in which she developed through her own theological and metaphysical phases finally emerging into the scientific and positive stage as a mature adult. It offered Martineau a very clear structure for looking at her own life – and it provided the framework for her autobiography. Martineau's autobiography, as Mitzi Myers says, 'is organized around a stage-by-stage pilgrimage from darkness to enlightenment ... delineating in vivid detail the progress of a Victorian woman's mind from the paralysis of childhood to the serene freedom of full self-government'.[99] Looking back on her life, she insisted on 'the surpassing value of philosophy which is the natural growth of the experience and study, – and perhaps I may be allowed to say, – the progression of a life'. And had 'opened my way before me, and given a staff into my hand, and thrown a light upon my path'.[100]

While not as introspective in its reflections on her feelings or development as Martineau's, Frances Cobbe's autobiography also offered a new way of constructing and indeed celebrating a sense of self. Her autobiography, she made clear, was intended to delineate her life, character and achievements.

---

[99]Meyers, 'Harriet Martineau's *Autobiography*', p. 54.
[100]Martineau, *Autobiography*, vol. II, p. 112.

Like Martineau, she was very interested in philosophy, and wrote quite extensively on ethical and moral questions. Cobbe did not draw on any philosophical method or approach in depicting her life, however, focusing rather on her sense of emotional and physical well-being, her competence and independence, her comfortable place in her various social worlds and her philanthropic and political activities and involvements. In place of the childhood terrors with which Martineau's autobiography began, Cobbe began hers by describing herself as 'well born' in two different ways, the first of which is the good sense and dependability of her parents while the second centres on the family's affluence and high social standing. She inherited from her parents, she says in her first paragraph,

> a physical frame which, however defective even to the verge of grotesqueness from the aesthetic point of view, has been, as regards health and energy, a source of endless enjoyment to me. From childhood till now in my old age, except during a few years of lameness from an accident, mere natural existence has always been to me a positive pleasure ... my spirits ... have kept a level of cheerfulness subject to no alternatives of depression save under the stress of actual sorrow.[101]

This picture of herself as a cheerful and positive person continued throughout her autobiography. Cobbe wrote about herself in different ways at different stages of her life. In her discussion of her early life, her childhood, school years and religious crisis, she wrote directly about herself and her feelings Once her inner struggles over education and religion were resolved, Cobbe's life seems to have been set. There is little introspection after this and the autobiography focuses on how she managed her social, professional and political life rather than how she felt about anything. The eschewal of the personal that has already been discussed meant that she said nothing about her feelings for Mary Lloyd. But what is notable in the way Cobbe told her life story is her emphasis on the qualities and capacities that she valued in herself and saw as important. These included her resilience, mental toughness, persistence and sense of duty. All of these qualities are much in evidence in her discussion of the way in which she approached and wrote her first book for example. Having come through her own religious crisis, she insisted, she felt that she owed it to others to offer them some ways forward. She was still her father's housekeeper when she wrote the book, so she could attend to it only in the hours when she was not required to perform domestic tasks, and she published it anonymously to avoid embarrassing her father. She took great pride in the skill with which she found an excellent publisher and relished the fact that no reviewer suspected it had been written by a woman. These qualities, combined with a spirit of adventure and a determination to

---

[101] Cobbe, *Life*, vol. I, p. 65.

make her own life are underlined in her discussions of how she decided to leave the family home, travel to the East and then set herself up as a single woman. While Cobbe did not provide a broad philosophical framework for interpreting her life in the way that Martineau did, she emphasized her deeply felt philanthropic concerns and the social and political commitments that led to activism on behalf of women and animals. Her feminism – or what she would have called her support for the claims and the rights of women – was also very important in the autobiography and in the way she establishes and elaborates her sense of herself. Her insistence that hers was a full and active life, despite the fact that no man sought to share it, is an underlying theme in a book that serves as a celebration of this kind of life.

The issue of religious faith that had been so important in the autobiographies of Martineau and Cobbe was even more important to Annie Besant. It provided the framework for her understanding and depiction of her sense of self in a couple of different ways. In her *Autobiographical Sketches*, Besant suggested that her religious yearning and desire underlie almost every aspect of her life. As we have seen, she stressed the close link between adolescent sexuality and intense Christian devotion, especially in a society that allowed neither any form of sexual education nor any close social interaction between adolescent girls and boys.

In her *Autobiographical Sketches*, Besant described the way in which she emerged from this innocence and unhappiness through her close reading of the Bible, her contacts with others who took a different approach to religion from the narrow one of her husbands, and then her pathway from Christianity and the expectations of a wife into her own independent activities and beliefs. Her turn to writing, her successful publications and her horror at realizing that what she earned belonged to her husband were important here as showing a stage of her move towards independence of thought and to the possibility of an independent life as she became involved in free thought and then in socialism. Although she used the title 'Sketches' for this first significant piece of autobiographical writing, the work is more than that. Ending as they do with the loss of custody of her daughter in 1879 because of her beliefs, the readership of these sketches, as Carol Mackay argues, recognize in them 'a coherent life story driven by a call for justice'.[102]

Almost a decade later, Besant wrote her second Autobiography. As we have seen, one major reason for writing this work was her conversion to Theosophy, so religion was a central issue in it. One key point in this work centres on Besant's insistence that her whole life centred on her religious and spiritual yearning until she found the fulfilment that she needed in Theosophy. It was this that gave her life meaning and coherence and that enabled her, as

---

[102] Carol Hanbery Mackay, 'Emerging Selves. The Autobiographical Impulse in Elizabeth Barrett Browning, Anne Thackeray Ritchie and Annie Wood Besant', in *A History of English Autobiography*, ed. Adam Smyth (Cambridge: Cambridge University Press, 2016), pp. 207–220.

Martineau had done, to explain her life as a search for enlightenment and the stages along the way.

> I have been told that I plunged headlong into Theosophy and let my enthusiasm carry me away. I think the charge is true, in so far as the decision was swiftly taken; but it had been long led up to, and realised the dreams of childhood on the higher planes of intellectual womanhood. And let me here say that more than all I hoped for in that first plunge has been realised, and a certainty of knowledge has been gained on doctrines seen as true as that swift flash of illumination.[103]

This later *Autobiography* as Carolyn Miller argues, also brought a new sense of self. In the *Sketches*, Besant's belief in science and socialist materialism went along with an idea of herself as an autonomous individual who can be described by rational exposition. Her conversion to Theosophy required that she gave up some of her earlier social beliefs and values, including her advocacy of birth control, and that she sees herself in communion with a wider universe. Hence the *Autobiography* began with a description and chart of the astrological conditions obtaining at her birth in a way that enables her to traverse space and time and connect herself with the wider universe. The concern here was not to produce a definitive self as much as an account of 'her conversions and deconversions to create the sense of a fluctuating, evanescent self'.[104] Besant's approach was particularly notable here precisely because of the way in which the different versions of her autobiography allow for and involve the construction and presentation of different selves, depending on the life trajectory that is of particular importance at the point of writing. The construction of self has moved from something to be avoided or dealt with only indirectly to becoming the major focus of women's autobiography.

Conclusion

There are changes in women's autobiography both within and across the 19th century as the idea of women's autobiography became more established and different kinds of women came to write their life stories. The continuities with the 18th century, evident in the autobiographies of courtesans and prostitutes early in the century gave way to significant change by the 1820s and '30s as new voices came to be heard, on the one hand, while new concepts of womanhood became increasingly dominant, on the other. These new voices include slaves and women of colour from the wider British

---

[103]Besant, *Autobiography*.
[104]Carolyn Elizabeth Miller, 'Body, Spirit, Print: The Radical Autobiographies of Annie Besant and Helen and Oliviarossetti', *Feminist Studies* 35, no. 2 (2009): 243–273.

world, whose stories are quite unlike any that have been heard within the British Isles. But while they were being heard, there were also new restrictions on the kinds of things that women could include in autobiography as ideas of womanly decorum made it unacceptable to discuss many aspects of adult life and particularly intimate relationships.

The contradictions that surrounded women became more pronounced in the second half of the 19th century. While domestic ideals of womanhood continued to be believed and articulated strongly, new avenues in terms of paid work expanded somewhat, especially in journalism and teaching, and in unpaid work, in philanthropy and political activity and campaigning. Small numbers of women became prominent in the public world through their intellectual and literary achievements, rather than as a result of sexual scandal. Feminist resistance to the legal and social confinement of women also emerged. Small numbers of Victorian women wrote autobiographies in which they sought simultaneously to mark and celebrate their achievements, while at the same time insisting that they accept and indeed embodied the appropriate norms of womanly conduct in every aspect of their lives. These autobiographies deal with their religious beliefs and spiritual crises, their education, their struggles to articulate their aspirations and to gain some independence, while still meeting parental demands – and showing how within their lives, as within their autobiographies, they are faced with many conflicting demands.

And yet, for all of these contradictions and limitations, it is clear that women's autobiography came of age in the 19th century. One can see this in many ways: in the refusal to apologize for writing such a work, in the stress on their capacities and achievements and above all in the ways in which the main concern of women's autobiography became the depiction of the author's life and the development and unfolding of her mind. Harriet Martineau set the pattern here. As we have seen, while concerned to discuss and describe events, institutions and significant individuals, her autobiography is fundamentally the story of an internal evolution, 'the active formation of a self as it responds to outer circumstances'. It was she who first seized on this as the way to write a woman's life and provided her successors with a model to negotiate and work with. Few of them shared her introspection and none agreed with her particular approach to development or to the ideal of a woman's life. But all of them continued in various different ways to place the formation of the self at the centre of their work.

Autobiographies Discussed in This Chapter

Besant, Annie Wood, *An Autobiography* (1893) (London: T. Fisher Unwin, 1908). Accessed through Nineteenth Century Collections Online.

Besant, Annie, *Autobiographical Sketches* (1885) (Peterborough, Ontario: Broadview, 2009).

Cobbe, Frances Power, *The Life of Frances Power Cobbe by Herself* (London: Richard Bentley & Son, 1894).

Elizabeth, Charlotte, *Personal Recollections* (London: R. E. Seeley and W. Burnside, 1847).

Johnstone, Julia, *Confessions of Julia Johnstone Written by Herself in Contradiction to the Fables of Harriette Wilson* (London: Benbow, Printer and Publisher, 1828).

Martineau, Harriet, *Autobiography*, 3 vols (1997) (London: Virago, 1983).

Prince, Mary, *The History of Mary Prince, a West Indian Slave, Written by Herself* (1831) (London: Penguin, 2001).

Seacole, Mary, *Wonderful Adventures of Mrs Seacole in Many Lands* (1857), ed. and with an Introduction by Sara Salih (London: Penguin Books, 2005).

Somerville, Mary, *Personal Recollections from Early Life to Old Age*, ed. Martha Somerville (London: John Murray, 1874).

Wilson, Harriette, *Harriette Wilson's Memoirs of Herself and Others*, 3 vols (London: T. Douglas, 1825). Accessed through Nineteenth Century Collections Online.

FIGURE 3 *Circa 1910: Fabian socialist thinker, historian, economist and writer Beatrice Webb (1858–1943). (Photo by Hulton Archive/Getty Images.)*

CHAPTER THREE

Autobiography as a Form of History

More women wrote autobiographies than ever before in the years after the First World War. In some cases, as in the 19th century, this was because of a sense of having lived remarkable lives and achieved significant objectives. A new note appeared at this time in women's autobiography, however, which came from those women who had been directly involved in major historical developments. The period from the late 19th century and through the First World War was the first in which women in significant numbers had been engaged in political campaigns or in national and international conflicts. They were well aware of the novelty of their experience, and many felt that their life stories had a new kind of importance and had to be told because they were not only interesting in themselves but offered historical insights that could not be gained in any other way. The idea that there was a close link between the history of a period and the writing of an autobiography was not new. Many autobiographies point to the social and political changes that have occurred in the life of the author, and some comment on particular issues and events. These works were different, however: their authors saw them not simply as commenting on recording historical events but as being themselves historical works.

In the last decades of the 19th century and the first of the 20th, the wider public world opened up to middle-class women in a number of different ways. There was a considerable expansion in their involvement in unpaid charitable and philanthropic work and in social reform campaigns. In addition, some women became involved in public administration as they began to be appointed or elected as Poor Law Guardians and members of school boards in the course of the 1870s and as factory inspectors in the 1890s. Women were also drawn into campaigning for the major political parties in national elections in the 1880s. The outlawing of paid political agents with their practice of bribing voters to turn up at elections led to the establishment of women's auxiliaries by the major political parties, like the

Primrose League and the Women's Liberal Federation, to provide support during elections. Trade unions and labour organizations and parties also offered new opportunities for women as paid workers and as volunteers.[1]

By far the most significant development, especially in providing a stimulus to autobiography, however, was the campaign for women's suffrage. Women had begun campaigning for suffrage in the 1860s, but in quite small numbers and in carefully managed and genteel ways. Interest in suffrage expanded in the 1890s, but it was the advent of the militant campaign in 1903 that galvanized the movement and brought it into the national spotlight. From the start, the militants, whether they were involved in interrupting political meetings, giving public speeches or holding largely carefully costumed demonstrations – or towards the end, were involved in the breaking of shop windows and acid burning of golf courses – sought and gained immense publicity, using courtroom appearances and any other opportunities to make speeches. Many were imprisoned and some who went on hunger strikes were brutally forcibly fed. The drama surrounding the militant campaign massively increased the numbers of women who became involved in all suffrage organizations.[2] For the militant suffragettes themselves, their involvement was often the most important episode in their lives and, in view of the extraordinary violence with which they were treated by the government, sometimes seemed like a form of martyrdom. A number wrote autobiographies, and their works, Maroula Joannou argues, 'differ radically from the usual autobiography of a middle-class subject which presents itself as the record of an unusual but exemplary life'.[3] They deal with an autobiographical 'I' but are written as both autobiography and history, telling a story that is shared collectively with other militants.

The militant suffrage movement came to an end with the outbreak of war in August 1914. The war too offered women new opportunities for direct involvement, however, as drivers, nurses and VADs on the battle front and in terms of new employments to replace men, especially in munitions factories and in agricultural work through the Land Army. As the first total war, the First World War impacted every aspect of their daily life, whether women were directly engaged in it or not. The catastrophic scale of male suffering and the terrible loss of life amongst soldiers, however, meant that, even when autobiographies dealing with the war began to appear in the 1920s, few women felt able to tell *their* stories of war. One who persisted

---

[1] See Patricia Hollis, *Ladies Elect: Women in English Local Government, 1865–1914* (Oxford: Oxford University Press, 1979).
[2] See Barbara Caine, *English Feminism, c 1780–1980* (Oxford: Oxford University Press, 1996), and Laura E. Nym Mayhall, *The Militant Suffrage Movement: Citizenship and Resistance in Britain, 1860–1930* (Oxford: Oxford University Press, 2020).
[3] Maroula Joannou, 'She Who Would Be Free Herself Must Strike the Blow. Suffragette Autobiography and Suffragette Militancy', in *The Uses of Autobiography*, ed. Julia Swindells (London: Taylor & Francis, 1995), p. 37.

was Vera Brittain. Brittain too saw the writing of her life, and especially her discussion of loss and of the way that her life had been torn apart by the war, as a kind of history: the history of her generation.

This new historical impetus meant that women of very different ages were engaged in writing autobiography. While Beatrice Webb, like Millicent Fawcett and Emmeline Pankhurst or Helena Swanwick followed a 19th-century pattern in writing autobiographies that involved looking back over their lives in their sixties, many women who published autobiographies in the 1920s and early '30s were much younger. Ethel Mannin wrote *Confessions and Impressions*, the first of her seven autobiographical works, at the age of thirty and Storm Jameson wrote her first autobiography at a similar age.[4] Others were a little older: Vera Brittain was in her mid-thirties when *Testament of Youth* was published,[5] while Annie Kenney was in her early forties when she published her *Memories of a Militant*.[6] Rather than telling a whole life story, these autobiographies focused closely on the brief period that was of most significance to their author at that point, and indeed some of these women, including Mannin, Brittain and Storm Jameson, went on to write additional volumes or works of autobiography dealing with their later years.

One novel feature of interwar autobiography that followed from the tendency for women of very different ages to write it, was the appearance of marked generational differences in works that are published at the same time. There are notable continuities with Victorian women's autobiography in the work of Beatrice Webb, Millicent Fawcett and Helena Swanwick, for example, all of whom grew up in Victorian households and retained a very strong sense of decorum and propriety. In so far as they discussed private matters in their autobiographies, they did so in limited and careful ways. The works of the younger women are often markedly different in tone, style and content. Generally, these women wrote far more openly and frankly about their sexual and emotional experiences. Brittain and Mannin, for example, were quite explicit about their struggle to gain sexual knowledge, the difficulties of their intimate relationships and the conflicts that they faced as women seeking independence and a career. The new tone and approach evident in women's autobiography were noted by readers. Virginia Woolf regarded the frankness and intimacy of Brittain's *Testament of Youth* as unprecedented. Her story 'told in detail, without reserve, of the war & how she lost her lover and her brother, and dabbled her hands in entrails, & was forever seeing the dead, & eating scraps, & sitting five on one WC, runs rapidly, vividly across my eyes'.[7]

---

[4] Ethel Mannin, *Confessions and Impressions* (London: Jarrolds, 1930).
[5] Vera Brittain, *Testament of Youth: An Autobiographical Study of The Years 1900–1025* (London: Virago, 1933, republished 1978).
[6] Annie Kenney, *Memoirs of a Militant* (London: Edward Arnold, 1924).
[7] Virginia Woolf, *The Diary of Virginia Woolf*, vol. 4, 1931–35, (Harmondsworth: Penguin Books, 1982), p. 177.

Alongside some continuity, one can also see several different issues coming to the fore in the shaping of lives in interwar autobiographies. The religious crises that loomed so large in Victorian women's autobiographies tended for the most part to disappear as different preoccupations came to the fore. The brutality of poverty was one of these, dominating some autobiographies. Another is the question of sexuality as more attention was now paid to the problem of sexual ignorance and the immense difficulties women faced in gaining sexual knowledge. This discussion was part of a conscious breaking of the Victorian taboo on the discussion of sex and it was extended in works like that of Ursula Bloom to depict what might now be regarded as a form of sexual abuse by her father. The struggles women faced to obtain the education they wanted that was evident in Victorian autobiography continue, sometimes now discussed in greater detail and linked more closely to the demand for personal independence and the ability to follow careers and to engage in a meaningful public life. This also means that the discussion of childhood was extended so that it encompassed not only early childhood but also adolescence, something that was coming to be seen as a separate and significant phase of individual development. Adult relationships were also given more attention than previously as several women novelists detailed the trials and difficulties of their marital and intimate lives.

Producing an Autobiography

The increase in the number of women's autobiographies published in the interwar period points not only to the new sense that many had of the importance of writing their lives but also to the new kind of support they received in producing these works. This support came in various forms: from organizations that encouraged women to write their life stories, from periodicals ready and willing to include them, and from friendship networks that helped in the task of finding publishers. There was also a growing number of publishers willing to include women's autobiographical writing in their lists. The autobiographies of several 'progressive women', including Vera Brittain, Helena Swanwick and Ethel Mannin were published by the leading left-wing and progressive publisher, Victor Gollancz, for example, while T. Fisher Unwin, who published the memoirs of the suffrage leader Millicent Garrett Fawcett, also published *The Letters of Olive Schreiner* and those of the founder of the Theosophical Society, H. P. Blavatsky.[8]

The feminist ideas and approaches that began to emerge in the 19th century became very important in this period, as one can see from the large number of autobiographies by women who had been involved in the suffrage

---

[8]Advertisement for T. Fisher Unwin, *The Book Man*, vol. 77, no. 399, Dec 1924, p. 85.

movement. Many of these women were encouraged to write autobiographies by feminist organizations and were first given a voice in feminist periodicals.[9] In the 1860s, at the start of the campaigns for women's suffrage, employment and higher education, new feminist periodicals and presses were established in order to record the actions of those in the women's movement and to correct and expand the historical record by publishing biographical sketches of notable – and often forgotten – women from earlier periods. As the suffrage movement gathered energy in the later 19th and early 20th centuries, the number of feminist periodicals publishing women's comments and stories increased.[10]

By the turn of the 20th century, there was an assumption amongst those concerned with women's rights that the women who had led feminist campaigns should write autobiographies detailing their struggles and their activities. When they did not do so, others stepped in to do it for them. This was the case with Josephine Butler, the charismatic leader of the campaign for the repeal of the Contagious Diseases Acts, for example. Butler had written about that campaign and also published memoirs of her husband and her favourite sister, but had not written an autobiography. After her death, however, the organization that she had led asked one of her nephews to remedy this situation, which he and his wife did. As they indicate in the preface, they 'tried to tell her life story as far as possible in her own words, by means of extracts from her writings, with just sufficient thread of explanation to hold them together'. Hence, they insisted, their book was 'to a large extent an autobiography'.[11] In producing this book, they were following a pattern that, as we have seen, had already been established in the 19th century.

While Butler's autobiography was produced posthumously, that of Emmeline Pankhurst was written for her during her lifetime. As the leader of the militant Women's Social and Political Union and the leading spirit in the militant campaign, Pankhurst was probably the most prominent woman in the suffrage campaign. She was, as her biographer, June Purvis notes, a doer rather than a thinker and showed no inclination to write her life story – and especially not at the height of the suffrage campaign. 'Oh, dear', she is quoted as saying once, 'why do I always feel as if I were in the dentist's chair when I try to write?'[12] In 1913, however, the editor of the American journal *Good Housekeeping* wanted to include articles about her in his journal and sent a young journalist with feminist sympathies, Rheta Childe Dorr, to

---

[9] Maroula Joannou includes twenty of these published suffrage autobiographies in her article on 'Women's Struggle for the Vote and the Autobiographical Subject'.
[10] See Barbara Caine, *English Feminism, c. 1780–1980* (Oxford: Oxford University Press, 1998), and Barbara Green, *Feminist Periodicals and Daily Life: Women and Modernity in British Culture* (London: Palgrave Macmillan, 2017).
[11] Josephine E. Butler, *An Autobiographical Memoir*, edited by George W. and Lucy A. Johnson (Bristol: J. W. Arrowsmith, 1909), p. i.
[12] Simone Murray, '"Deeds and Words":The Woman's Press and the Politics of Print', *Women: A Cultural Review* 11, no. 3 (2000).

write them. Dorr felt it imperative that Pankhurst produce an autobiography – and suggested that Pankhurst tell her life story which she would then write up. Pankhurst who was recovering from a period of imprisonment in which she had gone on a hunger strike, agreed to do this while she was on a trip to the United States, telling Dorr her story on the voyage to and from New York and in her spare time while there. Dorr added information that she got from suffrage newspapers and then published *My Own Story* by Emmeline Pankhurst, the work that has been regarded as Pankhurst's autobiography ever since.[13] Pankhurst certainly approved it and, as Purvis notes, 'through it her voice sounds loud and clear'. This book was serialized both in *Good Housekeeping* and in *The Suffragette* before appearing in book form. It was not the only autobiography of a suffrage leader that was serialized in suffrage publications prior to being published as books. Constance Lytton's *Prisons and Prisoners: Some Personal Experience* was also serialized in *Votes for Women* in 1911 before appearing as a book.[14] And indeed, Lytton's work was probably more influential than that of Pankhurst. Her account of imprisonment and the torture of forcible feeding depicted as a form of martyrdom is powerful and compelling, and several historians like Laura Mayhall argue that Lytton's memoir came 'to stand as the representative experience of militancy, and indeed, participation in the suffrage movement'.[15]

Unlike Pankhurst, Millicent Garrett Fawcett, leader of the largest and longest-lasting women's suffrage organization, the moderate and constitutionalist National Union of Women's Suffrage Societies, was an experienced and accomplished writer who had published quite extensively on political economy as well as on women's suffrage and other issues of concern to women, over many decades. But Fawcett too was reluctant to write her life. After she revised her own account of the suffrage movement, *The Women's Victory and After* in 1919, friends and colleagues urged her to write her own reminiscences. For years, her biographer, Ray Strachey insists, Fawcett refused. 'The book would have to be an "I, I, I"', she said. 'I don't like that kind of book.' But friends were importunate and the editor of *The Woman's Leader*, the official paper of her own organization, persuaded her by saying how important it would be for that paper to be able to include her life story.[16] Fawcett acceded to this request and her autobiography, *What I Remember*, was serialized in the *Woman's Leader* in 1923 and appeared in book form a year later.[17]

---

[13]Emmeline Pankhurst, *My Own Story* (New York: Source Book Press, 1914, repr. 1970). June Purvis, *Emmeline Pankhurst: A Biography* (London: Routledge, 2002), pp. 7–11.
[14]Lady Constance Lytton, *Prisons and Prisoners: Some Personal Experiences* (London: Virago Press, 1914, repr. 1988).
[15]Laura E. Nym Mayhall, 'Creating the "Spirit": British Feminism and the Historical Imagination', *Women's History Review* 4 (1995).
[16]Ray Strachey, *Millicent Garrett Fawcett* (London: John Murray, 1931), p. 343.
[17]Millicent Garrett Fawcett, *What I Remember* (London: T. Fisher Unwin Ltd, 1925).

In the years after the war, suffrage autobiographies continued to appear in considerable numbers. The first of these works, Annie Kenney's *Memoirs*, was written soon after the war and expressed her sense that the history of the suffrage movement could only be written through individual stories. 'Believing it necessary', she wrote in her preface to *Memories of a Militant*, 'that a clear description should be given . . . of a certain but important part of the Militant Movement for Women's Suffrage, . . . I have concluded that the best way will be to write my Life.'[18] Kenney, who joined the Women's Social and Political Union (WSPU) in 1905 continued to work with it until the WSPU came to an end with the outbreak of war. Even after that, she continued to work with Christabel Pankhurst, supporting Pankhurst's unsuccessful campaign to be elected to parliament. Kenney was one of the small numbers of working-class women to be part of the inner group of WSPU leadership and her autobiography is essentially the story of a working-class girl whose life was completely transformed by the militant campaign.

Annie Kenney needed no encouragement to write her life story, but other former suffrage campaigners were encouraged in this endeavour by new organizations like the Suffragette Fellowship. Founded in 1926 by former militants, the aim of the Suffragette Fellowship was 'to perpetuate the memory of the pioneers and outstanding events connected with women's emancipation and especially with the militant suffrage campaign, 1905–14, and thus keep alive the suffrage spirit'.[19] Its members set up a number of forms of commemoration including a calendar of celebrations that noted the birthdays of prominent leaders and activists and other notable days especially taken from the militants. One of their key concerns was to document fully the militant campaign for women's suffrage, something that proved very difficult as there had been no systematic keeping of records. Individual stories that focused on the suffrage struggle provided a good alternative and women were encouraged to write their own stories. Emmeline Pethick-Lawrence, who published her autobiography in 1938, had been a founder member of the Suffragette Fellowship, for example.[20]

The relative ease with which former suffrage campaigners wrote lives was not shared by those who wanted to tell the story of their involvement in the war effort. In part, this is because the suffrage movement was always organized by and for women and automatically embodied their stories. The experience of the First World War, by contrast, was dominated by the horror of the battlefield and generally seen emphatically as a masculine one. Women wrote a number of novels about the First World War, but few autobiographies. It was this challenge of writing about the war as a woman had experienced it that was the driving force behind Vera Brittain's autobiography, *Testament*

---

[18]Kenney, *Memoirs of a Militant*, p. 5.
[19]Mayhall, 'Creating the "Suffragette Spirit"', p. 329.
[20]Emmeline Pethick-Lawrence, *My Part in a Changing World* (London: Victor Gollancz, 1938).

of Youth. The war was the dominant and catastrophic force in Brittain's life, interrupting her longed-for university education and turning her life upside down. As she says in her first line, 'when the Great War broke out, it came to me not as a superlative tragedy, but as an interruption of the most exasperating kind to my personal plans'.[21] Once the war began, one after another the men she loved volunteered and she was left alone at Oxford until she felt she could no longer bear it and became a nurse's aid (VAD or Voluntary Aid Detachment as these women were called during the war), helping to nurse injured soldiers both in London and in field hospitals in Etaples in northern France. She was close to the battle front and knew the horror of war – and during it her fiancé, brother and close friends were all killed, leaving her bereft.

Although committed to the war effort, Brittain was highly critical of the training and treatment of VADs including her own. She had begun trying to tell her story even before the war ended in the form of a novel called *The Pawn of Fate*, depicting the trials and abusive experiences of a young VAD, but was advised against publishing a book that was so critical of the medical and military system – and might lay her open to a charge of libel. She was establishing herself as a journalist and a novelist in these years and wrote a number of other works, attempting unsuccessfully to publish her war diaries. There was little appetite for war diaries and memoirs in the immediate years after the war and Brittain went back to thinking about telling her story as a novel. Towards the end of the 1920s, however, there was a sudden surge of interest in war memoirs and those of many men were published to great acclaim, including works by Edmund Blunden, Siegfried Sassoon and Robert Graves. Brittain deplored the way these works contrasted the desperate masculine struggle at the front with the loving, passive and often selfish mothers, wives, or sweethearts at home who had little understanding of the nature of war. She was irritated at the ways in which 'the woman is still silent'. In her diary in 1929, she wondered 'who, by presenting the war in its true perspective in her own life, will illuminate its meaning afresh for her generation'. As her biographers, Paul Berry and Mark Bostridge, make clear, by that time she had decided that she would be that woman.[22]

Brittain faced several challenges at this point, including an assumption amongst many men, including some she knew, that as a woman she could have nothing to say about the war. She also faced a writerly one: how to write a book that was 'as truthful as history, but as readable as a novel'. Brittain's post-war life, as the wife of an academic and the mother of young children, added additional challenges, as indeed did the resentment of her husband, George Caitlin, about the way in which he appeared in the book.

---

[21]Brittain, *Testament of Youth*, pp. 2–3.
[22]Paul Bostridge and Mark Berry, *Vera Brittain a Life* (London: Chatto & Windus, 1995), p. 241.

Once she was underway, however, Brittain faced considerable pressure to complete the book relatively quickly. In contrast to the early 1920s when there was little interest in her story, there was now interest from two British publishers. Brittain was pleased that Victor Gollancz took the book, giving it considerable advance publicity so that within a week of its publication on 28 August 1933, the entire first impression of 5,000 copies had sold. The book went through twelve impressions and sold some 120,000 copies before the start of the Second World War. Given the initial difficulties that Brittain faced in telling her war story, it is somewhat ironic that her memoir is now by the far the best-known memoir of the First World War. It has been continuously in print since its publication – as well as being the subject both of films and television series.[23]

The war was a catalyst even for autobiographies that do not deal with it directly. It inspired Beatrice Webb's *My Apprenticeship*, for example, although she makes no explicit mention of it. In her careful study of *My Apprenticeship*, Deborah Nord emphasizes the importance of the First World War to the book. In the course of the war, Webb suffered a kind of breakdown as so many of her once cherished ideals and her belief in the efficacy of the political and intellectual work that she and her husband, Sidney, had devoted their lives to was questioned and undermined.[24] The social progress in which she had believed and to which she had committed so much of her life no longer seemed credible and the war made her feel old and as if she were living out of her own time. Accordingly, she felt it imperative that she go back and re-evaluate her earlier life. In her diary for 3 January 1917, she noted, 'I have bought a small typewriter and am using up some of my spare hours in the afternoon in copying out and editing my mss diaries so as to make a book of my life.' The copying out was intermittent as she was called on to serve on several government committees. But she resented them, noting almost two years later that she was tired of investigating new subjects. 'I want to brood over the past and reflect on men and their affairs. . . . I want to summarise my life and see what it amounts to.'[25] As Nord and others point out, *My Apprenticeship* was the only book that Beatrice Webb wrote without Sidney, and it was not a project in which he took much interest. This is not surprising: Sidney Webb had little time for the kind of introspection in which Beatrice was engaged and this book explores at some length the spiritual, intellectual, and emotional journeys and crises that dominated her life in her thirty-five years before their marriage.

Webb herself was unclear as to whether it was an autobiography at all. 'I have neither the desire nor the intention to write an autobiography',

---

[23]Bostridge and Berry, *Vera Brittain*, p. 246.
[24]Deborah Epstein Nord, *The Apprenticeship of Beatrice Webb* (Basingstoke: Macmillan, 1985).
[25]Nord, *Apprenticeship of Beatrice Webb*, p. 231.

she wrote on her first page insisting rather that she wanted to write about her craft as a social investigator – and that this required her to quote from her diaries and to say something about herself. She must do this, she insisted, because as a social scientist, her

> main instrument is social intercourse; thus, I can hardly leave out of the picture the experience I have gathered, not deliberately as a scientific worker, but casually as child, unmarried woman, wife and citizen. For the sociologist, unlike the physicist, chemist, and biologist, is in a quite unique manner the creature of his environment.[26]

But elsewhere, and especially when musing over the process of writing *My Apprenticeship* in her diaries, she frequently referred to it as an autobiography, albeit one 'with the love affairs left out'. Webb herself saw the attempt to interrogate her own life as a social scientist – and indeed as she would interrogate someone else – as making it a very new kind of autobiography.[27] The novelty of *My Apprenticeship*, in her view, lay in the experimental approach that she took to her life, seeking to write about it as an outsider, a social scientist interrogating her own experiences and ideas. And indeed, Webb was writing a new kind of autobiography. Although it is not yet widely recognized, in her approach Webb anticipates the use of autobiography within academic disciplines like history and sociology as a way to offer new social insights by interrogating a particular set of life experiences.

At the same time, as several of those who have written about *My Apprenticeship* agree, it fits more neatly within the Victorian autobiographical tradition than its interwar counterpart. This is most evident in the way that it deals with her loss of religious belief. Deborah Nord stresses the need to see *My Apprenticeship* within the context of the patterns of de-conversion, dealing with the loss of orthodox religious belief followed by a period of crisis, a search for a new faith and finally a re-birth in a new faith and vocation that is so important in Victorian autobiography.[28] The work that is often seen as closest to Webb's is John Stuart Mill's *Autobiography* and especially his moving account of his own mental and spiritual crisis and of the importance to him of attending to the 'internal culture of the individual' rather than relying on the Benthamite utilitarianism endorsed by his father. But Webb had also to deal with the distinctive problems faced by women who had not only to try to resolve intellectual and spiritual crises but also to reconcile their sense of their own intellectual and spiritual identity and work with the demands made on them

---

[26]Webb, *My Apprenticeship*, p. 1.
[27]Beatrice Webb, Diaries, 21 July 1925. *The Diaries of Beatrice Webb*, eds Norman and Jeanne McKenzie (London: Virago, 2000).
[28]Nord, *Apprenticeship of Beatrice Webb*, pp. 58–63.

as women by their families and the wider society. Nord notes Beatrice Webb's reading of other women's diaries and memoirs, and particularly her interest in Harriet Martineau's autobiography.[29] In her diaries, Webb commented on how Martineau's long illness in the 1830s gave her 'immense opportunities for quiet and serious thought' and relieved her of the burden of constantly attending to her mother.[30] This was of particular significance to Webb who spent several years caring for her father in the last years of his life as he became increasingly incapacitated and dependent. Webb's entire sense of herself, as Samuel Hynes, Ira Nadel and Debra Nord all agree, especially her sense of the importance of duty and service, was completely Victorian.[31] As a young woman, she thought of becoming a novelist, something that her diaries suggest she might have done well. But writing novels seemed to her a form of self-indulgence that had to be relinquished and replaced with something more serious and scientific that accorded better with her sense of duty. The conflicts she describes between Self and Service, or Art and Science were, as Webb herself realized, deeply embodied in Victorian life and thought.[32]

Although the number remains limited, there is a marked increase also in the number of autobiographies by working-class women in the interwar period. Prior to this period, the number was very small indeed: David Vincent suggests that no more than 3 per cent of 19th-century working-class autobiographies were written by women.[33] This figure has been disputed, but the dispute really focuses on questions of form and on whether very brief sketches of a life and unpublished work should be included under the heading 'autobiography' or whether it should apply only to more substantial works.[34] Although the overall percentage remained small, in the interwar period a number of full-length autobiographies by working-class women were published, appearing under the imprint of notable publishing houses. Kathleen Woodward's *Jipping Street* is the best known now, as it was at the time.[35]

---

[29]Nord, *Apprenticeship of Beatrice Webb*.
[30]Nord, *Apprenticeship of Beatrice Webb*, p. 71.
[31]Samuel Hynes, *Edwardian Occasions: Essays on English Writing in the Early Twentieth Century* (London: Routledge & Kegan Paul, 1972), Ira Bruce Nadel, 'Beatrice Webb's Two Voices: My Apprenticeship and Victorian Autobiography', *ESC: English Studies in Canada*, vol. 2, no. 1 (1976): 83–98; Nord, 'Victorian Autobiography: Sons and Fathers', in *The Cambridge Companion to Autobiography*, edited by Maria and Emily O. Wittman DiBattista (Cambridge, 2014).
[32]Hynes, *Edwardian Occasions*, p. 154.
[33]David Vincent, *Bread, Knowledge, Freedom a Study of Nineteenth-Century Working Class Autobiography* (London: Europa Publications Limited, 1981).
[34]Jane Rendall, '"A Short Account of My Unprofitable Life": Autobiographies of Working-Class Women in Britain c. 1775–1845', in *Women's Lives/Women's Time: New Essays on Auto/Biography*, edited by Trev Lynn and Linda Anderson Broughton (Albany: State University of New York Press, 1997), pp. 31–50.
[35]Kathleen Woodward, *Jipping Street* (London: Virago, 1928, repr. 1983).

Woodward was already well known as a journalist and as the author of a popular biography of *Queen Mary* when it was published. Much was made in contemporary reviews of the way that, unlike most accounts of slum life that were written by philanthropic or other outsiders, *Jipping Street* was an insider report that disposed of comfortable illusions. 'Miss Woodward writes as a child of the slum, who was unhappily aware that cold and hunger and overcrowding, fatigue, monotony are not miraculously deadened by familiarity', wrote one reviewer. It is a 'human document ... that everyone should read'.[36] For some, as Carolyn Steedman points out, there was also the romance involved in thinking of Woodward 'as the daughter of a washerwoman who grew up to be a biographer of a queen' and had made the fairy tale journey across the river to the other side.[37] *Jipping Street* is not a simple life story. It quite consciously uses an individual story as a way to illustrate the experience of slum life from within. Woodward altered the details of her family life in order to provide a picture of more extreme poverty and to locate it in a real slum. She was born in Peckham, a lower-middle-class neighbourhood. But her story is located in Bermondsey, a poorer neighbourhood, closer to the river and a slum that had been previously almost unexplored in literary texts. Like Woodward, Annie Kenney also described her working-class childhood and with the support of the Women' Institutes, Louise Jermy depicted the poverty, brutality and manipulation that she had endured in a working-class home and at the hands of a cruel stepmother.[38]

The other group of women who moved into the writing of autobiography were popular novelists. While few 19th-century writers of fiction turned to autobiography, tending rather to use aspects of their own stories in fiction, a large number of 20th-century novelists chose both to do this and to write more directly about their own lives in autobiographical form. Vera Brittain had written novels and tried her story in fictional form before turning to autobiography, and several other novelists did so too. Ethel Mannin was one of the first to do so, publishing several successful novels before *Confessions and Impressions*. Mannin was by then very well known, both as a novelist and as a woman of radical political, sexual and educational views. Andy Croft insists that she was already a celebrity whose views were sought on a wide range of political and personal matters.[39] *Confessions and Impressions* was the most popular autobiography of the interwar period. First published in 1930, it went into its fiftieth impression in 1936 when it came out in a Penguin edition.

---

[36] Anon., 'Jipping Street', *The Sketch*, 28 Nov 1928: 144.
[37] Carolyn Steedman, 'Introduction' to Woodward, *Jipping Street*, p. xi.
[38] Louise Jermy, *The Memories of a Working Woman* (Norwich: Goose & Son, 1934).
[39] Andy Croft, 'Ethel Mannin: The Red Rose of Love and the Red Flower of Liberty', in *Rediscovering Forgotten Radicals: British Women Writers. 1889–1939*, edited by Angela Ingram and Daphne Patai (London and Chapel Hill: University of North Carolina Press, 1993), p. 210.

Mannin had begun life working in an advertising agency and as a copywriter. She had married young, writing novels as a way to earn the rent and ending her marriage after five years as she preferred freedom and independence to married life. She continued to write to support herself and her daughter. Mannin was well known for her radical views. She was a defender of avant-garde art and artists, an advocate of a more open approach to life and sexuality, and a strong believer in the need for a more progressive and liberal way of treating and bringing up children. A major feature of her autobiography is her advocacy of a freer approach to sexuality. Not one in ten women, she insisted, 'has ever had full sexual satisfaction', including married women with children and those who had had several lovers. 'The ignorance of civilized people concerning physiology and its significance in this business of living fully is as astounding as it is pitiful.'[40] In a way that was unusual at the time, especially for women, Mannin offered something of her own sexual history in her autobiography.

Other contemporary novelists, Ursula Bloom[41] and Marjorie Bowen,[42] felt a rather stronger need to tell their own sad stories, ones that included childhood exploitation of various kinds and a need to provide financially for mothers and siblings at an early age. Both deal in some detail with very unhappy marriages, Bloom to an alcoholic and Bowen to an Italian suffering from both mental illness and tuberculosis. But while offering some detail about the unhappy nature of their married lives, neither of these women deal with it in the explicitly sexual terms suggested by Mannin. They are rather tales of survival in very difficult circumstances.

Shaping a Life

Childhood continued to be important in women's autobiographies – and often to be seen as miserable. For some, however, there was a stronger emphasis now on the differences between what was possible or made available to the authors in their girlhood, in contrast to their brothers. Early childhood played a smaller part in most of these autobiographies than do the years from around ten through adolescence. It is here that one begins to see the most significant change from nineteenth-century autobiographies in relation to discussions of education, on the one hand, and sexuality on the other. Several autobiographies treated school days at some length, some because of the pleasure that they experienced in the atmosphere and the learning, others

---

[40]Mannin, *Confessions and Impressions*, pp. 41–45.
[41]Ursula Bloom, *Without Make-Up* (London: Michael Joseph, 1938).
[42]Margaret (pseud Marjorie Bowen) Campbell, *The Debate Continues, Being the Autobiography of Marjorie Bowen* (Heinemann, 1939). Marjorie Bowen's work is complicated by the fact that Bowen was only one of the pseudonyms she used – and in the autobiography she writes both as Bowen and as Campbell.

rather because of the inadequacy of their education – and their sense that it was not preparing them for university or for careers. The sexual curiosity of adolescent girls was an issue here too, with some women echoing Annie Besant's cry for more enlightenment and understanding, while others pointed rather to the information forced on them by older girls at a time when they were not ready or able to understand it.

Childhood

The childhoods depicted in some interwar women's autobiographies resemble very closely those of their Victorian predecessors. Lonely and sometimes miserable childhoods of a kind familiar to readers of Harriet Martineau continue to feature prominently in middle- and upper-middle-class women's autobiography. This continuity is marked not only in Beatrice Webb's *My Apprenticeship*, but also in the autobiographies of Emmeline Pethick-Lawrence, Helena Swanwick and Evelyn Sharp, all of whom were only a few years younger than Beatrice Webb and came from similar upper-middle-class families. The absence of parental attention suffered by the daughters of large families in which the births and deaths of other infants meant that they were of little account is underlined here. Beatrice Webb described herself as 'creeping up in the shadow of my baby brother's birth and death'.

> I spent my childhood in a quite special way among domestic servants, to whom as a class I have an undying gratitude. I was neither ill-treated nor oppressed: I was merely ignored. For good or for evil I was left free to live my own little life within the large and loose framework of family circumstance.[43]

Her poor health interrupted the few attempts that were made to provide her with a formal education. She was aware that her education received less attention than was accorded to her sisters and quoted a passage from her mother's dairy in which she wrote that Beatrice 'is the only one of my children who is below the average in intelligence', which Webb realized may have explained her indifference. So, Beatrice Webb educated herself, reading what was in the family library and keeping from a very early age, diaries in which she paid particular attention to her own failings, especially her inclination for 'building castles in the air' at the age of ten and for her vanity at the age of fourteen.

Emmeline Pethick-Lawrence too commented on the misery of her childhood. Her parents were loving, but their mother was too absorbed in pregnancy and the births and deaths of younger children to attend to the

---

[43]Webb, *My Apprenticeship*, p. 78.

older ones. Two younger sisters were born before she was three and then two brothers died and a final sister was born when she was eight. As a result, she was banished to a lonely nursery, where she spent 'the only unhappy part of my life'. Like Webb, she was grateful to 'the two faithful servants who were our friends and protectors and ran the kitchen and the parlour' and Charlotte, the cook, who stayed with the family for forty years and returned after she had retired to nurse Emmeline through a serious illness. But this benevolence did not extend to the nursery. That,

> was ruled by a changing succession of ignorant and inefficient nursemaids who cared neither for their jobs nor for their charges.... Nurseries in those days were prisons, as I realized when I found myself for the first time in Holloway jail and reverted at once to the old sense of hopelessness and misery. We were in the hands of those who possessed delegated authority over us, and from that authority there was no appeal. In one sense it was worse than prison, for there was no public opinion to check abuses. Nursemaids could be tyrants exercising favoritism and venting personal prejudices, unlike the warders in prison who were themselves under discipline.[44]

Some late Victorian women continued to voice the explicitly feminist criticism of their childhood and their treatment as compared with their brothers evident in Victorian women's novels and suggested in some autobiographies. Helena Swanwick who depicted the most intense unhappiness as a child saw this not in terms of the absence of her parents, but of how they treated her when they were present. One reason she gave for writing her autobiography was the 'wish to express the intense desire which possessed me all my youth, for more opportunities for concentration and continuity'.[45] As a girl, she was constantly being distracted by her mother who demanded all her attention and companionship, seeking always to limit what she could do and to distract her from anything she was interested in. 'Until a girl is given the same respect for her personality as a boy', wrote Swanwick, 'we shall not know the best of which women are capable.' Her father, although usually absent, also had a negative impact on her life.

> He rarely spoke to me except to give an order or make some sarcastic comment on my appearance, clumsiness, ineptitude – although I was not inordinately ugly or clumsy. He seemed to be possessed by the notion that it was salutary for me to be systematically belittled, lest I should become conceited, vain or insubordinate. I was always tremblingly nervous and therefore clumsy in his presence and avoided it as much as I could.[46]

---

[44]Pethick-Lawrence, *My Part in a Changing World*, pp. 24–25.
[45]H. M. Swanwick, *I Have Been Young* (London: Victor Gollancz Ltd, 1935).
[46]Swanwick, *I Have Been Young*, pp. 15–16.

While both Webb and Pethick-Lawrence came to love and feel close to their parents in later years, Swanwick never did. It was only when she married that she was able to stop battling her mother and was allowed to follow her own path.

As more autobiographies came to be written by women who did not belong to the privileged middle and upper-middle classes, aspects of childhood and family life that had not previously been discussed entered this genre. Poverty and the different ways in which it was experienced and dealt with in working-class families, on the one hand, and socially marginal middle-class ones, on the other, is one of these aspects. Material deprivation and physical discomfort were an integral part of the childhoods described in Kathleen Woodward's *Jipping Street* and a few years later also in Louise Jermy's *Reminiscences*.

Woodward described how her father, who came from a higher social class than her mother and was quite genteel, became an invalid shortly after her parents married. Woodward's mother cared for him while also working as a cleaner and doing laundry to support her children. From an early age they were expected to help and Woodward recalled having to get up early in the cold to get a place in the wood line in order to get the daily ration of firewood. She worked alongside her mother later in the day, collecting the clothes to be washed, turning the wringer as the washing was done and walking with her to return the finished washing and to collect more.[47] Her mother was burdened beyond her capacity to cope and was hopeless and sometimes violent. Nonetheless, Woodward's greatest terror was the fear of having to go beyond her mother's strong presence to get other work, something that happened when she was twelve and had to walk from Bermondsey to Jewin Street where she was employed in a factory making men's collars, preparing the machinery and running a variety of errands – a life she hated and from which she was eventually able to escape.[48]

Louise Jermy too was subject to physical violence from her irritable stepmother, often as a punishment for something that she had not done. 'I've been beaten with stair-rod, poker, broom handle, knocked down and kicked up again', she wrote, 'often for things I could not help, such as not being able to find things.' When a set of teaspoons that her stepmother had been given by a former employer disappeared, one by one, she was savagely beaten each time one could not be found. Some years later, her stepmother told her they had been taken by an acquaintance who removed one each time she came to tea. Jermy was required to help in the laundry work her stepmother did to support the family when her father's business ventures continued to fail. From the age of eleven, she was required to turn the mangle for hours and then to deliver baskets of washing. She was a frail child and felt that this

---

[47]Woodward, *Jipping Street*, pp. 12–13.
[48]Woodward, *Jipping Street*, p. 58.

excessive labour contributed to – or even caused – the tubercular hip disease which required hospitalization and left her unable to walk properly for the rest of her life.[49]

Poverty and the difficulty in making ends meet were central to the childhoods of Ursula Bloom and Marjorie Bowen too. In Bloom's case, her father's clerical stipend just about covered the family's needs, but when her parents separated, money became very short indeed. In the case of Marjorie Bowen too, her parent's separation, possibly as a result of her father's alcoholism, meant that the family had a very limited income. Her childhood years involved constantly moving house, either to find cheaper lodgings or to move in with wealthier friends. In either case, Marjorie and her younger (and prettier) sister were left in the charge of an aged and incompetent nanny. Even when they lived in affluent households where their mother dined lavishly, little notice was taken of the children and Bowen suggests that she was hungry throughout most of her childhood. Like their working-class counterparts, both Bloom and Bowen began working while adolescents to support their mothers and siblings.

These autobiographies are also amongst the first to tackle the question of marital separation and family breakdown and to look both at the economic and personal consequences of these events. These discussions include not only the question of poverty and social stigma but also the emotional and psychological strain that family breakdown often imposed on an older daughter who, in the cases of both Bloom and Bowen, felt responsible for managing the aftermath. This discussion of the impact of particular events and developments on the life and emotions of a child was accompanied in the interwar period, by the depiction of rather more complex relationships with parents than had been evident earlier. The depiction of these relationships took a number of different forms. Some women used a language derived from psychoanalysis in describing these relationships, especially those with their mothers. Ethel Mannin's *Confessions and Impressions* offers one example. 'Throughout my childhood', she wrote,

> I had what the psychoanalysts today called a 'fixation' on my mother. She could not enter into the secret world of my imaginings, and I hid it away from her, yet I literally could not bear her out of my sight.[50]

Ursula Bloom too referred to her 'mother-fixation' and the closeness to her mother that developed as she became more and more aware of her father's infidelity and distanced herself from him. This fixation took over her life – and her sense of responsibility for her mother she later realized, denied her a childhood. It,

---

[49] Jermy, *Memories of a Working Woman*, p. 45.
[50] Mannin, *Confessions and Impressions*, p. 12.

was to develop into a passionate love which has lasted through the years. In my anxiety for the future that menaced her ... I dug myself into a rut; in that rut I most successfully buried my childhood. At thirteen I was a woman.[51]

There are other works which, while not using this language are nonetheless concerned to provide a psychological analysis of the mother-child relationship. One of these is Kathleen Woodward's *Jipping Street* which, Carolyn Steedman suggests, 'should be read as case-history rather than history'. Woodward's narrative is a psychological one in which the primary relationship depicted is that between Woodward and her mother. Woodward's story goes directly counter to any notion of mother-daughter relationships as nurturing ones, Steedman argues, as Woodward makes very clear her knowledge from early childhood that she had been a burden to her mother, that she need never have been born. 'Fearless and without hope mother was', she notes, 'flinty, enduring, strong, proud.'

> Six children she reluctantly bore, and she was in the habit of saying in a curiously passionless tone that if she had known as much when her first child was born as she learned by her sixth, a second child would never have been.[52]

Her mother's lot might have been less hard without her unbending nature and pride, Woodward suggests, and along with it, especially when she was tired, went great anger. 'In her anger', she notes, 'which was frequent and violent ... she aimed her blows without feeling or restraint.' She split Woodward's head open on one occasion and threw a fork at her on another. She made it clear that, while she did her best to meet the physical needs of her children, she had no love to give them. 'At home it was always wintry', Woodward notes – and she took refuge when she could in the homes of other women who offered her something of the kindness and warmth that her mother denied. The portrait of the mother-daughter relationships offered here, Steedman argues,

> is about the ambivalence and restriction of the relationship between mother and daughter, about a mother and daughter no longer split into good and bad as in the fairy tales and psychoanalytic theory, but powerfully integrated, terribly confining.[53]

---

[51] Bloom, *Without Make-up*, p. 46.
[52] Woodward, *Jipping Street*, p. 7.
[53] Steedman, 'Introduction', *Jipping Street*, pp. xiv–xv.

Education

The struggle for an education continued to occupy a significant place in women's autobiographies, and here too there is marked continuity in the largely haphazard arrangements that were made for educating girls. Schooling was not made compulsory in Britain until 1918 and several of the women who wrote autobiographies in the interwar period had little or no experience of it. Beatrice Webb's only experience of school was a few months 'as a "parlour boarder" in a fashionable girls' school' in Bournemouth where she was sent at the age of fourteen and when her ill health and her moral scruples made her want to avoid the London Season. While there, she seems to have focused her attention on questions of morality and religion. She undertook some private study on Jewish History and English Law, choosing two subjects that were so different from each other that each 'employs a different set of muscles'. She does not suggest that there was any assistance in her study. The passages she quotes from her diary deal rather with her concern about her own pride and vanity, on the one hand, and the difficulty she felt in accepting the doctrine of atonement, on the other, including a description of the terrible meeting she had with the resident clergyman when she tried to explain her views on the atonement to him.[54]

Some autobiographies still bemoaned the inadequacy of the education provided in Continental finishing schools or in English private schools designed for 'the daughters of gentlemen', for intelligent young women, seeking some kind of career or public life. But one also begins to see new experiences as those who attended girls' day schools concerned to provide an academic education described their time there. After her four miserable years in France, for example, Helena Swanwick went to Notting Hill High School and loved it from the first moment. It stood in complete contrast to her unhappy home life.

> Perhaps most people would think it exaggerated if I said that, while I was in school, I lived in an almost constant state of bliss. But it would be true. I was ravenous for discipline, teaching, books, friends and leaders. The simple commonplaces of an orderly education were a delight to me, and I was gluttonous for friends after my own heart.[55]

Swanwick's days were not entirely easy: she had to get up early every day to practise the piano and was required to mend and darn her own clothes in addition to extensive homework. She loved the sociability of school – and felt that some of her teachers were exceptional women who managed what she came later to see as her arrogance and often difficult behaviour well and

---

[54] Webb, *My Apprenticeship*, pp. 78–81.
[55] Swanwick, *I Have Been Young*, p. 73.

taught her to think about the importance of social order and personal conduct.[56] Evelyn Sharp too enjoyed her brief period at a boarding school. The four terms she spent at Strathallan House School were very liberating for her and a change from her austere and regimented life at home. She regarded her time at this school as 'the only supremely satisfactory experience of childhood'. It was a place where she could read and study, unimpeded by the needs and demands of younger siblings.[57] Even some women who were very happy in their home life enjoyed being at academically directed schools. Lady Rhondda was one of these, devoting three and a half chapters of her autobiography to the wonderful years she spent as a boarder at St Leonard's School for Girls in St Andrews in Scotland.[58] This was a new school, established in 1877 with the avowed aim of giving girls as good an education as their brothers – or indeed a better one. It encouraged competitive sports, introduced debating and allowed the girls a great deal of freedom. Lady Rhondda greatly valued her time there and acknowledged her indebtedness, especially to her housemistress. Indeed, her autobiography grew out of her attempt to record her gratitude to her.

Here too, the autobiographies of women who came from working-class or more generally from poorer families offer a very different picture of the educational possibilities available to girls. Neither Ursula Bloom nor Marjorie Bowen had any formal education at all. In both cases, this was deemed a necessary economy. Bloom's brother was sent to a boarding school, but she had to make do with the books in the house. She claims that she had read Shakespeare and all of Dickens by her teens, but she knew little else. Nor, although she began writing stories at an early age, had she any knowledge of grammar or spelling. She had to work hard to make up for these deficits.[59] Bowen too had no education apart from a few chaotic lessons from her mother – who gave up in despair. She was more disciplined in her efforts at self-education than was Bloom, making considerable use of libraries when there was one close to where she lived and teaching herself to read both French and Italian.[60] But both were bitterly aware of the obstacle they faced through the lack of formal schooling.

One gets a very different picture of school, and one that focuses rather more strongly on questions of sexuality and bodily constraints, in the autobiography of Ethel Mannin. Mannin's father was a postal worker with a limited but regular income, so the family had a settled home, and as conscientious parents, the Mannins sought to ensure the education of their

---

[56]Angela John, *Turning the Tide* (London: Parthian Books, 2013), p. 39.
[57]Evelyn Sharp, *Unfinished Adventure: Selected Reminiscences from an Englishwoman's Life* (London: John Lane, 1933). Angela John, *Evelyn Sharp* (Manchester: University of Manchester Press, 2009), pp. 9–10.
[58]Viscountess Rhondda, *This Was My World* (London: Macmillan and Co., Ltd, 1933).
[59]Bloom, *Without Make-Up*, p. 265.
[60]Campbell, *The Debate Continues*, p. 78.

daughter. But Mannin's description of her schooling is damning. Initially, when she was six, her parents decided to send her to a small private school. It was supposed to be preparatory, 'but for what it could possibly prepare anyone, it would be impossible to say'. History lessons involved learning by heart passages from various books, and other learning was by rote. Mannin suggests that it was appalling in every conceivable way.

> I would feel dazed by all that I was told and required to commit to memory. Various small boys would create a diversion in the midst of this welter of tediousness by exposing their little genital organs under the desks for the amusement of the little girls.[61]

It was in her view appalling in other ways too in its often-sadistic treatment of children. 'A child would be refused permission to "leave the room" until the little over-strained bladder began to relieve itself and the poor child suffer agonies of shame by being sent home for the offence.' After a year, her parents decided that they were not getting results for their money and sent her to the local board school. Mannin's depiction of this school too is, in part, an indictment of the board school system, with its mechanical curriculum constantly moving children from one subject to another, its use of corporal punishment if a child's mind wandered and its lack of any attention to the development of the child's imaginative or thinking capacities. Mannin notes with particular distaste the ways in which poverty was stigmatized by the condescending way that poor children were given a midday meal. The school had a separate section for children with special needs – who were often taunted by the other pupils. 'Fortunately for myself', she noted, 'I lived too much shut up in my fantasy world for much harm to be done me from outside and at fourteen I left school and began getting educated in the real sense.'[62]

At the same time, she recognized that the school 'made three important contributions to my education' – although none was linked to the actual syllabus. 'My socialism was fostered in secret by a communist teacher; I discovered poetry by accident, and I fell in love.' Mannin engaged in 'flagrant subversion', writing an essay in which she quoted Johnson's dictum 'patriotism is the last refuge of the scoundrel', a statement that did not go down well in 1914! As punishment, she was required to kneel in the hall all day – to be seen by every class as it moved through the school. She read and loved a great deal of poetry – and wrote some herself. Not knowing what to do, and with little desire for education and a great desire to avoid the civil service, Mannin sought and won a scholarship to a commercial school. At the age of fifteen, she was sent as a stenographer to the advertising agency,

---

[61] Mannin, *Confessions and Impressions*, p. 31.
[62] Mannin, *Confessions and Impressions*, p. 36.

Charles F. Higham Ltd – and stayed for quite some time as, while many of his regular employees were engaged in the war effort, Higham encouraged her to try copywriting.[63]

For some of these women, going to university was also a possibility. The first women's colleges at Oxford and Cambridge opened their doors in 1869. They seem never to have been thought of by Beatrice Webb, but they were on the agenda of younger women – although often in the face of parental opposition. Both Helena Swanwick and Vera Brittain describe at length their desire to go to university and the pain of paternal refusal – especially as it was assumed their brothers would go. Even though she won a scholarship, Helena Swanwick was only able to go to college when her godmother offered to pay all the living expenses not included in the scholarship. She loved her time at college, noting especially the freedom to do as she pleased – and the capacity to put a notice 'Engaged' on her door if she wished to remain undisturbed. The college environment and her pleasure in it shocked her mother.[64] Vera Brittain too fought bitterly to be allowed to go to university as her brother was expected to do – and eventually when a lawyer friend of her father spoke in support of women's university education was allowed to go.[65] Her university time was quite unlike what she had anticipated: she enrolled in 1914, shortly after the outbreak of the war – and at a time when her beloved brother and Roland Leighton were both enlisting in the army. Brittain lasted only a few months before she too felt it necessary to leave in order to contribute to the war effort.

Religion

One aspect of the depiction of childhood in almost all interwar women's autobiographies that differs markedly from their Victorian predecessors is the place and importance of religion. Although they do not entirely disappear, the religious crises of the 19th century diminish very considerably. Most interwar women's autobiographies, especially those by younger women discuss religious belief, observance and the relinquishing of it quite briefly. Almost all autobiographies contain a description of the familial observances in which they were expected to participate, often pointing out how perfunctory they were. Vera Brittain described the family prayers she was expected to attend every morning before breakfast – and her father's explosion as her brother Edward was always late. It was his discourtesy that her father minded, however, rather than his lack of religious devotion! Ethel Mannin too describes the nightly ritual of prayers before bedtime but notes that her mother couldn't conceal her impatience when she took her time

---

[63]Mannin, *Confessions and Impressions*, p. 65.
[64]Swanwick, *I Have Been Young*, p. 117.
[65]Brittain, *Testament of Youth*.

over her nightly prayer. Mannin was sure that she and her brother 'had religion inculcated into us because it was "the proper thing" for properly brought up children'.[66] Helena Swanwick wrote of her regular Sunday church attendance with her mother – but noted that her atheist father never came. There was little feeling amongst these women that these family observances reflected any deep religious belief, and Swanwick, like Mannin and Brittain, became an agnostic in the course of her adolescence.

This comparatively casual approach to religion is evident in the autobiographies of working-class women too. Annie Kenney, for example, grew up attending Sunday School and church regularly and having frequent conversations with God. She was confirmed, but even as she prepared for confirmation, the discussions about science that were occurring in her own home made her question whether one could believe anything without proof. Shortly after her confirmation, she read some 'sayings of Voltaire' and began to question many aspects of her life and faith, turning first to a belief in the importance of reform of Labour under the influence of Robert Blatchford – and then to women's suffrage under the influence of Christabel Pankhurst.[67]

Sometimes religion and questions of religious observation became enmeshed in a wider familial situation. For Helena Swanwick, for example, it seems to encapsulate other forms of distress rather than to be a matter of importance in itself. As a very unhappy adolescent who felt completely unloved by her parents, Swanwick found a way to assert herself by refusing to be confirmed, although this meant missing out on the usual gift of a watch and incurring the immense displeasure of her mother who refused to talk to her. For the only time in her life that she could remember her father, not a believer, intervened to support her and said she needn't be confirmed if she didn't want to – but she had to accompany her mother to church. Her mother refused to go to church with her – which gave Swanwick the supreme pleasure of Sundays as days when she could do as she chose.[68] For Louise Jermy, by contrast, attending Sunday school and church, something her family did not do, became very important indeed. She met a Sunday school teacher she liked and who encouraged her to read and offered her warmth and sympathy. Attending Sunday school and church every week offered her not only the comfort of faith but also the one place where she could escape from her family and their surveillance and brutality and meet up with people who really seemed to care about her well-being.[69]

The one notable woman's autobiography in which religion remains central is that of Beatrice Webb. The importance of religious belief and the difficulties that accompanied and followed its loss are amongst the key

---

[66]Mannin, *Confessions and Impressions*, p. 13.
[67]Kenney, *Memoirs of a Militant*, pp. 22–25.
[68]Swanwick, *I Have Been Young*, p. 91.
[69]Jermy, *Memories of a Working Woman*, pp. 55–57.

concerns of *My Apprenticeship*. Webb details the extensive reading and the pain associated with the process by which she came to cease believing in Christianity. This is followed by a discussion of the complicated steps that took her through a religion of science and towards her belief in socialism and social reform. Even as a non-believer, Webb retained a sense of the efficacy of prayer. This emphasis on religion is one of the many reasons why *My Apprenticeship* is often seen as the last of the great Victorian autobiographies.[70]

Sexuality

The decline in concern about religion in interwar women's autobiography was effectively replaced by a much greater emphasis on questions about sex and sexuality. This was a complex question, addressed in a number of different ways. Many women expressed resentment about the taboos that surrounded sex and made it into a mystery which meant that they had immense difficulty in gaining any accurate sexual knowledge. For some, this taboo extended into early adult life where their own sexual ignorance made their first romantic relationships or their marriages much more difficult than they might otherwise have been. Others talked about the way that a fascination with sexuality manifested itself at their schools, where in their early adolescence, some were rather brutally told something of the 'facts of life' but could get neither confirmation nor clarification at home.

Not everyone acquired sexual knowledge or was exposed to sexual curiosity at school. Helena Swanwick, for example, insists that she,

> did not have any of the experiences in regard to sex which modern psychologists record as common among adolescents. None of the girls I associated with at Notting Hill even so much as mentioned sex, and we dismissed as disgusting any evidences of schoolgirl flirtations and premature passions.[71]

It was impossible to raise this question with her mother and so she 'absorbed what I could from such scientific books and medical journals as I could lay my hands on and I puzzled much over the Bible, Shakespeare, Chaucer and La Fontaine, none of these being kept from me'.

A rather different picture of how sex was approached in school is offered by Vera Brittain. She hated the small private school she was sent to at the age of 11, of which she had only two memories. One was of the extreme disapproval she faced when one day, on the way to school she stopped to talk to Edward and introduced herself to his friends – only to be 'severely

---

[70]Nadel, 'Beatrice Webb's Two Voices', pp. 83–96.
[71]Swanwick, *I Have Been Young*, p. 83.

reprimanded for her naughtiness' in doing so. The event 'aroused in me a rebellious resentment that I have never forgotten'. The other was of her being bullied by two older girls, 'who soon tired of the easy physical advantage given them by their superior age and stature and instead endeavoured to torment my immature mind by forcing upon it items of sexual information in their most revolting form'.[72]

What they actually told Brittain was insufficiently accurate and detailed to be of any use to her. Brittain's is one of the few interwar autobiographies to address the question of sexuality in her own intimate life – rather than in very general terms. She makes it clear that at the time of her engagement to Roland Leighton, when she was nineteen, she had no clear idea what the sexual act was. This was a problem when she began nursing because she had to deal with a case of venereal disease, having no idea what it was or how it occurred. 'Throughout my two decades of life', she noted, 'I had never looked upon the nude body of an adult male; I had never even seen a naked boy-child since the nursery days when at the age of four or five, I used to share evening baths with Edward.' She was relieved that neither she nor the men she had to nurse were embarrassed or nervous as she attended to their intimate needs and was thankful to them for the knowledge that they allowed her of 'masculine functioning' and 'the early release from sex-inhibitions' that afflicted so many of her contemporaries who were brought up in Victorian traditions of female ignorance.[73]

Not everyone saw this issue as problematic. Lady Rhondda, for example, argues that the mystery that everyone made about sex and the fuss that was made about it so aroused her curiosity that while in her very early teens, she set out to discover what it as all about. She succeeded after much difficulty in finding out what the sexual act was – but remained puzzled about why it occasioned so much fuss. The question of sex did lead to her first concern about the status and situation of women: when, at the age of thirteen or fourteen, she discovered the existence of prostitutes as a 'class set apart', she 'took a vow to myself that all my life I would do what I could to see that the terrible injustice of scorning them and treating them as untouchables simply because they performed the sexual act for money should be done away with'. Her knowledge of the existence of prostitutes made her mother's attempt to persuade her that no young girl was ever kissed by a man to whom she was not engaged absurd.[74]

The double standard in sexual morality was integrally connected to the gaining of sexual knowledge also for the expatriate Australian artist, Stella Bowen. Bowen came to understand what sex was about at a very early age, she insists, exercising her embryonic reasoning power to connect

---

[72]Brittain, *Testament of Youth*, p. 28.
[73]Brittain, *Testament of Youth*, pp. 165–166.
[74]Rhondda, *This Was My World*, pp. 37–39.

reproduction in the animal world with human life. 'If hens laid eggs, then it was logical to suppose that puppies and even babies came from inside their mothers. And the idea that you had to be married in order to have children did not seem reasonable in face of the fact that dogs and cats evidently had no need of the ceremony.' All that was needed was simply some act of intimacy. Stories of fallen women – and their shameful maternity bore this out. While Rhondda confessed herself unable to understand why people made such a fuss about sex, Bowen suggests rather that she came to realize the pleasure and importance of physical passion when pondering why women would engage in acts of sexual intimacy when they were not married and when the penalties for doing so were so harsh. She was puzzled 'until I hit upon the explanation that it must be highly pleasurable'. At that point, she felt she had solved the sexual puzzle – and her only concern was to spare her mother the embarrassment of feeling she needed to enlighten her.[75]

It was not only in the middle and upper-middle class that sexuality was a problem for girls and young women. But their exposure to it came in different forms. Ethel Mannin describes the extensive discussion of sexual questions at her board school. All the little girls

> were morbidly interested in parturition, menstruation and procreation. The older girls talked of little else. We raked the Bible for information and those of us who came from homes in which there were books did endless research, looking up . . . such words as 'confinement', 'miscarriage' etc.[76]

Neither school nor home provided any detailed information. This autobiographical account underlines the need for sex education that Mannin later sought to provide. Her own sexual ignorance lasted until she was eighteen when she finally entered into a sexual relationship with a nineteen-year-old cadet.

The discussion of sexuality in interwar women's autobiography also addresses the sometimes questionable sexual behaviour of parents for the first time. When she was scarcely in her teens, Ursula Bloom saw her clergyman father passionately kissing a parishioner. He noted that she had seen him – and took this as an invitation to discuss his extramarital sexual relationships with her.

> I hated him to speak of the physical longing he felt for this friend, but not understanding my feelings, and probably aching for a confidante, he told

---

[75] Stella Bowen, *Drawn from Life* (Collins, 1940), p. 22.
[76] Mannin, *Confessions and Impressions*, p. 41.

me everything. He assured me that the natural desires of a man for a woman were something I should understand and was impatient of my lack of knowledge. He had no idea that he was instilling in me a very strong inhibition, or that he was making me terrified that one day I might be married and have this horrible intimacy come closer into my life.[77]

His confidences also meant that Bloom was forced to hide things from her mother, to whom she was very close. At some point, her mother discovered his infidelities and separated from her husband, increasing the family poverty as two households had to be maintained from a small clerical stipend. Later still, Bloom became furious when her father refused to help support her mother through her final illness – and wrote to the bishop about his many affairs. She later came to regret this step as it led to him losing his clerical living.

The Struggle for Independence

One theme of great importance in interwar women's autobiography is the struggle that they waged for independence. This struggle did not necessarily occur at any particular age, although it was often most pronounced in their adolescent and early adult years as they sought the freedom to follow a life of their own choosing, free from the constraints of family and for some, also free of the normal expectations of womanhood. Here too there are generational differences as the older women, like Webb and Swanwick, tell stories that follow lines similar to those of Victorian women's autobiography. Their freedom from familial demands came only with the death of parents – or with their marriage to a sympathetic man. But a very different approach is evident amongst younger women, many of whom fought for independence from their family of origin before they married and indeed from husbands who had different marital ideas to their own after marriage. For some, like Helena Swanwick and Vera Brittain, this struggle is articulated in explicitly feminist terms, although some others, while demanding similar things, do not describe their lives in these terms.

There is an echo of Harriet Martineau in Beatrice Webb's account of her adolescence and her struggles. Like Martineau, Webb immersed herself in religious and philosophical works in her late adolescent and early adult years as she sought both intellectual and spiritual independence and solace. She was seeking ways to deal with her loss of religious belief, on the one hand, and her strong sense of the need for some form of faith, on the other. She moved from religion and philosophy to more scientific approaches as she tried to master algebra, the natural sciences and positive philosophy, the

---

[77]Bloom, *Without Make-Up*, p. 35.

subjects that seemed to be most important in the intellectual world that she came to know through her family's close friendship with the philosopher, Herbert Spencer. Her mother's death, which occurred when Beatrice was thirty-four, 'revolutionised my life'.

> From being a subordinate carrying out directions . . . I became a principal, a person in authority, determining not only my own, but other people's conduct; the head of a large household perpetually on the move . . . busy hostess in town and country . . . (and) my father's counsellor and my youngest sister's virtual guardian.[78]

For her, as for Cobbe and Martineau, the first point to settle was 'how to reconcile the rival pulls on time and energy, on the one hand of family affection, backed up by the Victorian code of feminine domesticity and, on the other, of a domineering curiosity into the nature of things, reinforced by an awakening desire for creative thought and literary expression'.[79] With these new demands on her, Webb suddenly found that she had more energy than ever before so she managed to combine her own desires with her family duties by 'getting through my intellectual work in my own room between five and eight in the morning, leaving the rest of the day for domestic cares and social duties'. Aware that she lacked formal education, Webb noted with some regret 'that the circumstances of my life did not permit me to seek entry to one of the few University institutions then open to women'.[80] Nonetheless, Webb began to push out in her own intellectual direction: she came to realize that what interested her particularly was not sociology or even psychology as it was then understood.

> What roused and absorbed my curiosity were men and women, regarded – if I may use an old-fashioned word – as 'souls', their past and present conditions of life, their thoughts and feelings and their constantly changing behaviour.[81]

Novels and literary works proved far more helpful than psychology texts as she tried to work out a path into the kind of detailed social investigation that interested her. Although Webb's sisters were unsympathetic when it came to her desire for self-education, they did see that she needed some respite from her domestic role and freed her every now and again to leave home and begin to work out what it meant to be a social investigator. She went first to visit Bacup, the area from which her mother's family came with an old family retainer and assumed a different identity so that no one knew

---

[78] Webb, *My Apprenticeship*, p. 113.
[79] Webb, *My Apprenticeship*, p. 117.
[80] Webb, *My Apprenticeship*, p. 134.
[81] Webb, *My Apprenticeship*, p. 13.

that she actually had connections to the place so that she could interview people. A subsequent venture came through Charles Booth, who was married to a cousin, and who welcomed her assistance in his massive survey of London Life and Labour. It was only after her father's death in 1892, however, that Webb was able to live independently and engage both in social investigation and in her growing interest in trade unions and Fabian socialism. Her meeting with and marriage to Sidney Webb, a man deeply unacceptable to her affluent sisters and their husbands, occurred within this framework and established the working partnership that continued for the rest of her life.

Webb was perhaps the last autobiographer to accept familial rules and constraints as not only unavoidable but in some way reasonable. Helena Swanwick, by contrast, felt nothing but despair at having to comply with her parents' expectations. The sense of frustration and distress and the inner revolt against her mother's demands that began when she was a small girl who was never allowed to concentrate on anything or develop her own interests – unlike her brothers – is expressed powerfully in her autobiography. The only happy periods of childhood, adolescence or early adulthood she records are those when she was away from home, either at school or at university. Even then, her mother sometimes intervened: when she discovered that her daughter had been seeing Frederick Swanwick, she refused to let them meet or correspond until they were formally engaged. This intervention occurred in the course of Swanwick's last year at Girton. After it, she 'went back to "keep my term" at college, firmly resolved, when that was completed, to make my own living, leave home and have what friends I pleased'.[82] Unfortunately for her, her father died suddenly at around this time and she had to return home.

> My mother was nearly mad with grief, and it happened that I was the person she wished to have constantly with her and the one upon whom fell the burden of her unreason. She had never slept alone, so I felt obliged to share her bed-room and I had no privacy, night or day.[83]

Swanwick's mother wept if her daughter even left the room, so Swanwick had to do her best to work in the drawing room amidst the constant conversation. She took up the piano and enjoyed it – but the sound irritated her mother. She had begun to undertake paid work, teaching at Westfield College, doing some private coaching, and giving courses of lectures on Economics at Hampstead and Kensington. 'I had a gruelling time preparing these lectures in the bosom of my family', she notes, and 'earned more than I had expected, and paid into the house, a matter about which my mother

---

[82]Swanwick, *I Have Been Young*, p. 135.
[83]Swanwick, *I Have Been Young*, p. 137.

was uncertain: sometimes she resented it and sometimes she was proud of it.' Swanwick always felt that her mother took no more pleasure in their close contact than she did, and a friend confirmed it, telling her 'during that wretched year after my father's death, that I would be obliged to go, and that, in reality, my mother wished me gone'. But her mother refused to let her go – and her freedom only came when Frederick Swanwick finally proposed and they married. Swanwick's mother felt that her husband now had first claim to her time and attention. Marriage to Frederick Swanwick was for her an absolute liberation.

> I found him exactly what I most needed. After my harassed youth it was balm to my spirit to live with a man consistently reasonable, and to be able to feel that I could lighten and warm an existence which had become rather drab.[84]

Vera Brittain too writes of herself as having been in some kind of rebellion against her family from the time of her adolescence – and over similar issues. Although Brittain did not feel belittled and constantly negated by her parents, as Swanwick did, she resented intensely the assumption that she would fit into the pattern of a provincial young lady. She was not allowed to travel to Europe and for years refused the university education that she wanted. But she did not ever see marriage as resolution.

> The desire for a more eventful existence and a less restricted horizon had become an obsession, and it never occurred to me to count on marriage as a possible road to freedom . . . it seemed only too likely that a husband would yet further limit my opportunities.[85]

As we have seen, Brittain did eventually get to university, although she left in her first year to become a VAD in order to contribute to the war effort. But here too, she had to combat parental concerns and their belief that she would be better off at home. Brittain, although very critical of the ways that VADs were housed and generally treated, relished being 'an unprotected female', dashing around the London streets at night, and 'seeing life'. Her parents, however, were not happy about this life. She quotes a letter she sent to her father refusing to return home. 'Nothing', she wrote,

> would induce me to stop doing what I am doing now. . . . I honestly did not take it up because I thought you did not want me or could not afford to give me a comfortable home. . . . I do not agree that my place is at home doing nothing or practically nothing, for I consider that the place

---

[84]Swanwick, *I Have Been Young*, pp. 141–142.
[85]Brittain, *Testament of Youth*, p. 53.

of everyone who is young and strong and capable is where the work that is needed is to be done.[86]

Even though Brittain trained and learnt what was required of a nurse and spent years dealing with injured soldiers close to the battlefront, this did not suffice to win her independence. While she was nursing in France in 1917, she received a letter from her father saying that her mother was not well. 'As your mother and I can no longer manage without you', he concluded, 'it is now your duty to leave France immediately and return to Kensington.'[87] Brittain was in despair, and made to feel that she was deserting her post at an important time – but there was no appeal against this kind of familial demand, made worse by the fact that when she got home, she found there was little wrong with her mother that sounder domestic management could not cure. She remained at home for a time and then returned to nursing and when the war ended to Oxford. At that point, her freedom from family was secured. Her parents recognized that after four years of war service and three at university,

> my return to a position of subservient dependence at home would be tolerable neither for them nor for me. . . . They understood now that freedom, however uncomfortable, and self-support, however hard to achieve, were the only condition in which a feminist of the war generation . . . could do her work and maintain self-respect.[88]

Familial demands and manipulation were by no means confined to the middle class. If anything, it was worse in some working-class and marginal poor families where the daughter's earning capacity made her necessary to the family's economic well-being and even survival. When she was sixteen, Marjorie Bowen, much to her own surprise, published a successful novel and was given a cheque for sixty pounds, and other publishers made offers for her future works. 'I thought then in my very youthful folly, that this might be the end of the bad times. I imagined that we could leave the squalid London flat and rooms and perhaps go to the country.' But this was not to be. Her money was banked in her mother's name and she became from then on the family provider, required to publish the historical novels that made her name on a very regular basis in order to supply the constant income that her mother needed – and in her view squandered. When she attempted to move away and live with friends and separately from her mother and sister,

> My mother came to see me, ill, fretful, exhausted. How could we afford to run two establishments? What was the sense of my staying there?

---

[86]Brittain, *Testament of Youth*, pp. 213–214.
[87]Brittain, *Testament of Youth*, p. 421.
[88]Brittain, *Testament of Youth*, p. 536.

What good was I doing? It was not fair, I had no right to break away. And so on through all the sad changes of possessiveness, frustration and disappointment.

I felt her tragedy so keenly that there was nothing to do but to return.[89]

So for several years, she remained in an unhappy home with her mother, her sister and their ageing maid, moving from one house to another as everything seemed to be inadequate or haunted. She was so involved in the miseries of her family that she had little time for other intellectual or social interests. Although she was earning a good livelihood from her writing, at the age of twenty-three she had 'a sense of withering'. Eventually the strain of living at home and dealing with the constant quarrels that her mother and sister provoked with neighbours and old friends became intolerable and she decided to marry, accepting the proposal of a young Italian man she had met at one of the few parties she attended in London. She did not love him – and promised her mother that her financial contribution to the household that she was leaving would not be reduced. The marriage turned out to be disastrous: her husband had little earning capacity and soon showed signs of the tuberculosis that killed him within a few years. But it did take her away from her thraldom to her mother.

Parental manipulation and attempts to thwart a young girl's freedom were evident across the social scale. Louise Jermy too wrote of the immense difficulties that she had in freeing herself from her father and stepmother. They made her leave places where she was an apprentice seamstress because they deemed her pay insufficient. Indeed, it seemed that almost every time she found a job she liked, especially one that offered her a live-in position, they would find a way to make her relinquish it – and then return to the home where she had been so unhappy. One mistress in a home where she had really enjoyed working commented on her excessive obedience. 'Well Louisa,' she said when she found Jermy crying over having to leave,

> You are a very silly girl to let your people over-rule you so much, if you were happy with me, because I did not ask you to go, but I've engaged someone else now so there is no going back is there?[90]

After an unhappy time at home, Jermy got another job as a nursemaid but noted that 'it was dreadful' and needed a really strong woman to manage the eighty stairs in the house and clean the daughters' bicycles. Although by nature diffident and timid, Jermy had eventually to fight her stepmother to be allowed to work where she chose – and her father to be able to marry the agricultural labourer who became her husband.

---

[89]Campbell, *The Debate Continues*.
[90]Jermy, *Memories of a Working Woman*, p. 83.

The struggle for independence in Kathleen Woodward's *Jipping Street* takes a very different form. She did not have to fight her mother to be able to work or leave home. On the contrary, she was expected to begin working independently at the age of thirteen and was pleased that her contribution reduced the hours of labour required of her mother. Moving out of home and finding a room closer to her work was something that was expected. For her, the struggle was rather a political one, to break away 'from that attitude of accepted misery that encompassed us'. Quite early in her working life, she met a woman she calls 'Marian Evelyn', who supported trade unions and the suffrage agitation, and took Woodward to their meetings as well as to those of an ethical society. She also persuaded her to attend night school, where she studied both shorthand and English. After classes, they had long discussions as they 'fumed and fretted and raged and swore that we would not tread the path of our neighbours'. Under her influence, Woodward joined an organization that she calls 'The sons and daughters of revolt' with whom she discussed different possibilities and alternative lives.

Woodward contrasted the 'long summer nights when we sought to free ourselves from the prevailing attitude of being thankful for any slavery so long as it gave us bread and a measure of security', with the recognition that anyone who showed more brains or initiative 'soon turned this advantage to battening on his neighbours as a moneylender or bookmaker'.[91] The fierce evening discussions seemed to amount to little by the morning when Woodward realized that 'our aspirations availed us little without a plan'. And that no one had. Woodward retreated into a life of reading that encompassed the historical writing of Gibbon and Macaulay, Shakespeare, Elizabeth Barrett Browning and the American transcendentalists. 'If only there were not Jipping Street, and the factory, and mother;' she wrote, 'I could read all day and set down my dreams.' Eventually, after the tragic deaths of several of the women she had loved, Woodward felt the bonds that had held her to Jipping Street lessen – and a need to move on. But she had no one to talk to about it and no idea where to go. Her dreams beckoned on and she knew she must go on. But, as she wrote in the final sentence of her book, she was 'following without seeing where they lead'.[92]

The Turn to Personal Life

Not all interwar autobiographies deal with personal life. Few of those concerned with the suffrage campaigns chose to include discussion of their personal lives in their autobiographies, for example. Marriage was mentioned by the suffrage leaders Emmeline Pankhurst and Millicent Garrett Fawcett, as indeed it was later by Emmeline Pethick-Lawrence, but mainly in order to

---

[91] Woodward, *Jipping Street*, p. 108.
[92] Woodward, *Jipping Street*, p. 151.

show how supportive their husbands were of their activities. Others omitted any reference to their personal lives. Annie Kenney was married with a child when she wrote her reminiscences but didn't once mention this fact. Evelyn Sharp never even hinted at the fact that Henry Nevinson, to whom she refers often as a colleague and friend, was her lover and subsequently became her husband. Lady Rhondda included a brief discussion of her marriage in her autobiography, but only because friends insisted. She had not mentioned it in her first draft: 'One's marriage seems to me a purely private matter, unsuitable for discussion in print.' But friends who read her work suggested that she should include it: if she said nothing at all, people would make their own assumptions and assume a level of unhappiness which was not the case in what was, she insisted, 'the plain and simple story of a misfit – a misfit likely enough to happen under the social conditions of pre-war days when most protected girls married before they knew what they themselves were really like, leave alone their future husbands'.[93] There were others too who eschewed any mention of their adult or married lives, including Kathleen Woodward and Louise Jermy.

Other women did deal with marriage and sometimes also other aspects of personal life, however, in new and interesting ways. The treatment of marriage in women's autobiography is one that shows very clearly the importance of generational differences. Beatrice Webb and Helena Swanwick, for example, like Pethick-Lawrence and Fawcett, discuss their marriages briefly, depicting them as completely harmonious – even idyllic. Webb is particularly interesting here. *My Apprenticeship*, the first volume of her autobiography – and the only one she completed – ends with her meeting and marrying Sidney Webb. She quoted passages from her diaries to indicate how she met him as she was becoming interested in socialism and how important their shared interests and work were. What she doesn't include, however, are the passages that have fascinated her biographers in which she describes how unattractive she found him at the start and how disinclined she was for any kind of intimate relationship with him.[94] His persistence won out, however, and finally, they married. 'Here ends *My Apprenticeship*', she wrote,

> and opens *Our Partnership*; a working comradeship founded in a common faith and made perfect by marriage; perhaps the most exquisite, certainly the most enduring, of all the varieties of happiness.[95]

Long before she formally introduced Sidney Webb to the reader, he had become a familiar figure in *My Apprenticeship*, referred to always as 'The

---

[93]Rhondda, *This Was My World*, p. 10.
[94]Barbara Caine, 'Beatrice Webb and the "Woman Question"', *History Workshop Journal* 14, no. 1 (1982): 23–44.
[95]Webb, *My Apprenticeship*, p. 108.

other one'. Although Deborah Nord insists that Sidney Webb was not involved in writing *My Apprenticeship*, he seems sometimes to be sitting beside Beatrice, encouraging and supporting her: pointing out that she needed a partner to assist in her attempts to teach herself algebra and in her early social investigation, for example, and pleased that no one had claimed her for a wife before he came on the scene!

There seems never to have been any question of Helena Swanwick's attraction to her husband: the barriers they faced were rather imposed by her mother who refused to let them meet for some time until they actually became engaged. Marriage was her refuge against her mother and seems always to have been idyllic. Emmeline Pethick-Lawrence depicted her marriage in similarly idyllic terms. She describes her meeting with and engagement and marriage in 1901 to Frederick Lawrence, making clear his commitment not only to the cause of women's emancipation generally but to hers in particular. When they married, they merged their surnames and both became Pethick-Lawrences. This step was not the only one he took to protect her independence. On their first wedding anniversary, he gave her the key to a garden flat which had a bedroom, bathroom and sitting room. 'This is your very own apartment', he said, 'no one else has keys and no one needs to know about it. When you are here, staff can say you are out.'[96]

A very different note is struck by Vera Brittain in *Testament of Youth*. Despite the intensely romantic tone of her description of her relationship with Roland Leighton, Brittain does not hide the difficulties she experienced in it. She and Leighton became engaged early in 1915, just before Leighton was sent to the front. Around New Year's Eve of 1914, they had two wonderful days in London, chaperoned throughout by her aunt. When they met for dinner, Roland 'gave me a bunch of tall pink roses with a touch of orange in their colouring and the sweetest scent in the world.... In the warm atmosphere of the restaurant, their wistful, tender perfume clung about us like a benediction.'[97] Their two unforgettable days together 'seemed to relegate the whole of our previous existence into a dim and entirely insignificant past'. Once Leighton went to the front, however, Brittain soon came to feel that the war was changing him and she struggled to maintain a sense of the person she had known before. Brittain was very much aware of the contrast between the rapport they seemed to find in their letters – and the awkwardness of their actual meetings. As Lynn Pearce points out, in the course of a relationship that lasted for two and a half years, Brittain and Leighton met only seven times.[98] Hence theirs was largely an epistolary relationship and Brittain struggled to reconcile the person that she knew through her letters with the one she encountered in the flesh in their

---

[96]Pethick-Lawrence, *My Part in a Changing World*, p. 131.
[97]Brittain, *Testament of Youth*, p. 116.
[98]Lynne Pearce, *Romance Writing* (Cambridge: Polity Press, 2007), pp. 119–121.

occasional and usually uncomfortable meetings. Even in the letters, however, one senses a growing distance between them as Roland was changing under the strain of war in ways that Vera sought not to acknowledge, becoming more religious even, without telling her, converting to Roman Catholicism. Sometimes his letters or silences made her angry. However, as she noted in a letter to him: 'One cannot be angry with people at the front – a fact which I sometimes think they take advantage of'... 'for thinking that the world might end for you on that discordant night.'[99] The tragic ending of this relationship with Leighton's death in 1915, consigned it to an even more romantic level in which their youthful passion was saturated with longing and sacrifice.

Brittain found it very hard to resume any kind of normal civilian life when the war ended, feeling that no one understood the depth of her sorrow and suffering. She felt increasingly that her work as a writer was the most important thing to her and marriage was not on her agenda. She began a relationship with George Caitlin, a political scientist, in 1923 after he wrote to her about liking one of her novels and sought a meeting. This relationship too began through letters and the couple only met after some months of correspondence. Caitlin who was planning to take up an academic post in the United States wanted Brittain to marry him and go with him. It took a long time to persuade her. So long as I remained unmarried, she noted,

> I was merely a survivor from the past – that wartime past into which all those whom I loved best had disappeared. To marry would be to disassociate myself from that past, for marriage inevitably brought with it a future.[100]

The impact of the war on her own life and on that of her generation, made Brittain question the whole notion of private life. As a girl, she noted,

> I imagined that life was individual, one's own affair; that the events happening in the world outside were important enough in their own way but were personally quite irrelevant. Now, like the rest of my generation, I have had to learn again and again the terrible truth of George Eliot's words about the invasion of personal preoccupations by the larger destinies of mankind, and at last to recognise that no life is really private, isolated, or self-sufficient.[101]

Brittain's sense of the close connection between personal life and wider issues is very evident in her depiction of her relationship with George Caitlin, who was only too aware that he was for her a second best, described always

---

[99] Brittain, *Testament of Youth*, p. 217.
[100] Brittain, *Testament of Youth*, p. 651.
[101] Brittain, *Testament of Youth*, pp. 471–472.

in terms that underlined how much he differed from the adored Leighton. When she hesitated over whether or not to accept his proposal, she explained that one of the problems she saw in marrying was the feminist one. 'I want to solve the problem of how a married woman, without being inordinately rich, can have children and yet maintain her intellectual and spiritual independence as well as having . . . time for the pursuit of her own career.'[102] This insistence that her life was bound up with the feminist cause was evident subsequently too when Brittain refused to remain with Caitlin and insisted on devising a 'semi-detached marriage', in which she was based with her friend Winifred Holtby, in London, with him joining them for holidays. Her insistence on forging a new feminist pathway was used also as an argument to prevent his forming other sexual relationships in her absence! From the start, as this suggests, their marriage was a compromise that Brittain did not embrace wholeheartedly. Caitlin in turn was deeply unhappy about how he was presented in her autobiography.

Intimate life was depicted in many different ways in the autobiographies of interwar women novelists. Ethel Mannin followed her description of the sexual interests and behaviours of her schoolmates with details of the many attempts at seduction made by her first employer, Charles F Higham, and various colleagues. She was one of the first women to describe her first sexual encounter, one involving a young provincial bank clerk who was nineteen at the time, while she was a year younger. It was 'the most extraordinarily naïve affair, as clumsy and disappointing as our joint inexperience could make it',[103] and came to an end when his Primitive Methodist parents found out about it. Soon after, she fell seriously in love with a man she subsequently married – although their five years of her marriage, during which she lived in dreary rental rooms and apartments, had a daughter, and became a novelist, did not live up to the promise of their first year together.

Her later relationships are dealt with in a rather sketchier way. She makes it clear that she had several sexual encounters and relationships after her marriage ended but offers little information about them. One chapter of her work, dealing with the trip to America she made shortly after the end of her marriage is titled 'American medley: Some Indiscretions and Impressions'. It deals with her impressions of New York, the ease with which one could obtain alcohol despite prohibition, the way that New York businessmen behaved in the summer months while their families went away – and certainly suggests that she had several affairs, beginning on the ship on which she left England. Mannin offers oblique hints, however, rather than saying anything specific or explicit about these relationships. She follows the same pattern in relation to a very sad relationship with a man she loved who

---

[102]Brittain, *Testament of Youth*, p. 653.
[103]Mannin, *Confessions and Impressions*, pp. 67–71.

committed suicide. Reading her autobiography now, what is notable is how coy and uninformative it is about her intimate life and relationships. When it was published, however, its relative openness about sexual questions shocked many. Under the heading 'wildly indiscreet' book, the anonymous reviewer for the *Daily Mail* made this very clear. 'Writers have before now undressed in public', he or she noted, 'but this process has seldom been carried so far as by Miss Ethel Mannin, the novelist, who has written her outspoken, sex-obsessed autobiography at the early age of 30.'[104]

The most graphic depictions of unhappy marriages and the links between them and their equally miserable childhoods occur in the autobiographies of Ursula Bloom and Marjorie Bowen. Having looked after her mother both financially and physically from her early teens, Bloom was cajoled into what her mother thought of as a great match to a man from a wealthy and propertied family toward the end of the First World War. Bloom's mother was dying of cancer at the time, which gave her wishes greater power. But the marriage was a disaster from the start. The Denham-Cooke family, into which Bloom was marrying wanted nothing to do with her. She was not in love with her husband – and was both ignorant of many details about sexual intercourse and generally terrified of sex after her adolescent exposure to her father's revelations of his sexual encounters. She described her honeymoon as a nightmare and after it, felt that she ought never to have married. After it, 'I saw men in a new light, the world had altered for me and not for the better. Marriage was a ghastly shock to me, and I was facing an experience which might last the rest of my life and which I felt I could not possibly endure.'[105] She resented and blamed her mother for her marriage – something that made her want not to see her in some of the last months of her mother's life. Bloom became pregnant – and while pregnant discovered that her now abusive husband was an alcoholic. He died within a year of their marriage leaving her with a child to support through her writing.

Bowen too describes in considerable detail the misery of her marriage to an Italian man with whom she shared little. Her marriage was bitterly opposed by her mother who, Bowen thought, feared mostly losing her access to Bowen's income. The marriage was in some ways an escape for her from her own family, and in its early years – ones she spent with her husband in Italy – this was the case. Within a short time, however, the marriage itself became increasingly difficult. Her husband's lack of education and inability to earn an income, his violent temper and what she came increasingly to recognize as his mental illness, posed immense problems. He also suffered from tuberculosis, and she spent terrible months separated from her child while nursing him until his death in Italy.

---

[104]'Miss Ethel Mannin in Love.' *Daily Mail* (London, England), Issue 10656, Friday, 20 June 1930, p. 7.
[105]Bloom, *Without Make-Up*, p. 156.

Public Life

Involvement in public life, more especially political life, provided both the reason for writing an autobiography and the core activity in it for many of the women who wrote autobiographies in the interwar period. This was not so for all: the novelists Ursula Bloom and Marjorie Bowen, and sometimes a working-class woman, like Louise Jermy, whose main preoccupation was the revelation of their private pain and anguish, never so much as suggest any form of public life. But it is important for almost everyone else.

Public life obviously provides the major focus for the women writing autobiographies that included or centred on their suffrage activity. Involvement in the suffrage campaign demanded many participants. For many, it amounted to full-time work – sometimes paid but more often not – as they were required to organize, publicize and address meetings, go on demonstrations and marches, solicit membership and support and attend innumerable meetings of many different kinds. Although suffrage campaigning was public and political in its aim and its activities, engagement in it usually involved intense emotion and affected every aspect of private life. Some women describe how their lives were taken over and transformed by the suffrage campaign, others simply write their lives as histories of the suffrage movement assuming that little else needs to be known about them.

Emmeline Pankhurst and Millicent Fawcett both told their stories as histories of their particular organization and its place in the suffrage movement. These organizations are covered in great detail, while little attention is paid to any other aspect of their lives. Both women emphasized their sense of the historic importance of their life and cause by linking their births or earliest memories with wider histories of reform. In Pankhurst's case, it is the struggle for the emancipation of slaves that is important. Her earliest recollection

> is of a great bazaar which was held in my native city of Manchester, the object of the bazaar being to raise money to relieve the poverty of the newly emancipated negro slaves in the United States. My mother took an active part in this effort, and I, as a small child, was entrusted with a lucky bag by means of which I helped to collect money. Young as I was – I could not have been older than five years – I knew perfectly well the meaning of the words slavery and emancipation.[106]

Fawcett too began by stressing the connection between her life and the great liberal reforms, although it was free trade that she wrote about rather than slavery. 'The year of my birth was the year of the Irish Famine and the Repeal of the Corn Laws, and the following year saw the downfall of half

---

[106] Pankhurst, *My Own Story*, p. 2.

the autocratic governments of Europe.'[107] She does not, of course, remember these events, but is sure they had 'an electrifying effect on the whole atmosphere in which I found myself as a child'. These memories underline the extent to which the women were drawn into their political campaigns from their earliest years, and they frame the ways in which their families of origin, their education and marriages are dealt with. Pankhurst talks about the liberal sympathies of her parents and the constant support she received from her husband. Fawcett says a little more about her family of origin and their community, but also stresses the strength and independence of her father and his support for his daughters, a support that was also extended by her blind husband, Henry Fawcett. Their children too only fit into their autobiographies through their suffrage involvement. Thus, Pankhurst omits any mention of two of her children, mentioning Sylvia (who was ejected from the WSPU) very briefly and concentrating on Christabel, her favourite child and partner in leading the WSPU. Pankhurst introduces Christabel with her recollection of an incident when Christabel was still a child and startled me one day with the remark: 'How long you women have been trying for the vote. For my part, I mean to get it.'[108] From that point on, her story becomes effectively a joint autobiography of mother and daughter. Fawcett's only child, Philippa, only enters her autobiography in an extended way when, although unable as a woman to take out a degree, she completes her mathematical tripos at Cambridge with results better than that of the top male student!

For Annie Kenney too, it is her involvement in the militant suffrage campaign that both explains and dominates her autobiography. She was one for whom that involvement offered extraordinary opportunities and a completely new life. She came from a working family and although her older siblings spent time at school, a period of intense economic hardship during her childhood meant that Kenney had been sent to work in a factory at the age of ten, joining an army of half-timers who worked in the factory half the day and attended school the other half. A couple of chapters are devoted to her family and community, her early interest in labour questions and her involvement in a choir and with fellow workers. In 1905, however, her mother died and 'the cement of love that had kept the home together disappeared'. It was in that year, Kenney explains, and in her state of bereavement that she met and became enthralled by Christabel Pankhurst. Kenney attended a talk that Christabel Pankhurst gave to Oldham women workers. She went up to Christabel after her talk and

> before I knew what I had done, I had promised to work up a meeting for Miss Pankhurst with the factory women of Oldham and Leeds. I walked

---

[107] Fawcett, *What I Remember*, p. 10.
[108] Pankhurst, *My Own Story*, p. 36.

to the station with her, and before we separated she had asked me to spend the following Saturday afternoon with them at their home at Nelson Street, Manchester.

The following week I lived on air; I simply could not eat.[109]

Kenney was soon involved in organizing local meetings for the WSPU, in regular weekend discussions with the Pankhursts and then in the first of Christabel's militant demonstrations in Parliament, after which they were both arrested. She became a full-time organizer for the WSPU, leading demonstrations and giving many public lectures. Like others, she was arrested and went on a hunger strike and endured forcible feeding, often addressing public rallies immediately on her release. Becoming a full-time suffrage worker released her from working in a mill. She was taken into the Pankhurst home where she lived for several years, becoming a close companion and confidante not only of Christabel Pankhurst but for a time of other leading militants as well, including the Pethick-Lawrences who took her to Europe for holidays. As others were arrested and imprisoned and Christabel went to Paris to avoid arrest, Kenney became more and more central to the movement, travelling often to Paris to see Christabel and get her orders.

It was not only women whose earlier lives had been both limited and, in many ways, very hard who felt themselves to be transformed by the suffrage campaign. This was the case also for very privileged women who had enjoyed school and sometimes even university. This sense of deep involvement and of transformation was more pronounced amongst those who became militants. Evelyn Sharp sought in her autobiography to explain why some women, of whom she was one, felt it imperative to join the militants rather than the moderate and constitutional wing of the movement – and why, once this was done, radical action and even the courting of imprisonment was inevitable. There were two lines of approach to the suffrage question:

> Either you saw the vote as a political influence, or you saw it as a symbol of freedom. The desire to reform the world would not alone have been sufficient to turn law-abiding and intelligent women of all ages and all classes into ardent rebels. Reforms can always wait a little longer, but freedom, directly you discover you haven't got it, will not wait another minute.[110]

Moderates, seeking reform had campaigned for a long time and would continue to do so. But militants were those who, suddenly made aware of an imperative need, 'could not wait another minute'. The intensity of this involvement made public disobedience – and the courting of arrest inevitable.

---

[109] Kenney, *Memoirs of a Militant*, p. 30.
[110] Sharp, *Unfinished Adventure*, p. 128.

Lady Rhondda, who came from an even more privileged background and made the same choice as Sharp described in particularly evocative terms what the militant suffrage movement meant to her. She was an affluent young woman without a career or other immediate interests. She married a local landowner while very young and, especially as she did not fall pregnant, was very bored. When she was taken by a relative to a suffrage demonstration, she was entranced and decided immediately to join the WSPU. Her father disapproved, but she decided not to discuss it with him. She joined the militants and soon began to make public speeches, finding that it offered a life she had never dreamt of.

> Militant suffrage was the very salt of life. The knowledge of it came like a draught of fresh air unto our padded, stifled lives. It gave us a release of energy, it gave us that sense of being of some use in the scheme of things.... It made us feel we were part of life, not just outside watching it. It made us feel that we had a real purpose and use apart from having children.[111]

Many other women who had been involved in the suffrage campaign also produced autobiographies that dealt with their suffrage activities but presented them as one episode in busy and active lives. Evelyn Sharp was one of these. Her autobiography, *Unfinished Adventure*, places her suffrage activity in the context of her earlier courageous decision to leave home and settle alone in London seeking to make a career as a teacher and writer. Important as the suffrage campaign had been to her, commemorating it and her own part in it was not her primary reason for writing an autobiography. According to her biographer, Angela John, it was rather the need to earn more as a writer when other sources of income dried up, combined with the fact that her partner, Henry Nevinson, had been engaged in writing his autobiography that turned Sharp's attention to writing her own life story in the early 1930s.[112] Sharp's suffrage involvement occurs in the first section of her autobiography, in the years after she had established herself as an avant-garde writer. Unlike other militants, she became a pacifist during the First World War and remained one, moving on to other social and political causes, including the Save the Children Fund, human rights organizations and helping provide relief for impoverished communities in Germany, Hungary, Ireland and the Soviet Union in the 1920s and early '30s.[113]

A similar sense of the suffrage campaign as being an important part of a life that remained very full and active is evident in the autobiography of Lady Rhondda. Although written and published in the early 1930s, the book, which was titled *This was My World*, ended in 1919, just prior to her

---

[111] Rhondda, *This Was My World*, p. 12.
[112] John, *Evelyn Sharp*, pp. 187–188.
[113] Sharp, *Unfinished Adventure*.

establishing the very successful journal, *Time and Tide*, by which she is best known.[114] Indeed, Angela John, who wrote her biography as well as that of Evelyn Sharp, suggests that it was the very prominence that she had gained as the editor and owner of *Time and Tide* that made her think her readers might be interested in an account of the world of her youth. Rhondda devotes three chapters to the suffrage movement, discussing her family's involvement – and her husband's opposition and concern that she not be arrested, her involvement in meetings and visits to cabinet ministers and finally her militant actions and imprisonment. Joining the WSPU also forced her to educate herself, to read the books and read pamphlets of earlier feminists including J. S. Mill. She moved from feminist literature into political science, economics, different systems of government and political history. Her reading extended even to Havelock Ellis' *Psychology of Sex*. In addition, she began to read newspapers in a new way – and even to read weeklies, like *New Statesman*. But this was only the start. She had then to learn how to organize meetings and events, to campaign and 'often the most terrifying thing, to defy the conventional rules of womanhood and speak in public'. For Lady Rhondda, suffrage was both an education and an initiation into a new kind of life. It receded from importance when, during the war, her father, who was a very successful businessman and Liberal politician, at the suggestion of her mother, asked her to become his assistant and to help run his coal businesses. Her involvement in her father's world makes up another substantial part of her autobiography.

For some women, involvement in suffrage or in the War led almost automatically to public and political engagement after the War. Brittain, for example, describes her interest and involvement with the League of Nations Union, an organization that many feminists joined in the hope that an international organization of this kind would take up the question of women's rights at a time when few nations seemed inclined to do so. This involvement was also a step on the way to the pacifism that Brittain came to espouse. By contrast with Brittain, Helena Swanwick had been a pacifist during the First World War and had been in serious disagreement with others in the suffrage movement who strongly supported the war effort over this matter.[115] Swanwick belonged to the Women's International League which had sought to oppose the war and attempted to hold a conference in Zurich in 1915 to discuss ways of opposing and if possible ending the war. She was very critical of the war guilt clauses in the treaty of Versailles and of the terms on which the League of Nations was set up. Hence, she describes in some detail in her autobiography her amazement when the new Labour government rang to ask her if she would go as a 'substitute delegate' to the fifth assembly of the League in Geneva in 1924. She was initially aghast at the idea, but her husband insisted that it was her duty to go – and she sought

---

[114] Rhondda, *This Was My World*.
[115] Swanwick, *I Have Been Young*.

to obtain the appropriate clothes and to prepare herself by reading all the necessary reports. While women had initially had high hopes for the possibilities of the League in terms of women's issues, in fact, it was as discriminatory and male-dominated as any other institution. Swanwick knew that,

> as a woman, I was predestined for the Fifth Committee, a sort of rag-bag of miseries and forlorn hopes, and there were some six or seven subjects with which I would have to deal, and which required much study. A woman, it appeared, was assumed to be well-informed about Opium, Refugees, Protection of Children, Relief after Earthquakes, Prison Reform, Municipal Co-operation, Alcoholism, Traffic in Women. I did know something about this last, but of the other questions I was as ignorant as the rest of the delegation.[116]

Swanwick was again invited to be a delegate to the 10th Assembly of the League in 1929, although she felt very old and unconnected to politics at the time and thought this assembly lacked the vitality of the earlier one she had attended. Swanwick ends her autobiography with this chapter. In it, she deals with her sense of the inadequacy of the League, of the appalling treatment of Germany by the allies – and her sense of how this contributed to the rise of Nazism. Her own sense of affinity with Germany, from where her father had come, made current political developments very painful to her. Swanwick describes all of this as the prelude to the great tragedy in her life, the death of her husband in 1931. Like other women in this period, for Swanwick public and private worlds were very closely connected. Her despair at the international scene makes a fitting introduction to her discussion of Frederick Swanwick's final illness and death that effectively ends her autobiography. 'I will not write of the next five months;' she writes as her concluding statement. 'I had lost not only my life-companion, but myself. I seemed to be living with a stranger whose chief capacity was to make me suffer.'[117] Swanwick was an increasingly isolated figure in the course of the 1930s, and the final pages of her autobiography make it unsurprising that she could not bear the thought of another war and committed suicide in November 1939, just after it had begun.

A Sense of Self

It was the novel, and especially those that focused on introspective and self-aware heroines, like Charlotte Brontë's *Jane Eyre*, that offered the language that helped in constructing a particular sense of self for Victorian women

---

[116] Swanwick, *I Have Been Young*, p. 385.
[117] Swanwick, *I Have Been Young*.

autobiographers. But while there is a close link between autobiography and the novel in the 20th century, fiction was no longer a key source for those seeking to articulate a sense of self.[118] New approaches and new vocabularies had become available. Both psychology and psychoanalysis are important here. We have already seen the casual references to Freud and the use of psychoanalytic terms that some women used to describe aspects of their childhood and their complex feelings about their mothers. And, although none of the autobiographers discussed in this chapter was directly engaged in psychoanalysis or claimed any special knowledge or understanding of psychology, one does begin to see the influence of both in the new sense of how complex the relationships and feelings depicted in autobiographies are. One of the most significant terms that enters into the language generally in the early decades of the 20th century is 'ambivalent'. As a term describing the 'coexistence in one person of profoundly opposing emotions, beliefs, attitudes, or urges (such as love and hate, or attraction and repulsion)', it came from psychoanalysis, but it was increasingly being used in a more general way to describe mixed, uncertain or contradictory feelings.[119] Several women describe not only this sense of mixed or contradictory feelings but also, and associated with it, a sense of themselves as divided and as feeling a sense of inner struggle or division about themselves and their aims and objectives.

One of the clearest depictions of this sense of division is that offered by Beatrice Webb in *My Apprenticeship*. The work begins with a statement of her sense of the inner conflict that seems universal.

> Beneath the surface of our daily life, ... there runs a continuous controversy between the Ego that affirms and the Ego that denies. On the course of this controversy depends the attainment of inner harmony and consistent conduct in private and public affairs.[120]

At this point, Webb insisted that for her, this conflict centres on the struggle between science and religious faith that took the form in her own life of the question of whether it was possible for there to be a science of social organization that could not only enable people to predict what was going to would happen, but 'to alter the event by taking appropriate action or persuading others to take it' – and whether this was the only faculty needed. Do we, she wondered, 'need religion as well as science, emotional faith as well as intellectual curiosity'. But as Nord argues, and as Webb herself recognized, she was facing other conflicts as well.

---

[118] Max Saunders, *Self-Impression: Life-Writing. Autobiografiction, and the Forms of Modern Literature* (Oxford: Oxford University Press, 2010).
[119] *'ambivalent'*. Oxford Dictionaries. Oxford University Press, n.d. https://premium.oxforddictionaries.com/definition/english/ambivalent, via Oxford Dictionaries Online.
[120] Webb, *My Apprenticeship*, p. xliii.

When Webb described the change in her life that occurred with her mother's death and her need to become her father's housekeeper and companion – while also seeking to keep alive her own intellectual interests and ambitions – she noted her new energy and that she was carrying on 'several separate, and in some ways conflicting phases of life – undergoing in fact, much of the strain of a multiple personality'.[121]

Looking back on her diaries to describe her observations of East End life a few years later, in the mid-1880s and her own sense of herself at that time, Webb noted 'a black thread of personal unhappiness'.

> From the entries in my diary I gather that I saw myself as one suffering from a divided personality; the normal woman seeking personal happiness in love given and taken within the framework of a successful marriage; whilst the other self claimed ... the right to the free activity of a 'clear and analytic mind'.[122]

A similar sense of division is evident in the autobiographies of several other interwar women who constantly asked themselves how they could reconcile the desire for free activity and a clear mind with the expectation – and often the desire – for personal happiness of a conventional kind involving marriage and probably children. Ultimately, Webb saw the divisions within herself, both those involving science and religion and those concerned with marriage versus intellectual work, as becoming integrated.

> A conversion to Fabianism, a political philosophy that ostensibly accommodated both science and faith, transcends the struggle between the two 'Egos', so marriage to Sidney Webb, a husband who was also a partner in work and faith, transcends the conflict between the 'masculine' and 'feminine' selves.[123]

But she was in a minority amongst interwar women autobiographers in seeing this inner conflict as one that came to be resolved on both the personal and the intellectual or spiritual level. In some ways, Helena Swanwick followed a similar path. She was not as introspective as Webb, and nor did she have the same sense of a need for resolution of the conflict between the religious and the spiritual. Her sense of inner conflict and unhappiness came largely from the sense of being unrecognized and undermined as a girl in a family in which personhood was really only recognized in men. But for Swanwick too, marriage to a supportive and sympathetic man provided a solution as it allowed her to develop her strong political interests in the suffrage movement, the Labour Party and the world of internationalism.

---

[121] Webb, *My Apprenticeship*, p. 114.
[122] Webb, *My Apprenticeship*, p. 279.
[123] Nord, *Apprenticeship of Beatrice Webb*, p. 82.

For many younger women, the inner conflict over who they were, where they belonged in the world and how they might find a way to live at ease with themselves within it was much harder to resolve. In part, this has to do with the ways in which they understood and thought about questions of gender and about their rights and responsibilities as women. Although the question of gender was important for Webb too, one of the questions about which she was clearly ambivalent was feminism. In 1889, while struggling with the question of her own independence, she had been a leading signatory of an appeal against women's suffrage, and although she subsequently changed her mind, she was never a committed feminist. By contrast, for many younger women, feminist commitment underlined the demand for their own autonomy and was accompanied by a much stronger sense of hostility to and resentment of familial demands and the expectation that they would conform to the expectations of womanhood held by their family and society more generally. The sense of rebellion that we have already seen in relation to Swanwick and Brittain was integral to their sense of self. From childhood, Swanwick and Brittain had felt at odds with their own families and the broader society in which they lived. Brittain dates 'the rebellious resentment that I have never forgotten' from the incident that occurred when she was eleven and was deemed to have behaved shamefully when she stopped on the way to school to talk to her brother and his friends.[124] Much of her account of her childhood, and especially of her adolescence, is centred around her discontent with how she, as a girl, was treated. While not always actively unhappy, she suffered constantly from the sense that her education was inferior and her opportunities narrower than was the case for her brother and his friends.

This sense of being at odds with the expectations and norms that dominated the Buxton world of her youth is the prelude for Brittain to a more general sense of herself as outside and at odds with the institutions and worlds in which she lives. This is the case in all the places and circumstances that she describes in *Testament of Youth*: at university when she began in 1914; sometimes as a VAD, close to the battlefront and experiencing a life quite outside the traditional norms of womanhood; back home when recalled by her parents; at university when she resumed her studies after the war – and in a most pronounced way when beginning her career as a writer and faced with the question of whether or not to marry. Brittain's descriptions of herself exude a sense of her inability to feel or to behave in ways that would be readily understood or evoke sympathy and her discomfort in almost all situations. This sense of being an outsider and unable to conform to expected norms was exacerbated by the war. In her early days at Somerville College, Brittain describes the enthusiasm with which she threw herself into all available activities and societies. But the war

---

[124]Brittain, *Testament of Youth*, p. 28.

had begun even before she began – and as her fiancé and brother and their friends enlisted, she felt more and more isolated until she too left in order to become a VAD.

As we have seen, engaging in the war effort enabled Brittain to demand and claim her sense of independence from her parents. At the same time, as Meg Albrinck argues, the denial and rejection of the behavioural standards and the feelings expected of women was confronting and sometimes terrifying for her. Even her fellow nurses were, she noted, baffled and appalled by her inability to mourn the loss of Roland in the way expected of a woman. They would have understood 'a sentimental, dependant sorrow', but were baffled by 'an aloof, rigid grief, which abhorred their sympathy, detested their collective gigglings and prattlings, and hated them most of all for being alive'.[125] But when she returned to college, Albrinck points out, her 'moment of gender ambiguity is terrifying' as she sees herself as having become an unnatural woman. She explains the transformation that she sees in the following way:

> I looked one evening into my bedroom glass and thought, with a sense of incommunicable horror, that I detected in my face the signs of some sinister and peculiar change. A dark shadow seemed to lie across my chin; was I beginning to grow a beard, like a witch? Thereafter my hand began, at regular intervals, to steal towards my face.

It is telling that Brittain accounts for the growing beard as the mark, not of a man, but of an unnatural woman – a witch.[126] Brittain sometimes sees herself as not fitting into a single gender, she argues, but as forming a connecting link between the women who have remained and the men who returned. This is an unstable, liminal and sinister position.

This sense of neither belonging nor of being quite whole pervades the final stages of Brittain's autobiography. It underlies her sense of one part of herself as being locked into the war and the world of those she has loved and lost, her finest world. To move beyond this is to betray it – and to compromise and accept second best. But for Brittain, there is also always the unresolved gender question and the conflicting sense that what is most important for her and makes the core of her identity is her sense of independence and her need for work – but there is also a need for acknowledgement from others and marriage and family.

There is a marked difference between the extended discussion of their own subjectivity and development of a sense of self in the autobiographies of middle-class women like Webb, Brittain, Swanwick, and the apparent lack of such a sense in the autobiographies of working-class women. One

---

[125]Meg Albrinck, 'Borderline Women: Gender Confusion in Vera Brittain's and Evadne Price's War Narratives', *Narrative* 6, no. 3 (1998): 283; Brittain, *Testament of Youth*, p. 247.
[126]Albrinck, 'Borderline Women', p. 284.

notable feature of Annie Kenney's *Memoirs*, for example, is her almost complete self-effacement. The story that she tells is primarily the story of her devotion to Christabel Pankhurst. There is a clear sense of a strong independent girl in the early chapters, dealing with family and community, with her early interest in labour questions and her involvement in a choir and with her fellow workers. But as she noted, once she met Christabel Pankhurst, 'all the old relationships slipped away'. She was, she noted 'one of the active, impulsive, intuitive temperaments of the world'. Hence,

> I naturally was drawn to a personality like that of Christabel Pankhurst. If I have faith in a person, no arguments, no persuasion, nothing outside can shake my faith. I had faith in Christabel. It was exactly the faith of a child – it knows but it cannot explain.[127]

Kenney's primary concern in her *Memoirs* is to tell the story of the militant campaign as she saw and understood it. For her, Christabel Pankhurst was the only person who could win the vote and she gave her complete and undivided loyalty. She accepted absolutely that a revolution of the kind the suffragettes were concerned to make required autocratic leadership, and that Christabel brooked neither opposition nor even questions. Although it often hurt her, as she was fond of some of those ejected by the Pankhursts, what she describes is her absolute adherence to them and their vision. Kenney was aware that others in the WSPU called her 'Christabel's blotting paper', but insists that this label neither flattered nor depressed her: 'I knew that blotters were useful things, and I had no ambition but to be of use to the only one that I believed could win the Vote.'[128] Kenney seems not to recognize the other point that emerges from her account: her immense talents as an organizer and a public speaker, the level of responsibility and potential of power that she had in the WSPU, especially in the years between 1911 and the outbreak of war. She was clearly a woman of great charm and persuasive power. She was one of the people who converted Constant Lytton to the militant cause and who drew the Pethick-Lawrences into it. Many others in the militant movement noted their deep affection for and trust in her. She was called on by Christabel to deal with formidable opponents like the press baron, Lord Northcliff, and William Hughes, the Australian prime minister. Kenney notes how she managed to get these men to meet with her and how nice they were to her – but she has no sense of the combination of charm and persistence that made this happen. Later historians have noted her immense abilities and importance as a strategist and as an administrator, but she never suggests these things about herself.

---

[127]Kenney, *Memoirs of a Militant*, p. 2.
[128]Kenney, *Memoirs of a Militant*, p. 193.

Kenney's lack of recognition of her own subjectivity is, Regina Gagnier insists, a characteristic feature of much working-class autobiography. The life course and the experiences of working-class writers did not produce the kind of subjectivity to find it comfortable to write about the development of the self. By contrast with the predominantly middle-class autobiographies that assume the uniqueness of their authors, most working-class autobiography begins by indicating how ordinary the lives that are being depicted are and how similar to those around them. They come slowly to differentiate themselves in some particular way as a result of some specific attribute or activity. In Kenney's case, this lack of a clear sense of herself is underlined by the way that her reminiscences end when she ceased to work for Christabel, ignoring entirely her subsequent marriage or the birth of her child and mentioning only in passing her taking up Theosophy and becoming a Rosicrucian. Her active political life ended at the point that she ceased working for Christabel Pankhurst – and the rest did not seem worthy of attention.

Kathleen Woodward's *Jipping Street* is another autobiographical work in which the author seems to lack a clear sense of self. While Woodward had considerable psychological insight into the nature of her relationship with her mother and understood well how her indissoluble ties to her mother gave her a strong desire for some other form of more sympathetic and nurturing maternal love that was satisfied to some extent by the affection she was offered her by the other women who serve as a contrast with her mother. She depicts clearly the gentle figure of Jessica Mourn, silent and loving and accepting of every pain; the laughing, careless Lil, whose love of life ends abruptly as she dies in childbirth; the supportive figure of Marian Evelyn, who introduces Woodward to women's suffrage, to the trade union movement, to night school and to the possibilities that exist of a life beyond Jipping Street. But Woodward's autobiography is not primarily concerned with explicating and showing the development of its author. Her work is not a chronological account of her life, but rather a series of sketches of other people and particular events. It is through her depictions of these others that Woodward illustrates her own life, underlining the poverty of her home, the hardship of her childhood, her early factory employment and the independence it allowed, and her move beyond this as she became involved in political debate and sought to educate herself through the books that opened to her the possibilities of another kind of life. She too serves as an illustration of Regina Gagnier's insistence on the absence from working-class autobiography of the subjectivity that is often taken as standard but is a product of a middle-class life and education.

Conclusion

The many changes evident in women's autobiography in the interwar period reflected wider changes in the status of women, many of whom became citizens in this period. Their political citizenship was hard fought, and, in many cases, it was accompanied by a battle for personal freedom and independence from family and from conventional expectations of womanhood. It also gave some women a new sense of their involvement in major historical developments, and conversely of the historical significance of their own lives. This sense extended beyond those women who had been involved in the suffrage campaign and the war effort and can be seen also in the autobiographies of many who had no direct connection with them – including working-class women who saw the writing of their lives as a way to make the wider society aware of their lives and circumstances.

The writing of one's autobiography as history was but one of the changes that can be seen in the interwar period. There were others that were equally important, including the ending of Victorian taboos on discussing intimate aspects of adult life and relationships. Women who had been born and grown up in the 19th century remained fixed within this framework of Victorian reticence when it came to dealing with intimate life. But younger women did not and in their work one begins to see the discussion of sexuality, including their battle to gain sexual knowledge, the traumatic sexual experiences some had in childhood, the difficulties of negotiating sexual relationships and their way of coping with unhappy married lives.

The framing of lives, including the stress on the importance of childhood that had emerged in the 19th century, continued in the interwar period. But new models and new issues also came to the fore. The realist novel that was so important in shaping lives for Victorian women, was giving way to new ideas and new discourses about the inner life and personal development. Although few autobiographies written in this period suggest an extensive or detailed study or understanding of psychology or psychoanalysis, the popularization of some of their concepts and of their language provided new ways for thinking about the relationships between a young girl and her parents and indeed about herself and some of her own ideas and approaches. This knowledge and interest in psychology was evident in some working-class as well as middle-class women, in their discussions of their family lives and childhood pain in dealing with harsh and unloving parents.

Autobiographies Referred to in This Chapter

Bloom, Ursula. *Without Make-Up*. London: Michael Joseph, 1938.
Bowen, Stella. *Drawn from Life*. Collins, 1940.
Brittain, Vera. *Testament of Youth: An Autobiographical Study of The Years 1900–1025*. London: Virago, 1933, republished 1978.
Campbell, Margaret (pseud Marjorie Bowen). *The Debate Continues, Being the Autobiography of Marjorie Bowen*. Heinemann, 1939.
Fawcett, Millicent Garrett. *What I Remember*. London: T. Fisher Unwin Ltd, 1925.
Jermy, Louise. *The Memories of a Working Woman*. Norwich: Goose & Son, 1934.
Kenney, Annie. *Memoirs of a Militant*. London: Edward Arnold, 1924.
Lytton, Lady Constance. *Prisons and Prisoners: Some Personal Experiences*. London: Virago Press, 1914, repr 1988.
Mannin, Ethel. *Confessions and Impressions*. London: Jarrolds, 1930.
Pankhurst, Emmeline. *My Own Story*. New York: Source Book Press, 1914, repr 1970. www.gutenberg.org/files/34856/34856-h/34856-h.htm.
Pethick-Lawrence, Emmeline. *My Part in a Changing World*. London: Victor Gollancz, 1938.
Rhondda, Viscountess. *This Was My World*. London: Macmillan and Co., Ltd, 1933.
Sharp, Evelyn. *Unfinished Adventure: Selected Reminiscences from an Englishwoman's Life*. London: John Lane, 1933.
Swanwick, H. M. *I Have Been Young*. London: Victor Gollancz Ltd, 1935.
Webb, Beatrice. *My Apprenticeship*. London: Longmans, Green and Co., 1926.
Woodward, Kathleen. *Jipping Street*. London: Virago, 1928, repr 1976.

FIGURE 4 *British novelist Doris Lessing in her north London flat, March 2003. (Photo by John Downing/Getty Images.)*

CHAPTER FOUR

The Personal is Political

The decades from the 1970s until the end of the 20th century are often referred to as a boom period in women's autobiography. This boom was evident in the increasing numbers of autobiographies that appeared, written by a much wider range of women and offering quite new stories.[1] Novelists contributed significantly to this number. In marked contrast with the 19th century, during which not a single leading woman novelist wrote an autobiography, by the late 20th century, there were few who did not. They included popular novelists like Catherine Cookson, along with writers of literary fiction like Naomi Mitchison, Storm Jameson and Doris Lessing. Increasing numbers of working-class women, who had been poorly represented in autobiography prior to this point, now wrote their life stories too, detailing their daily lives and often difficult circumstances. Several of these autobiographies were widely read and reviewed both in major literary journals like the *Times Literary Supplement* and in more popular venues. This was the case not only for Kathleen Dayus's award-winning *Her People: Memoirs of an Edwardian Childhood*, for example, but also for Margaret Powell, whose *Below Stairs* has been seen as the inspiration for the popular television series *Upstairs Downstairs*, and Rosina Harrison, whose *My Life in Service* offered unique insights into the life of her long-term employer, Nancy Astor.[2] Other groups of women who had rarely figured in autobiography prior to this point were academics from different disciplines, especially history and sociology, who also became very prominent as writers of autobiography and memoir.

---

[1] There is a short list of these works in Kate Douglas, 'British Women's Autobiography', in *Encyclopaedia of Women's Autobiography*, eds Victoria Boynton and Jo Malin (Greenwood Press: Westport, CT, 2005), p. 123.
[2] Dayus won the J. R. Ackerley Prize for Autobiography in 1982.

There were a number of major social, political and intellectual developments in the post-war period that encouraged or provided an impetus for the writing of women's autobiography, especially from women who did not come from the literary circles in which the writing of memoir was becoming a norm. The war itself was important here. Unlike the First World War, which stimulated the writing of autobiography because it involved women directly in a major national crisis for the first time, the Second World War saw the development of a new interest in the daily lives and experiences of 'ordinary' women who were being encouraged by a range of organizations to record and write about them. The most important organization here was Mass Observation. Formed in 1937 by Charles Madge and Tom Harrison, Mass Observation was a research hub with a particular interest in collecting details about daily life. A major purpose of this research was to gauge the views and values of the majority of the British public, with a view to making them more engaged and active citizens. The outbreak of the Second World War brought a new urgency to this task and led to the recruitment of vast numbers of volunteers who were asked to provide detailed accounts of various aspects of their daily life throughout the war. Sometimes they were sent specific questions to answer or directives about what to discuss, but many also wrote regularly in a more general and informal way about themselves and their lives. The Mass Observation directives and encouragement of diary writing emphasized the importance of the quotidian and led to reflection on every aspect of a person's life and sense of self.[3] The subjective element in this writing and the personal revelation in some of it clearly displays autobiographical elements, Dorothy Sheridan argues, it led on to more autobiographical work.[4] Some of the reports and diaries written for Mass Observation have been published as if they were a form of autobiography, while others who wrote for Mass Observation, like Naomi Mitchison, moved from this form of writing to their own autobiographies.

There were other new organizations that also encouraged people who did not see themselves as part of an educated literary elite to write. As Chris Hilliard and others have shown, even prior to the outbreak of war, one can see a 'democratisation of literature' in the growing numbers of working-class and lower-middle-class men and women with limited formal education who sought to write and publish their own work.[5] They formed or joined writing circles and clubs with others who shared their interests and in which the members encouraged each other to write. Some of them sought and found ways to publish their work in left-leaning journals or through radical publishers. These writing groups continued and expanded around the

---

[3] James Hinton, *Nine Wartime Lives: Mass Observation and the Making of the Modern Self* (Oxford: Oxford University Press, 2010).
[4] Dorothy Sheridan, 'Writing to the Archive: Mass-Observation as Autobiography', *Sociology* 27, no. 1 (1993): 27–40.
[5] Christopher Hilliard, *To Exercise Our Talents: The Democratization of Writing in Britain* (Cambridge, MA: Harvard University Press, 2006)

country after the war, often meeting in local libraries and continuing to provide a supportive framework for aspiring writers. Catherine Cookson was a founder member of one that was established in Hastings and continues to flourish. Cookson found it essential in the writing of her early novels and her autobiography. Adult education discussion groups all over Britain also encouraged women to write their autobiographies and memoirs.

The re-emergence of feminism in the late 1960s and '70s served as another important stimulus to women's autobiography. Here too, an important element was the new emphasis on women's daily lives and experiences. The extensive discussion of the problems and difficulties faced by women that became prominent in the press and in society generally at this time encouraged women to talk about matters that they had long been taught to shroud in silence. Bodily experiences once regarded as shameful and something that should never be discussed, including menstruation, sexuality, childbirth and domestic violence all became things to talk and write about. The emergence of 'consciousness-raising', a group activity in which women sought to explore the ways in which they experienced subordination and oppression in their own daily lives, as daughters, housewives, mothers, lovers or girl-friends encouraged women to reflect on their own lives and to articulate their own stories. Feminist theory offered a useful framework for articulating issues of power and subordination and for explaining how differently women saw, experienced and wrote about their lives from men. Autobiographical writing, Lynda Anderson suggests, 'encouraged as praxis as much as studied as texts – became allied with the idea of "finding a voice", of putting an identity into words or telling a life story which challenged the ready-made stereotypes of women within a patriarchal order'.[6]

As we will see, Feminism encouraged autobiographical writing in other ways too. In seeking out women's stories, younger feminists turned to an older generation of women who had been actively engaged in feminist campaigns earlier in the century, including marriage reform and the advocacy of birth control, encouraging them to write their life stories. The interest taken in their lives by younger women was particularly important to women like Naomi Mitchison and Dora Russell, who wrote their autobiographies in the 1970s when they were already in their eighties. The energy in the feminism of the 1970s can also be seen in the emergence of the feminist publishers who played a crucial role in the development of women's autobiography. Both Virago and the Women's Press are important here: Virago republished the work of earlier women writers and encouraged contemporary women of many different ages to write their life stories, while the Women's Press published the life stories of women from the wider British world.

---

[6]Lynda Anderson, 'Life Lines: Auto/Biography and Memoir', in *The History of British Women's Writing, 1970–Present*, ed. Mary Eagleton and Emma Parker (Houndsmills, Basingstoke: Palgrave Macmillan, 2015), p. 183.

The emergence of feminism intersected with developments in academic disciplines to encourage the autobiographical writing of women academics. The decline of Marxism and the emergence of postcolonialism at much the same time as the re-emergence of feminism led to a questioning of once widely held views about the nature of social development and historical progress. The general patterns, or what some had seen as 'laws' of social development were shown increasingly to be limited and partial, depicting a world as seen by privileged western men, but ignoring entirely the very different historical experiences of women and of entire populations who had been subjected to imperial control. Individual life stories came to be seen in many disciplines, especially history and sociology, as a way to understand different perspectives and different experiences. They came to be seen as providing the most effective way of showing how different economic and political forces and forms of oppression, including colonialism, racism and gender, impacted on those who were subjected to them. Many women academics concerned to explore questions about class or gender or sexuality came to see that reflecting on their own experiences and their own stories, using the tools and methods of their discipline as well as other theoretical insights, offered new ways to understand their own lives while also offering insights into important general questions about the nature of history and memory, and of many social institutions.[7] It was in the work of these academic women that some of the most important innovations in women's autobiographical writing appeared.

The boom in women's autobiography involved not only more books, but also new ideas about how autobiography could be written. Traditional autobiographies continued to appear, but so did others that questioned and undermined these traditional approaches. The idea that an autobiography should encompass the whole life of the author from childhood to the time of writing was also rejected by many who chose to focus on specific episodes or aspects of their life which made their experiences more meaningful. Childhood seemed to many the most important part of their lives and the one that best explained the kind of person they became as an adult. Other episodes, however, such as emotional or intellectual crises, like a mental breakdown, or the ending of a marriage could also be the focus of special attention. In a similar way, some authors rejected the notion of writing a life as a linear narrative. They sought rather to offer perspectives from different chronological points in their lives, describing the process of looking back on their earlier lives in ways that combined a sense of themselves in the present with their reconstruction or interpretation of their younger selves. Rejecting any attempt at narrative, some of these women chose to write their lives in the form of themed essays. Other forms of writing, including fiction and

---

[7]Diana P. Freedman and Olivia Frey, eds, *Autobiographical Writing Across the Disciplines: A Reader* (Duke University Press, Durham, NC, 2004).

myth that emphasized the importance or inner meaning of particular experiences or episodes in the life of the author, were included in some autobiographies, alongside narrative sections. The importance of factual truth or details was questioned by authors who stressed the importance of feelings and beliefs and the significance of stories they had been told as children that framed their sense of identity, whether or not they were true.

Both individual development and family life came to be seen and understood in different ways by some authors, as they sought to understand the parent-child relationships and the family dynamics that had dominated their lives. One can see clearly here the increasing recognition of psychoanalysis and of a range of different forms of psychology and psychotherapy. The first translation of Freud's complete works into English was undertaken between 1943 and 1974, years in which, alongside considerable very public divisions within the psychoanalytic community in Britain, psychoanalytic practice flourished, and terms and concepts derived from it became widely accepted and disseminated. This increased psychological awareness is evident in the ways in which many women described their writing of autobiography as therapeutic, seeing it as a way to deal with a traumatic past and to gain a clearer sense of themselves. One can see it also in the ways that women wrote about themselves, especially about their own sense of identity and sometimes their sexuality, but also in the ways in which they discussed their parents, particularly their mothers and the importance of their early relationships with them. Psychoanalytic insights also frame many discussions of memory in women's autobiographies and can be seen in their most extensive form in the suggestion of authors, like Carolyn Steedman, that their autobiographies might be seen as a form of psychoanalytic case study.

Producing an Autobiography

There is some continuity alongside much change in the production of autobiographies in this period. The continuity is evident amongst established novelists, most of whom followed familiar writing practices in the ways they wrote their autobiographies and sent them to their regular publishers. Those women who had not written before, by contrast, illustrate some of the new developments in writing and publishing. They were often assisted by recently formed writers' groups, for example, or by particular mentors and publishers eager to expand their range of women's autobiographies. Several were also assisted by the new feminist publishers seeking to make women's voices more prominent in the world of books.

There were changes too in the reasons cited by women for writing an autobiography. The importance of the author's achievements and their connection with major historical developments, which had been so important before, was much less evident. Doris Lessing was one of the very few to cite her standing and prominence as a reason for writing an autobiography, but as we will see, even she added others. Lessing was unquestionably the most prominent novelist to write an autobiography at this time and suggested that it was this very prominence that made her undertake it.[8] Writing her life, she insisted, was 'a form of self-defence', as five others were apparently working on her biography, some without even contacting her and hence with no real knowledge or understanding of her life.[9] Few of these planned biographies actually appeared, however, and some critics have suggested that Lessing decided to write an autobiography as a way to bring herself back into the limelight after she had passed the peak of her appeal.[10]

This reference to her own prominence was unusual, however, and other writers often suggested more intimate reasons for writing their lives. In dedicating her autobiography to 'granddaughters who ask questions', for example, Naomi Mitchison suggested that family interest in her story was a major reason for writing it. In a similar way, Kathleen Dayus who also dedicated her autobiography to her granddaughter, Christina Rainey, made it clear that her book was a response to the questions about her life that her granddaughter asked. It was not only family interest, but the trauma of family life that was cited by others as a reason for writing their lives. Catherine Cookson, for example, saw the writing of her autobiography as therapeutic and something that would help her recover from a serious breakdown and come to terms with her terrible familial past, especially her illegitimacy and her violent and painful relationship with her mother. The therapeutic value of writing an autobiography was suggested to Janet Frame by her psychiatrist who thought it could help her come to terms with the horror of the lengthy incarceration in a mental hospital she had endured as the result of a false diagnosis of schizophrenia. The Nigerian-born author Buchi Emecheta, like Doris Lessing, thought writing an autobiography might help her to come to terms with her painful relationship with her mother.

If Lessing refused to recognize that interest in her other writings was waning before she turned to autobiography, others were much more willing to accept that it was happening to them. Once widely read and well-reviewed novelists, both Storm Jameson and Naomi Mitchison were very much aware that their literary reputations had peaked long before they decided to write their autobiographies. Born in the 1890s, they were at their most prominent as authors in the 1930s, the decade in which Mitchison produced her major historical novels and Jameson hers dealing powerfully with contemporary life and society.[11] By the 1960s and '70s, Mitchison was writing very little,

---

[8]The award of the 2007 Noble Prize to Lessing indicates her international stature as a novelist.
[9]Doris Lessing, *Under My Skin: Volume One of My Autobiography to 1949* (London: Harper Perennial, 1994), p. 14.
[10]Susan Watkins, *Doris Lessing* (Manchester: Manchester University Press, 2010), William Pritchard, 'Looking Back at Lessing', *Hudson Review* 48, no. 2 (1995): 317–324.
[11]Maroula Joannou, ed. *Women Writers of the 1930s: Gender, Politics, History* (Edinburgh: The Edinburgh University Press, 1999).

and Jameson's novels were rarely well-reviewed. In the course of the 1960s, Jameson noted in her diary that she was forced to recognize 'my own invisibility' when, even while she was chairing a dinner of the Pen Club, she was not included by the speaker amongst the distinguished women writers present.[12] Jameson was anxious about writing an autobiography and sought feedback and advice from many friends. Her two-volume autobiography, *Journey from the North*, was extremely well received, however.[13] In part, this reception reflected Jameson's concern to produce a new kind of autobiography, one which included reflections on the problems involved in writing such a work within the text, resonated with her readers. 'It is not possible, in a personal memoir, to be truthful', she wrote to a close friend. 'That's one thing I learned as I went on. One tells the truth, but all the time there is a contradictory or different-in-some way truth being ignored.'[14] She was determined to try and offer an intimate and very critical self-portrait, however discomforting her readers might find it.

> Nothing would have been easier for me than to write one of those charming poetic memoirs which offend no one and leave a pleasant impression of the author. I am trying to do something entirely different. Trying in short to eat away a double illusion: the face I show other people and the illusion I have of myself – by which I live. Can I?[15]

In her endeavour to remove this 'double illusion' and offer a truer version of herself, Jameson interrogated her early memories, her dreams and her sense of time, attempting to gather together the bits that somehow made her own sense of herself. Her harsh self-criticism and her presentation of her failings, evident particularly in her inability to feel as much as she felt she should, her dislike of domesticity, her behaviour during her first marriage and her sense of inadequacy as a mother, were seen as offering a new frankness in autobiography and an unusually revealing insight into her own psychology. Each volume got a separate and positive review in the *Times Literary Supplement* in which the contrast between the first volume, focusing largely on her private life, and the second, dealing with her public life, especially her work with refugees in the late 1930s and '40s, the period when she was president of the Pen Club, was noted. So too was the general way in which Jameson linked her own life with the major political developments of the mid-20th century. The review of the first volume praised her honesty in describing her agonizing sense of guilt over having to leave her son in Whitby

---

[12]Margaret Storm Jameson, *Journey from the North*, vol. II (London: Virago, 1984).
[13]Jennifer Birkett, *Margaret Storm Jameson: A Life* (Oxford: Oxford University Press, 2009), p. 328.
[14]Elizabeth Maslen, *Life in the Writings of Storm Jameson: A Biography* (Evaston, IL: Northwestern University Press, 2014), chapter 28.
[15]Jameson, *Journey from the North*, vol. I, p. 16.

in order to work in London and linked the lengthy confession of this continuing anguish with her own intense and difficult relationship with her mother.[16]

Naomi Mitchison, a contemporary and a friend of Jameson's, also offered something new in her autobiographical works. She too raised questions about how it was possible to write an autobiography, pondering the problem of memory and noting how selective and partial hers was. Sometimes she could supplement it with notebooks and diaries, she noted, but these had been written at the behest of her mother and read by others. They were intended to sharpen her skills at observation and said nothing about her feelings. What worried her most was how hard it was to think her way back to the earlier stages of her life: she noted how much clearer her memory of her childhood was than that of her teenage years. How could a woman of mature years still know and understand her younger self, she asked, or explain her own behaviour when she could no longer understand it? Why, for example, had she so often told her mother things it would have been better to keep secret? How could she deal with the person who did that and who seemed so alien to her now? Interrogating her memories was a complex process.[17]

> Looking back, it seems to me in the main that I only remember accurately and in detail times when there has been this tension of delight, of fear, of pain, of action, when I have been most clearly myself. Yet what is remembered is not the content of the tension, but the facts that aroused it, the people and places and smells. Why did some things trigger it off and some not? Psychologists would have different theories about this.[18]

Mitchison attempted to resolve this problem by writing about herself externally as it were, focusing on her behaviour and making clear as she described particular episodes in her life how hard it was to recall her feelings. She constantly commented as an adult on her childish and adolescent self. Her somewhat fragmented sense of herself, in contrast with her very clear recollection and knowledge of how her family had lived, led her to avoid any kind of linear narrative and to write short thematic or episodic pieces that dealt with particular matters of importance. Sometimes, as Helen Lloyd notes, she rejects 'the notion of a fixed temporal chronology to produce an almost scrap-book effect of people, events and impressions'. The period 1897 to 1940 is clearly covered, but the individual chapters are arranged by theme and subject: 'Becoming oneself', for example, or 'Real and not Real' or 'Boy into Girl', 'Books & Plays', 'Politics & People'.

---

[16]Anon, 'The need to be uprooted', *Times Literary Supplement*, 2 Oct. 1969, pp. 1125–1126.
[17]Mitchison, *All Change Here Girlhood and Marriage* (London: The Bodley Head, 1975), pp. 9–11.
[18]Mitchison, *All Change Here*, pp. 26–27.

In the process, Mitchison provided a very clear and detailed portrait of the upper-middle-class world in the first few decades of the 20th century, linking her depiction of herself closely to it.[19]

Coming as she did from a very distinguished and wealthy family against most of whose political and religious views and moral values she fought throughout her adult life, Mitchison included in her autobiographical writing a detailed picture of the society from which she came and extensive criticism of the prejudices of her mother and her class. She also wrote unusually frankly about some aspects of her own personal life including the sexual inadequacy of her marriage, her sexual radicalism and her belief in open marriage. At the same time, she worried about revealing things that had been secret. Hence while she was prepared to broach the sexual problems in her marriage and the decision to make it an open one, as her biographers point out, she drew back from detailing the very complex way in which her open marriage developed and its impact on her close friends.[20]

While Jameson and Mitchison sought to avoid making things that had been secret public, the impetus for the popular novelist Catherine Cookson was quite the reverse. Cookson experienced a severe nervous breakdown in 1945, after her third miscarriage. Unimpressed with the therapy she received, she read extensively in the general field of psychoanalysis and mental illness and came to feel ever more strongly that she would never fully recover from this breakdown until she was able to reveal the most shameful secrets of her life: her illegitimacy and the violent and drunken behaviour of her mother.[21] Cookson had already published several widely-read novels that dealt with the kind of impoverished family and community she had come from in the north of England and addressed the problematic family life that she had known including its drunkenness, violence and dysfunctional relationships. This fictional revelation was not sufficient, however, and she felt the need to write about these matters directly. She began writing the autobiography in the mid-1940s but could not complete or publish it until after her mother's death in 1957.

The therapeutic nature of Cookson's autobiography can be seen very clearly in the process of its composition. She wrote eight drafts, insisting that each one was more therapeutic as her bitterness towards her mother decreased. There is no question that she gained a greater sense of control as the drafts emerged.[22] Rather than offering a coherent narrative, the first draft consisted of a series of notes and descriptions of particularly painful episodes in her life. It begins with the heading FEAR...FEAR...FEAR, in

---

[19]Helen Lloyd, 'Witness to a Century the Autobiographical Writings of Naomi Mitchison' (University of Glasgow, 2005), p. 24.
[20]Jill Benton, *Naomi Mitchison: A Biography* (London: Pandora, 1992).
[21]Kathleen Jones, *Catherine Cookson: The Biography* (New York: Random House, 1999).
[22]Barbara Caine, 'The Making of Catherine Cookson's Autobiography', *Women's History Review* 22, no. 1 (2013).

large black capital letters, under which is a list of these fears presented in point form. Her opening statements: 'Fear of being different – fear of drink – of a woman drunk', and the subsequent one, 'Fear of loving in case I slipped and went the way of my mother', make very clear her constant preoccupation with her mother's drinking and her own illegitimacy.[23] Other fears are listed too, including her various physical ailments, her marriage, her desire to be a mother, her sense that a miscarriage was somehow equivalent to an abortion which, as a Catholic, she abhorred, and the religious difficulties she faced as a once devout Catholic just beginning to doubt the teachings of the church. By the second draft, she had decided that some of these fears should be excluded, ruling a line through them and indicating to her typist that they should be omitted. The whole issue of fear subsequently became a very minor issue, discussed towards the end of the book. As the fears diminished and her memories of her mother became calmer, she moved beyond the earlier episodic notes and began to write her story in a chronological way.[24] The final version, Cookson later suggested, made her mother softer and kinder than she really was, as she forced herself to write with pity and compassion about one who had damaged and hurt her deeply, but whose own life had been extremely hard. Writing in this way, Cookson insisted, freed her of what she had seen as a ruinous hate.[25]

By the time Cookson's autobiography was published in 1969 she was a very successful novelist, with twenty-six books to her name and some notable awards.[26] There is no mention of her literary success in the autobiography, however, which emphasizes, rather, how hard it was to establish herself as a writer. She had always wanted to write and completed her first novel in her teens. Her very limited education, however, meant that she lacked both elementary grammar and the self-confidence that she needed to do so. Extensive efforts at self-education made up for the former, while the latter was provided by a local writers group. Cookson had moved from Jarrow in the north of England to Hastings in the south, partly in order to escape her family. In 1947 she became a founder member of the Hasting's Writers group where she first tried out the story 'She had no da', that dealt with an illegitimate child and served to tell her own story in a fictionalized form. The warmth of the response she received from the group encouraged her writing generally and her attempt at autobiography in particular.

The idea of writing an autobiography as a therapeutic exercise was central also for the New Zealand author Janet Frame. Indeed, the very idea that she should do it was first suggested to her by Robert Cawley, the very

---

[23]Cookson, 'Autobiography 1958', Cookson Collection, Gottlieb Archive, Boston University, Box 30.
[24]Caine, 'The Making of Catherine Cookson's Autobiography', pp. 10–11.
[25]Jones, *Catherine Cookson: The Biography*, pp. 235–238.
[26]Catherine Ann Cookson, *Our Kate: Her Personal Story* (London: Macdonald, 1969, repr. 1973, 1969).

sympathetic and supportive psychiatrist whom she worked with in London and to whom she dedicated one volume of her work. Frame had been misdiagnosed as a schizophrenic when she was a university student and was subsequently incarcerated in brutal psychiatric hospitals in New Zealand for some eight years. Convinced by living amongst people who *were* schizophrenic that she was not, Frame had taken herself to the Maudsley hospital when she was living in London seeking to have the diagnosis investigated. Tests done at the Maudsley showed conclusively that she had never suffered from schizophrenia. In the view of her medical team, it was what she had endured in the terrible years in hospital from which she needed to recover. Cawley suggested she write her story of the hospital years to give her a clearer sense of herself and her future.[27] She followed this suggestion, although initially in the form of a novel, *Faces in the Water*. The fiction of the book, she later noted, 'lies in the portrayal of the central character, based on my life but given largely fictional thoughts and feelings, to create a picture of the sickness I saw around me'.[28] In the late 1970s, when Frame decided to return to New Zealand, Cawley again suggested that she write about her life, possibly through a series of essays, that might be followed by comments taken from documents in his possession. He saw this work both as an occupation for her and as a way to clear away any misunderstandings about her 'illness' that still haunted her.[29] In February 1980, having established a comfortable home in New Zealand, Frame did indeed begin to write her autobiography, but in a form quite unlike that suggested by Cawley.[30]

One can see something of the growing importance of autobiography at this time in the way that Frame's autobiography, rather than her novel, established her literary reputation. Although she had published critically acclaimed novels and short stories, she was very much a minor author in the 1970s. The publication of her autobiography established both Frame's dominant place in New Zealand literature and her standing as one of the great writers of the 20th century. Released in three separate volumes by the Women's Press in the UK and Hutchinson in New Zealand, it met with immediate acclaim, not only in those countries but also in the United States. Its depiction of her hard early life, the appalling years of incarceration in mental hospitals, her recovery and her courageous taking up of her life moved readers everywhere. Michael Holroyd described it as 'one of the greatest autobiographies written this century', and Patrick White declared it as 'among the wonders of the world'.[31] As the book was being published, Frame talked at many literary festivals and won prestigious awards including

---

[27]Michael King, *Wrestling with the Angel. A Life of Janet Frame* (Sydney: Pcador, 2000), pp. 204–207.
[28]Janet Frame, *An Angel at My Table* (London: Virago, 1989), p. 262.
[29]King, *Wrestling with the Angel*, p. 429.
[30]King, *Wrestling with the Angel*, p. 433.
[31]King, *Wrestling with the Angel*, p. 470.

the Commonwealth Writer's Prize. Her story attracted the attention of the New Zealand filmmaker Jane Campion, who eventually persuaded Frame to help her produce the award-winning film of her life, *An Angel at my Table*. The three separate volumes were subsequently combined into a single publication with the same title as the film.[32]

Although she had not suffered a breakdown or been in any major form of therapy, the Nigerian novelist Buchi Emecheta too saw the writing of her autobiography as therapeutic. It helped her to answer questions that had been nagging at her for a long time, particularly her tendency to trust the men around her more than the women – something that she came to see as linked to her mother, especially to her mother's lack of understanding of her desire for education and for a life outside the accepted limits of her tribe. Writing the autobiography helped her to forgive both herself and her mother.[33] Emecheta began writing her autobiography in the early 1980s, less than ten years after the publication of her first book, *In the Ditch*, and when she was just beginning to be recognized as a significant novelist in Britain.[34] In the autobiography, she also suggests that one impetus for it was her desire to record how hard and unremitting her struggle to make a life for herself in London with five small children had been. Emecheta had published ten novels, all of which dealt with aspects of her heritage and her experience of migration.[35] She wanted now 'to stop looking back into the past of too long ago'. She wanted in her autobiography to write about 'me in the almost now: the last twenty years during which time I made England's North London my home'.[36] The autobiography allowed Emecheta not only to detail her struggle but to stress her absolute determination to make a success of her life. She included extensive discussion of the immense difficulties she had faced as a young Black woman in dealing with and being accepted by the British literary and publishing establishment. At the time when she was completing the autobiography, she was just beginning to earn enough to support herself and her family through her writing. It was a precarious existence, she wrote at the end of the book, but she could just keep her head above water.

While all the established authors drew on existing connections with publishers in order to produce their autobiographies, this resource was not available to the growing numbers of working-class women who now wished to write their lives. Most of these women depended on intermediaries: individuals with contacts or writing and reading groups connected to small

---

[32] Frame's combined autobiography, *An Angel at My Table*, was initially published by Hutchinson in Auckland and the Women's Press in London in 1989. It was subsequently republished as a Virago Classic with an Introduction by Jane Campion in 2008.
[33] Buchi Emecheta, *Head Above Water* (London and Nigeria: Heinemann, 1986), pp. 3–4.
[34] Buchi Emecheta, *In the Ditch* (London: Allison and Busby, 1972).
[35] Buchi Emecheta, *Second Class Citizen* (London: Allison and Busby, 1974).
[36] Emecheta, *Head Above Water*, p. 2.

publishers. This role of intermediary was also taken on, somewhat unexpectedly, by the BBC. It provided the stimulus and the support that made possible the publication of Margaret Powell's *Below Stairs*, for example, a very popular autobiography that appeared in 1968, the year before the publication of Cookson's *Our Kate*. Like Cookson, Powell had left school at the age of thirteen and gone into domestic service. After some years in service, she married and had three sons. In an attempt to keep up with the sons as they went through their grammar school education in the 1960s, she enrolled in evening classes. At one of these classes on debating, she was spotted by a BBC producer, Leigh Crutchley, and invited to talk about her life in service on the radio series he produced, *It Takes All Sorts*.

The BBC archive records some twelve interviews between Crutchley and Margaret Powell, covering a range of topics including her educational progress and how it felt to be taking exams and trying to keep up with her sons between 1964 and 1968.[37] The talks led directly to her writing her autobiography: after hearing one, the publisher Peter Davies approached Powell and persuaded her to write about her experiences. Although there are no documents to indicate the precise nature of their collaboration, Crutchley seems to have written the book with her. It is dedicated to him 'with gratitude and affection', and his name appears on the title page as a joint holder of the copyright.[38] The BBC also helped with publicity, broadcasting a talk between Powell and Antonia Fraser shortly after it came out. Powell's book sold well. Peter Davies issued it in 1968, but it was republished by Pan Books in 1970 and then again in 2012.

The BBC and Leigh Crutchley were involved in the publication of other working-class women's autobiographies too. Rosina Harrison, for example, talked to Crutchley about her life in service to Nancy Astor a few years after Powell had described hers and he helped her to turn it into a book. Here too, the precise nature of the collaboration is not clear, but the dedication, 'To Leigh "Reggie" Crutchley who made it possible' suggests that his was an important role.[39] The BBC also published Rose Gamble's account of her impoverished working-class childhood, *Chelsea Child*, after she had described it on radio, although Crutchley does not seem to have been as closely involved in this work.[40]

Sometimes the intermediaries who facilitated the publication of the memoirs of otherwise unpublished women were enterprising family members. Kathleen Dayus, for example, wrote her story at the request of her granddaughter. She wrote it in an exercise book in 1970 and put it away for

---

[37] BBC Archive, Margaret Powell, A/132 11–63, A106506 and A/132 11–64 9965. Powell also published a menu and discussion of it in a BBC volume called *Come for a Meal*.
[38] Margaret Powell, *Below Stairs* (London: Pan Books, 1968 (Pan 1970)).
[39] Rosina Harrison with Leigh Crutchley, *My Life in Service* (New york: Viking Press, 1975). Crutchley was joint copyright holder.
[40] Rose Gamble, *Chelsea Child* (London: British Broadcasting Corporation, 1979).

several years until her granddaughter asked to read it.[41] This granddaughter took the hand-written story to her teacher who was impressed by it and passed it on to her husband, John Rudd, a local historian who thought this story of an impoverished Birmingham childhood worth publishing. It was he who contacted Virago Press, who published the book in 1982. Dayus's *Her People* appeared, as Sharon Ouditt has pointed out, just at the point when Virago was publishing 'what was to become a game-changing list of books', giving voice to working-class women and their history in a quite new way.[42] It was published also in the year that the Pen Ackerley Prize 'for a literary autobiography of excellence' was established and was a joint winner of that prize.

As this last example suggests, the resurgence of feminism and the establishment of new feminist publishers was a major factor in the production of women's autobiography. Virago, the first and most successful of these feminist publishers, and the only one still in existence, paid a great deal of attention to women's autobiography. They republished earlier women's autobiographies, as well as encouraging contemporary ones. Some years prior to the appearance of Dayus's work, for example, Virago had published Dora Russell's autobiography, *The Tamarisk Tree*, as well as republishing Vera Brittain's *Testament of Youth* and her *Testament to Friendship*, the account of her relationship with the novelist Winifred Holtby. Shortly after Dayus's book appeared, they republished Kathleen Woodward's *Jipping Street* and Storm Jameson's *Journey from the North* as well as the autobiographies of other little-known working-class women like Grace Foakes, whose *Four Meals for Fourpence* appeared in 2011.

Virago was also proactive in encouraging contemporary women to write their own life stories, sometimes in quite new ways. In the early years of the press, for example, one of its founders, Ursula Owen, brought together a collection of autobiographical writings called *Fathers: Reflections by Daughters*. Much had been written about fathers and fathering, she argued, but there had rarely been an attempt to 'gain information from the receiving end of this embattled and intense relationship. What do daughters feel about their fathers?'[43] This collection was followed by several other Virago anthologies: *Truth, Dare, Promise*, edited by Liz Heron in 1985, focused on women's recollections of their childhood, for example, while Sara Maitland's *Very Heaven: Looking back at the 1960s* looked at women's stories of society beyond the immediate family.[44] Some of Virago's early publications

---

[41]Kathleen Dayus, *Her People: Memoirs of an Edwardian Childhood* (London: Virago, 1982).
[42]Sharon Ouditt, 'Kathleen Dayus: The Girl from Hockley', in *A History of British Working Class Literature*, ed. John and Bridget Keegan Goodridge (Cambridge: Cambridge University Press, 2017).
[43]Ursula Owen, ed. *Fathers: Reflections by Daughters* (London: Virago, 1983), p. x.
[44]Liz Heron, ed., *Truth, Dare or Promise* (London: Virago, 1985); Sara Maitland, *Very Heaven: Looking back at the 1960s* (London: Virago, 1988).

of autobiographies and memoirs drew in academics and writers who subsequently went on to write their own life stories. The historian Carolyn Steedman's interest in working-class subjectivity and writing made her an obvious person to write the introduction to Kathleen Woodward's *Jipping Street* when Virago republished it in 1983. In this introduction, Steedman made very clear her own sense of connection, as one who had grown up in a working-class family and felt, as Woodward did, that she was a burden to her mother. As Steedman later wrote, Carmen Callil, another of the founders of Virago, 'saw from reading the introduction to . . . Jipping Street that there was much more to say' and encouraged Steedman to go on writing about herself.[45] A couple of years later, Steedman included a piece on her childhood in *Truth, Dare, Promise*. Ten years later in 1986, she published her own epoch-making autobiographical story of her mother and herself, *Landscape for a Good Woman*, which Ursula Owen edited. Ursula Owen also persuaded Elizabeth Wilson, an academic already well known for her writing on style and popular culture but who grew up in a very eccentric family that was still deeply enmeshed in the works of the Raj, to write her unusual and innovative autobiography, *Mirror Writing*.

Wilson and Steedman were only two of the feminist academics who became involved in writing autobiography in the 1980s and '90s.[46] They reflect significant changes in academic approaches and ideas. As I have already said, one of these was the growing recognition amongst those involved in the humanities and social sciences that the large-scale interpretive frameworks and narratives once seen as a way to understand both history and contemporary social life ignored the many different experiences of groups and individuals outside the mainstream, especially those of women. Another was the rejection of the impersonal and authoritative stance and voice that had long been accepted in academic writing, in favour of a much more reflective approach in which the author included her own standpoint, experiences and assumptions in her work, while at the same time seeing her own life as a case study for some of the issues being investigated. Those academic authors who sought to explore their own lives within the broad framework of their academic research, usually examined the importance to them of questions of gender and identity, drawing on a range of psychoanalytic and other social theories in their work. Sometimes, they used their own story to question or critique these theories. It is these works by academic women that offer some of the most important new ways to think about and write autobiography, as they interspersed personal narrative with other kinds of writing: fiction, historical analysis, reflective essays dealing with psychological, sociological or philosophical questions. Some also drew on poetry and myth to illustrate their stories, while others drew on art and

---

[45]Carolyn Steedman, *Landscape for a Good Woman* (London: Virago, 1986), Acknowledgements.
[46]Freedman and Frey, *Autobiographical Writing Across the Disciplines*.

especially photography. Steedman's work is particularly notable here, as is *Taking it Like a Woman*, the autobiography of the sociologist Ann Oakley.

Wilson's *Mirror Writing* was the first of these innovative academic autobiographies to appear, focusing primarily on her search for a sense of identity. It was followed shortly after by Ann Oakley's *Taking it Like a Woman* and Steedman's *Landscape for a Good Woman*. There were several others in the following decade, including that of the cultural historian Annette Kuhn whose *Family Secrets: Acts of memory and imagination*, made considerable use of photographs and images and Lorna Sage's award-winning *Bad Blood*, focusing entirely on her childhood and adolescence. These women were well aware of the unusual nature of their undertaking in integrating their lives with their academic disciplines, most of which had until this time eschewed any reference to individual experiences, let alone making them a primary focus. All of them, as Annette Kuhn argues, were producing 'revisionist autobiography', as they sought to negotiate the formal conventions of autobiography and to find new ways to write about the self that offer moments of insight within a broad interpretive structure.[47]

Mirror Writing is the only one of these works to use the term *Autobiography* as a subtitle. But as Wilson was well aware, hers was a very unusual kind of autobiography concerned not so much to tell her life story as to detail the ways in which she sought to establish a sense of her own identity. Her rejection of the standard form of autobiography and her focus on the struggle for identity are made clear from the very start. Rather than beginning with her childhood, the book begins with a description of radical demonstration in which she was involved in 1971. Her sense of living in the present in this demonstration is then contrasted with the extraordinary family and home from which she came, the existence of which she sought to deny in her attempt 'to pose as a normal teenager'.[48]

Ann Oakley, a feminist sociologist, was concerned not only to depict her own life but to use her life as a way to address the dilemmas of other contemporary women of a similar class and social background to her own. In order to do so, she produced a kind of hybrid that mixed together fiction, life narrative and essays, stating at the beginning that 'some of the characters in this book are real, and some aren't'.[49] Her first chapter offers a fictional scene, the first of several dealing with a middle-aged couple whose intense and highly charged extramarital affair ultimately could not withstand their other commitments or the demands of family life. Alongside these scenes, Oakley includes chapters titled 'Chronology' that provided a direct narrative of her life starting with the marriage of her parents and continuing up to the present. These chronologies include commentary on the many emotional

---

[47]Annette Kuhn, *Family Secrets: Acts of Memory and Imagination*, (London: Verso, 1995, 2nd edition), p. 5.
[48]Wilson, *Mirror Writing: An Autobiography* (London: Virago, 1982), p. 36.
[49]Oakley, *Taking It Like a Woman* (London: Jonathan Cape, 1984), author's note.

difficulties she has experienced from childhood, on her depression, on how hard she found the birth of her first child and on the challenge of bonding with him. Then there are the essays that focus on the family, entitled 'The War between Love and the Family' and making clear her sense both of the importance of the family and its oppressive force for women.

Writing a few years after Ann Oakley, Carolyn Steedman contrasts herself with her, rejecting Oakley's claim that she felt herself an outsider when young. Oakley may have felt excluded by particular groups, Steedman argues, but as a privileged middle-class woman, she was able to draw on all the resources of the dominant culture including the outlines of conventional romance to tell her story.[50] This was not something that the working-class Steedman felt able to do. Stories are central to her work too, however, but rather than creating her own fictional ones, she devotes her first chapter to a discussion of the stories she heard in childhood, pointing to the importance of such stories in how she understood her own life. These stories include ones her mother had told her about her childhood and early youth and about their current life. It is in telling these stories that Steedman reconstructs aspects of her childhood: particularly the sense she was given early about how hard life is and how she mustn't cry or complain.[51] Steedman also draws on fairy tales that had been particularly important to her in her childhood and that serve to illustrate her own feelings and sense of self. When thinking about particular stories to link with her own life, she goes to Hans Christian Anderson, to 'The Snow Queen', and the image of Kay (her childhood nickname) with the lump of ice in his heart or to 'The Little Mermaid': 'I knew one day I might be asked to walk on the edge of knives, like the Little Mermaid, and was afraid I might not be able to bear the pain.'[52]

Shaping a Life

Childhood assumed greater significance in the autobiographies of many women in this period. A significant number focused almost entirely on the childhood of the author, saying almost nothing about their adult lives. Carolyn Steedman's was the first of these, but it was followed by others: the novelist Penelope Lively's explorations of her childhood in Egypt in *Oleander Jacaranda*, or that of the literary scholar Lorna Sage in *Bad Blood*. The new emphasis on childhood also introduced a new way of looking at it primarily in psychological terms, with a close focus on family dynamics and their impact. The relationship of the author with her parents, usually her mother, although in Sage's case it was her grandfather, was seen as integral to her emotional development and to the formation of her personality. It

---

[50]Steedman, *Landscape*, p. 17.
[51]Steedman, *Landscape*, p. 38.
[52]Steedman, *Landscape*, p. 46.

explained, to use Steedman's phrase, how she became the women that she was. This psychological approach and concern with relationships between the child and parents is central not only to the work of Steedman and Sage, but also to that of Ann Oakley, Carolyn Steedman, Catherine Cookson, Storm Jameson and Doris Lessing.

Family dynamics were given much less attention in the autobiographies of working-class women, few had either the theoretical knowledge of psychoanalysis or the experience of psychotherapy which these authors drew on. Working-class women sometimes noted maternal neglect or cruelty, but had little to say about family dynamics and the development of their personalities. They were more concerned to discuss their lives and expectations in relation to their working-class origins and to describe the nature of working-class life in terms of housing, food, family structures, work and community, as they sought while writing their own lives, to show what an early 20th-century working-class life was like to a readership that would know little about it.

Childhood

Very different kinds of childhood are depicted in these autobiographies. Class was clearly an important factor here, determining not only the experiences of a child in terms of their home and family life but also the expectations they faced about contributing to the family and how long childhood lasted. All working-class girls were expected to do unpaid household work, something never expected of their middle-class counterparts. In the early decades of the century, most were also expected to leave school and become financially independent when they were thirteen or fourteen. The educational reforms of the 1940s meant that later generations of working-class girls had the opportunity of gaining scholarships to grammar schools and to universities. The childhoods of women who grew up outside Britain, in Africa, in the case of Lessing and Emecheta, or New Zealand, in the case of Janet Frame, were also very different in terms of culture and expectations.

It is in their discussions of childhood that one can see most clearly the contrast between those women who stressed the centrality of their relationship with their mothers and those more concerned to describe their class and wider social context. For the former, it was this relationship that determined the nature of their childhood, and sometimes their adult life too. Storm Jameson's was one outstanding example of an autobiography in which the life of the author was dominated by her mother. Jameson began her autobiography by discussing her mother, emphasizing both how hard and lonely her life was and how violent she was to her children. Jameson's mother had also known violence in her youth. Her father, a wealthy shipbuilder, was a violent and taciturn man who disciplined his children harshly but showed little affection to them. Marriage did not provide an escape for her: Jameson's father was a sea captain, also a hard and taciturn man who was rarely home and whom his wife came to despise. In a very abrupt transition from the description of her family of origin to her own world, Jameson noted that in the days of her own childhood as of her mother's 'it was the custom to thrash children. Few people imagined they could be trained by any means other than those used on unbroken horses'. Jameson's mother resorted to this method often. Any act of carelessness or disobedience outside the house merited it and some inside. It was a form of cruelty, Jameson insisted, because of how deliberate it was. '*I shall thrash you when we get home* had the ring of a death sentence.' Jameson was aware that the violence her mother visited on her children was often provoked not by any specific thing the children did, but by her own unhappiness, loneliness and frustration. But while sometimes resenting her, she felt protective towards and somehow responsible for her mother. Rather than seeking escape from her, she sought for most of her life to assuage her unhappiness.

> It seemed that a nerve led direct from my young mind to hers: I knew instantly what she wanted me to say, what it would please her to hear, what she wanted. . . . I cannot remember a time when I was not aware, and with that helpless pity, that her life disappointed her.[53]

Ironically, as Jameson noted that while her mother always insisted on honesty, her concern to say what she thought her mother would want to hear led her often to lie. But it is this relationship rather than any of Jameson's childhood activities that has central place.

One issue on which Jameson and her mother agreed was the importance of her education. Jameson had taught herself to read before she went to school and was both able and ambitious from an early age. From the start, she knew that the local school in Whitby was a poor one, and not adequate for her needs. Her mother, who shared her ambition, sent her to the County School in Scarborough in order to learn the mathematics she needed for the Cambridge entrance examination. When Jameson began attending that school, her mother made it clear to the headmaster that her daughter needed to get one of the three available county scholarships that would enable her to go to university, which, to his surprise, she did. Education took precedence over everything else and Jameson travelled for over an hour by train to Scarborough to prepare for the scholarship examinations. For her last two terms at school, she lived alone in lodgings in Scarborough, relishing the freedom that this offered. Jameson gained the scholarship she needed to get into Leeds University and went there to read English for her first degree.

A very different kind of relationship between a daughter and her mother is depicted by Doris Lessing. Her mother was never violent. On the contrary,

---

[53] Jameson, *Journey from the North*, vol. I, p. 32.

she always insisted that a child should be governed by love and was, Lessing insists, an absolutely brilliant educator, although her obsession with toilet training her children from their earliest babyhood was problematic! From the start, however, Lessing felt that her mother did not love her. The love that was so much talked about bore no resemblance to her own early experience.

> What I remember is hard bundling hands, impatient arms and her voice telling me over and over again that she had not wanted a girl, she wanted a boy.... The fact was, my early childhood made me one of the walking wounded for years.[54]

This sense of being unloved was exacerbated when her baby brother was born and she could see the unconditional love lavished on him in contrast to how she was both treated and talked about. This difference between herself and her brother was made even more pronounced when at the age of eight or nine, Lessing was sent to a convent for several years, where she had to get special permission to read *Vanity Fair* in the library, while her brother remained at home. Her solace throughout her early life, and especially during her school years, came from the solitary time she was able to spend in the African bush. She took great pleasure in learning about how to survive in it.

Catherine Cookson places an even greater emphasis on the centrality of her mother and their painful relationship in her autobiography than Lessing or even Jameson. It is her mother, rather than herself, who features in the title of her autobiography, and it is her story with which the book begins, as Cookson explains how Kate went into service as a very young woman and was seduced and then abandoned when she became pregnant. Her bigoted, impoverished and violent family never forgave Kate for the shame that her pregnancy brought on them. Catherine was passed off by her grandparents as their child and while Kate was treated with extreme cruelty, she was much beloved. Kate's story provides the framework for Cookson's discussion of her own illegitimacy. Cookson introduces herself into the story through an altercation she had with local children at the age of seven. In the course of an argument, one of the children told her that the woman she called 'ma' was her grandmother, adding 'your Kate's your ma and she drinks ... and YOU haven't GOT NO DA'.[55] Cookson was appalled. When she next looked at Kate, however, she realized this story was true – and the shame associated both with having no da and Kate's drinking was almost unbearable. This realization occurred shortly before Kate returned to live with the family as her own mother needed care. Her arrival had a dramatic

---

[54]Lessing, *Under My Skin*, p. 25.
[55]Cookson, *Our Kate*, p. 24.

impact on Cookson. The indulgence with which she had been treated by her grandparents gave way to constant beating and humiliation at Kate's hands. Like Jameson, Cookson realized that Kate's beatings, were not always as a result of her own behaviour, but rather of Kate's general frustration.[56] They finally stopped in Cookson's early adolescence – apparently when she threatened to hit Kate back. But they built up a powerful resentment and she often felt that she hated Kate.

Cookson's story, as Carolyn Steedman noted, depicted powerfully the terrible experience of exclusion that she suffered as a poor working-class child who was also illegitimate.[57] She was also picked on by the other children and excluded from their activities. Her autobiography includes a very poignant description of a day when she was not invited to a birthday party that all the other children in the neighbourhood attended and spent an hour standing outside the party, sure that at some point she would be admitted. Cookson's illegitimacy had an impact on her schooling too, especially when her nominally Catholic grandfather insisted that she leave the local school which she quite liked and went to a series of Catholic schools. She hated these schools, recalling that there was little interest in teaching either literacy or numeracy as their primary concern was the state of religious knowledge and belief amongst their pupils. The emphasis on confession and sin became a source of almost lifelong fear and nightmares for Cookson. There is a strong sense in Cookson of the impact of the combination of extreme poverty, illegitimacy and violence on her physical and emotional development. Although she did not use the same language as Steedman, there is certainly some recognition in her work of the psychic dimension of class.

This insistence on the psychic dimension of class is a central issue in Steedman's *Landscape for a Good Woman*, something that she makes very clear in her insistence that there is a psychological as well as a material dimension to class and that a childhood of deprivation has lasting consequences. A key impulse for Steedman in writing her own life was her wish to reject the psychological simplicity attributed to working-class families in much social history. Her story and that of her mother are depicted in a way that underlines the importance of longing and fantasies in their lives and the immense complexity involved in their relationship. Steedman's childhood, she insists, was framed by the longings and disappointment of her mother, and by the knowledge that her mother hadn't wanted children and felt she would have been better off without them. Steedman used stories to explain and illustrate the psychic underpinning of her childhood, repeating the

---

[56]Cookson, *Our Kate*, p. 8. The early version suggests that Kate beat her particularly often during the First World War when Kate herself was 'working like a black'. 'Autobiography 1958', #102, Cookson Papers, Box 31. The word 'buttocks' is replaced by 'backside' in the published version of this comment. Cookson, *Our Kate*, p. 73.
[57]Steedman, *Landscape*, p. 9.

stories (not always entirely true) that her mother told about her own childhood and early adult life that helped to explain her sense of disappointment. Her mother's story, told in bits, about being sent away at the age of eleven to go into service far from home and crying as she waited on the railway platform is central here. The lesson was clear, Steedman realized, 'I must never, ever, cry for myself, for I was a lucky little girl: my tears should be for all the strong, brave women who gave me life'.[58] As a literary child, Steedman turned to Grimm's fairy tales which offered other versions of the suffering of women and young girls. Steedman drew on earlier depictions of working-class girlhood: those of Kathleen Woodward and Catherine Cookson as she stresses the ways in which she, like other working-class girls, grew up knowing they too were a burden to their mother's whose lives would have been much better without them. The importance of domestic labour in the childhood of working-class girls is stressed also by Carolyn Steedman. She was aware of the precise calculation of the cost of the food she and her sister ate – and how there was also a pattern in their usefulness.

> At six I was old enough to go on errands, at seven to go further to pay the rent and the rates, go on the long dreary walk to the Co-op for the divi. By eight I was old enough to clean the house and do the weekend shopping. At eleven it was understood that I washed the breakfast things, lit the fire in winter and scrubbed the kitchen floor before I started my homework.[59]

Steedman was well aware that this depiction of the work she was expected to do differentiated her childhood from those of her middle-class counterparts (including Oakley) for whom any form of work would have been unthinkable.

School was an oasis for Steedman. While every aspect of her home life was overseen by her mother and inflected with her unhappiness, her school life was her own.[60] No questions were asked about it: it was just what she did. The material things she needed – a table in her room and a pattern of domestic work that allowed for homework – were provided. Although often sharing the widespread criticism of the state made by contemporary academics, she insists that she experienced the intervention of the state into her childhood in the 1950s as 'entirely beneficent', arguing that she would have been a very different person 'if orange juice and milk and dinners at school hadn't told me, in a covert way, that I had a right to exist, was worth something'.[61] Steedman's success, especially her selection for a grammar school, was also a source of pleasure and pride to her mother – and the fact

---

[58]Steedman, *Landscape*, p. 30.
[59]Steedman, *Landscape*, pp. 42–43.
[60]Steedman, *Landscape*, p. 36.
[61]Steedman, *Landscape*, p. 122.

that she was sitting this exam enabled her teachers to persuade her mother that she needed glasses to deal with her short-sightedness when she was ten.

Most women's autobiographies emphasize the relationship between daughters and their mothers, but there are a couple that extend this framework to include fathers as well. Ann Oakley's *Taking It Like a Woman* is the most notable of these. As a sociologist herself and the daughter of Richard Titmuss, one of Britain's pre-eminent sociologists, Oakley had to deal with the issue of following in the footsteps of a famous father while also being a woman expected to marry and focus on family life. She wrote movingly of the intense conflicts that she faced as a woman wanting both a profession and a family, in the years before the resurgence of feminism had made this a common problem amongst women. This was the more important because of the way that gender played out in her family and the relationship of her parents.

Although her parents began their courtship and married life writing together, Oakley's mother gave up any kind of outside work when she was told by her eminent gynaecologist that 'busyness may prevent conception'. This sacrifice did not endear her to her daughter who regarded her non-working mother as a very ordinary parent – in contrast with her extraordinary father. Indeed, one key part of the web of contradictions that Oakley saw herself bound in as a child, and one that differentiates her from many other women who wrote autobiographies, is the absolute centrality to her life of her father. 'Although I loved both my parents', she wrote, 'I identified with my father and felt ambivalent towards my mother.'[62] Oakley's relationship with her parents was made more complex by the way that her father took on aspects of the female role: from her early childhood he was the patient one, with open arms and ready sympathy, while her mother was often impatient. He seemed 'wholly good' to her so she was bound to him by a moral passion as well as by her immediate feelings. At the same time, while he had great ambitions for her, he was totally opposed to married women working, something that set the framework for the terrible struggle Oakley had to decide what kind of woman she wanted to be.

These accounts of childhood that centre on relationships with parents differ markedly from those of the working-class women concerned to emphasize their class as determining the nature of their childhood. In their works, a description of their physical surroundings usually precedes and frames the discussion of both their families and their childhood. Kathleen Dayus, for example, called her first chapter 'Our yard'. It was a district,

> so crammed with humanity it was more like a rabbits' warren. There were still factories and lots of small workshops and foundries and the same pubs were crowded all day long ... this was what people today

---

[62]Oakley, *Taking It Like a Woman*, p. 13.

would call a 'slum', I suppose, and the people who lived there would be pitied as the 'have-nots', but then there was no pity and we were left to sink or swim, rise or fall, as best we could.[63]

The other autobiographies by working-class women also described their homes in some detail often explaining where people slept and the nature of their meals, as well as the surrounding areas and usually also the ways in which people made their livings.

Even memories, which for Jameson and others encapsulate feelings about themselves or their parents, are presented in these autobiographies as social rather than personal ones. Margaret Powell, for example, claimed that her 'earliest recollection is that other children seemed to be better off than we were'.[64] This led her into a discussion of her father's difficulty in getting work as a house painter in winter, the size of her family, the lack of any idea of birth control and her own tasks in supporting her mother in feeding and caring for her younger siblings from the time she was seven. Powell also offered a description of life in Hove, where the family lived, listing the kinds of entertainments they enjoyed, especially the circus, the cinema and various family games.

Powell says little about her relationship with either parent or about herself at all, until she got to a critical issue: the fact that she was unable to take up the scholarship she was awarded to continue her education. Powell was clearly an exceptional student and at the age of thirteen won a scholarship to a secondary school, but she was not able to accept it.

> My parents saw my headmistress but when they found out that I couldn't possibly earn any money till I was eighteen and up to that time they would have to keep me, and not only keep me, but buy my books and clothes, they just couldn't do it.... Looking back, I wish it had been possible to have gone on with my education but at that time I didn't mind in the least. I didn't think my parents were hard because I knew I had to go out to work. I knew we needed the money so desperately.[65]

Although she understood her parent's decision, Powell referred often to this crucial event that determined her whole future. Ironically, she was allowed to leave school even earlier than the normal age because she had performed so well: 'I was in the top class and if I had put in another year it would have been the same work over again.' She left school at the age of thirteen to go into domestic service.

Important as class was in the childhoods of these women, it did not preclude their recognition of other important aspects of their lives, including

---

[63]Dayus, *Her People*, p. 1.
[64]Powell, *Below Stairs*, p. 15.
[65]Powell, *Below Stairs*, p. 27.

their relationships with their parents. Here, as in the autobiographies of other women writing at this time, it is the relationships between the authors and their mothers that are given the greatest emphasis. Kathleen Dayus, for example, detailed her mother's cruelty and negligence towards her children, as she beat them continually and took little care to feed them so that they were often dependent on school lunches as their only daily meal. 'Neither our parents nor the neighbours had any time to give us any love or affection', she notes, 'and they didn't listen to our troubles.'[66] Dayus saw her mother as particularly cruel to her. By contrast, Margaret Powell and Rosina Harrison suggest a much more supportive relationship between their mothers and themselves.

All working-class women's autobiographies stressed that they were expected to help and detail the amount of unpaid labour required of them from their earliest years. 'From the time any of us can remember', wrote Rosina Harrison, 'we were expected to play our part in the running of the house.' Her first job was laying kindling and getting the fire going, before fetching the water and helping to prepare breakfast.[67] In a similar vein, Margaret Powell described how, at the age of seven, she was expected to give her younger siblings their breakfast as her mother was already at work. She would take them to their school before going to her own and would run home at midday to get the dinner ready.[68] The kind of work required was somewhat different in less well-regulated working-class families. In her very impoverished family, rather than helping with the housework, Catherine Cookson was expected to fetch drinks from the pub or kept home from school to pawn the family's clothes, activities that she hated and that filled her with shame. Another of her regular tasks was getting out of bed late at night to help put her drunken grandfather to bed. She was chosen for this task as the one most able to cajole him – and least likely to be hit.[69] As we have seen, the importance of domestic labour in the childhood of working-class girls is stressed also by Carolyn Steedman.

The Teen Years

One notable feature of this group of autobiographies is the recognition in many of them of a period between childhood and adulthood as a separate and important stage of life. At the time these autobiographies were being written, there was considerable discussion of teenagers in the media and

---

[66]Dayus, *Her People*, p. 5.
[67]Harrison, *My Life in Service*, p. 2.
[68]Powell, *Below Stairs*, p. 5.
[69]Cookson, *Our Kate*, p. 65.

amongst psychologists and educators. The new forms of work that became available to young people in the decades after the Second World War brought them into prominence as it expanded their power as consumers and brought a new awareness of and concern about their tastes, desires and activities. The notions of 'teenage rebellion' and 'generational conflict' that emerged at the time showed how widespread anxiety about adolescent sexuality and the forms of independence that now became possible were. The whole question of what teenage rebellion meant and how extensive it actually was, has recently become the subject of historical discussion and there is only a very limited sense of such rebellion in any of these autobiographies.[70] The stronger suggestion in these autobiographies is that it was a complex stage of life involving physical changes and for some a new kind of life, but one that was not yet fully independent. Several women, especially working-class ones, discuss their difficulties in coming to terms with bodily changes, including menstruation, and in dealing with the constant warnings about pregnancy which, in view of their complete sexual ignorance, meant little.

Adolescence as a significant stage in life is discussed in most detail by Doris Lessing, Janet Frame and Ann Oakley. All of them note their strong sense of a growing separation between themselves and their parents. Lessing depicts it most emphatically in terms of adolescent or teenage rebellion. She left school, with a feeling of some relief, at the age of thirteen. Once home, however, the conflictual relationship she had always had with her mother became even more pronounced. 'I was in nervous flight from her ever since I can remember,' she wrote, 'and from the age of fourteen I set myself obdurately against her in a kind of inner emigration from everything she represented.' Why, she wondered, was the battle between mothers and adolescent daughters so implacable?[71] Ultimately, she saw it as something distinctly female and centring on the ways that adolescent daughters become aware of – and obsessed by – their own sexuality. Eventually her usually mild father 'said he could not stand one more day of a ringside seat at the quarrels between his two females . . . and why didn't I leave'.[72] Lessing did so, taking up a position as a nursemaid in a family living near Salisbury where she took pride in her domestic skills – and as a demonstration of her own obsession with her body and sexuality, attempted to seduce the reluctant brother-in-law of her employer. 'I was in a fever of erotic longing, which had succeeded the romantic fevers of my childhood,' she wrote, noting that while she could say that 'I spent my adolescence in a sexual trance', she also spent much of her time reading and discovering the world of books and wandering about the bush.[73]

---

[70] Selina Todd and Hilary Young, 'Baby-Boomers to "Beanstalkers"', *Cultural and Social History* 9, no. 3 (2012).
[71] Lessing, *Under My Skin*, p. 15.
[72] Lessing, *Under My Skin*, p. 179.
[73] Lessing, *Under My Skin*, p. 185.

There is little suggestion of sexuality in Janet Frame's account of her adolescence. What mattered most to her was rather how much unhappier her home life became. In childhood, while her family was extremely impoverished and chaotic, she had felt at ease within it, threatened only by the outside world. During her adolescence, the dysfunctional nature of her family became much more evident: home was seldom happy, she noted, and the cherished festivals and events of childhood had lost their joy. Her father's violence and appalling treatment of her epileptic brother, and his insistence that he could get over the epilepsy if only he tried, became unbearable. Her parents receded and became less important in her own life, but there was little to take their place. School became increasingly difficult for Frame too, not because of the actual work which she managed well, but because the family's poverty meant she could not get new uniforms or clothes that fitted her. Her final year at school was 'the cruellest I had known'. The shy and anxious Frame could cope with the traditional school pattern of sitting silently at a desk, but the new one for senior pupils involved sitting in groups and working at tables, something that terrified her. Her body was a huge issue too. 'My school tunic was so tightly fitting that it pressed on all parts of my body. It was torn and patched again and again.' Frame was never selected as a partner – even when standing in a line, people avoided the space next to her. She concluded that the reason for this had to do with the question of personal hygiene, especially during her menstrual periods. 'I knew that my home-made sanitary towels showed their bulk, and the blood leaked through, and when I stood up in class, I'd glance furtively at the desk seat to see whether I was bloody.' No one would stand next to her in line, she decided, because she stank.[74]

Becoming an adolescent some decades later than either Frame or Lessing, Ann Oakley also found this a particularly difficult time. It was one, she notes in the section entitled 'Chronology' in her autobiography, when she felt even more alone and excluded by her classmates, especially as they began to menstruate earlier than she did. She was excited when her periods finally began. At around the same time, she fell in love with the son of a social worker friend of her parents and entered into an intense, if unconsummated, relationship that lasted for three years and was exhaustively documented. These years were ones during which Oakley became an angry teenager, openly disobedient at school until she moved from her private girls' school to 'the more liberal atmosphere of a polytechnic in West London', which she enjoyed more and where she made new friends.[75] Her involvement in politics, especially the campaigns for nuclear disarmament and for the abolition of capital punishment, brought contact with new people and romantic entanglements as well as intellectual engagement. In the course of all of this, Oakley finally sorted out the details of sexual

---

[74]Frame, *An Angel at My Table*, p. 189.
[75]Oakley, *Taking It Like a Woman*.

reproduction and lost her virginity. In this chronological discussion of her teenage years, Oakley omits the important detail that she focuses on in her reflections on 'Family': the fact that when she was eighteen, she experienced 'something that resembled what is popularly called a nervous breakdown'. Its symptoms were 'uncontrollable hysteria and unmanageable weeping' and, when her father resisted getting outside help, she took to her bed, refusing to eat or get up. In due course, her father called his friend, the child analyst Donald Winnicott, who referred her to another analyst whom she saw for several months. Although they didn't use these terms, she realized that they both recognized that the 'real dilemma was being born female in a man's world', an issue that Oakley took years to resolve – and that constitutes the central point of her book.[76]

These years presented very different issues and problems for many working-class women. Oakley clearly knew about menstruation before her periods began – unlike Kathleen Dayus who knew nothing when she had her first period.

> I was scared to death. I ran all the way home from school thinking I was going to bleed to death. I burst into tears when I saw Mum and told her what had happened. But all the explanation she gave me was 'Now yow keep away from the lads an' never let them kiss yer or the next thing yer know yer'l be 'aving a baby'.[77]

She tried repeatedly to find out where babies came from but was told she would find out when she got older. A friend whose mother was pregnant said that after a woman carried a baby for nine months, 'when the time comes their belly goes pop with a bang and the baby pops out'.[78]

The lack of support and indeed cruelty of her mother in terms of menstruation and sexual maturation was evident also, Dayus notes in relation to the other major demand on her as on other working-class girls around the age of thirteen: the need to leave school and get a job. She wanted work in the enamelling trade rather than in domestic service and had a difficult time negotiating terms – as well as being sexually abused in the course of the medical examination she was required to have. It was generally expected that a girl would be helped to get a job by her mother, but Dayus's mother simply told her she had to stand on her own two feet. There is a marked contrast here with Margaret Powell, for example, whose mother came with her to her first interview and spoke for her, as well as ensuring that she had everything she needed for her job. It was some years later that she decided she wanted to go to London and find a job for herself. Rosina Harrison too notes how her mother helped to prepare her to become a lady's

---

[76] Oakley, *Taking It Like a Woman*, p. 77.
[77] Kathleen Dayus, *Where There's Life* (London: Virago, 1985), p. 95.
[78] Dayus, *Where There's Life*, p. 193.

maid by learning dress-making and cooking and played a supervisory role in her early working years, waiting until she felt that she was able to manage herself.

This sense that young working women were not children but not yet adult was evident in the workplace, especially for those involved in domestic service. This point is made somewhat bitterly by Margaret Powell in her discussion of how concerned middle-class employers were if their young maids showed any sign of 'flightiness' – such as wearing make-up or stockings or having your hair waved – even on days off.[79] Flightiness was feared because it suggested the possibility that a maid might have a young man or become pregnant, the cause of instant dismissal – and of disruption in the household. As Powell makes clear, however, this constant concern about the behaviour of servants amongst their employers set very considerable limits on what she and her fellows could do in their late teen years.

It is those women fortunate enough to be university students in the early decades of the 20th century, who depict these years, especially their late adolescence, as the ones of greatest freedom and pleasure. Jameson emphasizes this sense of freedom during her undergraduate years in Leeds and even more during those that followed when she was enrolled for a master's degree in London. To her surprise, her mother agreed to her sharing rooms with her close friends, the Harland brothers, and for a couple of years, Jameson relished a life filled with friendship, ideas, conversation and the long walks necessitated by their lack of money for public transport. They lived happily on a pittance, she recalled, often toasting muffins in the fireplace of their shabby lodgings and filling them with sardines.

> Our freedom intoxicated us; there was nothing we should not be able to attempt, no road not open to us, no barriers in the world that we children of farmers and seamen were going to walk about in as equals.[80]

Jameson managed to complete her degree while in London and offered free tutoring in a working women's college. On the whole, these years were the happiest she ever had. 'No life I have lived since has come so close to satisfying me', she wrote later, 'a life, that is, without possessions, above all without responsibility, to things or people.'[81] Dora Russell too wrote at length about how much she relished both the intellectual and the personal freedom of these university years.[82] Although Jameson was a student in the years just before the First World War, she and her friends had little sense of the impending catastrophe. Although not a student herself, Naomi Mitchison was able to take advantage of her brother's student years as she was allowed to be with him and with a few other close family friends unchaperoned. But

---

[79]Powell, *Below Stairs*, p. 80.
[80]Jameson, *Journey from the North*, vol. I, p. 66.
[81]Jameson, *Journey from the North*, vol. I, p. 70.
[82]Dora Russell, *The Tamarisk Tree 3 Vols* (London: Virago, 1978–1985), vol. I, pp. 13–32.

even when she spent time at his college chaperoned, she was not particularly bothered by it as it didn't interfere with her freedom to talk to other students. 'The excitement was in the conversation between young people, spiced with clever quotations and local jokes or witty remarks.'[83]

Few younger women experienced anything like Jameson's sense of freedom or pleasure at university or while undertaking other forms of tertiary education. Their discussions suggest that university years were seen as much more complicated by a younger generation of women who were at university in the 1960s. Although she doesn't depict her university life in any detail, Carolyn Steedman makes it clear that she never felt at home at the University of Sussex where she met no women with a similar background to her own.[84] Ann Oakley 'wept with loneliness into my already diluted tomato soup and rang home frequently' when she was first at Somerville and found it very hard indeed. Learning how to be a proper undergraduate and accommodating herself to the Oxford educational system were both difficult – and emphasized the difficulties women faced in what remained a man's world.[85] Oakley married while at university, a marriage that worked, although it did not resolve her fundamental problem of how to be a woman in a man's world, or to combine marriage, motherhood and a career. Her university years were on the whole unrewarding, with the crowning insult the fact that she '"only" got a second-class degree'.[86]

Sexuality

Just as these autobiographies depict a wide range of childhood and educational experiences, so too they offer very different accounts of experiences and understandings of sexuality. Sexual ignorance continued to be a major concern for some, while others talked in a more open way about the sexual problems that they faced in marriage and how they sought to deal with them by establishing new kinds of marital relationships. What is most noticeable, however, is the preparedness of women to talk about their own sexuality, including their sense of their own sexual development, their recognition of their own sexual needs and in some cases, their sexual identity. The preparedness of some women to discuss their own sexuality and the general question of sex and sexual problems in a marriage reflected the attention that was being paid to these questions in the wider world. Naomi Mitchison and Dora Russell, for example, who wrote much more openly about these questions than many others, had both been closely involved in organizations to promote birth control information and to reform sexual

---

[83]Mitchison, *All Change Here*, p. 70.
[84]Steedman, *Landscape*, p. 15.
[85]Oakley, *Taking It Like a Woman*, p. 36.
[86]Oakley, *Taking It Like a Woman*, p. 48.

relations and marriage in the 1920s, when both were experiencing their own sexual difficulties.

Sexual ignorance was discussed particularly by working-class women for whom it was a problem, not just in adolescence, but also when they were courting or in the early stages of their married life. Grace Foakes, for example, noted the anxiety she felt when she was being courted by Reuben, the man she subsequently married, when he kissed her goodnight after an outing. 'So great was my ignorance of the facts of life', she noted, that she feared that the consequences of these kisses would be a baby.[87] It was not only working-class women for whom it was a problem, however. Naomi Mitchison, for example, insisted that her own sexual ignorance and that of her husband, Mitch, prevented them from establishing a satisfactory sexual relationship. Mitchison waited until after her husband's death before writing about the sexual difficulties that she had faced in the early years of her marriage.

> I got little or no pleasure, except for the touch of a loved body and the knowledge that for a time he was out of the front line. The final act left me on edge and uncomfortable. Why was it so unlike Swinburne? Where were the rapture and the roses? Was it going to be like this all my life? I began to run a temperature.[88]

Eventually, Mitchison read Marie Stopes and found out about foreplay and other 'elementary sexual techniques', sending the book to her husband as well. There was 'a marked increase in happiness' after this, she noted. 'But some damage had been done. We were both, so to speak, open to something better.' After some twelve years, they both agreed to begin seeking other lovers.

The question of sexuality is addressed in very different ways by Janet Frame and Doris Lessing. Sexual ignorance was apparently not an issue for them and they wrote rather about how important sex was to them and what it meant. In Frame's case, it was an important part of her need to catch up on all the experiences she had missed out on in her years of incarceration. In the 1950s, in search of new experiences, she went to London and then for some months to Ibiza, partly because it was a cheaper place to be. Once there, she lived a full and rich life, accepted by the locals and becoming friendly with a number of visiting Americans. One of the Americans became her lover. Amongst other things, she noted, this relationship offered 'the satisfaction of having yet another first experience' and she clearly enjoyed it.[89] She describes the times she spent with her lover with great warmth and

---
[87] Foakes, *Four Meals for Fourpence*, pp. 244–245.
[88] Mitchison, *You May Well Ask*, p. 69.
[89] Frame, *An Angel at My Table*, p. 460.

enjoyed her growing sense of sexual confidence. The relationship came to an end, however, when she suggested that she might be pregnant. Her lover's insistence that, if she were pregnant, it would be terrible for them both, made her end the relationship. Frame was in fact pregnant at that point and miscarried a few weeks later. She does not describe any subsequent sexual relationship, or even suggest there was one. This one sexual experience seems to have brought her a sufficient sense of being an adult woman to enable her to lay the whole issue to rest and concentrate her life on writing.

Lessing discussed sex quite extensively in her autobiography and in a variety of different ways. The lack of interest in sex in her mother and many other married women she met and the sexual unhappiness of her father, for example, is an integral part of her discussion of her own family. She wrote about it in relation to herself too, delineating both the nature of her various sexual experiences and her sense of herself as a sexual being. As we have seen, she emphasized her own adolescent sexuality and desire for sexual experience, and this desire continued in her adult life. Neither of her marriages brought her either great sexual satisfaction or knowledge. Her first marriage was better than her second in this respect. Thus, when she decided to leave her first husband and everyone assumed that their sexual relationship was a failure, she insists that this was not the case: 'our sex life was, as they say, satisfactory'. Her second marriage was worse: Gottfried Lessing was so sexually repressed that it was almost intolerable. 'As for subtle and refined sex', Lessing wrote, 'it was years before I discovered it. I am sure many people never do.'[90] Her later relationships revealed much more to her about sex and about her own sexuality. This was particularly the case with the man only identified as Jack, the love of her life, but a man who would not commit to a relationship with her. The sex here was much more compelling, but that itself proved problematic. 'It is my belief', Lessing wrote, 'that energetic and frequent sex breeds sudden storms of antagonism.' It produced great jealousy in Jack and did not in any way solidify or support their relationship.[91]

Lessing provided an unusually full description of herself and her sense of herself as a sexual being, but there was no questioning of her heterosexuality. For some younger women who were entering into adulthood in the course of the 1960s, the sexual revolution, the movement for gay liberation and the early stages of women's liberation brought to the fore new ideas about the different kinds of sexual desire and sexuality that women might experience along with the whole question of sexual identity. These issues were central in Elizabeth Wilson's *Mirror Writing*, and it was her treatment of them that served to make it such an important and innovative work. The question of her own identity, and how she sought to construct or understand it provides the organizing principle for *Mirror Writing*, and the question of her sexual identity is a key part of it. Drawing on the love of fashion and the fascination

---

[90] Lessing, *Under My Skin*, p. 266.
[91] Lessing, *Walking in the Shade*, p. 816.

with style, which she would later write about extensively in academic work, Wilson described how she sought both to display and to screen herself in her adolescence, using the fashions of the 1960s so that she could be simultaneously 'doll and pretty boy', fusing narcissistically 'the glamour of the sexual object with the glamour of the sexual predator'.[92] The sexual confusions of these adolescent years seemed to be resolved when she came to see herself as a lesbian at the age of eighteen. But this too ultimately raised as many problems as it seemed to solve as there were soon so many other issues to resolve: was she a butch lesbian or a femme? Did she want a stable monogamous lesbian relationship that mirrored marriage when she was so attracted to others that threatened it? Her sexual identity seemed constantly to undermine her social identity and her acceptability to others. As a woman of the 1960s and '70s, questions of sexuality and sexual identity involved a political as well as a personal dimension for Wilson and she sought to come to terms with her understanding of her lesbianism and her attitude towards it through psychoanalysis and through her involvement in Women's Liberation and in the Gay Liberation Movement. When Gay Liberation was at its height in 1971, for a time, she noted, 'my lesbian identity achieved a kind of unitary coherence because it fused my socialism and my sexual politics'. But even at this time, she was aware it was not enough to say 'I'm gay and I'm proud . . . it left too many questions unanswered'.[93]

Marriage and Family Life

Often presented in fiction as something anticipated with pleasure and indeed the crowning moment of a woman's life, marriage was rarely depicted in this way in these autobiographies. For middle-class women, especially those with a reasonable education and a desire to establish a career, marriage was a problem and an obstacle that they had to face and find some way to deal with. Several women make it clear that they had not sought marriage but were cajoled or pushed into it by parents or importunate suitors. Even where the women had chosen to marry and selected a partner these autobiographies suggest that some realized even before it happened that it was a mistake, while others became aware of it soon after. Class is an important issue here, however, as few working-class women's autobiographies echo this sense of marriage as a trap. On the contrary, while some described difficult marriages or ones in which they were forced to be the breadwinner, their autobiographies suggest that most saw marriage as the entry into adult life, or as a way to leave service and paid work to establish the kind of family life they wanted.

Although the volume of her autobiography dealing with her marriage was published in the 1950s, Vera Brittain's *Testament to Experience* serves

---

[92]Wilson, *Mirror Writing*, p. 15.
[93]Wilson, *Mirror Writing*, pp. 129–130.

well to illustrate the problem posed by marriage to women who became adults around the time of the First World War. Faced with the great desire to marry her expressed by George Caitlin, Brittain had succumbed to his wishes. On her wedding day, however,

> I realised as I removed my wedding dress that in the near future lay another conflict as harsh as any I had faced in the past, for I knew that, even if I would, I could not lay down my work unless everything that mattered to both G and myself was to die.[94]

Brittain explains how she resolved this problem by devising a semi-detached marriage, which involved her remaining in London and sharing an apartment with her close friend Winifred Holtby when her academic husband was teaching at his American University. Although they experienced difficulties, Brittain and Caitlin's marriage lasted throughout their lives. This was not the case for Dora Russell, however, who also resisted marriage for as long as she could. As a self-consciously modern woman who believed strongly in sexual freedom and careers for women and a Girton graduate who had been offered a college fellowship, she might have had an academic career had she not met and fallen in love with the much older and already very distinguished philosopher, Bertrand Russell. They became lovers quite early in their relationship. Dora wanted to maintain a free relationship, but Bertrand Russell wanted marriage. She prevailed initially and the couple lived together for a couple of years during which time they travelled in Russia and China. The problem came with children: two months after their first son was born, Russell who had finalized his divorce from his first wife, insisted that they marry. The marriage was not a success. From the start, Russell expected more domestic service than Dora was willing to offer – and his friends patronized her.[95] Her compromise was to attempt to make their marriage an experiment in a new morality that would combine sexual freedom and commitment. Dora Russell also makes clear that as Bertrand Russell was often impotent, theirs was not a sexually satisfying relationship for her and that she wanted other sexual partners. The experiment was a dismal failure: Russell could not accept her sexual freedom – or the thought that she would have children with another man – and the marriage came to a bitter end.[96]

Unwelcome and problematic marriages were forced on others too who made their objections clear, although not in the explicitly feminist terms used by Brittain and Russell. Storm Jameson, for example, was pushed into a marriage she did not want by her mother. Early in her time at Leeds

---

[94]Vera Brittain, *Testament of Experience* (Bath: Cedric Chivers Ltd, 1957, repr. 1971).
[95]Deborah Gorham, 'Liberty and Love? Dora Black Russell and Marriage', *Canadian Journal of History* 46, no. 2 (2011).
[96]Russell, *The Tamarisk Tree*, vol. I.

University, she met and fell in love with a young theology student whom she designates only as 'K'. Jameson insists on her complete sexual innocence at this stage. However, when her mother discovered 'K's' letters to her, letters that she thought erroneously suggested the possibility of sexual intimacy, she insisted that Jameson marry at once. She did this, Jameson noted, although 'she knew she was saving my moral being at the expense of my future'. Even at the time of the marriage, Jameson insisted that 'some submerged current had begun to set against him in my mind. . . . Given time, I should have become critical of him and in the end the obsession would have died and I should have been free.' Her mother would brook no opposition, however.

> There I was, back where I had so often stood, cowered, as a child crushed by guilt for a half-realized crime. I was neither hard enough, nor adroit or single minded enough, to withstand the force of her anger and grief. I had nothing to set against it except my deep inarticulate reluctance to be married, my profound instinct to keep my freedom.[97]

Throughout her autobiography, Jameson downplayed her mother's cruelty, stressing rather her own weakness and dark side, including her inability to love sufficiently. But it is hard to overlook the deliberate cruelty evident in the way her mother forced her into a deeply unhappy marriage that soon made her effectively a single mother, responsible for the entire financial support of herself and her son.

Jameson wrote openly and at some length about this terrible first marriage, making clear the lack of companionship between her and her husband, her absolute hatred of domesticity, the misery of their surroundings and the separate lives they came to lead. She suggests its sexual inadequacy by inference in her description of an American soldier with whom she became obsessed. She described its breakdown and how hard she found it to leave in painful detail. She could not, however, bring herself to write in the same detail about her second marriage to Guy Chapman, to whom she was still married while writing the autobiography. She described her meeting with Chapman in this work, noting it provoked the sharpest personal crisis in her life. Yet she refuses to elaborate. 'Like my happy difficult second marriage', she says, 'it is part of the nervous system of my mind: to draw it out would kill me. What little could safely be turned into phrases has been told once already.'[98] Jameson had drawn closely on her own story in her novel *Love in Winter*, the second volume in a trilogy, *The Mirror in Darkness*, in which she traced the life of Hervey Russell Vane who was effectively her alter ego. Here, she explored in considerable detail the pain and anguish suffered

---

[97] Jameson, *Journey from the North*, vol. I, p. 72.
[98] Jameson, *Journey from the North*, vol. I, p. 409.

by the fictional character, Vane, when she meets and falls in love with her cousin, Nicholas Roxby, a man who, like Chapman, feels that he is emotionally dead and that his affective life is over after the First World War.[99] She reproduced almost verbatim passages from the novel in *Journey from the North*, underlining the extent to which this novel is autobiographical – but avoiding the need to write all this detail in her own voice.

Naomi Mitchison too was pushed into marriage by her mother. Her relationship with Dick Mitchison, the man she married, a close friend of her brother's, began during her adolescence. They met at a picnic when she was just sixteen. A few months later, in August 1914, the war began. Naomi was invited to the Mitchison family home, where Dick proposed, and she accepted. Although she did not know it, before she made the visit his mother and hers 'had spoken' and she was invited specifically in order for Mitch to propose. She makes very clear her lack of any deep feeling for Mitch and her sense that everything was taken over and organized by her mother. It was her mother who felt the romance of her impending marriage. 'I remember with such embarrassment and distaste that my memory shies away', she wrote,

> how much mother seemed determined to share all emotional passages with me. It was as though Dick's presence stirred her in a way it did not stir me. He was certainly very fond of her and always nice to her, but that was not at all the same thing. . . . I also remember very clearly being told that the period of her engagement was the happiest time in a girl's life. This seemed to me to bode ill for marriage.[100]

Marriage usually signalled the start of adult life, but this was emphatically not the case for her. On the contrary, her engagement, her early married life and even the start of motherhood seemed to be a continuation of her childhood, controlled entirely by her mother. As we have seen, her foreboding was justified and, although they worked out a way to remain together, theirs was a difficult relationship.

Writing about herself in Nigeria and in a very different context some decades later, Buchi Emecheta too described living in a community that pressured her very strongly to marry at the age of sixteen. She agreed to do so, rejecting all the possible young men suggested by her extended family, and marrying 'a dreamy, handsome local boy' to whom she became passionately attached. It was not a good choice: once married, she discovered that 'under his handsome and strong physique was a dangerously weak mind'.[101] She became pregnant soon after marriage – and then again shortly

---

[99]Storm Jameson, *Love in Winter* (London: Capuchin Classics, 1935 repr. 2009).
[100]Mitchison, *All Change Here*, p. 108.
[101]Emecheta, *Head Above Water*, p. 25.

after the birth of her first baby. After a couple of years, her husband left Nigeria for England, ostensibly to continue his studies. Her family wanted Emecheta to stay in Nigeria, but she insisted on following her husband. Her education stood her in good stead: she had completed English O and A levels and found herself a good job at the American Embassy in Lagos where she quickly saved the fare for herself and her children. Going to London brought her further pregnancies but did not help her marriage. Her husband continued to be unreliable, refusing to work or to place supporting her and the children ahead of his studies – although he seemed to make little progress there. Emecheta had to get a job to support herself and her children, of whom there were soon five. Although wishing to remain married, and pressured to do so by the Nigerian community, she realized she could not do so if she wanted to be a writer and so left her husband only a couple of years after arriving in London.

Although not in any way pressured into it, Doris Lessing too found marriage oppressive and antithetical to her desires for freedom and a life in Britain as a writer. Lessing had moved to Salisbury at the age of sixteen where she got a job as a telephonist and became involved with what she describes as 'a country club crowd'. At the age of eighteen, she agreed to marry a civil servant ten years older than she. She was not in love with her husband, nor he with her, and in her autobiography, she was unable to explain why she had married him. It was part of the 'general delirium' of the post-war moment, she suggests, a period when many of the young people she mixed with in the white country clubs of Rhodesia were becoming engaged. Even before the wedding, she wished her father had told her not to do it, but he said nothing. Lessing never really expected the marriage to last. They set up home in a small flat, owned by one of his friends – and close enough to the country club to enable him to continue his familiar social life while she kept house – and devoted herself to married life, dreaming all the time of escape.[102] This dream of escape sustained Lessing during her second loveless marriage to the East German communist Gottfried Lessing and provides the framework for the intense sense of freedom she experienced when she finally left him and made her way to London.

Marriage brought the question not only of how to deal with a husband but also of how to manage motherhood. Jameson, for example, faced much less conflict in dealing with her first husband than she did in managing her son, especially given that she needed to establish a career, not only for herself but in order to support him financially. Her solution was first to board him out and then to leave him with her mother in Whitby, while she established herself as a writer in London. The guilt and anguish she felt over leaving him and her sense of constantly disappointing him when she cut short her visits and was unable to bring him back to London with her continued throughout her life and is powerfully expressed in her autobiography.

---

[102]Lessing, *Under My Skin*, p. 209.

Kathleen Dayus faced a more intense form of grief and anguish and a much harsher separation from her children. As a result of her lack of any knowledge of contraception, Dayus was pregnant when she married. Money was scarce from the start of her married life and as her husband found it harder and harder to get a proper job, and began to drink more and more heavily, it became ever more so. Dayus had five children within ten years, one of whom was run down and killed by a butcher's delivery van when he was five. Her husband died on their tenth wedding anniversary, shortly after the birth of their last child. Neither her mother nor her older brother was prepared to offer her any help, and, determined that her children would be properly looked after and not left to experience the kind of struggle she had known when young, Dayus made the hard decision to take them to Barnardo's and leave them there while she established herself in the kind of work that would enable her to support them properly. She visited the children weekly until, without asking her, Barnardo's sent the children south to be fostered. It took her eight difficult years to get them back. Dayus was regarded as a bad mother by her own mother and their neighbours, but when she established herself as an enameller and was able to buy a house and reclaim her children, she felt that she had made the right decision.

Work

It is in dealing with work that one sees one of the most valuable additions made to women's autobiography by the growing number of working-class women writing it. The depiction of domestic service from the perspective of those who were employed in it was particularly important here. All the women who discussed domestic service stressed how very arduous it was. When they began work, domestic servants were given no induction or support and usually found themselves expected to undertake excessive amounts of labour, including many tasks that had not been mentioned when they agreed to accept a position. When she left school, Catherine Cookson, for example, accepted a job said to be that of a companion to an elderly woman, only to discover that she was also expected to do copious amounts of basic household labour. When Margaret Powell first looked at the list of tasks she was expected to do as a kitchen maid 'I thought they had made a mistake. I thought it was for six people to do'. She was expected to rise at 5.30 a.m. to clean the house, clean the boots of her employers, prepare the kitchen and lay out the servants' breakfast all before 8 o'clock. Powell offers the most detailed analysis of domestic labour including how servants were engaged, the lack of induction or training, the hierarchies amongst the servants themselves. She was very much aware of the power dynamics and hierarchy within domestic service and the various ways that senior servants, like cooks, exploited and ill-treated those over whom they held authority, like kitchen maids. Servants always presented a united front when dealing with upstairs, however.

We always called them 'Them'. 'Them' was the enemy, 'Them' overworked us, and 'Them' underpaid us and to 'Them' servants were a race apart, a necessary evil. As such we were their main topic of conversation. . . . It was the opinion of 'Them' upstairs that servants couldn't appreciate good living or comfort, therefore they must have plain fare, they must have dungeons to work in and to eat in, and must retire to cold spartan bedrooms to sleep.[103]

The immediate dismissal of servants who became pregnant appalled Powell. On one occasion when this happened, she was sure that the father was the nephew of the owner of the house – and that the owners thought that too. But it made no difference. The pregnant girl was dismissed and the other young women in service in the house lectured on the evils of wanton behaviour and told that no decent girl would ever let a man take advantage of her. In Powell's view, this was 'another ridiculous remark'. Powell's insistence on the fierce antagonism between servants and their employers in the homes she had worked in, and the lack of consideration that servants almost always experienced, was the source of many concerned and critical comments from readers, all of whom insisted on the care with which they had always treated their own servants.

Rosina Harrison offered a similarly graphic picture of the difficulties of domestic service, but she stressed the ways in which it was possible to negotiate it. She worked for the Astor family for most of her adult life and became deeply attached to Nancy Astor – as indeed Astor did to her. This relationship, however, as she notes in her Foreword was one 'of constant conflict and challenge'. As we have seen, Harrison prepared herself carefully for this role and she insisted that it involved terms that were acceptable to her. When she began working for Astor, she found her often unpredictable, unappreciative and sometimes both sadistic and sarcastic. Harrison, who felt that she carried out her work thoroughly and well, was determined that she would not be spoken to rudely, have unreasonable demands made on her, or be put down in front of others. Once, when she made her opinion known, Astor remonstrated with her. Harrison countered:

'My lady', I said, 'from now on I intend to speak as I'm spoken to. Common people say please and thank you, ordinary people do not reprimand servants in front of others, and ladies are supposed to be an example to all, and that is that.[104]

Instead of sacking her, as Harrison had half expected, Astor apologized and the confrontation proved a turning point, establishing the basis on which they were able to live together for thirty-two years.

---

[103]Powell, *Below Stairs*, p. 94.
[104]Harrison, *My Life in Service*, p. 83.

One particularly interesting feature of these autobiographies is the clarity with which these authors explain how they had planned and managed their working lives, gained necessary skills, and worked out when to leave, seek new employment or negotiate improved conditions. Margaret Powell and Rosina Harrison, for example, detail how they planned their careers in domestic service and the importance of the help they received from their mothers. Powell's mother insisted that, as Margaret hated needlework, she would have to go into the kitchen. She accompanied her to her first interview, did all the talking in it, accepted the job on her daughter's behalf, organized her uniforms, and facilitated her move to the house where she was employed.[105] As we have seen, Harrison's mother approached the task somewhat differently ensuring at the outset that her daughter had the kinds of skills she would need to be an invaluable lady's maid who would be asked to accompany her mistress on her travels. This proved an excellent strategy, and from the start, Harrison found jobs as a lady's maid in wealthy titled families. Kathleen Dayus never contemplated domestic work, choosing rather to work in factories as a metal press worker and then turning to enamelling. Her working life was constantly interrupted by childbirth, but when Dayus was widowed and needed to make a proper living to support her children, she planned her future carefully, working out how best to learn every aspect of the trade so that eventually she could set up her own enamelling workshop, thereby earning enough to purchase a house for herself and her children.

While working-class women born in the early decade of the 20th century describe themselves as carefully preparing themselves for their working lives and taking some pride in their work, this was not always the case for their middle-class contemporaries who sought and developed a career as writers. Neither Storm Jameson nor Naomi Mitchison, for example, suggest that they had a long-term ambition to become writers and certainly not that they were driven to write. Although setting out to explain why she and others chose to write, Mitchison was unable to offer much more than a general sense that 'because story telling has been part of the human environment for so long that we feel lost without stories'. Some of her novels originated as dreams and she had then to fill in some of the historical context that would make them intelligible, while not particularly enjoying reading history. She makes it clear that she enjoyed writing, taking pride in the fact that 'I was the first to see that one could write historical novels in a modern idiom'.[106] In her writing, as in her private life, she had to deal with the way her values conflicted with those dominant amongst the middle class, noting the difficulties she sometimes had with what she referred to as 'the decencies': those surrounding what could and could not be discussed in literature and

---

[105]Powell, *Below Stairs*, pp. 36–39.
[106]Mitchison, *You May Well Ask*, pp. 161–170.

demanding both a decorum in regard to language and a refusal to treat sexual questions. Mitchison did not need to earn her living as a writer and talks little about her literary successes and failures. Writing was undertaken alongside mothering and she wrote often while walking her children. As a woman with a household staff, however, there is no suggestion that she had to struggle to find time to write.

If Jameson minded not being considered one of the distinguished writers of her time, her own account of her writing career hardly offers a countervailing story or sense of her importance. There is no suggestion that writing was a passion or that she felt a need to say particular things or discuss particular issues. On the contrary, she suggests rather that, as a young and deeply unhappy married woman who found her only solace in reading – and who had been forced to give up the offer of a position writing critical essays for the advanced magazine *The Egoist*, because it meant leaving her mother alone, she began to write a novel, 'since there was nothing else I could do'.[107] In the self-deprecating way that she so often writes about herself, Jameson explains that she was always prepared to cut novels if publishers wanted because of her 'deep unrealized contempt for novel-writing as a serious use for energy and intellect'.[108] She admired the great novelists, but something kept murmuring in her ear: 'Only an artist without the wit to become a poet ... becomes a novelist.'[109] Her discussion of her writing and the sequence of her novels is interspersed with the agonizing story of the breakdown of her marriage, the start of her relationship with Guy Chapman and her continued guilt and anguish over her son. In the course of the 1930s, the political situation in Europe occupied more of her time and energy – and while Jameson continued to produce novels, the actual writing of them is rarely discussed. Far more detail is provided of the kind of work she had to do when her son was born to support them both, first by working in an advertising agency, which she loathed, and then as the British representative for the publishers Alfred Knopf. In characteristically judgemental terms, she ascribes her success as a publisher's agent not to her literary judgement or interpersonal skill, but rather to her unscrupulous capacity to use people.

The contrast between this approach and those of the younger women novelists who published autobiographies in the 1970s and after could not be more marked. Frame, Lessing and Emecheta, for example, all make it clear that their literary interests and their determination to be writers began in their childhood and was a guiding force in their lives. Janet Frame stresses that her passion for language, for learning new words and working out how to use them, was evident from her earliest childhood. Her desire to become

---

[107] Jameson, *Journey from the North*, vol. I, p. 84.
[108] Jameson, *Journey from the North*, vol. I, p. 84.
[109] Jameson *Journey from the North*, vol. I, p. 116.

a writer was clear soon after. She started writing in adolescence, publishing poems in the school magazine. She continued to write and publish short stories in her student years and right through her psychiatric incarceration. From adolescence, she recognized the importance of her writing, not only as a form of creative expression but because it gave her a kind of standing that was available in no other way. In her early adult years, her writing was literally a lifesaver. In her long years of incarceration, Frame's desire to be a writer was mocked and scorned by nursing staff. A leucotomy was suggested by them as a way to make her 'normal', give up 'fancy intellectual notions of being a writer', and her mother agreed to it. Fortunately for Frame, her book of stories, *The Lagoon*, received the Hubert Church prize when it appeared in 1951. Her name was already on the surgical list for a leucotomy and there seemed no way out when she was visited one evening by the new hospital superintendent. To her amazement, he spoke directly to her, pointing to the notice in that day's paper about her prize. 'I've decided that you should stay as you are. I don't want you changed', he said, and then began the process of moving her towards discharge from the hospital.[110]

This book and the prize helped when she left hospital too. At the time, she notes, she was 'outwardly smiling and calm, but inwardly with all confidence gone, with the conviction at last that I was officially a non-person' – and with no ongoing support or plan of management. She was given a lifeline by the established New Zealand writer Frank Sargeson, who, impressed by her writing and horrified by her life, invited her to live in a hut in his garden and devote herself to writing. Sargeson also managed to obtain a health pension so that she could concentrate on her writing. While working in Sargeson's garden, Frame wrote her first novel, *Owls do Cry*. He also helped her get a travelling grant to England where her life began again in many ways. In her early years in England and Ibiza, as Frame noted, she was too busy living life to the full to write. When she came back, she bought herself an encyclopaedia of sex so that she could fully understand and articulate the sexual experiences she had had and took herself to the Maudsley. When she finally left the Maudsley, she was 'no longer, I hoped, dependent on my "schizophrenia" for comfort and attention and help, but with myself as myself, I again began my writing career'.[111] The demands of her writing determined where and how Frame lived in England: in the country for a time, but then when she felt the need of its stimulation, in London. It also provided the reason for her to return to New Zealand. A few years after she had moved to London, her father died and as she was his executor, there were family reasons to return home. While others, including Dr Cawley, thought she should remain in London where she had been able to flourish, rather than return to New Zealand where she had had such a damaging experience, Frame did

---

[110]Frame, *An Angel at My Table*, p. 300.
[111]Frame, *An Angel at My Table*, p. 501.

not agree. Her ongoing development as a writer, she insisted, made it imperative that she return. She knew New Zealand in a way that she could never know another country, and her stories and novels all depended on that knowledge. She could also make a mark of greater significance writing about New Zealand than about anywhere else. Europe was already on the map of the imagination, she insisted, while New Zealand was not. It would be for her,

> like living in an age of myth-makers; with a freedom of imagination among all the artists because it is possible to begin at the beginning ... and to help form them, to be a mapmaker for those who will follow, nourished by this generation's layers of the dead.[112]

Although Lessing was a much better-known author than Frame when she wrote her autobiography, her sense of herself as a writer was less pronounced, especially in her early life. She relies on the testimony of friends to illustrate the fact that she had always planned to write, rather than seeing it as a core of her own early self, as it was for Frame. What she stresses rather is her love of reading and the way in which, especially in her adolescence, she discovered the world of books. In her early adult years, however, the desire to write took hold and the lack of interest in literature or writing within Rhodesian society, and the explicit hostility towards it evident amongst her communist friends and colleagues increased her strong sense of the need to escape from this narrow colonial world and to get to England. Lessing wrote her first book, *The Grass is Singing*, in Rhodesia, stressing that there was nothing autobiographical about it as a way of emphasizing that it was her first major literary work. It did indeed establish her career. She had signed a contract to publish it but on very unfavourable terms in Rhodesia. Shortly after her arrival in England, however, she found an agent who rejected this contract and got her another with Michael Joseph and set her up with writing projects that supported her while she wrote her later novels.

While Janet Frame's literary skills and ambitions were recognized from childhood onwards and framed her life, this was not the case for Buchi Emecheta. As we have seen, her literary ambitions were ridiculed at school and not accepted within her family or her marriage. Seeking to show her husband that she had aspirations beyond motherhood, basic paid work and housework, she gave him the manuscript of her first novel, *The Bride Price*, to read – and he responded by burning it.[113] It was that act that finally made Emecheta leave her marriage and become a sole parent.

As a Black woman, Emecheta had a much harder time establishing herself as a writer than did Lessing or Frame. She makes very clear how hard she

---

[112]Frame, *An Angel at My Table*, p. 541.
[113]Emecheta, *Head Above Water*, p. 32.

found it to negotiate the English literary world and its social mores – and the way in which she was treated as a Black woman. She disliked the editing process involved in preparing her first book, *In the Ditch*, and resented the fact that her editor wrote of her as 'that intelligent African girl with little self-control', called her 'little Buchi' and seemed to want to look after and devote himself to her. She later felt that she had let her anger get the better of her and regretted cutting her ties with this first editor and others who had helped her initially because 'those people at the top stick together. A few months before, most of them were saying how clever, how promising, but now it seemed, because of telling one of the clan to go home with his red rose, the rest seemed to clam up on me.' Publishers no longer seemed interested and she had difficulty in publishing her second book, *Second-Class Citizen*. Although she continued to write, there was insufficient interest in her work to enable her to live by writing. She published her major novels *The Slave* and *The Bride Price* in the mid-1970s, however, for some years Emecheta supported herself with other paid work, initially in youth clubs catering for Black adolescents and then working in mother-and-child groups for the local council. Emecheta includes detailed descriptions of the process of getting these jobs and of the work, along with her ongoing difficulties with publishers and agents in her autobiography. As she got more and more work in the late 1970s, writing plays for television and being commissioned to write books for young readers in West Africa by Oxford University Press, she began to win awards. Emecheta began to establish herself as an independent and full-time writer. She felt she had done so by the time she finished her autobiography, but that, even though she now owned a house, her life was not yet secure. 'Living off writing is a precarious existence and money is short', she wrote in the last sentence to her autobiography. 'But with careful management and planning, I found I could keep my head and those of my family, through God's grace, above water.'[114]

A Sense of Self

Exploring and articulating a sense of self was an increasingly important issue in many women's autobiographies in the late 20th century. Informed by a range of psychological theories and by new approaches both to sexuality and to the notion of identity, many women were more introspective and concerned to analyse themselves and their own feelings and behaviour than had been the case earlier. Indeed, for some women, a search for the self or for a sense of identity was a primary objective within the autobiographical project. This search for a sense of self, or the feeling of a need to articulate it, however, was often fraught and painful and not everyone felt that they had managed to achieve it.

---

[114]Emecheta, *Head Above Water*, p. 96.

The self had greater prominence in these autobiographies because most of them involved a strong sense of the struggle the author engaged in to overcome the many obstacles they faced as women in order to pursue the life they wanted and to become the person that they sought to be. These obstacles took different forms: class was one, sometimes discussed in terms of the poverty that it entailed for working-class women, and at others in terms of the way it made them feel like outsiders. Provincial and colonial life was another, bringing its own expectations and limitations that women had to challenge. All of these women see their own capacities and strength and determination as enabling them to challenge the conservative worlds from which they came and to take their place in a changing world. There is sometimes a tension here between the emphasis on the importance of history and class and the expectations of womanhood, the framework that set up the idea that the personal is political, on the one hand, and the depiction of each individual author in psychological terms that underline her individuality and the importance of her particular personality and set of intimate and familial relationships, on the other.

The new urgency in describing a sense of self can be seen very clearly in Storm Jameson's autobiography. It is evident from the question that she poses at the start of her autobiography about how she can write about someone she knows only from the inside and continues throughout in the way in which, while depicting the particular episodes or experiences that make up the story of her life, she emphasizes the specific characteristics, in herself that are exhibited by it, characteristics that made her an uncomfortable companion as well as causing her pain and difficulty. Her frequent sense of intolerable boredom, hatred of domesticity and lack of capacity to organize her life or manage her money are referred to often. 'I cannot explain my pathological hatred of domestic life and frantic need to be free', she wrote when describing the unhappiness of her first marriage.

> Not free to write, to be amused, or famous. To be free. To call it spiritual nausea only pushes it further out of reach. A crazy violent character, a tramp, or a lunatic, shares my skin with a Yorkshire housewife.[115]

The other side of the desire to be free was the constant sense she had of being trapped. Sometimes she describes herself as feeling like a trapped animal, an image that she uses to describe herself in childhood while expecting a beating[116] and then again when describing living with her first husband in Kettering where he was employed as a schoolmaster.[117] She trapped herself into this marriage, she insists, exonerating her mother from any blame, as she so often did, although her description of how the marriage

---

[115]Jameson, *Journey from the North*, vol. I, p. 88.
[116]Jameson, *Journey from the North*, vol. I, p. 24.
[117]Jameson, *Journey from the North*, vol. I, p. 82.

came about makes it clear that it was driven entirely by her mother's fury and against her wishes. At the same time, and clearly illustrating her general understanding of psychology, Jameson describes some of her adult responses as those of a beaten child. As a writer, she insists, she was indifferent to the opinions of others about her work. 'The person in my skin who flinches when damned or mocked is not the writer.... The one who flinches is a beaten child, afraid with an old fear.'[118] The reverse of this is her sense that she is responsible for everyone else, for the unhappiness of her mother and son and sometimes even her first husband. The self-flagellation that early readers and critics noted in her autobiography is clearly evident in the frequency with which her description of her characteristics become failings. Even things that might be seen as a success and indicating her abilities: her early success acting as an agent for the publisher Alfred Knopf, for example, was an illustration not just of her competence, but of her unscrupulousness. That, alongside her ambition, selfishness and incapacity to live sufficiently were underlying failings.

Jameson was clearly both psychologically informed and aware at some level of the importance of her mother in producing her painful and conflicted sense of herself. The next generation of women writers, however, talked far more explicitly both about a sense of self and about the importance of relationships with parents in producing it. In the case of Doris Lessing, for example, this awareness is threaded throughout her autobiography. It underlay her insistence, when describing her childhood and how unloved she felt that these early childhood experiences 'made me one of the walking wounded for years', and her discussion of the need to revolt against her mother that was so central to her adolescence.

Part of Lessing's depiction of herself includes the way in which she adopted different persona as a way to manage her life, especially in the years before she was able to leave Rhodesia. When the family was reading A. A. Milne, 'just as if we had never left England', they each adopted a character. She became 'Tigger' and adopted a particular personality that helped her to manage her life and her sense of alienation from white Rhodesia and its lifestyle and institutions.

> I remained Tigger until I left Rhodesia, for nothing would stop friends and comrades using it.... This personality was expected to be brash, jokey, clumsy and always ready to be a good sport, that is to laugh at herself, apologise, clown, confess inability. An extrovert. In that it was a protection for the person I really was.[119]

After she married, as the wife of a central member of the country club set, Lessing was expected to entertain and added the role of Hostess to the

---

[118] Jameson, *Journey from the North*, vol. I, p. 143.
[119] Lessing, *Under My Skin*, p. 89.

persona of Tigger, again with the sense that her real self was hidden from view. Lessing dispensed with Tigger the moment she arrived in England. The question of who she was, however, continued to be an important one that resurfaced in different ways, in her personal life, in relation to her writing and in the course of her political activities. In her dislike of the imperialism and racism of the white Rhodesia in which she grew up and into which she married, Lessing began in her early adult life to gravitate towards left-wing groups including the Rhodesian Communist Party. But she was never quite comfortable in the left-wing groups she joined. Many of the Communists were hostile to her ambition to write so that she was again facing a critical world that required struggle or subterfuge. This ambivalence continued when she was in Britain where she continued her left-wing activities and decided to join the Communist Party. This decision, she noted in her autobiography, was 'probably the most neurotic act of my life', especially as she had decided to do so 'at a time when my "doubts" had become something like a steady private torment'.[120] Lessing was no more able to explain this decision than she was her first marriage: if the former was simply something that went with the *zeitgeist*, the latter was 'some kind of social psychosis or self-hypnosis' that she shared with the many others in her generation who became involved in communism.[121]

The question of her sense of self came most strongly to the fore for Lessing when, having realized that her own life was an extraordinary one and would make a good subject, she was beginning to work on the Martha Quest novels. She was looking back on her early life and seeing it in different ways, questioning things she had taken for granted. The process left her confused. 'While I certainly "knew who I was" (to use the American formula), I did not know how to define myself as a social being.' This whole business of 'finding out who I am', she noted, always left her wondering what people meant by it. 'Surely they can't be without a sense of self. A sense of: Here I am, inside here.' She repeated that she did not know 'how to define myself in a social context'. Lessing makes clear what she meant by this context.

> Easy enough to say I was a child of the end of the Raj. . . . Yes, I was one of a generation brought up on World War I and then as much formed by World War II. But there was hiatus, a lack, a blur – and it was to do with my parents and particularly my mother. I had fought her steadily, relentlessly, and I had had to – but what was it all about. . . . I was not able to answer that, entirely, until I was in my seventies, and even then perhaps not finally.[122]

---

[120]Lessing, *Under My Skin*, p. 862.
[121]Lessing, *Under My Skin*, p. 901.
[122]Lessing, *Under My Skin*, p. 253.

Although she was sceptical about and resistant to psychotherapy, Lessing did see a therapist when she was in London, distraught both at the prospect of a visit from her mother and because the most important sexual relationship in her life was going badly. Her therapist, she insists, mainly offered support – but it is hard not to see her portrait of herself as informed by it. The same point could be made about Janet Frame, who was well aware of the importance to her of her psychiatrist, Michael Cawley. It was experiencing life in London and working the experiences through with him, Frame suggests, that helped her develop a sense of who she was. 'My London days were full of experience', she wrote,

> museums, galleries, libraries, people; and underlying all was a gradual strengthening of me in my place through my talks with Dr Cawley as if he was a bespoke tailor helping to reinforce the seams of my life and now I was putting on my own garment to try it.[123]

Dr Cawley also seems to have helped Frame to understand and come to terms with her family difficulties, her unhappy adolescence, her years in psychiatric hospitals, and with the ways she had dealt with her own anxieties. A key part of Frame's development, as she later saw it, was her realization of the extent to which she had allowed others to make her decisions. She recognized also how important a protection her illness and the diagnosis of schizophrenia had been to her in enabling her to withdraw from difficult situations and how hard it was to relinquish.

One of Dr Cawley's most important contributions to Frame was his insistence that she was primarily a writer. It is this sense of herself that underlies the coherent picture of herself that Frame delineated throughout her autobiography, even as she shows how hard she found it to deal with the social world outside her home and the different demands made on her. Her family was clearly very important to her and to how she developed, but as she made very clear, her relationships with them did not define her. On the contrary, she stresses the importance of her imagination and of external events and experiences from her earliest years. As a child, she recalls asking huge existential questions: 'why was the world?', for example, to which she later added 'and where was my place?'[124] Her first memory, she insists, was of a day when she stood by the long white dusty road and listening to the wind – feeling a burden of sadness and loneliness. Until then, she insists, 'I don't think I had thought of myself as a person looking out at the world, until then, I felt I *was* the world. In listening to the wind and its sad song, I knew I was listening to a sadness that had no relation to me, which belonged to the world.'[125] Her fascination with language and the meaning of words

---

[123]Frame, *An Angel at My Table*, p. 544.
[124]Frame, *An Angel at My Table*, p. 61.
[125]Frame, *An Angel at My Table*, p. 29.

was something that made the world interesting and exciting for her from her earliest years. This sense of her early literary interest provides a balance to Frame's description of herself as a shy anxious, often embarrassed child, concerned mainly not to draw attention to herself and allowing others to decide what she should do. As we have seen, it was this sense of herself as a writer that made her.

While Lessing regarded discussions about knowing who one was and about a sense of self as very American in the 1950s, by the 1970s and '80s these issues, often now talked about in terms of subjectivity and a sense of identity were widespread. One can see this clearly in the academic autobiographies that I have been discussing, in which involvement with feminism or sexual and gay liberation linked political action with new forms of identity. Sometimes these were linked also to theoretical developments and debates in specific disciplines. And yet, for all the theoretical and disciplinary armoury that is at their disposal, these women rarely came to feel that they had established a sense of self or an identity that encompassed their entire lives or with which they were satisfied.

The importance of her search for a sense of identity is evident from the first page of Elizabeth Wilson's *Mirror Writing*. The book begins with a description of her finding a sense of identity in a radical demonstration in which she was involved in 1971.

> It was not until I became involved in radical political movement that I ever felt I lived fully in the present or was fully myself. All those years before I'd felt that my identity was suppressed, that I was confined to some self-created psychic prison. What was I? I didn't know. I had not 'found myself'. I looked in all the wrong places, of course – that was my psychic prison, if there was one.[126]

As she shouted and performed her street theatre with others, she came to feel herself and the importance of her connection with the others: 'my identity expands into the group identity with its subjective sense of potency.' As we have seen, contemporary political movements and activities were of immense importance in her search for her sense of self. In contrast with her experience of home, school and even university, it was only when she was involved in radical politics, she insisted, that she felt fully herself. But this was a fleeting feeling and not one that could always be sustained. This statement, however, serves to introduce the issue of identity as the one that structures every aspect of Wilson's story. Her sense of distance and alienation from her family and home are important here. Making no attempt to describe her childhood as she experienced it, she chose rather to look back on it as if through a telescope in a way that emphasizes how odd it was.

---

[126] Wilson, *Mirror Writing*, p. 1.

With its background in the world of empire and a house full of souvenirs of the Raj, her family seemed not to belong in the real world. It was an embarrassment and Wilson devoted 'much energy to the attempt to conceal, even deny, the existence of this strange home', from which she sought to emerge as a 'normal teenager of the 1950s'. One way Wilson found of dealing with this strange world was to establish a public persona that helped her to interact without revealing herself. She talked incessantly, becoming known as 'Chatterbox'.

Wilson set about escaping her home and family as early as she could, not by leaving physically, but rather by attempting to transform her image and assume new identities. Her interest in style and in culture, evident when she was quite young, was important here. As an adolescent, she developed a love of style and hoped her investment in clothes and fashion would enable her to transform herself into a work of art. This proved impossible and a series of other identities followed: her love of Latin at her grammar school suggested the identity of an intellectual. Her involvement in same-sex relationships at university brought a new identity as the 'glittering, snaky, sinister "lesbian" cut through my confusions at the age of eighteen. If I was *that*, then I could wash my hands of social success or failure.'[127] But this was not sufficient and was followed by an attempt to see herself as a writer. Eventually, having worked her way through social work, psychoanalysis and intense involvement in both the women's movement and the movement for gay liberation, Wilson came to recognize that the notion of a fixed and all-encompassing identity was illusory and that, as Brian Finney suggests, one should rather see 'individual identity as a process, a continual becoming which can therefore only be discerned by retrospective reflection, by a leap into a room of mirrors which reflect back the leaper's image into infinity'.[128]

Where Wilson describes an essentially isolated struggle, Ann Oakley insists rather on the extent to which the key features of her life and her dilemma are shared with other women. Both her own disciplinary training in sociology and her involvement in feminism play a part in the formulation of her autobiographical project. 'This book is about my life', Oakley noted, 'but it is also about others. . . . I know I am living and writing about something which is recognizable to others. I have thus tried self-consciously to draw together . . . some of the connecting threads between my life and the lives of others.'[129]

The key question she needed to address was what kind of woman she was, especially given her sense of her mother's ordinariness and her attraction to career women, on the one hand, and her father's support for her – but disapproval of married women working, on the other. The link that Oakley drew between her life and the lives of other educated middle-class women

---

[127]Wilson, *Mirror Writing*, p. 38.
[128]Finney Brian, 'Sexual Identity in Modern British Autobiography', *Prose Studies* 8, no. 2 (1985): 34.
[129]Oakley, *Taking It Like a Woman*, p. 3.

reflected also the extensive theoretical discussion amongst feminists of the ambiguities in the very notion of 'feminine' and the difficulties and contradictions that women faced in their daily lives. Oakley incorporated these feminist insights and arguments into her discussion, of the conflicts she and other women faced when seeking further education and a career but dealing also with the demands of marriage and an all-encompassing family life.

Nonetheless, as Oakley was well aware, her story also had very particular features. Writing about the period of her life that occurred before the re-emergence of feminism in the early 1970s, Oakley stresses her intense unhappiness and her sense of being an outsider who didn't fit into her school life or the society around her. The particular problems that she faced reflected the contradictory nature of her position within her own family. There was not only the problem of her identification with her father, despite his belief that women should devote themselves to motherhood, but also a kind of gender confusion as her father was the more overtly loving and nurturant parent, often apparently taking on a maternal role. The question of who she was and what kind of woman she wanted to become dominated Oakley's life for many years. It led to a breakdown at university and years of unhappiness. Eventually after years of psychotherapy, with the help and support of a loving husband and with the knowledge she gained through her own involvement in feminism, she felt she had resolved it more or less satisfactorily, establishing a very successful career, and managing to mother her two children. Nonetheless, she insists at the end of her book, neither feminism nor any of the other avenues she followed offered a comprehensive identity. One thing in her life remained unresolved. 'What I most of all want that I don't have is something very fundamental and very surprising. I want a concept of myself.'[130]

Like Wilson and Oakley, Steedman's *Landscape for a Good Woman* is preoccupied with questions of identity, linked closely to her sense of being an outsider. Her mother's sense of unfairness and of loss, the stories that her mother told and that she read about sad, forsaken and lost children, the misery of her childhood, combined with the constant re-iteration that hers was not the saddest life and that she could neither complain nor shed tears for herself – but only for her mother and others whose lives were harder left Steedman with a sense of the pain of her childhood and the need not to draw attention to herself or be a nuisance. But they also made her feel even more of an outsider when she went to university and met up with people who wanted to talk about themselves and their early lives. She found it almost impossible to explain to the middle-class women that she met at university and in her adult life how difficult and painful her childhood was. 'My childhood was like yours', they would say.

---

[130]Oakley, *Taking It Like a Woman*, p. 186.

What they cannot bear, I think, is that there exists a poverty and marginality of experience to which they have no access, structures of feeling that they have not lived within (and would not want to live within for these are the structures of deprivation).[131]

As an historian interested in working-class life, and especially here in the lives and experiences of working-class girls, she sought stories of lives that might link more closely with hers, reading the small number of earlier working-class women's autobiographies obsessively during their twenties and thirties. Although the lives depicted in them were very different from hers, she found links of an important kind in Kathleen Woodward's *Jipping Street*. Woodward's description of feeling herself as a burden to her mother was the first she had seen that resembled Steedman's. Cookson too was important, although her life was even more different. Her intense description of feeling an outsider as an illegitimate child offered an echo for Steedman when, in her adult life, she discovered that she too was illegitimate. Steedman's sense of herself as connected to these women, despite her differences from them, contrasts with her insistence that she felt completely excluded from the autobiographies of middle-class girlhood such as Oakley's *Taking It Like a Woman*.

One of the most powerful ways in which Steedman's sense of herself, and of other working-class girls who felt burdened and unloved by their mothers, as being outside the dominant culture can be seen in their disinclination to become mothers themselves. There is, she notes, an extensive literature on mothering and how it is reproduced in the daughters who in turn become mothers. These accounts of mothering, she argues 'need to recognize not-mothering too', including here the women who have children for specific economic or emotional reasons that make the child herself a secondary consideration. In her own case, she wonders if her mother's half-conscious reason for having her was the wish a baby might induce her father to marry her. Although her own mother insisted constantly that she was a good mother and provided more or less adequately for her daughters, Steedman identifies with Woodward's recognition that while her mother did what she could for her children she had no love to give them. Recognition of this refusal of love had its liberating aspect, but as Steedman's discussion makes clear, the refusal itself deprives the daughter of the 'the self-love that lies at the root of a wish for a child'. The child's incapacity to bring happiness to her mother produces a kind of guilt that cannot be removed – and shapes and limits the kind of woman she can become.

Conclusion

It is hard to overestimate the significance of the developments in women's autobiography that occurred in the 1970s and '80s. One can see them in the

---

[131]Steedman, *Landscape*, p. 17.

expanding range of women who wrote and published in these decades and that extended from obscure and completely unknown women whose often very hard lives had centred on family and work, on the one hand, to the most prominent and highly awarded novelists and extremely distinguished academics, on the other. Works from across this range not only sold well and found a substantial readership but were extensively reviewed and received notable awards. Indeed, the growing importance and recognition of women's autobiography and autobiography more generally was evident in the increasing amount of reviewing and writing about it in both academic and more general works and in the advent of autobiography prizes, like the Pen Ackerley Prize.

Many different social and intellectual developments contributed to the growing prominence of autobiography, and autobiography in turn serves to illustrate some of those developments. One can see this particularly clearly in terms of how history featured and was dealt with in these works. As we have seen, history was very important to those writing autobiographies in the interwar period, many of whom saw their work as important primarily because of their involvement in and experience of major historical events and movements, like the First World War or the militant suffrage campaign. It continued to be important in the later period too but was seen in very different ways. The basic experiences of women's lives were now seen as historically interesting and important because of the insight into the many facets of daily life that they offered, whether this was the life of privileged upper-middle-class families or extremely poor working-class ones or indeed imperial ones whether lived in settler communities or in tribal locations. The emergence of the new social history with its interest in 'life from below' and in the quotidian, offered an academic framework for this new approach to history, but it was evident equally in more popular fora like the various BBC programmes focusing on the daily life of ordinary people.

The question of changes within academic disciplines takes on an added significance because of the number of academic women who wrote autobiographies at this time. It was not only academic women who turned to autobiography at this time, as Jeremy Popkin has shown in his extensive analysis of the many male, as well as female, historians who turned to autobiography and as others have chronicled in terms of 'an autobiographical turn'. One could, however, argue that it is women academics who have posed the greatest challenge to traditional autobiography and offered the most significant innovations in thinking and writing about it. The work of Carolyn Steedman and Ann Oakley in particular served to transform autobiographical writing, in the way that they rejected a linear narrative as a way to depict their lives, choosing instead to intersperse sections that offered some kind of narrative with other kinds of writing that expanded on the meaning of their experiences by drawing on fiction, myths, fairy stories and other kinds of historical or sociological analysis.

Feminist insights and approaches to questions of gender were important here too. The importance of gender is evident throughout the history of women's autobiography, as all the women who wrote their life stories had something to say about the ways in which they experienced womanhood and about the limitations and difficulties that were imposed on them as women. This issue was formulated in a different way in this later period, partly as a result of feminist ideas and insights. Thus, the issue that was raised by several women, and most notably by Ann Oakley and Carolyn Steedman, was the psychic dimension of gender, in Steedman's case linked also to her analysis of the psychic dimension of class. It was not institutional barriers that Oakley noted, but the gender confusion in her home – and the difficulty of sorting out what kind of woman she wanted to be. The key issue in the breakdown she suffered as a late adolescent and that she dealt with in therapy, she noted, although these words were not used to describe it, was the dilemma of how to be a woman in a man's world. For Steedman too, the key issue was that of being a daughter taught always that she was a burden and that her mother would have been better off without her. This too raised the question of how to *be* as a woman – and the impossibility of thinking about herself ever reproducing.

This focus on questions of gender as ones primarily of psychological significance that required resolution in order for the author to have a sense of who she was and how to live also leads to a very different way of writing and thinking about autobiography. The focus on internal and emotional issues and problems, *albeit* ones that are seen as shared rather than important only for the individual writing about them, is new in autobiographical terms. Recognition of the problem of gender in earlier women's autobiographies was the prelude to stories of struggles in the public world: against unjust situations or brutal men, or laws and institutions that needed to be changed. Alternatively, there were stories of achievement of particular professional or philanthropic ends, or of active involvement and engagement in major political campaigns or events. There is here, one might argue, at least a tacit acceptance of the existing male autobiographical models and approaches that Virginia Woolf pointed to in her discussion of Rousseau in which the primary goal of writing an autobiography was the struggle to establish a sense of oneself as an autonomous being, capable of making significant public or intellectual contributions. While this struggle might incorporate sexual and moral issues, its resting point was public achievement. This model, however, has no place in some of the more innovative autobiographies of this period where little or no attention is paid to careers or to the mark that the author made in the world. The division between public and private is eroded in this insistence on the private and psychic aspect of these external circumstances and on the need for a private resolution of them. It is in this insistence on the psychic dimension of so many aspects of life: gender, class, the struggle to decide on a profession, that these works transformed women's autobiography showing through it the immensely important issues that underlay the problem of being a woman.

Autobiographies Referred to in This Chapter

Brittain, Vera. *Testament of Experience*. Bath: Cedric Chivers Ltd, 1957, repr 1971.
Cookson, Catherine Ann. *Our Kate: Her Personal Story*. London: Macdonald, 1969, repr 1973, 1969.
Dayus, Kathleen. *Her People: Memoirs of an Edwardian Childhood,* I. London: Virago: 1982.
Dayus, Kathleen. *Where There's Life*. London: Virago, 1985.
Emecheta, Buchi. *Head Above Water*. London and Nigeria: Heinemann, 1986.
Frame, Janet. *An Angel at My Table*. London: Virago, 1989.
Gamble, Rose. *Chelsea Child*. London: British Broadcasting Corporation, 1979.
Harrison, Rosina wih Leigh Crutchley. *My Life in Service*. New York: Viking Press, 1975.
Jameson, Margaret Storm. *Journey from the North*. 2 vols. London: Virago 1984.
Lessing, Doris. *Under My Skin: Volume One of My Autobiography to 1949*. London: Harper Perennial, 1994.
Lessing, Doris. *Walking in the Shade: Volume Two of My Autobiography, 1949–1962*. London: Harper Collins, 1998.
Lively, Penelope. *Oleander, Jacaranda: A Childhood Perceived*. London: Penguin Books, 1994.
Kuhn, Annette, *Family Secrets: Acts of Memory and Imagination*. London: Verso, 1995, 2nd edition.
Mitchison, Naomi. *Small Talk*. Oxford: Bodley Head, 1973.
Mitchison, Naomi. *All Change Here: Girlhood and Marriage*. London: The Bodley Head, 1975.
Oakley, Ann. *Taking It Like a Woman*. London: Jonathan Cape, 1984.
Owen, Ursula, ed. *Fathers: Reflections by Daughters*. London: Virago, 1983.
Powell, Margaret. *Below Stairs*. London: Pan Books, 1968 (Pan 1970).
Russell, Dora. *The Tamarisk Tree 3 Vols*. London: Virago, 1978–1985.
Sage, Lorna. *Bad Blood: A Memoir*. London: Fourth Estate, 2000.
Steedman, Carolyn. *Landscape for a Good Woman*. London: Virago, 1986.
Wilson, Elizabeth. *Mirror Writing: An Autobiography*. London: Virago, 1982.

FIGURE 5 *Sindiwe Magona, Festival Atlantide 2021, Nantes. (Courtesy of Wikimedia Commons.)*

CHAPTER FIVE

Autobiography and the Wider British World

The transformation of women's autobiography evident in Britain in the last decades of the 20th century can be seen also in the wider British world, in the appearance of large numbers of autobiographies by Indigenous women and women of colour from many parts of the empire including South Africa, Australia, Namibia, India, Pakistan, Egypt and Kenya. Imperial life had long provided a setting for women's autobiography. For the most part, however, these autobiographies were written by white Western women and described the hardships they experienced and the adventures they enjoyed when settling in far-flung and little-known places.[1] In the course of the 20th century, Kenya became prominent in these works, providing the setting for two of the most popular imperial memoirs: Karen Blixen's *Out of Africa* (1937) and Elspeth Huxley's *The Flame Trees of Thika* (1959).[2] Although Blixen herself was Danish and had a very strong sense of her own origin and cultural framework, she spent her sixteen African years growing coffee in a British colony and wrote her memoir in English, translating it into Danish later. Both women took a great interest in the local people, especially the Kikuyu, doing their best to get to know them and to understand their culture and beliefs. But theirs are autobiographies concerned with depicting how

---

[1] For Australia see Kay Walsh and Joy Hooton, *Australian Narrative Autobiography: An Annotated Bibliography*, 2 vols (Australian Scholarly Editions Centre, National Library of Australia, 1992); For South Africa see David Westley, 'A Select Bibliography of South African Autobiography', *Biography* 17, no. 3 (Summer 1994): 268–280. Siobhan Lambert-Hurley, *Elusive Lives: Gender, Autobiography, and the Self in Muslim South Asia*, South Asia in Motion (Stanford University Press, 2018).
[2] Karen Blixen, *Out of Africa* (Harmondsworth: Penguin, 1937, repr. 1952) and Elspeth Huxley, *The Flame Trees of Thika* (London: Catto & Windus, 1959). Both books sold very well and were adapted for screen. *Out of Africa* was made into a film starring Meryl Streep and Robert Redford and directed by Sydney Pollock in 1985. *The Flame Trees of Thika* was made into a five-part television series starring Hayley Mills in 1981.

they came to live in and understand an exotic and alien world. The imperial framework, and the sense of being civilized Westerners seeking to understand and describe the land, the fauna and flora and the curious customs of the native inhabitants in ways that would appeal to Western readers, dominates their work. Even African poverty is picturesque. Blixen describes the Swahili town outside Nairobi, for example, as 'built mostly out of old paraffin tins hammered flat, in various states of rust', and a 'lively, dirty and gaudy place'.[3] Women of colour too had occasionally produced autobiographies, as we have seen with the lives of Sarah Prince and Mary Seacole, usually when they were living in Britain, however, and in contact with the culture of autobiography established there in the course of the 19th century.

Nothing could have been less like these works than the autobiographies by Black African and Indigenous Australian women that appeared in the 1980s and '90s. These works described what it was like to actually live in buildings hammered out of old paraffin tins – or equally ramshackle alternatives. For them, the imperial world and colonial life was not exotic but impoverished, sometimes violent and very hard. There were marked differences amongst these autobiographies in terms of their literary style and the specific stories that they told. All of them, however, share a sense of the fundamental importance of the imperial political world, whether it took the form of discriminatory colonial policies or the practices of repressive regimes, in the shaping of their lives. These discriminatory structures and policies determined the basic shape of their lives, including where they could live, the kind of home they could live in, the education available to them, the kind of work they could do and the payment they could receive for it. For some, they extended to their capacity to marry or to have their children live with them. Unlike their contemporaries in Britain itself, these women did not argue that the personal was political, but rather that there was no aspect of personal life on which the political did not intrude.

These autobiographies illustrate one prominent aspect of the boom in autobiography, which was becoming a global phenomenon towards the end of the 20th century: the dramatic increase in accounts of experiences of severe forms of suffering, oppression and torture, some occasioned by war or repressive governments, but also as an ongoing part of colonial violence. The 20th century bore witness to destruction and suffering on an unprecedented scale. Starting with the appalling blood-letting of the First World War, imprisonment, torture and killing continued on a large scale with the rise of Fascism, the emergence of Communism and then the Second World War. War and violence on a horrific scale were evident in the post-war world too, in the Korean and Vietnam Wars and in the struggles for independence and an end to colonial and white rule in several parts of Africa, especially Kenya and South Africa. Some of these terrible experiences

---

[3] Blixen, *Out of Africa*, p. 10.

were recorded in autobiographies earlier in the century: those involving the First World War, for example, and some struggles for independence from colonial rule. From the 1970s and '80s onwards, this work proliferated especially in Britain and the United States. It was registered within autobiographical studies in a new interest in the study of autobiography and trauma.[4]

The appearance of a number of autobiographies of women of colour across the wider British world was unprecedented and a major turning point in the history of women's autobiography. These works were not, however, the first autobiographies to appear foregrounding the impact of colonial expropriation and oppression or depicting an individual life as an emblem of a political struggle. In the half-century before the 1980s, a number of leaders of independence and nationalist movements, most of whom had been imprisoned for their activity, published widely read autobiographies. Their personal struggles and suffering came to illustrate, even to stand for, the struggle for the independence of their people. These 'national autobiographies', Philip Holden argues, depict 'the growth of an individual implicitly identified as a national father in a way that explicitly parallels the growth of national consciousness and, frequently proleptically, the achievement of an independent nation state'.[5] The first of these works, Nehru's *An Autobiography*, written while he was in prison in 1936, became 'almost a template for future generations of nationalist leaders', including Kwame Nkrumah in Ghana, Jomo Kenyatta in Kenya and Nelson Mandela, whose *My Long Walk to Freedom* is probably the best known of these works. Autobiography has been recognized as particularly important in Kenya as 'one of the most prominent media through which the Mau Mau uprising has been explicated as a defining historical event in the history of Kenya and African nationalism', with many former Mau Mau writing about their lives.[6]

There was little place for women in these profoundly masculine works and some of the women's autobiographies written in the 1980s were intended not only to illustrate the harshness of colonial oppression but also to insert themselves and women more generally into this story of the struggle for independence. The Kenyan political activist Wambui Waiyaki Otieno clearly does so, even in the title of her autobiography, *Mau Mau's Daughter*, a work in which she stresses the independence and courage that she showed in her years of working with the Mau Mau.[7] While Wambui stresses her difference

---

[4]Nancy K. Miller and Jason Tougaw, eds., *Extremities: Trauma, Witnessing and Communities* (Albany: State University of New York Press, 2001).
[5]Philip Holden, *Autobiography and Decolonization: Modernity, Masculinity, and the Nation State* (Maddison, WI: University of Wisconsin Press, 2008), p. 5.
[6]Marshall Cough, *Mau Mau Memoirs: History, Memoir and Politics* (Boulder, CO: Lynne Rienner, 1998).
[7]Folasade Hunsu, 'Engendering an Alternative Approach to Otherness in African Women's Autobiography', *Life Writing* 10, no. 2 (2013): 177–179.

from most other women, other autobiographies were concerned rather to link the life of the author with the lives and activities of other women. One of the first and the best known of these autobiographies, that of the prominent South African social and community leader Ellen Kuzwayo, underlined this point by combining the discussion of her own life and activities with the stories of other Black women, insisting on the need for recognition of the immense contribution that they had made to the well-being of their people and the political struggle.[8] One can see a similar concern in the writing of the Namibian freedom fighter Ellen Ndeshi Namhila.[9] Her autobiography described her own life after she went into exile as a teenager and the difficulties involved in her return. Once she had re-established herself in Namibia, however, she spent years researching and writing the stories of other women whose contribution to the Namibia struggle for independence had been forgotten.[10] Few other women were concerned with this retrieval of women's stories, but many discussed the oppression of women and the specific forms of discrimination that they faced. The Egyptian feminist and doctor Nawal El Saadawi, for example, stressed in telling her own story the many forms of oppression and brutality suffered by women in Egypt, as the South African novelist Sindiwe Magona did in relation to South Africa or as Otieno did, in her critique both of traditional cultures and of the policies of the new Kenyan state once it had gained independence.[11]

These works are very different from those of their male contemporaries seen as 'national autobiographies' as few describe the birth or growth of a liberation movement in which they were closely involved. Nonetheless, they are all political autobiographies designed to highlight the ways in which the discriminatory and oppressive political regimes under which they live affect the lives of individuals. Their stories are personal and individual but also told in ways that illustrate situations and experiences of hardship and brutality that are widespread in their communities. Describing how painful it was to see her own son banned and confined to living in a small and remote town, unable to leave it or enter a public building within it, Ellen Kuzwayo, for example, insists that there was nothing unique about it: 'it is the torture and suffering of hundreds of black parents.'[12] In a similar way,

---

[8] Ellen Kuzwayo, *Call Me Woman* (London: The Women's Press, 1986).
[9] Ellen Ndeshi Namhila, *The Price of Freedom* (New Namibia Books: Windhoek, 1997).
[10] Ellen Ndeshi Namhila, 'Uncovering Hidden Historical Narratives of Village Women in Namibia', *Qualitative Research Journal* 14, no. 3 (2014); Ellen Ndeshi Namhila, *Mukwahepo. Women Soldier* (Windhoek: University of Namibia Press, 2014).
[11] Nawal El Saadawi, *The Daughter of Isis: The Early Life of Nawal El Saadawi* (London: Zed Books, 1999); Sindiwe Magona, *To My Children's Children: An Autobiography* (London: The Women's Press, 1991); *Forced to Grow* (London: The Women's Press, 1992); Wambui Waiyaki Otieno, *Mau Mau's Daughter. A Life History* (Boulder, CO: Lynne Rienner, 1998).
[12] Kuzwayo, *Call Me Woman*, p. 193.

Sally Morgan's report of her uncle's story, while very closely focused on his particular and painful experiences of being removed from his family and his battles when he tried to establish his own farm against constant attempts to defraud him by white farmers, includes his general comments concerning how colonialism isn't over yet. 'It's always been the same. They say there's been no difference between black and white, we are all Australian, that's a lie. I tell you, the Black man has nothin', the government's been robbin' him blind for years.'[13] Some of these women were involved in liberation struggles, as Wambui was working with the Mau Mau in Kenya, for example. But it was the writing of their autobiography that was both their major political statement and their most significant political act. All of their work, as Dorothy Driver argues of African women's autobiography, is not only a form of resistance but a way to write women back into history.[14] These women bring quite new voices into the writing of women's autobiographies while offering quite new ways of understanding and writing about their lives.

Producing an Autobiography

The significance of the political world in the lives of these women is clearly evident in the production of their autobiographies as many were impelled to write their stories after a particularly violent intrusion of the state into their lives. For some, this took the form of imprisonment on political grounds, usually as a result of their work or community activity rather than because they were actively politically involved, and for some their imprisonment ended without them receiving a formal charge or trial. For others, the key issue was rather the pain of being forced into exile and then feeling as if they did not belong when they returned to what had been their home. In other cases, the political intrusion was more complicated but no less important: the death of her sister in a car accident that may have been an intentional act directed at her father, in the case of Sara Suleri, or the Australian assimilation policy that led to her grandmother and mother being removed from their families and brought up in white institutions, thus depriving them and her of a sense of connection with their people and their heritage, in the case of Sally Morgan.[15]

For those whose autobiographies focused on imprisonment, writing their own story enabled them to describe the brutal and painful nature of this experience as well as offering a way to help them cope with and recover psychologically from the trauma involved. Ellen Kuzwayo, one of the first to write of this ordeal, insisted that she was not the same person when she

---

[13]Sally Morgan, *My Place* (Fremantle: Fremantle Press, 1987), *passim*.
[14]Dorothy Driver, 'Imagined Selves, (Un)Imagined Marginalities: Review Article', *Journal of Southern African Studies* 17, no. 2 (1991).
[15]Sara Suleri, *Meatless Days* (Chicago: University of Chicago Press, 1987), pp. 145–150.

came out of prison as she had been when she went in. Kuzwayo was imprisoned in 1977 along with all the other members of the committee that had been set up to investigate whether there might not be a better form of local administration in Soweto, the vast African township in which she lived, in the aftermath of student demonstrations there that had turned violent in the face of brutal police repression. She served five months in jail without actually being charged. While recognizing that the conditions of her imprisonment were much better than those of many others, including schoolgirls who were subjected to beating and torture, this was a terrible time and one that she felt changed her fundamentally, leaving her with 'dents' and 'unseen emotional scars'. As she watched her own responses to people and situations when she came out of prison, she came increasingly to feel that imprisonment had made her bitter and distrustful. Her decision to write an autobiography was an attempt to deal with these feelings and to gain a better sense of herself and her world.[16] Kuzwayo returned to her job teaching social work at the University of Witwatersrand when she was released from prison and waited some five years before she began this task. Her financial circumstances did not allow her to give up her paid work, but at this point she decided it was imperative to do so and mobilized her extensive political, education and community networks to get both the space in which to write and the financial support to be able to devote herself to writing.[17] The University of Witwatersrand gave her an office and the wealthy diamond magnate and philanthropist, Harry Oppenheimer, provided the sponsorship that replaced her salary for three years and enabled her to devote herself to the book.

Kuzwayo placed immense emphasis on the importance of women's activities in South Africa, naming and writing about several whom she feared may have been forgotten, like Charlotte Maxeke, the first Black woman to gain a university degree in South Africa and a teacher, missionary and founder of the Bantu Women's League.[18] She paid tribute also to her own contemporaries, like Winnie Mandela and Albertine Sisulu whose personal contributions to the political struggle and their own community she wanted to acknowledge. Her book ends with a whole section dealing with other women, naming and describing several who have shown great strength and been involved in the Black struggle and then with lists of the women who, against great odds, have qualified as doctors and lawyers in South Africa. While seeing her autobiography as a new kind of work in the way it claims her standing and importance as a woman, Julie Coullie points

---

[16]Kuzwayo, *Call Me Woman*, pp. 233–234.
[17]Cherry Clayton, 'Interview with Ellen Kuzwayo', in *Between the Lines: Interviews with Bessie Head, Sheila Roberts, Ellen Kuzwayo, Miriam Tlali*, ed. Craig and Cherry Clayton Mckenzie (Grahamstown, South Africa: The National English Literary Museum, 1989), pp. 66–67.
[18]Charlotte Maxeke (1874–1939), see entry in Henry Louis Gates et al. (eds.) *Dictionary of African Biography* (Oxford: Oxford University Press, 2011).

out that she also follows a long tradition of Zulu praise singers in the way that she uses the examples of admirable Black women to inspire others.[19] At the same time, Kuzwayo makes very clear her sense of her own standing and the importance of her book by including a preface by Nadine Gordimer and a foreword by Bessie Head, both of which pay tribute to her and her work.

Although never describing herself as a feminist and stressing always her sense of the importance of motherhood and family life, Kuzwayo does make clear the importance to her of a supportive international feminist network. The key figure was Elizabeth Wolpert, a filmmaker who had been a political activist in South Africa before going to London. In the early 1980s, Wolpert called on Kuzwayo both to participate in films about South African women and to head the trust she wanted to set up in memory of Maggie Magaba, a beloved Black nanny. Although initially suspicious of her, Kuzwayo came to like and trust Wolpert, whom she thanked for 'her encouragement and moral support and for her patience to listen with a critical ear to my work'. Wolpert also offered her a home base in London – and connected Kuzwayo with the Women's Press, which was headed at that point by Ros de Lanerolle, another former South African political activist.[20]

Although Kuzwayo was meeting her own psychological needs in writing her autobiography, it was emphatically a work in which the individual life is not only contextualized but serves to illustrate and amplify that context and the society in which she lived. Her own life, beginning with her childhood, only appears in the second section of the book which begins with a summary of the 'Principal legislation affecting the black community' and a history of Soweto, the vast Black township outside Johannesburg, where Kuzwayo lived. Her discussion of Soweto combined a description of the basic and impoverished nature of the homes of Black people in South Africa with an account of how Soweto was settled by Black families who were pushed out of Johannesburg and forcibly moved there. The harsh conditions of life there are shown in terms of poverty, inadequate housing, an appalling education system, violence and excessive police presence. As one deeply connected to and concerned about her community and the difficulties it faces, Kuzwayo emphasizes how hard it is for women in particular to live and manage their families.

> It is not easy to live and to bring up children in a community deprived of its traditional moral code and values – a community lost between its old heritage and that of its colonisers.[21]

---

[19] Judith Lutge Coullie, 'The Space between Frames: A New Discursive Practice in Ellen Kuzwayo's *Call Me Woman*', in *South African Feminisms*, ed. M. J. Daymond (New York: Garland Publishing Inc., 1996), pp. 139–140.
[20] Simone Murray, 'The Women's Press, Kitchen Table Press and Dilemmas of Feminist Publishing', *European Journal of Women's Studies* 5 (1998).
[21] Kuzwayo, *Call Me Woman*, p. 16.

This discussion of the history of Soweto and the South African treatment of its Black population provides the framework for Kuzwayo's depiction of her own life. There too, the intrusiveness of the wider political world and its racial discrimination is evident everywhere: in regard to her own family, it is evident in the expropriation of the family farm on which she grew up and part of which she inherited, for example.

Emma Mashinini was another South African woman who was traumatized by her imprisonment and saw writing an autobiography as a way to deal with it.[22] Mashinini, a prominent and effective trade union leader, was arrested in 1981 under a section of the Terrorism Act that allowed indefinite detention without trial. She had no idea that other trade union leaders had been arrested at the same time as her and felt completely isolated in prison where she constantly feared execution. Her trauma was exacerbated by the extensive time she was kept in solitary confinement, which she found so unnerving that she preferred even brutal police interrogations to being sent back to her cell. At times she felt that she was going mad: at one point she could not remember the name of her beloved daughter. Mashinini was encouraged to undergo trauma counselling subsequently in Scandinavia but found it useless. She too was helped and supported by Elizabeth Wolpert, Ros de Lanerolle and their contacts in both writing and publishing her autobiography. Wolpert met Mashinini when engaged in another film project about African women in which she wanted to include her, called 'Mama, I'm Crying'. While they were making the film, she persuaded Mashinini to write her own story and worked out a way to help her to do so. 'During the shooting of the film', Mashinini wrote, 'she interviewed me on every possible occasion.... She would then post them [the tapes] to Ruth Vaughan, her collaborator in London, who would rapidly transcribe them so that I could immediately work on the rough draft.' The story was very painful and Mashinini noted: 'There were times when Betty and I were both in tears ... but I must say that putting on paper some of these terrible times was therapeutic.' Wolpert arranged for her to work with an editor, Alison Mansbridge who 'helped to organise my hastily scribbled thoughts' and completed the book. Mansbridge took her manuscript to the Women's Press where it was published.[23]

It was not imprisonment but rather the attempt to avoid it by going into exile at the very young age of twelve and the difficulties she experienced on returning to Namibia nearly two decades later that impelled the Namibian author and librarian Ellen Ndeshi Namhila to write her autobiography, *The Price of Freedom*. Namibia had originally been a German colony, but after the First World War, the League of Nations gave South Africa a mandate over it. Seeking to resist demands for independence, the South African

---

[22]Emma Mashinini, *Strikes Have Followed Me All My Life: A South African Autobiography* (London: The Women's Press, 1989).
[23]Mashinini, *Strikes Have Followed Me*, p. 300.

Defence Force established camps in Namibia to maintain control. When one of these camps was set up in her village in the mid-1970s, Namhila wrote, life was turned upside down.[24] The extreme violence shown by the South African soldiers to locals, in the course of which she was shot and injured while riding and had to watch her teacher viciously beaten up in her classroom, made her and many other young people so fearful that they decided to leave secretly and to make their way to SWAPO camps in Angola. Namhila spent nineteen years in exile, first in Angola, then in the Gambia where she finished her schooling and finally in Finland, where she was awarded a scholarship to study library sciences. Although not without rewards, much of this time was painful and difficult, made more so, she points out, as there was neither any help in dealing with the early trauma of the violence and displacement she had experienced, nor any guidance on how to negotiate the different societies and cultures in which she lived as an adolescent and young adult. When she finally returned to the newly independent Namibia, it was to a very different country from the one she had left and one in which she did not feel at home. This sense of displacement was exacerbated by the lack of knowledge or interest in the new Namibia in the lives or experiences of the thousands who had gone into exile while fighting for independence and were now returning home. Namhila came to feel that her own identity crisis could only be solved if the lives and stories of exiles were known and recognized as part of Namibian history. 'I have now taken this identity crisis as my struggle phase two,' she wrote, and it was one that could be resolved by making her story and that of others involved in the liberation struggle part of the known history of Namibia.[25] She was the first of the exiles to write her story, but many others followed.[26]

While the burdens imposed by imperial rule and the struggle against it were major influences of these autobiographies, other major political issues, including different forms of tribal conflict, conflicts between tribal customs and modern expectations, and the difficulties of dealing with corrupt political regimes were also important. All of these issues were important in Wambui Waiyaki Otieno's decision to write her autobiography. As its title, *Mau Mau's Daughter: A Life History* suggests, Otieno's autobiography deals in some detail with her involvement as an adolescent and young woman in the Mau Mau campaign in which she worked as a scout, able as a woman to move around and pass information more freely than her male colleagues could. Her years in the Mau Mau were very hard ones and she was subject to restrictions on her movement, banning orders that required reporting daily to police offices for interrogation by police and district

---

[24]Namhila, *The Price of Freedom*, p. 8.
[25]Namhila, *The Price of Freedom*, p. 199.
[26]Kelly Jo Fulkerson-Dikuua, 'Conceptualising National Transition: Namibian Women's Autobiographies About the Liberation Struggle', ed. Sarala and Helen Vale Krishnamurthy, *Writing Namibia: Literature in Translation* (Windhoek: University of Namibia Press, 2018).

officers, constant harassment and ultimately to arrest and a period of imprisonment during which time she was raped by a police official. Her support for the Mau Mau was also linked to her horror at the terrible treatment and ultimately the murder of her grandfather by the British. Significant as these experiences were, it was not her early life that made her turn to autobiography but rather a later crisis in which she found herself opposing both the power of tribal custom and the new Kenyan State. After she was released from prison and left the Mau Mau, Wambui Waiyaki met and married a leading criminal lawyer, S. M. Otieno. As she was a member of the Kikuyu tribe, while he was a Luo, there was family opposition from the start. The tribal issue came to a head for her after Otieno's death. She wanted to bury him in the way she and he had agreed, but his family intervened and demanded that they be given the body and give him a traditional tribal burial. After a long dispute that included court appearances and government intervention and harassment of Wambui, it was his family that won and was allowed to conduct the burial as they chose. The case was widely publicized and discussed and has since been the subject of considerable academic interest.[27] It was the case and its aftermath, her horror at not being able to bury her husband as he had wished and her sense of how much her treatment by the family, the courts and the state demonstrated the low status of women in Kenya that finally made her write her story.

While the impulse to autobiography was not directly linked to political repression in Australia in quite the same way as it was in South Africa, the spate of Indigenous women's autobiographies that began to appear in the mid-1980s was very much a response to contemporary Indigenous struggles and debates. There was a resurgence of concern about the plight of Indigenous people, especially in terms of their extreme poverty, the high rates of their incarceration and deaths in prisons, and the removal of children that had been practised under an assimilation policy. An increased sense of the scale of Indigenous suffering and of the need to expose it emerged as white Australians began planning to celebrate two hundred years of colonial settlement in 1988.[28] These issues were individualized and personalized and made much more cogent when depicted in terms of their impact on particular individuals and families. The best-known of these works is *My Place*, the memoir of the artist, writer and dramatist Sally Morgan.[29] *My Place* is a quest narrative organized around Morgan's sense of confusion about who she was. She knew she was not white but had no clear sense of her ethnic origin until she

---

[27]Elsie Cloete, 'Wambui Otieno's Mau Mau', *Foreign Policy in Perspective* (30 October 2011); Ken Walibora Waliaula, 'The Female Condition as Double Incarceration in Wambui Otieno's *Mau Mau's Daughter*', *Eastern African Literary and Cultural Studies* 1, no. 1–2 (2014).
[28]Michele Grossman, 'Out of the Salon and into the Streets: Contextualising Australian Indigenous Women's Writing', *Women's Writing* 5, no. 5 (1998).
[29]Delys Bird and Dennis Haskell, eds, *Whose Place? A Study of Sally Morgan's 'My Place'* (Sydney: Angus & Robinson, 1992).

eventually came to understand her Aboriginal heritage largely through getting to know the stories of her grandmother, mother and uncle and what they had suffered under an assimilationist policy that had separated them from their kin and country. Eventually, she was able to connect with her Indigenous heritage and kin.

It was not the need to establish her own identity that prompted her to write her autobiography, Indigenous writer and activist Ruby Langford insisted, as she knew who she was and had a clear sense of heritage and kin.[30] Langford's book was rather driven by a concern to describe honestly the ups and downs of her very hard life as an Aboriginal woman, including periods of extreme poverty, isolation and alcohol abuse, her relationships with both Indigenous and white men, some of which were violent, and the attempt to care for her eight children, three of whom died tragically. Her story too, however, shows how hard it was for Indigenous people to survive when separated from family and kin as they so often were because of the paucity of employment opportunities available to them. Langford depicts clearly her peripatetic life, moving constantly as her partners sought unskilled work, regarding basic huts almost as a luxury after living in a car or a tent and trying to bring up and often support her eight children on minimal wages or welfare. Langford felt the need to finish her book,

> because it may help better the relationship between the Aboriginal and white people. That it might give some idea of the difficulty we have surviving between two cultures, that we are here and always will be.[31]

Writing their autobiography was the first literary venture for the great majority of these women concerned to describe their lives and the impact of colonialism and contemporary political developments on them. Several of them went on to produce other works: collecting folk stories and proverbs, in the case of Ellen Kuzwayo for example, writing more biographies of women in the case of Ellen Ndeshi Namhila, producing works on her people and their culture in the case of Ruby Langford, becoming a novelist in the case of Sindiwe Magona and a very prominent postcolonial theorist in the case of Sara Suleri. Writing their own stories paved the way for this later work as if it was the means they needed to find their own voice. Although some, like Magona and Suleri, were already engaged in other writing when they turned to autobiographies, for others, as for the working-class women discussed in the previous chapter, the writing posed a considerable challenge and was only made possible with various different kinds of assistance and support. A number of Black South African women, including Caesarina Makhoere and Maggie Resha, acknowledged the help they received from the cultural department of

---

[30]Ruby Langford, *Don't Take Your Love to Town* (Ringwood, Victoria: Penguin Books, 1988); Janine Little, 'Talking with Ruby Langford Ginibi', *Hecate* 20, no. 1 (1994).
[31]Langford, *Don't Take Your Love to Town*, p. 269.

the African National Congress.[32] Others, like Ellen Kuzwayo and Emma Mashinini, as we have seen, were given invaluable encouragement, and material help from a former political activist and filmmaker, Elizabeth Wolpert. In the case of Wambui Waiyaki Otieno, substantial help was provided by an American academic working in the field of African American studies and with specialist knowledge of the Mau Mau, Cora Ann Presley, who edited and introduced her autobiography when it appeared. As Sally Morgan made clear, she received immense help from Ray Coffey, her editor at Fremantle Press.

The nature of the assistance given to these women and the question of how much control over their work it involved is a complicated one, especially when that assistance came from editors who had a substantial say in whether the book would appear. In some cases, it seems to have been an easy, harmonious and supportive process. But this was not the situation in all cases. The easiest and most supportive relationship seems to have been that of Sally Morgan with Ray Coffey. When Morgan's manuscript landed on his desk, Coffey recalled 'it was only an idea and two draft chapters'. There was no synopsis or overall plan. He was taken with it, however: 'the style was engaging. I realized it had the potential to be an important book.'[33] He and Morgan worked closely for some eighteen months until the book was finished, and he is noted as its editor on the title page. Morgan greatly appreciated his approach and his contribution to the book. Editors didn't get sufficient credit, she insisted.

> Ray was very good in the sense that he has a sensitive, laid-back approach. If he had been a more aggressive person . . . it probably wouldn't have worked because the material I was working with was very sensitive . . . so he kind of stepped back and was very tactful.[34]

He was, she insisted, 'one of the great unsung heroes in literature'.

There is a very marked contrast here with the experience of another Indigenous autobiographer Ruby Langford, whose life story, *Don't Take Your Love to Town*, appeared a year after Morgan's.[35] Although Langford insists she had always wanted to write, the fact that she had to leave school at the end of her second year of high school made it hard to do so, as indeed did her family responsibilities. She finally began her autobiography when her children were grown up and she felt able for the first time to live away

---

[32]Maggie Resha, *Mangoana O Tsoara Thipa Ka Bohaleng. My Life in the Struggle* (Johannesburg: Congress of South African Writers, 1991); Caesarina Kona Makhoere, *No Child's Play: In Prison under Apartheid* (London: The Women's Press, 1988).
[33]David Clark Scott, 'Book Makes Big News on the "Bush Telegraph"', *Christian Science Monitor* no. 23 (November 1988).
[34]Bird and Haskell, 'Interview with Sally Morgan', in *Whose Place*, pp. 12–13.
[35]Tim Rowse, 'The Aboriginal Subject in Autobiography: Ruby Langford's "Don't Take Your Love to Town"', *Australian Literary Studies* 16, no. 1 (1993): 2.

from them and concentrate on her own life and needs. This was a bad time for her as she was recovering from surgery and suffering severe depression. The psychologist she was sent to was useless and she thought that writing about her life might be therapeutic. Reliving her painful life and especially the deaths of several of her children, however, nearly killed her.[36] Langford was heavily dependent on editorial help in writing her book. She worked closely for two years with an editor, Susan Hampton, and when the book was first published Hampton's name appeared under hers on the first page and they were listed as joint copyright holders. Some time later, however, Langford came to realize that Hampton's name as joint copyright holder meant that, in the event of Langford's death, the copyright and the royalties would belong to Hampton – rather than to Langford's children. She had no understanding, she later explained, of what copyright meant or of the difference between copyright and royalties, and while she didn't begrudge Hampton earning something from the book, she wanted to control it and to hand the copyright to her children. This was all the more important as the book was doing quite well: it won a human rights award and had reasonable sales. Ultimately Langford took Hampton to court and challenged the copyright. She won the case and Hampton's name disappeared completely from subsequent editions, as indeed did any acknowledgement for the immense amount of work she had done on the book.

This question of the editing of Langford's text has attracted attention from later scholars, some of whom see it as illustrating the whole question of Indigenous memoirs and writing and how they have been controlled and indeed expropriated. For much of the 20th century, the stories of Indigenous people were gathered in oral form and written down, and the white scholar who wrote them down was deemed to be their author and held the copyright. This colonial practice has continued, some critics suggest, in the editing of Indigenous women's autobiographies. Editors might see their work as neutral, Alison Ravenscroft argues, but the very language of editing, the 'cutting', 'cleaning up' and rendering a text orderly is itself redolent of colonial practices. This colonial situation is exacerbated by the way that the effort to render Indigenous colloquial speech into some more grammatical form of English seems to mirror how these women and their families were punished for speaking their own language in the schools and missionary homes to which some were sent as children, against their will and that of their families.[37] Langford insists she was always uncomfortable about some aspects of the editing process. She wanted her editor to recognize the way that she and other Indigenous people talked – rather than changing her language.

---

[36]Little, 'Talking with Ruby Langford', pp. 1–2.
[37]Alison Ravenscroft, 'Recasting Indigenous Lives Along the Lines of Western Desire: Editing, Autobiography, and the Colonizing Project', *a/b: Auto/Biography Studies* 19, no. 1–2 (2004); Gillian Whitlock, *The Intimate Empire: Reading Women's Autobiography* (London: Cassell, 2000), pp. 158–171.

Our voice is as valid as anybody else's and when we write we say comin and goin and gonna, hey bra, or tidda, something like that, and that's the way we talk. It's our voice, so when my editor was working on my first book I said to her 'Don't you gubba-ise my text!'[38]

It was not only in Australia that this question of editing texts was a difficult one. Indigenous Australians were not the only women for whom writing in English was a problem. It was often a second or third language for Black South African women too for whom writing in the master's tongue was also painful and difficult – as was the editing process. While recognizing the importance of the support she had received, Ellen Kuzwayo too pointed to the problems involved in accepting help in writing a book.

When you write your first book you are almost over trusting. You think that the people helping you have . . . I think they do have your welfare at heart. Let me give them that. But I think that sometimes they don't know what you want in the book. And if you are not careful people are going to put into your book things they think worthwhile, and push out the things you think are worthwhile.[39]

Morgan, Langford and Kuzwayo were all interviewed extensively after their books were published and hence their experiences and views can be ascertained. It is much harder to find or establish the author's view in other cases. The autobiography of Wambui Waiyaki Otieno, for example, was extensively edited. When she first read it in draft form Cora Ann Presley wrote that she was 'riveted by the events' in the life story and approached a publisher who in turn asked her to edit the work. As Hampton did with Langford, she worked on it with Otieno for two years, noting that she helped to add clarity by filling in background details and then undertook a line-by-line revision of the final manuscript. Presley's place in this work is evident in her being noted as Editor on the title page. She also explained her role in the Introduction that she wrote for the book. As there is no available comment from Otieno, it is impossible to know how she felt about that process.

Shaping a Life

The lives depicted in these autobiographies are shaped very differently from those discussed in the previous chapter. The political nature of these autobiographies is evident in their concern to frame their lives in terms of colonial experiences and contemporary political developments and struggles,

---

[38]Little, 'Talking with Ruby Langford', pp. 9–10. The term 'gubba' is used by some Indigenous Australians to refer to white people – or here to their language.
[39]Clayton, 'Interview with Kuzwayo', p. 67.

and to link them also with the history, heritage and traditions of their people. It is these issues that the works focus on rather than on the development of an individual personality. The dynamics of their immediate family were generally less important than extended kinship and family networks, especially in their early lives. Psychological discussion is rare, and where it does come to the fore, it too reflects the broader political framework: the impact of the loss of cultural heritage and consequently a sense of identity on people, or of arbitrary imprisonment, or the ways in which sometimes traumatized children in exile were treated by the organizations and families who cared for them.

Childhood and Adolescence

In their depictions of childhood, one sees immediately the contrasts between traditional customs and the expectations of a more modern world and the importance of colonial rule and discriminatory government policies or conflicts. Their autobiographies do not ignore the relationship of the author with her parents, but their presentation of this relationship serves to illustrate problematic aspects of the society in which they live, rather than seeing them as formative in the author's development. The traditional framework in which some authors grew up meant that parents were not the central figures in the child's early years at all. Grandparents and extended family were far more significant figures in the early years of some South African autobiographers, while the matrilineal system in which Ellen Namhila grew up in Namibia meant that her mother's brother was the authoritative male figure in her life and not her father. Even where parental figures are central, as her mother and grandmother were for Sally Morgan, the depiction of them and of the somewhat ramshackle family that they created ultimately serves to illustrate the impact that their early separation from their families and painful relationships with white authorities had on *them* rather than suggesting that it was important in her own development.

For some, memories of childhood served powerfully to show the value of their traditional heritage and culture as it still existed in their youth. The autobiographies of both Ellen Kuzwayo and Sindiwe Magona, in particular, provide pictures of happy traditional childhoods in South Africa. Both lived on family farms, supervised by grandparents, surrounded by cousins, embraced and cared for by an extended family in homes where there was plentiful food and easy access to the veld where they played freely. Kuzwayo's wealthy family owned a substantial farm – which was confiscated from them in the 1970s. 'Until I was about seven or ten years old', she wrote,

> we ate, drank, roamed, prayed and went to school together as old man Jeremiah's grandchildren, moving as freely on the farm as birds in the air.

It was common practice for we children to carry a mug and walk single file to the barn where they milked the cows, in order to get our ration of fresh milk direct from the udder.[40]

Magona's family was far less wealthy, but she too recalled the pleasure of her rural childhood spent with cousins who roamed in the countryside, swam in local rivers and relished the long stories told to them in the evenings as they waited for a meal. 'In such a people-world, filled with a real, immediate, tangible sense of belongingness, did I spend the earliest years of my life', wrote Magona, 'I was not only wanted, I was loved. I was cherished.'[41]

This idyllic early childhood stood in stark contrast to the very small home Magona moved into with her parents in an African location in Cape Town at the age of seven or eight when her grandmother died and this extended family life ceased to be possible. On her first night, there was a police raid searching for alcohol, which was illegal for Black South Africans to have, although many, including Magona's mother, made and sold it as their only source of income. None was found that night. But it was a rude introduction to a life that was much harder and poorer than that with her grandparents. Although her father had a good job, the only housing available to him was a single room in a 'lavatoryless slum', which involved walking through wet human dung every day on her way to school.

Not all depictions of childhood within a traditional African framework echo the sense of warmth and nostalgia that come from Magona and Kuzwayo. These traditional communities were very patriarchal and there were clear rules and hierarchies that discriminated against some members in favour of others. Kuzwayo was aware of this point: her parents had separated when she was a baby and her father had left. She knew that this made her status lower than that of her cousins. But she felt loved by her mother and stepfather and enjoyed her life on the farm. Buchi Emecheta, by contrast, felt that her life in Nigeria was forever marked by these patriarchal values, especially their preference for men over women and their powerful resistance to any hint of female independence. She had to work to overcome the shame that came to her parents when she was born – giving them a girl as a first child, rather than a boy. The death of her father while she was still very young, moreover, left her vulnerable to the violence of male relatives and to the expectation that she would marry very young, and made escape imperative. The brutal patriarchal nature of African societies was presented critically by Ellen Ndeshi Namhila too. Although she had enjoyed her early years with her parents and grandparents, she did not enjoy the life she led when sent to live with her uncle at the age of five. Ceaseless domestic toil was expected of her and exacted with severe corporal punishment.

---

[40]Kuzwayo, *Call Me Woman*, p. 56.
[41]Magona, *To My Children's Children*, pp. 3–4.

The expectation that children, especially girls, would undertake a significant amount of domestic labour was part of the Kenyan childhood depicted by Wambui Waiyaki Otieno too. She withdrew from primary school for a while to help care for younger siblings. She was expected to fetch water and firewood, clean the house and wash the clothes. Like Namhila, she had to run home from school to beat her mother's deadline as 'my authoritarian mother saw to it that we toed the line'. Namhila suggests that it was running home from school each day that might explain why she became so good at long-distance racing![42] Her childhood recollections are not happy and she resented the amount of labour expected of her, which included looking after a herd of cattle. But the hardest work was carrying water. 'The path to Kiharu was very steep, rough and winding', she noted, 'yet we made as many as ten round trips each day carrying big five-gallon tins of water.'[43]

All of the African autobiographies comment on the strictness and frequent use of corporal punishment that they knew in childhood. For some, this was simply a part of life. Ellen Kuzwayo, for example, notes how strict her grandmother was. She was the disciplinarian of the family, demanding the best from those required to do chores, and insisting on punctuality and cleanliness. When the children giggled and were disobedient, she spanked them. Nonetheless, Kuzwayo insists, 'we loved our granny very dearly', more she insists than their own mothers.[44] Sindiwe Magona inserts a slightly different and more critical note into her autobiography. Parenting did not involve much intimacy with children, she noted. She was sure her parents loved her and her siblings – most of the time.

> Their idea of raising children, however, was simple, direct, and innocent of ameliorating influence of any theory, psychological, sociological, anthropological or any other such profundity. They were staunch advocates of the adage: 'spare the rod and spoil the child' and beatings were frequent. Often a neighbour would intervene.[45]

Corporal punishment was common practice, she noted. 'We got it at home, at school, and even at Church on occasion.' Her father sometimes explained that such punishment was one of the ways that parents showed their love for their children and ensured they would not grow up wild. Magona and her siblings wailed often, she recalled, 'as we were much loved'.

Others were more forthright. Ellen Ndeshi Namhila was very critical of the kind of power her mother's brother had. He even had to give her permission to see her parents, something she particularly resented. She cites

---

[42]Otieno, *Mau Mau's Daughter*, p. 25.
[43]Otieno, *Mau Mau's Daughter*, p. 26.
[44]Kuzwayo, *Call Me Woman*, pp. 61–63.
[45]Magona, *To My Children's Children*, p. 24.

several situations in which she was beaten or threatened with beating unnecessarily. One particularly notable one was an incident in which she was refused permission to attend a wedding at which all of her family would be present, because she was required to attend on her grandmother who was too frail to go. With the help of other relatives, she did all the required work, left enough food and firewood for her grandmother and then went to the wedding. Her uncle was furious and would have beaten her publicly had her grandfather not intervened and said there would be no beating at the wedding. At the time, Namhila says she felt that her parents had let her become a slave to her uncle. 'Looking back at the harsh discipline under which I was brought up', she wrote, 'I wonder if it would not have been possible for my family to achieve the desired behaviour through a different approach, less forceful.'[46]

The disruption of Indigenous life by colonialization meant that there was little sense of a traditional childhood in Australian autobiographies. There is just a hint of an idyllic traditional childhood in the very early childhood years, described in *Aunty Rita*, that occurred in the 1920s, depicting the short time during which Rita and her family still lived in her 'born country', the area now known as Carnarvon Gorge, north of Brisbane. It was a place with 'waterfalls, waterholes and creeks where we swam and where the older people fished'. There was plentiful food, and the creeks and waterholes kept everyone cool on the hottest days. The Bidjara-Pitjara people were forcibly removed when Rita was still very small, however, and taken to Cherbourg reserve where, in place of this easy traditional life, they were placed in little, two-room cells, fenced off from each other and forcibly cut off both from their traditional way of life, their own language and from a sense of community.[47]

For the most part, other Australian Indigenous autobiographies describe childhoods spent on mission stations or in urban areas far removed from traditional country. Ruby Langford was born on an Aboriginal reserve at Box Ridge, Coraki, in the far north of New South Wales and then moved to another one near Kyogle. She describes an altogether more relaxed form of family life in her early childhood than any of the African women, especially in the six years with both parents before her mother left. She makes very clear how basic their life was and the poverty in which Aboriginal people lived: there was no lining in their four-roomed house, for example, cooking was done over an open fire while cups were made from old tin cans. Food seemed plentiful, however, and her parents caring and attentive. Langford's family life was peaceful and would have been happy, except for her anxiety about her mother's almost constant unhappiness, which was resolved when she left her family to live with another man. There was similar ease and sense of an affectionate community when she and her sister went to live

---

[46]Namhila, *The Price of Freedom*, p. 22.
[47]Rita Huggins and Jacki Huggins, *Auntie Rita* (Canberra: Aboriginal Studies Press, 1994), pp. 7–9.

with an uncle and aunt a few years later, after her mother had left and when her father's work made it impossible for him to remain with them.[48]

There was no suggestion of discipline or indeed of any kind of order in the somewhat chaotic family life described by Sally Morgan, in a home dominated in some ways by her white, shell-shocked father, and in others, by her grandmother whose home-making skills were very limited. This chaos underlined for Morgan the family's isolation and lack of connection to community. Her strongest sense was that of being an outsider, something she emphasizes from the beginning of the book, in her description of the discomfort she felt when having to visit her father in hospital, something she had to do often.[49] Both physically and mentally damaged by the First World War, her father was unable to pursue his trade as a plumber and drank very heavily, sometimes raiding his children's money boxes to buy alcohol.[50] He was a difficult presence in the home, sometimes violent and often unreliable. Wondering why her mother stayed with him, Morgan later realized that as a white man with an Indigenous wife, he had held the threat of having the children removed from her over her head to prevent her from leaving him. There is an immense difference between this unease and Morgan's attachment to and dependence on her loving mother and grandmother. Morgan's unhappiness is focused on her unease when she has to leave home. She hated having to leave it each day when she went to school where she was bored and intimidated and lonely. Her loneliness and sense of being an outsider were closely connected to her recognition that she was not white and her questioning of who she was, something she kept asking her mother and grandmother about, but neither of them would tell her anything.

Education

Schooling and the question of education feature prominently in all of these autobiographies. As in other women's autobiographies, education offered some the only possibility of pursuing an independent life, while others saw it as underlining their poverty and exclusion. Many of these authors stress the extent to which access to education and the kind of education they received were also linked to wider political issues. This was particularly the case in South Africa where the 'Bantu Education Act' of 1953 marked a watershed for the Black population. Prior to this point, Black children had access to the same curriculum as their white counterparts. As a key part of the apartheid policy of the Nationalist Party that came to power in 1948, this act instituted a separate curriculum and system of education for Black children, one designed to ensure that they received only a rudimentary

---

[48]Langford, *Don't Take Your Love to Town*, pp. 3–10.
[49]Morgan, *My Place*, pp. 6–10.
[50]Morgan, *My Place*, p. 53.

education, sufficient only to become unskilled or semi-skilled workers.[51] All of the Black South African women's autobiographies either note how fortunate they were to go to school before this legislation came into force, or describe the difficulties it posed for them and their children. Elsewhere in Africa too, Black children received a different and limited education and were discouraged from declaring any kind of ambition.

It is Ellen Kuzwayo who points most clearly to the contrast in the kind of education available to Black South Africans before and after 1953. Born in 1914, she went to school long before the rise of the Nationalist Party or the establishment of a separate educational structure and curriculum for Black children. The schooling she describes involved primary education while she was still living on the family farm, followed by higher primary schooling in a town nearby. A Catholic secondary boarding school followed and then teacher's training college and finally a couple of years at Lovedale College where she could concentrate on doing more intensive work in the subjects she would teach – and where she met future Black leaders. Kuzwayo noted that there were far more opportunities for Black men than for Black women, but the overall point she was seeking to make was that 'the black community had a long educational history before the Nationalist Party came to power in 1948, with educational institutions run by various churches all over the country' and to protest against the government attempt to create 'a community of poorly educated and ill-trained blacks to maintain the relationship of master to servant between whites and blacks'.[52]

While Kuzwayo avoided the Bantu Education Act, for Sindiwe Magona it was a major threat. Born in 1973, Magona avoided the provisions of the act in her primary school years, ones in which she did extremely well. She had difficulties with secondary school, however, and failed in her third year in 1958: 'a bad year to fail', she noted. While she had just avoided the new and reduced curriculum, if she repeated in 1959 she would be required to undertake her entire secondary education in the new limited curriculum, adding another two years to the time she needed to get her junior certificate.[53] Appalled by this prospect, Magona persuaded her parents to send her to a Catholic boarding school which was prepared to ignore this requirement and simply let her do her year three again. Unlike Kuzwayo, Magona liked the school and its Catholic ritual. 'I was fascinated by the sound, meaning (when I understood) and colour of the liturgy. Also, my Latin improved tremendously, thanks to the Mass (said in Latin). . . . The simplicity, rigid orderliness, and terrible diet . . . helped me focus in my studies.' These years 'were easily the most productive of my entire high-school career'.[54] She

---

[51]Tsoaledi Daniel Thobejane, 'History of Apartheid Education and the Problems of Reconstruction in South Africa', *Sociology Study* 3, no. 1 (2013): 1–12.
[52]Kuzwayo, *Call Me Woman*, pp. 80–92.
[53]Magona, *To My Children's Children*, p. 77.
[54]Magona, *To My Children's Children*, pp. 79–80.

passed well and went on to a college where she trained as a primary school teacher.

It was not only in South Africa that the education available to Black students was limited. Ellen Ndeshi Namhila experienced something similar in Kenya.

> The colonial education most of us received was not aimed at motivating African students to develop curiosity which would lead to independent thinking. In my case, I was taught to memorise things and to answer questions as I had been taught to, and not as I understood them. A student could be failed for answering questions from her own understanding. . . . [I]n Namibia, I was not taught to be an independent thinker, but a repeater of my teachers. This deliberate educational strategy for the so-called 'natives' demotivated students from developing independent thinking.[55]

Both Kuzwayo and Magona were supported in their educational goals by their parents. But as a niece living in her uncle's house and expected to provide extensive domestic and farm labour, Ndeshi was not so lucky.

> I was often late for school because I had to pound millet before I left every morning. During the rainy season I also had to weed the field before school. . . . It was at times like these I felt my parents gave me to relatives to come and be treated like a slave. . . . after school, I had to rush back home to help with household chores. I got a thrashing whenever I came home late from school. Often this would result in my not being allowed to go to school for days.[56]

The narrowness of her education and the limits of her knowledge were constant themes in her autobiography. They became particularly problematic when she went into exile, knowing nothing about the different language groups and cultures in Namibia, or African or European politics. Each new situation pinpointed her ignorance and the difficulties it posed for her: the differences in how boys and girls were supposed to interact when she was sent to undertake her secondary education in the largely Muslim Gambia, for example, as compared with what was acceptable in her own tribal culture in Namibia. Similarly, she was sent to Finland with no idea of Finnish culture or social expectations.

The experience of Wambui Otieno in Kenya stands in marked contrast to the others. Although her primary schooling was interrupted by the demand that she stays home to help her mother manage her younger siblings, when

---

[55]Namhila, *The Price of Freedom*, p. 25.
[56]Namhila, *The Price of Freedom*, p. 23.

she returned, she found she was bright and easily passed the Common Entrance Exam, which allowed her to enter the Mambere Girls' School and then the secondary school and finally the Tengeru College in Arusha, Tanzania. She was thus able to live away from her parents and develop her own interests and did well in everything except mathematics. Otieno especially appreciated domestic science because their headmistress 'answered all our questions and told us how a girl got pregnant, how the community reacted to such a pregnancy, and how the pregnancy ruined a girl's life'. But like Otieno's mother, she had strict ideas about conduct – and the girls were subjected to a virginity test after every holiday. Anyone found not to be a virgin was expelled.[57]

The question of schooling and education was treated differently in the Australian autobiographies, although here too there were political issues at play. Sally Morgan who really hated school, saw it as a place dedicated to belittling and demeaning her. As she presents it, the limited and impoverished nature of her primary education was a product of the lack of training of teachers and the scarcity of school resources, rather than being discriminatory. She learnt to read early, but rather than being rewarded, or given different books to read, she was required to re-read the same elementary texts over a couple of years. Unlike her siblings who seemed to manage and enjoy school, everything about it made her uncomfortable. It was there that she was most aware of her physical and psychological difference – and of her family's poverty. The horror and humiliation of her life at school are encapsulated in an incident when, unable to attract the attention of her teacher after what seemed hours in order to ask to be excused to go to the toilet, she wet herself. That this happened on a day when she had done well on a test and was the centre of attention, made it worse. 'My attitude towards school took an even more rapid downhill turn after that incident. I felt different from the other children in my class. They were the spick-and-span brigade. And I, the grubby offender.'[58]

Things did not improve in her teen years and school became the place where Morgan staged an adolescent rebellion by playing truant until the school began enforcing stricter attendance rules and threatening her mother with the Truant Officer. Ultimately, however, she was persuaded to complete her schooling and go to university.

As her depiction of her early years makes clear, the combination of poverty and politics dominated Ruby Langford's education too. Her first experience of neglect and brutality came from the mission school that her father was forced to send her and her sister to when their mother left and where the cruel reality of colonial rule became absolutely clear. Conditions in the

---

[57]Otieno, *Mau Mau's Daughter*, p. 29.
[58]Morgan, *My Place*, p. 27.

school were extremely harsh and care minimal. The children were bathed 'in the water that had been used to wash the linen, with handfuls of caustic soda added'. Was this because she wanted to turn us white, Langford asked. It certainly burnt their skin. No attention was paid to the children's health or medical needs. Langford's sister once cut herself badly and needed stitches, but no doctor was called, and she was left to heal as best she could. Ruby herself once poured kerosene on a fire and burnt her face very badly, but there was no recourse to medical help here either. When her father heard how they were being treated, he immediately removed Ruby and her siblings from the school and took them to Bonalbo to live with his brother and sister-in-law while he came to see them at weekends. Here they were able to attend a local day school where Langford was happy. Unlike Morgan, Langford loved her years at school, especially high school, and did well there. She was class captain and always top of her class, and her headmaster wanted her to continue to the Intermediate Certificate and then go on to teacher's college. He suggested this pathway to her father, pointing out that the Aborigines' Protection Board would probably pay for her to go to college. Ruby's father, however, refused this option. He explained his position to her. 'I'm not having any protection board put you through college. All the protection they've done so far is to take people from their land and split up families.'[59]

Langford accepted this position and left school at the age of fifteen, in the year she would have done her Intermediate Certificate. 'Dad had a lot of worry on his mind raising up us kids and I thought, what the heck, he'd been supporting me all this time and it was only fair I get a job and help out.'

Adolescence

If depictions of childhood allowed a sense of nostalgia for a traditional past, the discussion of adolescence and especially of the sexual issues connected to puberty underline the ways in which colonial dispossession and the break-up of communities, on the one hand, and the advent of Christianity, on the other, destroyed the traditional ways in which girls were prepared for adult life. In the African context, Kuzwayo and Magona, the two women who were most insistent on the value of their traditional family during childhood, stress most strongly the damage that conversion to Christianity did to them and others in adolescence. Both of their families had converted to Christianity and were devout in their beliefs. They retained some traditional practices, such as the extended-family life, evening storytelling

---

[59]Langford, *Don't Take Your Love to Town*, pp. 35–38.

and communal work camps on family farms, but they absolutely rejected traditional practice and ideas around puberty. Kuzwayo wrote at some length about how much she missed being able to attend Lebollo, the circumcision and initiation schools run separately for girls and for boys amongst her own tribe, the Basotho. Secrecy surrounded what the girls learnt there, but Kuzwayo knew it included sex education and 'played an important part in building up the personal standards and personal stability of young girls'. It also involved beautiful dance and movements which she watched with some envy when she stole out of her own home to watch the final ceremony at a Lebollo close to her family farm. This experience made Kuzwayo include traditional drama in the youth programmes she later ran in Johannesburg, but it produced a powerful sense of lack in her own adolescent years.[60] Sindiwe Magona too, noted the severe consequences she faced as her Christian upbringing meant that she was denied tribal initiation and left completely ignorant of sex, contraception and reproduction.

> We are a group which, as young people were caught up in transition, with sex having been reduced to a thin gold band minus apprenticeship and spontaneity. Previously, sex education for adolescents had been a fact of life. Both boys and girls were taught sex play that satisfied their urges with no risk of their being plunged into roles of parenthood prematurely. Then came the missionaries and sex disappeared from the agenda for educating the young.[61]

Having always felt ugly as a child, she was very happy when a handsome young man seemed to like her – and began a sexual relationship with him, only to find herself pregnant at the age of seventeen, just a few months after she had begun to work as a teacher.

The conflict between Christian expectations and traditional tribal ones and their impact on adolescents was evident in Kenya too. Amongst the Kikuyu tribe to which she belonged, Wambui Otieno notes that the circumcision of girls was as acceptable as it was for boys. Yet the ritual was anathema to missionaries who usually expelled any girls in their schools who were circumcised. Her mother, like many Kikuyu Christians, refused to have her daughters circumcised, a stance which led to immense problems for Otieno herself because her circumcised schoolmates would not associate with her and sang derogatory songs stating that 'the uncircumcised girl is evil'. In her family, as in Magona's, there was no discussion of puberty or

---

[60]Kuzwayo, *Call Me Woman*, pp. 72–73. The Basotho rite of passage ritual, unlike other practices in Africa, does not involve procedures which remove parts of the female genital organ. However, the inner folds of the labia are enlarged and elongated by stretching for a more pleasurable sexual experience. In areas where initiation is still valued, uninitiated girls are ridiculed by society.
[61]Magona, *To My Children's Children*, p. 106.

sexuality and she knew nothing about menstruation when she had her first period, nor would her mother help her. Later, however, when she studied mothercraft, she came to appreciate that her mother's stance on circumcision had saved her from genital mutilation.[62]

Not all the African women who wrote autobiographies were so lucky. Nawal El Saadawi, who grew up in an Islamic family in Egypt was subjected to clitoridectomy when very young, an experience that haunted her throughout her life. 'When I was six,' she wrote, 'The *daya* (midwife) came along holding a razor in her hands, pulled out my clitoris from between my thighs and cut it off. She said it was the will of God and she had done his will.'[63] In 1937, the year she was circumcised, all the girls in her society were too. 'Not a single girl, whether from city or village, from a rich or a poor family escaped.... Girls who believed in the Messiah did not escape any more than those who believed in Mohammed.' The pain of circumcision lasted throughout her life.

> Since I was a child that deep wound left in my body has never healed. But the deeper wound has been the one left in my spirit, in my soul.... Fifty-six years have gone by, but I still remember it, as though it were only yesterday. I lay in a pool of blood. After a few days the bleeding stopped, and the daya peered between my thighs and said 'All is well ...'. But the pain was there, like an abscess deep in my flesh.... I could not bear to see my body naked in the mirror, the forbidden parts steeped in shame and guilt. I did not know what other parts of my body there were that might need to be cut off in the same way.[64]

This process was not accompanied by any other instruction and El Saadawi too was entirely unprepared for menstruation, hiding it until the blood gushed out and stained a prayer rug, bringing additional humiliation to her and also increasing her own horror at the way that women's bodies and their reproductive systems were seen within Islam.

There is little suggestion of any traditional Indigenous knowledge of sexuality or contraception in most of the autobiographies of Aboriginal women, or of any coming from anywhere else. Ruby Langford began engaging in relationships with boys early – and received her first proposal at the age of fifteen. 'I was flattered', she noted, 'but I was only fifteen and had a lot of living to do yet.' Shortly after moving to Sydney for work and to be near her father, however, she met and fell in love with a man named Sam

---

[62] Otieno, *Mau Mau's Daughter*, pp. 28–30.
[63] El Saadawi, *Daughter of Isis*, p. 13.
[64] El Saadawi, *Daughter of Isis*, pp. 75–76.

Griffith. Although warned against him by her mother, Ruby was unable to resist as 'something made me really like him'. She was soon pregnant.

> I was throwing up every morning. I realised I was pregnant but I didn't know the facts of life. I told Sam and he was OK about it. I couldn't lie to Dad but I didn't want to bring any shame on him, so l told him I was going to Coonabarabran to stay with Sam's mother until I had the baby. Dad was very upset and didn't want me to go. He said, 'If everything doesn't turn out right you come straight back Ruby, you understand now, you come back'.[65]

Langford received no form of prenatal care. Sam's mother explained the kinds of pains she would have that would indicate that labour had begun. 'This was my only piece of information about birth, and I hung onto it.'

Marriage and Family Life

Marriage was as much a hurdle and an obstacle for some of these women as it was for those writing autobiographies in Britain at the same time – and something they sought to avoid even more fiercely as some were expected to marry very young. For others, it was a problem of a different order: several of these women had children in their late teens and those that were unmarried had to deal both with community disapproval and the need to support their children on what was often a very meagre wage. Others who had entered into marriage at what they saw as an appropriate time and with the desire to set up a home and family found themselves in violent relationships from which it was necessary to flee.

The difficulties that women faced in marriage was a key theme of Nawal El Saadawi's autobiography, illustrated by the discussion of laws and customs and by reference to the painful experiences of women in her own family. In a chapter entitled 'God Above, Husband Below', for example, she discusses the village custom that her grandmother was subjected to, requiring a husband to beat his wife on their wedding night as 'she had to try the taste of his stick before she could eat his food so that she would know that Allah was above, and her husband below, and she should be ready for a beating if she did not do as she was told.'[66] El Saadawi also offers an account of the stratagem she used to avoid being married while still very young. From the time she was ten, her grandmothers, aunts and uncles and the wider community all pushed for her to be married in accordance with community expectations, seeking suitable potential husbands and bringing them to meet her. Although not unsympathetic to her desire to finish school and to go to

---

[65]Langford, *Don't Take Your Love to Town*, pp. 53–55.
[66]El Saadawi, *Daughter of Isis*, p. 34.

university, her parents did not oppose the idea of her marrying early and she was subjected to a parade of potential suitors found for her by relatives. El Saadawi realized she would have to work out how to send them away, describing with much humour the extremely clumsy way she served coffee to them, shaking the tray as she sneezed incessantly, moving in such a clumsy way that she tipped over the tray so that both hot coffee and iced water fell on the chest of her suitor – who subsequently withdrew his suit.[67] This or similar performances were repeated several times until the family gave up. El Saadawi does not describe her own eventual marriage in any detail, simply mentioning at the end of the book that she had married a man who, like her, was a doctor and writer and an opponent of the government who had spent many years in jail, and with whom she had walked side by side for many years, including into exile.

In contrast with El Saadawi, who was extremely critical of the legal and social framework of marriage and saw it as oppressing women, Ellen Kuzwayo placed immense importance on family life for women and especially on the role of women as mothers. Her autobiography includes at the start, a letter from a young colleague of hers in the YWCA who was currently imprisoned and her immense concern about the impact of her imprisonment on her small son.[68] Kuzwayo had greatly valued her own family and home, and been deeply distressed when, after she had completed her training as a teacher, the aunt who had married her stepfather after her mother's death told her that she needed to leave their home and find her own. At the age of twenty-seven, having adequately established her career, Kuzwayo began planning to establish a secure home, for herself. She chose her own husband, selecting a new boyfriend, 'a handsome, well-built tall man'; amongst his attractions was the fact that 'he was reading for a Bachelor of Arts Degree ... spoke very good English ... and right through our courtship, he was gentle and appeared very polished in his manner'. The gentleness did not last, however, and the 'peaceful, loving, family life' she was seeking did not materialize. Although she does not provide explicit details, she makes it clear that violence and brutality that soon amounted to torture began early in their married life. Shortly after their wedding, she 'had to face the reality that marriage did not mean the pinnacle of life, but its stark beginning. It was a harsh, shocking discovery for me.' She had two sons in quick succession and without problems. During her third pregnancy, however, her husband's brutality was so great that it brought on a miscarriage. His family rescued her and ensured she had medical attention, but when the time came to return to him, she realized that his violence was a danger to her life and that she had to leave. Despite her devotion to her sons, there was no possibility of taking them with her.[69] Her very controlling husband did not want her to

---

[67]El Saadawi, *Daughter of Isis*, pp. 177–178.
[68]Kuzwayo, *Call Me Woman*, pp. 4–5.
[69]Kuzwayo, *Call Me Woman*, pp. 120–125.

leave and kept watch on the bus station. She decided nonetheless to go, taking nothing but the clothes she was wearing and hiding in a field overnight. The next day she returned to her father in Johannesburg and began yet again to make herself a new life. Leaving her young sons was a terrible loss, but she decided it was better for them if she went and thereby assured her own survival. Ultimately, moreover, she remarried happily, and her sons also left their father and came to be with her.

At this point, however, Kuzwayo confronted the obstacles that the South African government placed in the way of setting up and maintaining families for Black people. The residential laws and the group areas acts made it impossible for Black South Africans to live in an urban area unless they had either been born or worked there. Her first son was deemed to have been born in Johannesburg, but her second was not, and, try as she did, it was simply not possible for him legally to move in and share her home. On this occasion she notes, 'the instinct of motherhood had the better side of me and . . . I happily settled down, permission or no permission, with him and the rest of my family in the normal way families do all over the world.' She did wonder, however, if it was this refusal of formal permission to live with his mother that turned her son's attention to the Black Consciousness Movement, which was then becoming very prominent in South Africa.[70]

This legislation was at the base of the difficulties that Sindiwe Magona faced too, and it made her early adult life something of a nightmare. Having worked hard to gain qualifications as a teacher and then struggled to get a job, Magona was forced to give it up after only a few months when she found herself pregnant. As her boyfriend was a migrant labourer, he could not set up home with her in Cape Town, nor could he marry her properly as his family could not come to the ceremony. As a woman who was not 'properly married', however, Magona carried the stigma of being a single mother, a painful one within the Xhosa tribe. The Xhosa language had only derogatory terms to describe husbandless mothers, she noted, and she had to get over her sense that 'I was a has-been at the age of twenty-three . . . My alarm grew at the discovery that I was expected calmly and mother-like, to await old age and death.'[71] Once her teaching job came to an end, she became a dependant in her parent's home. When the baby was three months old, she found work as a domestic cleaner – work she continued for four years. While the residential laws did not allow her properly to marry her partner, according to tribal custom, to minimize her shame, she underwent a brief ceremony that constituted a partial marriage. Although not sufficient to qualify her properly as a wife, in terms of the South African legal system, this ceremony did transfer some authority over her from her father to her partner. He continued to visit – and to make her pregnant again on two

---

[70] Kuzwayo, *Call Me Woman*, p. 185.
[71] Magona, *Forced to Grow*, p. 79.

more occasions. When she was pregnant with her third child, he exercised his legal right to stop her working as a cleaner, hence removing her only source of income. Magona was forced to boil sheep's heads for a local butcher as the only paid occupation she could find. Shortly after, her partner went to visit his parents – and never returned. Although initially alarmed by his absence, she had long ceased to love him and came to relish the fact that 'my husband left me young enough still to be optimistic. . . . I was not just alone: I was free. Free of him. Free to be.'[72]

Magona managed her family life and supported her children, completing her education and gaining a university degree and much experience in the process. Looking back on her earlier life while writing the autobiography, she wondered if her children might have suffered from her preoccupation with providing for and disciplining, rather than mothering them.

> I was so busy being the breadwinner that I now know my children never had a mother. I was the head of the family. Their well-being depended on me. I worked. I dished out discipline. I created a place where they would grow up well mannered, purposeful. I was a father to my children. I shunned those things that mothers do . . . providing them with the gentler side of parenting.[73]

Having children out of wedlock was frowned upon in Aboriginal communities too, although the strictures seem to have been less severe. Both Auntie Rita and Ruby Langford describe leaving places where they and their family had settled to avoid bringing embarrassment to their families when they became pregnant. Auntie Rita had already had one child while living in Cherbourg and it had been taken by her parents and brought up as theirs. But she couldn't face telling them about a second premarital pregnancy and, as she was allowed to leave the reserve, 'did the disappearing act' and went north to a small town where a friend lived. When she returned three years later, she was welcomed by her mother, but her father would not allow her to return to the family, so she lived in a dormitory with other single mothers.[74]

Ruby Langford too left Sydney, where her father lived, in order not to embarrass him with her first pregnancy. He was more concerned about her well-being than about propriety, however, and made clear he would always stand by her. Langford entered into a number of different sexual relationships, something reflected rather ruefully in her choosing 'Don't take your love to Town' as the title of her autobiography. In a brief introductory section called 'Names' where she lays out her own various names and summarizes her story, she includes a paragraph on her partners and children that makes this clear. It also points to the fact that she had both Aboriginal and white partners.

---

[72] Magona, *Forced to Grow*, p. 182.
[73] Magona, *Forced to Grow*, pp. 47–48.
[74] Huggins, *Aunty Rita*, p. 47.

> I had my first three kids with Sam Griffin (Koori), but I didn't change my name. Bill, Pearl and Dianne are Andersons, named after me. The next three I had with Gordon Campbell (gubb), Nobby, David and Aileen. They're registered in his name. Then I married Peter Langford (gubb) and Ellen and Pauline were born. Now I'm Mrs Langford, my only name change. Later I had Jeff, my youngest with Lance Marriot (Koori), who took on all my kids and loved them all. But I stayed Langford. By now things were complicated enough.[75]

Langford describes in a very matter-of-fact and episodic way, the very hard life she lived over many years. Poverty was constant and housing was often limited: she describes living in a car or a tent when no other housing was possible and being offered welfare housing far from the community she knew and where she was the only Indigenous woman. The men she became involved with were often violent, especially when drunk, and she too drank too much and was sometimes extremely violent herself. Lack of employment opportunities in cities for her partners meant that her life involved constantly moving to new places as her partners searched for work or housing. She often found herself alone and with no extended family or supportive community. This was all the harder, as none of the men she was involved with seemed prepared to shoulder what she saw as their share of family responsibility, which increased her sense of isolation, especially when there was a crisis to deal with. 'I felt like I was living tribal but with no tribe around me', she wrote, after one crisis, with,

> no close-knit family. The food-gathering, the laws and the songs were broken up, and my generation at this time wandered around as if we were tribal but in fact living worse than the poorest of poor whites, and in the case of women living hard because it seemed like the men loved you for a while and then more kids came along and the men drank and gambled and disappeared. One day they'd had enough and they just didn't come back. It happened with Gordon and later it happened with Peter, and my women friends all have similar stories.[76]

Although Langford was involved with both Indigenous and white men and married to the white Peter Langford, she does not suggest that there were any tensions or repercussions from her choosing a white husband or partners who were not part of her own ethnic group. For some of the African women, by contrast, marrying a white man or indeed outside their own tribe posed marked problems. When she returned to Namibia planning to marry a white man, Ellen Namhila was subjected to much comment and hostility,

---

[75]Langford, *Don't Take Your Love to Town*, p. 2. Langford is using the terms gubba to refer to white men and koori for indigenous ones.
[76]Langford, *Don't Take Your Love to Town*, p. 96.

especially from her sister. It was not just marriage across the colour lines that was an issue but also marrying into different tribes. The core of Wambui Waiyaki Otieno's autobiography is concerned with the tribal conflict that came to a head when her husband died and his family insisted on claiming his body to bury according to Luo rites, disregarding her wishes entirely. As she knew, this tribal conflict had been evident from the start of their relationship, with hostility coming from both sides. She was anxious when she first took Otieno to meet her parents after having agreed to marry him. Her mother had not been exposed to people beyond the Kikuyu tribe and did not initially welcome her fiancé. 'Where did you find this one?' she asked, using an expression that 'could mean anything, including an animal, but never a human being'. She soon got over her hostility, Otieno notes, and made friends with her new son-in-law, but the hostility to her from his family remained.[77]

Work, Politics and Public Life

Just as their depictions of private life focus on the impact of discriminatory practices and occasionally on the importance of traditional beliefs and ideas, so too do their discussions of work. In some cases, this involves pointing out how limited the occupational opportunities were for Black and Indigenous people, how low the pay was and how common various forms of exploitation by white employers were. In others, the emphasis is rather on how their work revealed community problems that they had not been aware of before – or brought them into contact and conflict with governments and security services. El Saadawi's lectures in the College of Medicine at Aim Shams University in Cairo, in which she linked her ideas about women and their health with social and political questions, for example, led to her immediately being summoned and interrogated by the Security Police.[78] In a similar way, Mashinini's trade union work led to her arrest, and Kuzwayo's community work to hers.

The importance of work as a fundamental pillar of the South African system of racial discrimination is shown in most Black South African women's autobiographies, but nowhere more clearly than in the work of Sindiwe Magona. She describes carefully the ways in which the apartheid regime removed many possible forms of work from the Black population, reserving all permanent and well-paid work for whites and leaving Black men and women confined to low-paid, usually insecure and arduous labour. Although she fought to be able to qualify as a teacher, the minute she began teaching, she discovered that even here where people did the same work,

---

[77]Otieno, *Mau Mau's Daughter*, pp. 96–97.
[78]Nawal El Saadawi, *Memoirs from the Women's Prison*, trans. Marilyn Booth (London: The Women's Press, 1986), p. 3.

salaries followed the prevailing racial hierarchy so that white teachers earned considerably more than anyone else, and Indian and coloured teachers also earned more than Black ones.[79] So ingrained was this system of discrimination that some of her white colleagues sought to justify their higher pay on the basis that they had a higher standard of living to maintain. If teaching illustrated some of the key elements of racial discrimination, the work she had to do when her pregnancies temporarily brought her teaching to an end showed others. The only work Magona could find at this point was that of a domestic servant where, she noted, she truly came to understand what racism was. The way she was spoken to and treated by her employers and their children, the extraordinary expectations of how she would accommodate all of their needs, regardless of the hours of labour involved, all illustrated her point.[80] Subsequently, Magona returned to teaching, extended her qualifications by matriculating and going to university, and then moved into other forms of employment starting with local government administration. The only position available to her here was in the area of 'Bantu Administration': that which dealt with the Black population – and here she came fully to see the nature of the laws that prevented her and her partner from having a home together. Working in this area, she found herself coming to accept the rules and regulations that applied to her own people as ones they should understand and deal with – and left, horrified at the way it was, making her complicit with the racist state.[81] Magona moved back to teaching, but in a community school dealing with disaffected young Black students. Being employed as a teacher, however, did not stop her from being detained by security staff in department stores and accused of theft on more than one occasion.

Magona's depiction of her working life shows the obstacles placed in the path of a woman seeking to make a career for herself that would also enable her to support her children, and ultimately how impossible this was for a Black woman in South Africa. Frustrated in her working life, she began to involve herself in community activity, becoming a member of a multiracial Christian women's group that both expanded her understanding of South Africa and offered new opportunities. It enabled her to go overseas to attend conferences, suggesting the possibility of a quite different life. As her children approached adolescence, Magona applied for and was granted a scholarship to undertake a master's degree in social work at Columbia University, and there began what ultimately became her long-term occupation, working for the United Nations in New York. This job enabled her to leave South Africa and take her children into a world where they could receive a proper education and choose their own careers.

---

[79]Magona, *To My Children's Children*, pp. 95–102.
[80]Magona, *To My Children's Children*, pp. 118–138.
[81]Magona, *Forced to Grow*, pp. 82–93.

Ellen Kuzwayo's depiction of her own work and working life is very different from that of Magona. She carefully documents the development of her career, which, despite obstacles in the way, took her from teaching through community work to an academic position in the Social Work Department at the University of Witwatersrand. She notes how low the salaries of Black female teachers were, but rather than stressing the extent to which she faced discrimination everywhere, Kuzwayo emphasizes how much she enjoyed teaching and the many ways in which she augmented her teaching role. From the start, she added girl guide sessions and physical exercise classes to her role, relishing the enthusiastic response of her pupils.[82] Kuzwayo also found that there was a reformatory for delinquent boys near the school and went to do some teaching there. The plight of these boys, the number of boys who came from broken homes, and her concern to deal with the trauma of her own marriage led her to become involved in youth work training too. She explains also the ways in which the community aspect of her work became increasingly important, especially that involving women's organizations like the YWCA, of which she became the regional director before moving into social work.

Indigenous Australians too faced immense racism and discrimination which limited the kinds of work and the pay available to them. Sally Morgan depicts this very clearly in the stories of her uncle, her grandmother and her mother included in *My Place*. The assimilation policy, which not only involved the removal of half-caste children from their Indigenous families but also made domestic service one of the only occupations available to women, was a key issue here as she describes the way her grandmother became a servant while very young. There was massive exploitation here, masked with a discourse about her grandmother being part of the family. Rather than suggesting that she was well-treated, however, this familial rhetoric enabled her employers to demand ceaseless labour and deny her grandmother leave and pay. When she became pregnant, there was no suggestion that her daughter might become part of the family and she was forced to send her away to an institution where she had little access to her. Issues of assimilation, exploitation and indeed theft were prominent also in Morgan's telling of the story of her uncle Arthur, a hard-working man who was constantly being denied due wages when he worked for others. Discrimination continued when he finally managed to buy a farm. He was frequently embroiled in battles with neighbours, the bank and the police, who always took the word of white farmers against his. Fortunately, Arthur found a lawyer who intervened and stopped him from being forced to sell the farm or relinquish his cattle. 'They'll get you if they can', Morgan quotes him as saying. 'They'll follow you to the last ditch, even the government. You gotta be a blackfella to know what the pressure is from government.'[83]

---

[82]Kuzwayo, *Call Me Woman*, pp. 118–119.
[83]Morgan, *My Place*, p. 265.

While work is quite a separate thing from their political involvement for some of these women, for others the two are hard to separate. Wambui Otieno, for example, worked almost full-time for the Mau Mau in the early 1950s, scouting and gathering intelligence before raids and attacks and recruiting supporters. As a woman, she was seen as having greater freedom of movement and as arousing less suspicion than men did. It also meant that she led groups of women who gathered firearms by acting as prostitutes for British soldiers and then taking their guns when they were asleep. None of this work was paid, however, and she also did clerical work for a trade union and bookkeeping to earn some extra cash.[84] Subsequently, after her release from prison and marriage, she worked with her husband, a prominent criminal lawyer, managing his legal office and becoming actively engaged in politics.[85] Wambui was an active official of the Kenya African National Union and the first chair of its women's branch in Nairobi. She stood unsuccessfully for parliament in the Kenyan elections of 1969. After this, Wambui devoted herself to women's issues and was very active in the international arena, especially the UN International Women's Decade.

Although the awareness of discrimination and repression seems always to be present for many of these women, some also point to particular episodes or incidents that bring political questions to the fore and raise their consciousness and concern to a new level. In all the South African autobiographies, it was the crucial and violent events around 1976-7: the Soweto student demonstrations that began as a peaceful protest against the new government decree that Afrikaans should now become a language of instruction in Black schools. For many of the students, English was a second language and the burden of learning another was heavy, quite apart from the strong sense that this was the oppressor's language. The violent and brutal police response to these demonstrations increased the violence of the demonstrations and there was soon large-scale rioting accompanied by savage police repression. Ellen Kuzwayo offered the most detailed discussion of this episode in a chapter entitled 'Violence in the Community', as well as the one dealing with her own arrest and imprisonment. Her account indicates strong sympathy for the students and depicted her horror as she watched the growing police violence as students were met by armed police who shot at them, killing a ten-year-old boy, Hector Peterson. Kuzwayo stressed her horror at the violence of the police: the shooting of unarmed people from unmarked cars, the disappearance of students and the deaths in detention of so many young Black men who died mysteriously. Kuzwayo was concerned here to stress the extent to which violence 'is the ever-present background to life in Soweto'.[86]

It was these events that catapulted Kuzwayo into a new level of activity and led to her arrest. They were important too for Sindiwe Magona, but she saw

---

[84] Otieno, *Mau Mau's Daughter*, p. 44.
[85] Otieno, *Mau Mau's Daughter*, pp, 96–107.
[86] Kuzwayo, *Call Me Woman*, pp. 50–55.

them in a different way and from a different perspective. Magona too sympathized strongly with the initial demands of the students but was appalled not only at the government response but at how quickly violence and intimidation followed within Black communities. Magona was living in Guguletu in Cape Town at the time, working in a church-based education programme that sought to provide mature-aged students who had left the formal education sector a second chance at their final school examinations. As this was their last chance to complete their education, her students did not wish to join the demonstrations – but found it impossible to resist the pressure to do so.[87] Police brutality was extreme, and like Kuzwayo, Magona named and described young people who were either killed or permanently maimed and injured by police, often simply because they were standing in the street. Again, like Kuzwayo, Magona was asked to serve on a community committee to help manage the crisis. Although supportive at the start, she began to feel increasingly uneasy about the committee's proceedings. After a short time, she wrote, 'the three children of fear and confusion – Cowardice, Corruption and Colonisation – had arrived.'[88] Magona disliked much of what was being proposed in the community, including the insistence that everyone follows the same line and the refusal to tolerate differences of opinion. She opposed the boycotting of schools, feeling that it would deny her own and other Black children even the limited education allowed them by the state. She was appalled at the way anyone who disagreed with the majority was accused of being an informer, something that could have fatal consequences. At one point, she was accused of being an informer, an accusation she insists was made in spite by the former girlfriend of a man she was having a relationship with. What became clear to her was the breakdown in community relations that followed the political struggle of these years – and the need for herself to move outside the immediate local community and find an alternative way of life.

Sense of Self

Questions about a sense of self, of how these women thought about themselves and who they understood themselves to be, are complicated ones in all of these autobiographies. As several critics and commentators have noted, the sense of self articulated by African and Aboriginal women contrasts markedly with that evident amongst most white Western women writing at the same time. While the latter are generally informed by contemporary psychology and psychoanalysis and framed with some reference to a Western tradition of individualism, for the former, their senses of self are usually understood and written about within a wider community and cultural framework. The African saying, 'I am because we are, and since we are, therefore I am',

---

[87]Magona, *Forced to Grow*, pp. 151–152.
[88]Magona, *Forced to Grow*, p. 160.

Margaret Daymond argues, 'offers a very different basis for selfhood from the singularity, the uniqueness, that is emphasized in Western cultural tradition'.[89] A similar point could be made in relation to Indigenous Australian autobiography, in which links to country, mob and particular forms of Aboriginality are integral to any notion of self. At the same time, for some of these authors, the decision to write an autobiography entailed some kind of focus on an individualized self and sometimes also a struggle between the commitment to a notion of self, understood in terms of a connection to ethnic origin and heritage and community, on the one hand, and a rather more individualized sense of self linked to particular experiences on the other.

The work in which questions of heritage and connection to kin and community are most important, indeed effectively define a sense of self, is Sally Morgan's *My Place*. From the start of her book, Morgan makes clear the ways in which her shaky sense of identity and unhappiness in the outside world is linked to her questions about who she is and her frustration and distress at the way that her mother and grandmother will not discuss their past or provide any information about themselves to help her. An occasional slip in which her grandmother once said she was Black and her mother conceded that she was Aboriginal only increased her sense of being lost and her desire to know more. This knowledge finally became available when Morgan was already at university and her great-uncle Arthur, who had begun to visit more and more frequently, agreed to tell her his whole story. This story, including information about his parents: a prominent white man and an Indigenous woman, the way he was sent off as a very young child, as most 'half-caste' children were, to a mission school where he was brutally treated, and his very hard-working life after that offers a powerful picture of how discrimination in Australia worked. As Albert said, Morgan notes, colonialism wasn't over yet. That Morgan knew his story helped her to persuade both her mother and her grandmother to tell her their stories, ones which also revealed terrible suffering. Some things, her grandmother said, were too painful to recall. In the course of recording and writing up these stories, Morgan also visited the places where her mother and uncle came from and got to meet extended family and kin. Morgan's narrative depicts a quest that is ultimately successful: she discovers the Aboriginal heritage which she had been denied and gains a sense of the Aboriginal identity that she felt she needed to be at peace with herself. Both her quest and its resolution have proved very controversial in Australia, where several academics have questioned whether or not she was really entitled to claim an Aboriginal identity, given how small a percentage of her heritage was Aboriginal. The debate about Morgan has raised questions about whether her construction of Aboriginality is one that others accepted and indeed more broadly about the whole question of how the notion of Aboriginality

---

[89] M. J. Daymond, 'Siezing Meaning – Language and Ideology in the Autobiographies of Ellen Kuzwayo and Emma Mashinin', *Journal of Literary Studies* 9, no. 1 (1993): 26.

has been constructed.[90] What is most notable here, however, is precisely the way in which the discovery of her Aboriginal heritage resolved Morgan's questioning of who she is. Nothing else was required, and her story effectively comes to an end with the telling of the stories of her great-uncle, her grandmother and her mother.

The link to her Indigenous culture and sense of her own Aboriginality is crucial for the sense of self in other Indigenous women's autobiographies too. It is a key issue for Ruby Langford, although she did feel the need to establish her own individual subjectivity within a broader Indigenous framework. Unlike Morgan, Langford, in Tim Rowse's view, 'is apparently so confident of her Koori identity that she has no need to discover it, to convey it iconically or to protest it defiantly'.[91] At the same time, as Langford had white as well as Indigenous partners, some of her children were 'half caste', emphasizing the extent to which she and they lived between cultures. The question of quite how secure her Koori identity was, also came to the fore when, after she had already embarked on writing her autobiography, she travelled from Sydney and the urban world she was familiar with to Ayers Rock (now known as Uluru) where she met Aborigines who lived a much more traditional life in the outback. Their lifestyle was quite unfamiliar to her. When she returned to Sydney and wrote about the visit for the autobiography she noted how she,

> wished at that moment I'd been born fullblood instead of the degree of caste that I was. I had a longing for the relaxed tribal sense of time and of looking after the earth, but I knew I enjoyed luxuries like not having to boil the billy for a cup of tea . . . and the hot shower and watching TV. I'd become soft in the modern world.[92]

Langford did not describe or analyse her feelings very much within the text itself, tending rather to depict her life in an episodic way as it happened, introducing her various lovers and her children and the many hardships and tragedies that she experienced in a very matter-of-fact way, in the sequence in which they occurred. These include her desertion by her mother when she was very young, the realization of the infidelity of her partners, sometimes when she was pregnant and isolated, and the accidental deaths of three of her children. There is no suggestion of self-pity in her work. Rather, as Tim Rowse suggests, some of Langford's experiences were so painful that they could only be recited in this matter-of-fact way, and without dealing in detail with her actual feelings.[93] Despite the pain, the book was therapeutic. 'I knew when I finished this book a weight would be lifted from my mind', she wrote, 'not only because I could examine my own life from it and know who

---

[90]There is a very good summary of this debate in Hirokazu Sinoda, 'A Preliminary Study of Sally Morgan's *My Place*', *The Otemon Journal of Australian Studies* 35 (2009): 157–170.
[91]Rowse, 'The Aboriginal Subject', pp. 16–19.
[92]Langford, p. 236.
[93]Rowse, 'The Aboriginal Subject', pp. 20–21.

I was, but because ... it might give some idea of the difficulty we have surviving between two cultures.'[94]

The question of a sense of self is rather more complicated in some of the African women's autobiographies where, despite an insistence on service and connection to a Black community as the core of individual identity, there is also sometimes a struggle to fit entirely within the framework of community values – and an assertion of more individual self too. One can see all of this quite clearly in the writing of Ellen Kuzwayo, whose sense of self has been quite extensively discussed. Questions both about her endorsement of connection to community and her criticism of traditional and contemporary Black values begin with her title. *Call Me Woman*, Julie Coullie argues, immediately calls for a new discursive position for Black women, refusing the passivity and dependence of female subjectivity both in traditional Black ideologies and in racist white ones, and portraying a self who can speak in the imperative.[95] Gillian Whitlock agrees but suggests that it also offers a challenge to contemporary Black masculine political discourse. It was chosen, Whitlock argues, specifically in relation to Mathoba Mtutuzeli's book of short stories, *Call Me Not a Man*. Kuzwayo's book shapes a discourse of militant maternalism by inserting woman-centred concerns into discourses of Black consciousness.[96] There is a tension, she suggests, evident in Kuzwayo's concern to enunciate a critique of apartheid in terms that show her support for the Black Consciousness Movement, but does so in ways that raise issues of gender, emphasize her belief in the crucial importance of Black motherhood and her sense that this concept does not entirely encompass her. It is hard to overstate the importance to Kuzwayo of the notion of Black motherhood. Her book begins with a letter from a woman who is currently in prison on political grounds and whose main concern is the impact of her imprisonment on her young son. She wrote at length about the problems mothers faced and the heroic work they did. And of their pain and suffering when their children were arrested and murdered in the violent crackdown that followed the student demonstrations of 1975–6. She described her approach and many of her actions in her professional life as ones connected to maternal concerns: her treatment of her pupils, for example, as well as her concern for the young reformatory inmates that she teaches and her involvement in youth clubs. She took great pride in being greeted as a mother and seen as a mother of the community when she returned from prison. At the same time, in her personal life, Kuzwayo was unable to embody the values she endorsed so strongly. Her sense that her life was in danger from her husband's violence made her leave the sons whom she loved so dearly. Although she visited them regularly, they remained with their violent father for some years, until they were able to leave and come to her. She came to understand that her sons had suffered 'emotional, physical and psychological injuries' in the years

---

[94]Langford, *Don't Take Your Love to Town*, p. 269.
[95]Coullie, 'The Space between Frames', p. 148.
[96]Whitlock, *The Intimate Empire Reading Women's Autobiography*, pp. 150–152.

they were away from her.[97] She stressed her concern and involvement in their lives and the support she offered them through the trials of adolescence and early adult life, but cannot avoid recognizing also their suffering and the damage that her absence caused them.

While Kuzwayo's connection with and commitment to the Black community, her desire to serve that community and her concern to gain recognition for other Black women is immense, there is no question of her sense of her own importance and value, and of her recognition of her own needs. One can see this in the careful way in which she depicts the development of her career, the ways in which she enhanced her skills and moved from teaching to community work to a senior role in the YWCA and then into training in and teaching social work, and in her description of how she evaluated her marriage and decided to leave her first husband to save herself. She notes the high estimation others had of her abilities and her work and saw herself clearly as a woman of note, including herself when she drew up a list of notable contemporary women – noting amongst her other achievements that 'I am the author of this book'. There is a tension here for Kuzwayo, who, while extolling the importance of women and the value of their social and familial role, recognized that she moved beyond it. She insists, as far as possible, that doing so was not her choice, but rather something thrust upon her. She illustrates this point by describing an episode when she was called on by an advocate to speak on behalf of a group of students who had been arrested under the Terrorism Act and were facing long imprisonment and even possible death sentences. Here again, she insists, she is serving her community. The advocate explained that he saw her as the only person who could bring home to the judge the terrible conditions in which the young people lived, and which contributed to their negative behaviour. Kuzwayo found the court appearance an ordeal, although she established a rapport with the judge who protected her from the aggression of the prosecutor and offered her subtle support. When the case was over, Kuzwayo tells us, the father of one of the accused came over to her. All he said to me was, 'you are not an ordinary woman, you pleaded like a man, only a man could speak the way you did'.[98] That she found a way to mask the extent to which her own career and abilities made her move beyond the normal realm of women serves to underline the struggle involved for her here.

There is a much stronger assertion of an individualized subjectivity and sense of self in Sindiwe Magona's autobiography than there is in Kuzwayo's. This point is underlined by the title of the second volume of her autobiography, *Forced to Grow*, which depicts how, having been left as a single mother with three children, Magona re-established herself as a teacher and, with additional education and the seeking of new positions, builds an impressive career that takes her into public administration, social work, language teaching and

---

[97]Kuzwayo, *Call Me Woman*, p. 182.
[98]Kuzwayo, *Call Me Woman*, p. 227.

finally to a position at the United Nations in New York. Although Magona makes clear how important her mother and her friends are in enabling her to do all of this, there is little sense of her belonging to any community after her rural childhood came to an end. Indeed, throughout her work, one can see a much more difficult sense of connection to community than was the case with Kuzwayo. In her depiction of how appalling the conditions of Black South Africans were, Magona emphasizes how difficult and unpleasant her immediate environment was, not only physically in terms of its lack of any amenities and even the most basic hygiene, but also in terms of the constant threat to her safety. When she returned home having qualified as a teacher and was looking for work, she was constantly threatened by the thuggish young men who shadowed and bullied her, kept at bay only by the threat of reciprocal violence from her brother. This sense of community threat and violence to her as a woman has a tribal and traditional counterpart when Magona finds herself pregnant and becomes aware that she is seen as having no value and no prospects. Her maternity is not valued – but it is expected to prevent her from doing anything else. This sense of alienation from the Black community in which she lives is emphasized again in her account of the violence that erupted in Langa, the township where she lived, in the violence of the mid-1970s. Magona was so appalled by what was happening that she tried to prevent her own children from participating or going out at night, and her extreme protectiveness and limiting of their activity earned her scorn and the reputation of a counter-revolutionary. This became more threatening when Magona was named as an informer by a woman who was competing with her for the same man. Magona was not injured, but her sense of the need to move on in her life was greatly strengthened.

Like Kuzwayo, Magona sought a sense of meaning and self in community groups, but she did not find ones that met all her needs and interests within the Black community and looked to women's groups outside that offered her new connections, knowledge and insight. The first of these was a multiracial Christian women's group which brought her into close contact with white women for the first time and gave her some insight into how, despite their privilege, white women also experienced suffering and pain. This group also led to her being invited to address the International Tribunal on Crimes Against Women in Brussels, an extraordinary experience for her – although it pointed again to the extensive nature of discrimination Black people faced in South Africa: she was not deemed a citizen and had immense difficulty getting a passport. Magona also participated in a 'meeting of women of all colours, languages and races irrespective of class' which she described as 'the birth of the women's movement' in South Africa. Magona is quite clear about her own feminist commitment and it underlay much of her sense of herself and of the wider world in which she lived. It underlay her determination to take opportunities, such as the scholarship at Columbia, even though it meant leaving her children behind. Children grow up and become independent, she insisted, allowing her an independence too.

Conclusion

In writing their life stories in ways that focused attention on how their lives had been shaped, indeed dominated, by colonization and the dispossession, discrimination and political developments that followed from it, Indigenous women and women of colour across the wider British world were participating in the massive global expansion in autobiography that occurred in the last couple of decades of the 20th century. In many cases, the impulse to write an autobiography came from a particular confrontation with a repressive government or a realization of the full impact of colonization on their own lives and families. The use of individual stories to illustrate or depict wider historical events and developments was not completely new: as we have seen, it was a significant feature of interwar women's autobiography too. What was new here was the actual history that was being discussed and the stance taken by the author in relation to it. While women in interwar Britain sought to link themselves with the major events of national history that were quite widely known, these Black and Indigenous women were drawing attention to histories that were relatively little known to many readers and, in the process critiquing and talking back to the dominant historical narrative from the perspective of the silent and the oppressed. These books were usually designed to address the dominant white readership in their own country, to make them see how Black and Indigenous people lived and how these particular women felt about it. Their autobiographies all serve to show how important memoir and autobiography have become in the past few decades in the broader understanding of history.

While addressing their own particular situation and country, all of these books became known outside too. Most of them were published overseas, mainly in Britain, but occasionally in the United States. Many of these autobiographies were the subject of extensive discussion amongst scholars in a range of different disciplines. Wambui Waiyaki Otieno's *Mau Mau's Daughter*, for example, was the subject of much discussion amongst scholars of African history, as Sally Morgan's *My Place* and Sara Suleri's *Meatless Days* were amongst scholars interested in postcolonial studies. Nawal El Saadawi was a major figure in international feminism and all her autobiographical works were widely read. Although she was relatively unknown outside South Africa prior to the publication of *Call Me Woman*, Ellen Kuzwayo's book was also widely noticed. It was favourably reviewed in the *Times Literary Supplement* and extensively publicized elsewhere as Kuzwayo gave talks about it at book fairs and major literary and political events across Europe.[99] These works offered new ways of thinking about the writing of lives and of linking the personal to the political that had a major impact on the history of women's autobiography and on how it developed in an increasingly globalized world.

---

[99] Christopher Hope, 'In Undaunted Defence', *Times Literary Supplement*, 26 July 1985.

Autobiographies Discussed in This Chapter

El Saadawi, Nawal, *The Daughter of Isis: The Early Life of Nawal El Saadawi* (London: Zed Books, 1999).
Kuzwayo, Ellen, *Call Me Woman* (London: The Women's Press, 1986). This book has been re-issued with a new Introduction by Sindiwe Magona (Johannesburg: Picador Africa, 2018).
Langford, Ruby, *Don't Take Your Love to Town* (Ringwood, Victoria: Penguin Books, 1988).
Magona, Sindiwe, *To My Children's Children: An Autobiography* (London: The Women's Press, 1991).
Magona, Sindiwe, *Forced to Grow* (London: The Women's Press, 1992).
Morgan, Sally, *My Place* (Fremantle: Fremantle Press, 1987).
Namhila, Ellen Ndeshi, *The Price of Freedom* (Windhoek: New Namibia Books, 1997).
Otieno, Wambui Waiyaki, *Mau Mau's Daughter. A Life History*. (Boulder, CO: Lynne Rienner Publishers, 1998).
Suleri, Sara, *Meatless Days* (Chicago: University of Chicago Press, 1987).

Epilogue

The writing and publishing of British women's autobiography has shown no sign of diminution in the past couple of decades. On the contrary, in Britain as elsewhere, it has not only continued but expanded in number and range. Increasing numbers of prominent women of many kinds including actors, academics, entrepreneurs, philanthropists, politicians and professional writers have written their stories. Some have followed a traditional pattern, encompassing and summing up their entire life. More and more authors, however, have taken new approaches, seeking to do something rather different by focusing their attention on episodes or aspects of their lives that hold particular significance for them, including childhood, marital break-up, and bereavement and loss. There are also many authors who have shifted the focus away from themselves, embedding their story in a family memoir, often one that points to the domination of a particular parent or reveals long-held and painful secrets. This shift of focus is also evident in memoirs in which an author has sought to link her story with that of another: an institution, an historical figure who has particular importance for her, sometimes games or particular hobbies or pastimes that provide the framework for telling a life story. The impulse to autobiography has continued also amongst little-known women whose memoirs have brought them public attention for the first time. Accounts of personal trauma and suffering continue to bulk large here. In place of the political oppression that was so significant in the late 20th century, however, many of these accounts focus rather on traumas suffered within abusive families, especially on the sexual or emotional abuse suffered by women at the hands of a parent or on tales of illness and loss of loved ones.

The informality and episodic nature of much recent life writing has led to some debate about whether these works should be called memoir rather than autobiography. As we have seen, this distinction was important to those who established the field of autobiography as one deserving academic attention and who stressed the importance to it not only of offering a comprehensive depiction of a life but also a self-reflexive analysis of it.

Memoir, which they saw as simply recounting past experiences or people known or events remembered without this self-reflexivity seemed to them a lesser form, deserving little scholarly attention. In the recent debate about memoir and autobiography, however, this prioritizing of autobiography has been rejected as some now argue that memoir is the more revealing, innovative and important form. One recent commentator has suggested that in contrast to conventional autobiography, which is 'determined to cover the subject's entire life or career and show him or her in the most favourable light', a memoir 'is more tightly focused, more daring in construction, and (its author hopes) more penetrating. A memoir can be of one's self or of other people or of a particular decade – or of a particular place.'[1] The very looseness of memoir in structure and focus and its capacity to encompass innovative ways of telling life stories now gives it a particular value. Not everyone accepts this particular differentiation or evaluation of the two terms, however. At present, as in the past, the precise meanings of both terms are often contested while the practice of discussing them together and including both in the same general category continues. What is important here, it seems to me, is not the need to separate autobiography from memoir, but rather the increasing recognition that the ways in which people tell their life stories are changing and the meanings of both autobiography and memoir are changing too.

The importance and the nature of new approaches to writing a life story can be seen particularly clearly in the growing number of autobiographies and memoirs of established writers, especially novelists. Many prominent women novelists have published life stories in the past couple of decades, including Edna O'Brien, Margaret Drabble, Rose Tremain, Miranda Seymour, Hilary Mantel, Michelle Roberts, Jeanette Winterson, Maggie O'Farrell, Bronwyn Levy and Rachel Cusk. What stands out in all of them is their marked difference from the autobiographies of the major novelists of the late 20th century. There is nothing here that resembles the way that Storm Jameson or Doris Lessing or Janet Frame described their personal lives, showed how their literary careers developed – or discussed the ways that they drew on their personal lives in fiction and the relationships between fictional and autobiographical accounts. For the most part, the life stories recounted by contemporary novelists stand alone as stories that need to be told in their own right, rather than offering a commentary on their other work. Many of these works depict periods of considerable pain and sometimes hardship. Sometimes the painful episode centres on childhood, as it does for Rose Tremain and Jeanette Winterson, for example.[2] Equally, it

---

[1]Cited in Julie Rak, 'Are Memoirs Autobiography? A Consideration of Genre and Public Identity', *Genre* no. 3–4 (2004).
[2]Rose Tremain, *Rosie Scenes from a Vanished Life* (London: Vintage, 2018); Jeanette Winterson, *Why Be Happy When You Could Be Normal?* (London: Jonathan Cape, 2011).

might deal with a terrible marriage, as it does for Edna O'Brien, or the end and aftermath of a marriage or other intimate relationship, or motherhood, as it does for Debora Levy and Rachel Cusk.[3] Some deal also with illness, as Hilary Mantel does describing the undiagnosed endometriosis that crippled her and brought to an end the possibility of motherhood.[4] This episodic approach underlines the shift away from the psychological concern or desire to explore childhood and relationships with parents in relation to their own development that was so important in the later 20th century. There is certainly a desire to describe and depict particular experiences and feelings and to tell important stories, but rarely do these descriptions explain how the author came to be who she is. Rose Tremain's question about the distant and unloving mother who sent her and her sister to boarding school at the age of ten focuses on her mother's inability to love rather than the impact it had on her. In a similar way, while making clear the need for escape from her narrow, rigid and impoverished Catholic family, her occasional hatred of her mother, and the way her family's clumsy interference pushed her into a terrible marriage, in her memoir Edna O'Brien doesn't link her adult self to the earlier family dynamics. She is concerned, rather, to reveal a very painful world and a life that no longer exists.

While several of these women deal with the question of how they became writers, and some point to the way that a particular incident or person was incorporated into a novel, there is little general discussion of the relationship between their memoirs and their fiction and rather more of a sense that in the memoir, aspects of their lives that have not been addressed in fiction are important. The changing nature of fiction is of course important here too: the detailed study of a character such as Lessing's *Martha Quest* is as much a thing of the past as her autobiography. Even those few works that do reflect on the way the author has depicted her life in fiction do so in a different way from twentith-century autobiographies. Jeanette Winterson's provides a striking example. Winterson's first novel, the award-winning *Oranges Are Not the Only Fruit*, was clearly autobiographical. As she made clear in her autobiography, *Why by Happy When You Could Be Normal*, it did not tell her whole story. The life she lived in her adoptive home as depicted in her autobiography was a much harder and harsher life than the one she created in her novel. 'I suppose the saddest thing for me', she wrote when commenting on the novel in her autobiography, 'is that I wrote a story I could live with. The other one was too painful. I could not survive it.'[5] The version provided in the novel and the one that she could live with at that

---

[3]Edna O'Brien, *A Country Girl* (London: Faber and Faber, 2012); Deborah Levy, *Things I Don't Want to Know*, Living Autobiography 1 (London: Penguin Books, 2018); *The Cost of Living* (London: Penguin Books, 2019); Rachel Cusk, *A Life's Work* (London: Faber, 2001); *Aftermath: On Marriage and Separation* (London: Faber, 2012).
[4]Hilary Mantel, *Giving Up the Ghost* (London: Fourth Estate, 2003).
[5]Winterson, *Why Be Happy When You Could Be Normal?* p. 7.

early stage of her writing life included a fictional character, Elsie, who was an imaginary friend. 'There was no one like Elsie', she noted. 'Things were much lonelier than that.' Rather than offering the kind of discussion about literal and fictional truths that Doris Lessing did, Winterson simply pointed to the importance of stories and storytelling in her own life – and to the links between fiction and autobiography. 'Part fact, part fiction is what life is', she wrote. 'And it is always a cover story.'

Several authors have found more oblique ways to frame their memoirs and address their life stories. Some raise questions, as many earlier authors did, about whether their work is actually an autobiography or a memoir, or something else. The novelist, Margaret Drabble, for example, insisted that *The Pattern in the Carpet: A Personal History with Jigsaws*, was 'not a memoir, although parts of it may look like a memoir. Nor is it a history of the jigsaw puzzle, although that is what it was once meant to be. It is a hybrid.'[6] It is through discussing the jigsaws, something she often did with a beloved aunt, that she recalls and reveals aspects of her life. In one of the most celebrated works to approach a life through a pastime, *H is for Hawk*, Helen McDonald makes her passion for goshawks, for finding and describing them, something she had done from childhood with her father, into the framework for the memoir she wrote after her father's death, one that, while providing much fascinating discussion of goshawks, is dominated by her father and the grief of her bereavement.[7] Another and more recent memoir which was also the recipient of several awards, Doireann Ni Ghriofa's *A Ghost in the Throat* links her own story, and especially that of her daily life as a mother of several small children, with her quest to discover all the details she can of the life of the 18th-century poet, Eibhlin Dubh Ni Chonaill, by whom she has become completely obsessed.[8]

This range of different approaches to the telling of life stories is evident beyond the literary world too as women of many different educational levels, professions and occupations and of many different social classes and ethnic backgrounds have continued to write their life stories. Like professional writers, these women focus attention on a very broad range of issues and experiences. Dominating parents, destructive family lives, sexual abuse and violent marriages feature, as do newer experiences, including surrogacy and gender transition. Individual lives are depicted in relation to extended family and community, to institutions like churches and synagogues as well as hospitals and care homes. Matters that were once excluded or dealt with briefly in memoirs and autobiographies, sexual harassment including family quarrels, periods of mental as well as physical illness, at one extreme and cooking and collections of recipes or love of and care for

---

[6] Margaret Drabble, *The Pattern in the Carpet: A Personal History with Jigsaws* (London: Atlantic Books, 2009).
[7] Helen Macdonald, *H is for Hawk* (London: Jonathan Cape, 2014).
[8] Doireann Ni Ghriofa, *A Ghost in the Throat* (Dublin: Tramp Press, 2020).

pets at the other, have become the primary subject of fascinating and widely read works. As the range of autobiographies and memoirs has expanded so too have the ways in which they can be published, with self-publishing and online venues becoming more and more widely used, and tips and advice for how to write a memoir available in many different forms. After a long period of exclusion from the writing of autobiography and memoir and restrictions on what could be written, the writing and publishing of memoirs is now available to all.

BIBLIOGRAPHY

Albrinck, M. 'Borderline Women: Gender Confusion in Vera Brittain's and Evadne Price's War Narratives', *Narrative* 6, no. 3 (1998): 271–291.
Anderson, Lynda. 'Life Lines:Auto/Biography and Memoir'. In *The History of British Women's Writing, 1970–Present*, edited by Mary Eagleton and Emma Parker, 182–192. Houndsmills, Basingstoke: Palgrave Macmillan, 2015.
Anon. 'Jipping Street', *The Sketch*, Nov 28, (1928): 144.
Autobiography: A Collection of the Most Instructive and Amusing Lives Ever Published, Written by the Parties Themselves, 33 volumes. London: Whittaker, Treacher, Arnott, 1920–32.
Bellamy, George Anne. *An Apology for the Life of George Anne Bellamy*. London, printed for the authors, 1785.
Benton, Jill. *Naomi Mitchison: A Biography*. London: Pandora, 1992.
Besant, Annie Wood. *An Autobiography* (1893). London: T. Fisher Unwin, 1908. Accessed through Nineteenth Century Collections Online.
Besant, Annie. *Autobiographical Sketches*, edited by Carol Hanbury. Peterborough, Ontario: Broadview, 1885, repr 2009.
Binhammer, Katherine. *The Seduction Narrative*. Cambridge: Cambridge University Press, 2009. doi:https://doi-org.ezproxy.library.sydney.edu.au/10.1017/CBO9780511635496
Bird, Delys, and Dennis Haskell. ed. *Whose Place? A Study of Sally Morgan's 'My Place'*. Sydney: Angus & Robinson, 1992.
Birkett, Jennifer. *Margaret Storm Jameson: A Life*. Oxford: Oxford University Press, 2009.
Blixen, Karen. *Out of Africa*. Harmondsworth: Penguin, 1937, repr 1952.
Bloom, Ursula. *Without Make-Up*. London: Michael Joseph, 1938.
Bostridge, Paul, and Mark Berry. *Vera Brittain: A Life*. London: Chatto & Windus, 1995.
Bowen, Stella. *Drawn from Life*. Collins, 1940.
Breashears, Caroline. 'Scandalous Categories: Classifying the Memoirs of Unconventional Women'. *Philological Quarterly* 82 (2003): 187–202.
Breashears, Caroline. 'The Female Appeal Memoir: Genre and Female Literary Tradition in Eighteenth-Century England'. *Modern Philology* 107, no. 4 (2010): 607–631.
Breashears, Caroline. '"Justifying Myself to the World": Paratextual Strategies in Teresia Constantia Phillips's Apology'. *Script & Print* 35, no. 1 (2011): 7–22.
Breashears, Caroline. *Eighteenth-Century Women's Writing and the 'Scandalous Memoir'*. London: Palgrave Macmillan, 2016.
Brittain, Vera. *Testament of Experience*. Bath: Cedric Chivers Ltd, 1957, repr 1971.

Brittain, Vera. *Testament of Youth: An Autobiographical Study of The Years 1900–1025*. London: Virago, 1933, republished 1978.
Broughton, T. L. 'Life Writing'. In *Routledge Companion to Victorian Literature*, edited by Dennis Denisoff and Talia Schaffer. New York: Routledge, 2019.
Butler, Josephine E. *An Autobiographical Memoir*, edited by George W. and Lucy A. Johnson. Bristol: J. W. Arrowsmith, 1909.
Caine, Barbara. 'Beatrice Webb and the "Woman Question"'. *History Workshop Journal* 14, no. 1 (1982): 23–44.
Caine, Barbara, *English Feminism, c 1780–1980*. Oxford: Oxford University Press, 1996.
Caine, Barbara. 'The Making of Catherine Cookson's Autobiography'. *Women's History Review* 22, no. 1 (2013): 2–18.
Campbell, Margaret (pseud Marjorie Bowen). *The Debate Continues: Being the Autobiography of Marjorie Bowen*. Heinemann, 1939.
Charke, Charlotte. *A Narrative of the Life of Mrs Charlotte Charke (1755)*, edited and with Introduction and Notes by Robert Rehder. London: Pickering & Chatto, 2016.
Cholakian, Patricia Francis. *Women and the Politics of Self-Representation in Seventeenth-Century France*. University of Delaware Press, 2000.
Churchill, Sue. '"I Then Was What I Had Made Myself": Representation and Charlotte Charke'. *Biography* 20, no. 1 (1997): 72–94.
Clarke, Norma. *The Rise and Fall of the Woman of Letters*. London: Pimlico, 2004.
Clarke, Norma. *Queen of the Wits: A Life of Laetitia Pilkington*. London: Faber and Faber, 2008.
Clayton, Cherry. 'Interview with Ellen Kuzwayo'. In *Between the Lines: Interviews with Bessie Head, Sheila Roberts, Ellen Kuzwayo, Miriam Tlali*, edited by Craig and Cherry Clayton Mckenzie. Grahamstown, South Africa: The National English Literary Museum, 1989.
Cloete, Elsie. 'Wambui Otieno's Mau Mau'. *Foreign Policy in Perspective* (30 October 2011).
Cobbe, Frances Power. *The Life of Frances Power Cobbe by Herself*. London: Richard Bentley & Son, 1894.
Colley, Cibber. *An Apology for the Life of Mr Colley Cibber*. London, printed for the author, 1840.
Cook, Daniel, and Amy Culley, ed. *Women's Life Writing, 1700–1850: Gender, Genre and Authorship*. London: Palgrave Macmillan, 2012.
Cookson, Catherine Ann. *Our Kate: Her Personal Story*. London: Macdonald, 1969, repr 1973.
Cough, Marshall, *Mau Mau Memoirs: History, Memoir and Politics*. Boulder, CO: Lynne Rienner, 1998.
Coullie, Judith Lutge. 'The Space between Frames: A New Discursive Practice in Ellen Kuzwayo's *Call Me Woman*'. In *South African Feminisms*, edited by M. J. Daymond. New York: Garland Publishing Inc., 1996.
Croft, Andy. 'Ethel Mannin: The Red Rose of Love and the Red Flower of Liberty'. In *Rediscovering Forgotten Radicals: British Women Writers 1889–1939*, edited by Angela Ingram and Daphne Patai. London and Chapel Hill: University of North Carolina Press, 1993.
Culley, Amy. *British Women's Life Writing, 1760–1840*. London: Palgrave Macmillan, 2014.

Cusk, Rachel. *A Life's Work*. London: Faber, 2001.
Cusk, Rachel. *Aftermath: On Marriage and Separation*. London: Faber, 2012.
Danahay, Martin. *A Community of One: Masculine Autobiography and Autonomy in Nineteenth-Century Britain*. The Margins of Literature, edited by Miha I. Spariosu. New York: State University of New York Press, 1993.
David, Deirdre. *Intellectual Women and Victorian Patriarchy: Harriet Martineau, Elizabeth Barrett Browning, George Eliot*. London: Macmillan, 1986.
Davidoff, Leonore. *Thicker Than Water: Siblings and Their Relations, 1780–1920*. Oxford: Oxford University Press, 2012.
Daymond, M. J. 'Siezing Meaning – Language and Ideology in the Autobiographies of Ellen Kuzwayo and Emma Mashinini'. *Journal of Literary Studies* 9, no. 1 (1993): 24–35.
Dayus, Kathleen. *Her People: Memoirs of an Edwardian Childhood I*. London: Virago, 1982.
Dayus, Kathleen. *Where There's Life*. London: Virago, 1985.
Demos, John, and Virginia Demos. 'Adolescence in Historical Perspective'. *Journal of Marriage and Family* 31.4 (1969): 632–638.
Douglas, Kate. 'British Women's Autobiography'. In *Encyclopaedia of Women's Autobiography*, edited by Victoria Boynton and Jo Malin. Greenwood Press: Westport, CT, 2005, p. 123.
Drabble, Margaret. *The Pattern in the Carpet: A Personal History with Jigsaws*. London: Atlantic Books, 2009.
Driver, Dorothy. 'Imagined Selves, (Un)Imagined Marginalities: Review Article'. *Journal of Southern African Studies* 17, no. 2 (1991).
Eakin, John Paul. *How Our Lives Become Stories*. London and Ithaca: Cornell University Press, 1999.
El Saadawi, Nawal. *Memoirs from the Women's Prison*. Translated by Marilyn Booth. London: The Women's Press, 1986.
El Saadawi, Nawal. *The Daughter of Isis: The Early Life of Nawal El Saadawi*. London: Zed Books, 1999.
Elizabeth, Charlotte. *Personal Recollections*. Third edition. London: Seeley Burnside & Seeley, Fleet Street, 1847.
Emecheta, Buchi. *In the Ditch*. London: Allison and Busby, 1972.
Emecheta, Buchi. *Second Class Citizen*. London: Allison and Busby, 1974.
Emecheta, Buchi. *Head above Water*. London and Nigeria: Heinemann, 1986.
Fawcett, Millicent Garrett. *What I Remember*. London: T. Fisher Unwin Ltd, 1925.
Feather, John. 'British Publishing in the Eighteenth Century: A Preliminary Subject Analysis'. *The Library* s6–VIII, no. 1 (1986): 32–46.
Finney, Brian. 'Sexual Identity in Modern British Autobiography'. *Prose Studies* 8, no. 2 (1985): 29–44.
Folkenflik, Robert. 'Introduction: The Institution of Autobiography'. In *Culture of Autobiography*, edited by Robert Folkenflik, 1–20. Stanford: Stanford University Press, 1993.
Frame, Janet. *An Angel at My Table*. London: Virago, 1989.
Freedman, Diana P., and Olivia Frey, eds, *Autobiographical Writing Across the Disciplines: A Reader*. Durham, NC: Duke University Press, 2004.
Friedman, Susan Stanford. 'Women's Autobiographical Selves: Theory and Practice'. In *The Private Self: Theory and Practice of Women's Autobiographical*

Writings, edited by Shari Benstock, 34–62. Chapel Hill and London: University of North Carolina Press, 1988.
Fulkerson-Dikuua, Kelly Jo. 'Conceptualising National Transition: Namibian Women's Autobiographies About the Liberation Struggle'. In *Writing Namibia: Literature in Translation*, edited by Sarala and Helen Vale Krishnamurthy. Windhoek: University of Namibia Press, 2018.
Gamble, Rose. *Chelsea Child*. London: British Broadcasting Corporation, 1979.
Gates, Henry Louis et al., eds., *Dictionary of African Biography*. Oxford: Oxford University Press, 2011.
Gates, Henry Louis Jr., ed. *The Classic Slave Narratives*. New York: Penguin Books, 1987, p. xv.
Gerard, Christine. 'Laetitia Pilkington and the Mnemonic Self'. *The Review of English Studies*, New Series 70, no. 295 (2018): 489–508.
Gibson, Anna. 'Charlotte Brontë's First Person'. *Narrative* 25, no. 2 (2017): 203–226.
Gooch, Elizabeth. 'The Life of Mrs Gooch (1792)'. In *Memoirs of Scandalous Women*, edited by Dianne Dugaw. London: Pickering & Chatto, 2011.
Gooch, Elizabeth. *The Life of Mrs Gooch. Memoirs of Scandalous Women*, edited by Dianne Dugaw. London: Pickering & Chatto, 1792, repr 2011.
Gorham, Deborah. 'Liberty and Love? Dora Black Russell and Marriage'. *Canadian Journal of History* 46, no. 2 (2011).
Green, Barbara. *Feminist Periodicals and Daily Life: Women and Modernity in British Culture*. London: Palgrave Macmillan, 2017.
Grosskurth, Phyllis. 'Where Was Rousseau?' In *Approaches to Victorian Autobiography*, edited by George P. Landow, 26–38. Athens, OH: Ohio University Press, 1979.
Grossman, Michele. 'Out of the Salon and into the Streets: Contextualising Australian Indigenous Women's Writing'. *Women's Writing* 5, no. 5 (1998): v.
Gusdorf, Georges. 'Conditions and Limits of Autobiography (1956)'. In *Autobiography: Essays Theoretical and Critical*, edited by James Olney, 28–48. Princeton: Princeton University Press, 1980.
Harriette, Wilson. *Harriette Wilson's Memoirs*, edited by Lesley Blanch. London: Century Publishing, 1825, repr 1985.
Harrison, Rosina, with Leigh Crutchley. *My Life in Service*. New York: Viking Press, 1975.
Hendrick, Harry. 'Review: The History of Childhood and Youth'. *Social History* 9, no. 1 (1984): 87–96.
Heron, Liz, ed. *Truth, Dare or Promise*. London: Virago, 1985.
Hinton, James. *Nine Wartime Lives: Mass Observation and the Making of the Modern Self*. Oxford: Oxford University Press, 2010.
Holden, Philip. *Autobiography and Decolonization: Modernity, Masculinity, and the Nation State*. Maddison, WI: University of Wisconson Press, 2008.
Hollis, Patricia. *Ladies Elect: Women in English Local Government, 1865–1914*. Oxford: Oxford University Press, 1979.
Hope, Christopher. 'In Undaunted Defence'. *Times Literary Supplement*, 26 July 1985.
Huggins, Rita, and Jacki Huggins. *Auntie Rita*. Canberra: Aboriginal Studies Press, 1994.

Hunsu, Folasade. 'Engendering an Alternative Approach to Otherness in African Women's Autobiography'. *Life Writing* 10, no. 2 (2013): 171–185.
Huxley, Elspeth. *The Flame Trees of Thika*. London: Catto & Windus, 1959.
Hynes, Samuel. *Edwardian Occasions: Essays on English Writing in the Early Twentieth Century*. London: Routledge & Kegan Paul, 1972.
Ingrassia, Catherine. 'Elizabeth Thomas, Laetitia Pilkington and Competing Currencies of the Book'. *Women's Writing* 23, no. 3 (2016): 312–234.
Jameson, A. *Commonplace Book of Thoughts. Memories and Fancies*. London: Longman, Brown, Green and Longmans, 1854.
Jameson, Margaret Storm. *Journey from the North*. 2 vols. London: Virago, 1984.
Jameson, Storm. *Love in Winter*. London: Capuchin Classics, 1935, repr 2009.
Jelinek, Estelle, C. *The Tradition of Women's Autobiography: From Antiquity to the Present*. Boston: Twayne Publishers, 1986.
Jermy, Louise. *The Memories of a Working Woman*. Norwich: Goose & Son, 1934.
Joannou, Maroula, ed. *Women Writers of the 1930s: Gender, Politics, History*. Edinburgh: The Edinburgh University Press, 1999.
Joannou, Maroula. 'She Who Would Be Free Herself Must Strike the Blow. Suffragette Autobiography and Suffragette Militancy'. In *The Uses of Autobiography*, edited by Julia Swindells. London: Taylor & Francis, 1995.
John, A. *Evelyn Sharp*. Manchester: University of Manchester Press, 2009.
John, A. *Turning the Tide*. London: Parthian Books, 2013.
Johnstone, Julia. *Confessions of Julia Johnstone Writte by Herself in Contradiction to the Fables of Harriette Wilson*. London: Benbow, Printer and Publisher, 1825.
Jones, Kathleen. *Catherine Cookson: The Biography*. New York: Random House, 1999.
Kenney, Annie. *Memoirs of a Militant*. London: Edward Arnold, 1924.
King, Michael. *Wrestling with the Angel. A Life of Janet Frame*. Sydney: Picador, 2000.
Kuhn, Annette. *Family Secrets: Acts of Memory and Imagination*. London: Verso, 1995, 2nd edition 2002.
Kuzwayo, Ellen. *Call me Woman*. London: The Women's Press, 1986. This book has been re-issued with a new Introduction by Sindiwe Magona. Johannesburg: Picador Africa, 2018.
Lambert-Hurley, Siobhan. *Elusive Lives: Gender, Autobiography, and the Self in Muslim South Asia*. South Asia in Motion. Stanford University Press, 2018. doi:https://doi-org.ezproxy.library.sydney.edu.au/10.1515/9781503606524.
Langford, Ruby. *Don't Take Your Love to Town*. Ringwood, Victoria: Penguin Books, 1988.
Leeson, Margaret, *Memoirs of Mrs Margaret Leeson Written by Herself; in Which Are Given Anecdotes, Sketches of the Lives and Bon Mots of Some of the Most Celebrated Characters in Great Britain and Ireland, Particularly of All the Filles Des Joys and Men of Pleasure and Gallantry Which Have Frequented Her Citherean Temple for These Thirty Years Past*. 3 vols. Dublin: The Principal Booksellers, 1797.
Lessing, Doris. *Under My Skin: Volume One of My Autobiography to 1949*. London: Harper Perennial, 1994.
Lessing, Doris. *Walking in the Shade: Volume Two of my Autobiography, 1949–1962*. London: Harper Collins, 1998.

Levy, Deborah. *Things I Don't Want to Know*. Living Autobiography 1. London: Penguin Books, 2018.
Levy, Deborah. *The Cost of Living*. London: Penguin Books, 2019.
Lewes, George Henry. 'Recent Novels: French and English'. *Fraser's Magazine* 36 (December 1847): 686–695.
Linda, Peterson H. *Victorian Autobiography: The Tradition of Self-Interpretation*. 1986. http://www.victorianweb.org/genre/peterson/5.html.
Linda, Peterson H. 'Institutionalizing Women's Autobiography'. In *Culture of Autobiography*, edited by Robert Folkenflik, 80–103. Stanford: Stanford University Press, 1993.
Linda, Peterson H. *Traditions of Victorian Women's Autobiography: The Poetics and Politics of Life Writing*. Charlottesville: University Press of Virginia, 1999.
Little, Janine. 'Talking with Ruby Langford Ginibi'. *Hecate* 20, no. 1 (1994).
Lively, Penelope. *Oleander, Jacaranda: A Childhood Perceived*. London: Penguin Books, 1994.
Lloyd, Helen. 'Witness to a Century: The Autobiographical Writings of Naomi Mitchison'. University of Glasgow, 2005.
Lobban-Viravong, Heather. 'The Theatrics of Self-Sentiment in a Narrative of the Life of Mrs. Charlotte Charke.' *a/b: Auto/Biography Studies* 24, no. 2 (2009): 124–209.
Loftus, Donna. 'The Self in Society: Middle-Class Men and Autobiography'. In *Life Writing and Victorian Culture*, edited by David Amigoni. London: Routledge, 2006, reprint, e-book 2017.
Logan, Deborah, and Valerie Sanders, eds., *The Collected Letters of Harriet Martineau*. London: Routledge, 2021.
Looser, Devony. *British Women Writers and the Writing of History, 1670–1820*. Baltimore: Johns Hopkins Press, 2000.
Lynne, Pearce. *Romance Writing*. Cambridge: Polity Press, 2007.
Lytton, Lady Constance. *Prisons and Prisoners: Some Personal Experiences*. London: Virago Press, 1914, repr 1988.
Macdonald, Helen. *H is for Hawk*. London: Jonathan Cape, 2014.
Mackay, Carol Hanbery. 'A Journal of Her Own: The Rise and Fall of Annie Besant's Our Corner'. *Victorian Periodicals Review* 42, no. 4 (2009): 324–358.
Mackay, Carol Hanbery. 'Emerging Selves. The Autobiographical Impulse in Elizabeth Barrett Browning, Anne Thackeray Ritchie and Annie Wood Besant'. In *A History of English Autobiography*, edited by Adam Smyth, ch. 15, 207–220. Cambridge: Cambridge University Press, 2016.
Magona, Sindiwe. *To My Children's Children: An Autobiography*. London: The Women's Press, 1991.
Magona, Sindiwe. *Forced to Grow*. London: The Women's Press, 1992.
Maitland, Sara. *Very Heaven: Looking Back at the 1960s*. London: Virago, 1988.
Makhoere, Caesarina Kona. *No Child's Play: In Prison under Apartheid*. London: The Women's Press, 1988.
Mannin, Ethel. *Confessions and Impressions*. London: Jarrolds, 1930.
Mantel, Hilary. *Giving Up the Ghost*. London: Fourth Estate, 2003.
Martin, Robert B. 'Charlotte Brontë and Harriet Martineau'. *Nineteenth Century Fiction* 7.3 (1952): 198–201.
Martineau, Harriet. *Autobiography*. 3 vols. London: Virago, 1877, repr 1983.

Mascuch, Michael. *Origins of the Individualist Self: Autobiography and Self-Identity in England 1591–1791*. Cambridge: Polity Press, 1997.

Mashinini, Emma. *Strikes Have Followed Me All My Life: A South African Autobiography*. London: The Women's Press, 1989.

Maslen, Elizabeth. *Life in the Writings of Storm Jameson: A Biography*. Evaston, IL: Northwestern University Press, 2014.

Mayhall, Laura E. Nym. 'Creating the "Suffragette Spirit": British Feminism and the Historical Imagination'. *Women's History Review* 4 (1995): 319–344.

Mayhall, Laura E. Nym. *The Militant Suffrage Movement: Citizenship and Resistance in Britain, 1860–1930*. Oxford: Oxford University Press, 2020.

Meyers, Mitzi. 'Harriet Martineau's *Autobiography*: The Making of a Female Philosopher'. In *Women's Autobiography: Essays in Criticism*, edited by Estelle C. Jelinek, 54–70. Bloomington: Indiana University Press, 1980.

Miller, Carolyn Elizabeth. 'Body, Spirit, Print: The Radical Autobiographies of Annie Besant, and Helen and OliviaRossetti'. *Feminist Studies* 35, no. 2 (2009): 243–273.

Miller, Nancy K., and Jason Tougaw, eds., *Extremities: Trauma, Witnessing and Communities*. Albany: State University of New York Press, 2001.

Mitchell, Sally. 'Frances Power Cobbe's *Life* and the Rules for Women's Autobiography'. *English Literature in Transition, 1880–1920* 50, no. 2 (2007): 131–157.

Mitchell, Sally. *Frances Power Cobbe: Victorian Feminist, Journalist, Reformer*. English Literature in Transition, 1880–1920. Charlottesville: University of Virginia Press, 2004.

Mitchison, Naomi. *Small Talk*. Oxford: The Bodley Head, 1973.

Mitchison, Naomi. *All Change Here: Girlhood and Marriage*. London: The Bodley Head, 1975.

Morgan, Sally. *My Place*. Fremantle: Fremantle Press, 1987.

Murray, Fanny. *Memoirs of the Celebrated Miss Fanny Murray*. 2nd edition. London: J. Scott, 1759.

Murray, Simone. 'The Women's Press, Kitchen Table Press and Dilemmas of Feminist Publishing'. *European Journal of Women's Studies* 5 (1998): 171–193.

Murray, Simone. '"Deeds and Words":The Woman's Press and the Politics of Print'. *Women: A Cultural Review* 11, no. 3 (2000).

Nadel, Ira Bruce. 'Beatrice Webb's Two Voices: My Apprenticeship and Victorian Autobiography'. *ESC: English Studies in Canada* 2, no. 1 (1976): 83–98.

Namhila, Ellen Ndeshi. *The Price of Freedom*. Windhoek: New Namibia Books, 1997.

Namhila, Ellen Ndeshi. *Mukwahepo: Women Soldier Mother*. Windhoek: University of Namibia Press, 2014.

Namhila, Ellen Ndeshi. 'Uncovering Hidden Historical Narratives of Village Women in Namibia'. *Qualitative Research Journal* 14, no. 3 (2014): 243–258.

Neeley, Kathryn A. *Mary Somerville*. Cambridge: Cambridge University Press, 2001.

Ni Ghriofa, Doireann. *A Ghost in the Throat*. Dublin: Tramp Press, 2020.

Nord, Deborah Epstein. *The Apprenticeship of Beatrice Webb*. Basingstoke: Macmillan, 1985.

Nord, Deborah Epstein. 'Victorian Autobiography: Sons and Fathers'. In *The Cambridge Companion to Autobiography*, edited by Maria and Emily O. Wittman DiBattista. Cambridge, 2014.

Nussbaum, Felicity. *The Autobiographical Subject: Gender and Ideology in Eighteenth-Century England*. Baltimore: Johns Hopkins University Press, 1989.

Nussbaum, Felicity. 'Eighteenth-Century Women's Autobiographical Commonplaces'. In *The Private Self*, edited by Shari Benstock, ch. 6, 146–171. Chapel Hill: University of North Carolina Press, 1988.

Nussbaum, Felicity. 'Afterword: Charke's Variety of Wretchedness'. In *Introducing Charlotte Charke*, edited by Philip E. Baruth, 237–244. Chicago: University of Chicago Press, 1998.

O'Brien, Edna. *A Country Girl*. London: Faber and Faber, 2012.

O'Connell, Lisa. 'Authorship and Libertine Celebrity: Harriette Wilson's Regency Memoirs'. In *Libertine Enlightenment*, edited by Peter Cryle, 161–181. London: Palgrave Macmillan, 2003.

Oakley, Ann. *Taking It Like a Woman*. London: Jonathan Cape, 1984.

[Oliphant, Margaret]. 'Harriet Martineau', *Blackwood's Edinburgh Magazine*, 121 (1877): 472–475.

Olney, James, ed. *Autobiography: Essays Theoretical and Critical*. Princeton University Press, 1980.

Olney, James. '"I Was Born": Slave Narratives, Their Status as Autobiography and as Literature'. *Callaloo* no. 20 (1984): 46–73.

Otieno, Wambui Waiyaki. *Mau Mau's Daughter. A Life History*. Boulder, CO: Lynne Rienner Publishers, 1998.

Ouditt, Sharon. 'Kathleen Dayus: The Girl from Hockley'. In *A History of British Working Class Literature*, edited by John Goodridge and Bridget Keegan, 339–351. Cambridge: Cambridge University Press, 2017.

Owen, Ursula, ed. *Fathers: Reflections by Daughters*. London: Virago, 1983.

Pankhurst, Emmeline. *My Own Story*. New York: Source Book Press, 1914, repr 1970. http://www.gutenberg.org/files/34856/34856-h/34856-h.htm.

Payne, K. *Between Ourselves: Letters between Mothers and Daughters 1750–1982*. London: Michael Joseph, 1983.

Peakman, Julie. '"Blaming & Shaming" in Whores' Memoirs: Sex, Scandals and Celebrity'. *History Today* 59, no. 8 (2009).

Peakman, Julie, ed. *Whore Biographies in the Long 18th Century*. London: Pickering & Chatto, 2007.

Pethick-Lawrence, Emmeline. *My Part in a Changing World*. London: Victor Gollancz, 1938.

Phillips, Constantia. *An Apology for the Conduct of Mrs Teresia Constantia Phillips*, 3 vols, 2nd edition, printed for the Booksellers of London and Westminster, 1847. Accessed through Eighteenth Century Collections Online, Gale Primary Sources.

Phillips, Mark Salber. *Society and Sentiment*. Princeton: Princeton University Press, 2000.

Pilkington, Laetitia. *Memoirs of Mrs Laetitia Pilkington, Wife to the Rev. Mr Matthew Pilkington, Written by Herself, Wherein are occasionally Interspersed all her Poems, with Anecdotes of several eminent Persons, Living and dead*, 20 vols. Dublin: Printed for the Author, 1748. Accessed through Eighteenth Century Collections Online, Gale Primary Sources.

Powell, Margaret. *Below Stairs*. London: Pan Books, 1968, 1970.

Prince, Mary. *The History of Mary Prince, a West Indian Slave, Written by Herself*. London: Penguin, 1831, repr 2001.

Pritchard, William. 'Looking Back at Lessing'. *Hudson Review* 48, no. 2 (1995): 317–324.
Purvis, June. *Emmeline Pankhurst: A Biography*. London: Routledge, 2002.
Pyrne, Paula, *Perdita: The Life of Mary Robinson*. London: Harper Perennial, 2001.
Rak, Julia. 'Are Memoirs Autobiography? A Consideration of Genre and Public Identity'. *Genre* XXXVI (2004): 305–326.
Rasmussen, Bryan B. 'From God's Work to Fieldwork: Charlotte Tonna's Evangelical Autoethnography'. *ELH* 77, no. 1 (2010): 159–194.
Ravenscroft, Alison. 'Recasting Indigenous Lives Along the Lines of Western Desire: Editing, Autobiography, and the Colonizing Project'. *a/b: Auto/Biography Studies* 19, no. 1–2 (2004): 189–202.
Rendall, Jane. '"A Short Account of My Unprofitable Life": Autobiographies of Working-Class Women in Britain c. 1775–1845'. In *Women's Lives/Women's Time: New Essays on Auto/Biography*, edited by Trev Lynn and Linda Anderson Broughton, 31–50. Albany: State University of New York Press, 1997.
Resha, Maggie. *Mangoana O Tsoara Thipa Ka Bohaleng. My Life in the Struggle*. Johannesburg: Congress of South African Writers, 1991.
Rhondda, Viscountess. *This Was My World*. London: Macmillan and Co., Ltd, 1933.
Robinson, Mary. *Memoirs of the Late Mrs Robinson Written by Herself* (1801). London: Cobden Sanderson, 1930.
Rosenthal, Laura J. *Infamous Commerce: Prostitution in Eighteenth-Century British Literature and Culture*. Ithaca: Cornell University Press, 2015. doi: https://doi.org/10.7591/9780801454356
Rowse, Tim. 'The Aboriginal Subject in Autobiography: RubyLangford's *Don't Take Your Love to Town*'. *Australian Literary Studies* 16, no. 1 (1993): 14–30.
Russell, Dora, *The Tamarisk Tree*, 3 vols. London: Virago, 1978–1985.
Sage, Lorna, *Bad Blood: A Memoir*. London: Fourth Estate, 2000.
Salih, Sara. 'The History of Mary Prince, the Black Subject, and the Black Canon'. In *Discourses of Slavery and Abolition: Britain and Its Colonies, 1760–1838*, edited by Brycchan Carey, Markman Ellis, Sara Salih, 123–138. Basingstoke, Hampshire: Palgrave Mcmillan, 2004.
Sanders, Valerie. *The Private Lives of Victorian Women: Autobiography in Nineteenth-Century England*. New York: St Martin's Press, 1989.
Scott, David Clark. 'Book Makes Big News on the "Bush Telegraph"'. *Christian Science Monitor* no. 23 (November 1988).
Seacole, Mary. *Wonderful Adventures of Mrs Seacole in Many Lands* (1857), edited and with an Introduction by Sara Salih. London: Penguin Books, 2005.
Seacole, Mary. *Wonderful Adventures of Mrs Seacole in Many Lands*. Schomburg Series of 19th Century Black Women Writers, edited by Henry Louis Gates Jr. Oxford: Oxford University Press, 1988.
Setzer, Sharon M. 'The Memoirs of Harriette Wilson: A Courtesan's Byronic Self-Fashioning'. In *Women's Life Writing, 1700–1850*, edited by Daniel Cook and Amy Culley, 150–164. London: Palgrave Macmillan, 2012.
Sharp, Evelyn. *Unfinished Adventure: Selected Reminiscences from an Englishwoman's Life*. London: John Lane, 1933.
Sheridan, Dorothy. 'Writing to the Archive: Mass-Observation as Autobiography'. *Sociology* 27, no. 1 (1993): 27–40.

Shuttleworth, Sally. *Charlotte Bronte and Victorian Psychology*. Cambridge: Cambridge University Press, 1996.
Shuttleworth, Sally. 'Victorian Visions of Child Development'. *Lancet Perspective: The Art of Medicine* 379, no. 9812 (2012): 212–213.
Sinoda, Hirokazu. 'A Preliminary Study of Sally Morgan's *My Place*'. *The Otemon Journal of Australian Studies* 35 (2009): 157–170.
Smith, Sidonie. *Subjectivity, Identity, and the Body: Women's Autobiographical Practices in the Twentieth Century*. Bloomington: Indiana University Press, 1993.
Smith, Sidonie. 'The Transgressive Daughter and the Masquerade of Self-Representation'. In *Introducing Charlotte Charke*, edited by Philip E. Baruth, 83–106. Chicago: University of Chicago Press, 1998.
Smyth, Adam, ed. *A History of English Autobiography*. Cambridge: Cambridge University Press, 2016.
Somerville, Mary. *Personal Recollections from Early Life to Old Age*, edited by Martha Somerville. London: John Murray, 1874.
Spacks, Patricia Meyer. *Imagining a Self: Autobiography and Novel in Eighteenth-Century England*. Cambridge, MA: Harvard University Press, 2013. doi: https://doi-org.ezproxy2.library.usyd.edu.au/10.4159/harvard.9780674435780
Spedding, Patrick. 'The Publication of Teresia Constantia Phillips's Apology (1748–49)'. *Script & Print* 35, no. 1 (2011).
Stanton, Donna C. 'Autogynography: Is the Subject Different'. In *The Female Autograph*, edited by Domna C. Stanton, 30–20. Chicago and London: University of Chicago Press, 1984.
Steedman, Carolyn, *Landscape for a Good Woman*. London: Virago, 1986.
Stephen, Leslie. 'Autobiography'. *Cornhill Magazine* LXIII (1881): 410–429.
Stone, Lawrence. *Uncertain Unions: Marriage in England 1660–1753*. Oxford: Oxford University Press, 1992.
Suleri, Sara. *Meatless Days*. Chicago: University of Chicago Press, 1987.
Swanwick, H. M. *I Have Been Young*. London: Victor Gollancz Ltd, 1935.
Taylor, Charles. 'The Politics of Recognition'. In *Multiculturalism and the Politics of Recognition*, edited by Amy Gutmann, 25–73. Princeton: Princeton University Press, 1992.
The Parallel; or Pilkington and Phillips Compared, being Remarks upon the Memoirs of those two Celebrated Writers, by an Oxford Scholar. London, printed for R. M Copper, 1848.
Thobejane, Tsoaledi Daniel. 'History of Apartheid Education and the Problems of Reconstruction in South Africa', *Sociology Study* 3, no. 1 (2013): 1–12.
Thomas, Sue. 'Pringle V. Cadell and Wood V. Pringle: The Libel Cases over the History of Mary Prince'. *Journal of Commonwealth Literature* 40, no. 1 (2005): 113–135.
Thomas, Sue. '1831 Reviews of the History of Mary Prince'. *Notes and Queries* 66, no. 2 (2019): 282–285.
Thompson, Lynda M. *The Scandalous Memoirists: Constantia Phillips, Laetitia Pilkington and the Shame of 'Publick Fame'*. Manchester: Manchester University Press, 2000.
Todd, Selina, and Hilary Young. 'Baby-Boomers to "Beanstalkers"', *Cultural and Social History* 9, no. 3 (2012): 451–467.
Tremain, Rose. *Rosie Scenes from a Vanished Life*. London: Vintage, 2018.

Turley, Hans. '"A Masculine Turn of Mind": Charlotte Charke and the Periodical Press'. In *Introducing Charlotte Charke*, edited by Philip E. Baruth, 180–199. Urbana and Chicago: University of Illinois Press, 1998.

Vane, Frances. 'Memoirs of a Lady of Quality' first published as chapter LXXXI of Tobias Smollett, *The Adventures of Peregrine Pickle* (London, 1751), edited by J. L. Clifford. Oxford: Oxford University Press, 1969.

Vincent, David. *Bread, Knowledge, Freedom: A Study of Nineteenth-Century Working Class Autobiography*. London: Europa Publications Limited, 1981.

Waliaula, Ken Walibora. 'The Female Condition as Double Incarceration in Wambui Otieno's Mau Mau's Daughter'. *Eastern African Literary and Cultural Studies* 1, no. 1–2 (2014): 71–81.

Walsh, Kay, and Joy Hooton, *Australian Narrative Autobiography: An Annotated Bibliography*, 2 vols, Australian Scholarly Editions Centre, National Library of Australia, 1992.

Watkins, Susan. *Doris Lessing*. Manchester: Manchester University Press, 2010.

Webb, Beatrice. *My Apprenticeship*. London: Longmans, Green & Co., 1926.

Webb, Beatrice. *The Diaries of Beatrice Webb*, edited by Norman and Jeanne McKenzie (London: Virago, 2000).

Webb, R. K. *Harriet Martineau: A Radical Victorian*. New York: Columbia University Press, 1960.

Westley, David. 'A Select Bibliography of South African Autobiography', *Biography* 17, no. 3 (Summer 1994): 268–280.

Whitlock, Gillian. *The Intimate Empire: Reading Women's Autobiography*. London: Cassell, 2000.

Wilson, Elizabeth. *Mirror Writing: An Autobiography*. London: Virago, 1982.

Wilson, Frances. *The Courtesan's Revenge: Harriette Wilson, the Woman Who Blackmailed the King*. London: Faber and Faber, 2004.

Wilson, Harriette. *Harriette Wilson's Memoirs of Herself and Others*, 3 vols. London: T. Douglas, 1825. Accessed through Nineteenth Century Collections Online.

Winterson, Jeanette, *Why Be Happy When You Could Be Normal?* London: Jonathan Cape, 2011.

Woodward, Kathleen. *Jipping Street*. London: Virago, 1928, repr 1983.

Woolf, Virginia, *The Diary of Virginia Woolf, Vol. 4: 1931–35*. Harmondsworth: Penguin Books, 1982, p. 177.

Woolf, Virginia. 'Laetitia Pilkington' *The Common Reader, Series I*.

INDEX

Illustrations are shown in *italic* figures.

Aboriginal women 222–3
  adolescence 243–4
  childhood 236–7
  education 240–1
  family life 247–8
  production of memoir 228–9, 230–2
  sense of self 254–6
  working lives 251
Aboriginality 254–5
academic women 163, 166, 177–8, 215, 224
  see also Oakley, Ann; Steedman, Carolyn; Wilson, Elizabeth
additional material 27–8, 66, 72, 178–9
adolescence
  'British World' autobiographies 241–4
  eighteenth-century autobiographies 37–41
  nineteenth-century autobiographies 80–1
  twentieth-century autobiographies 112, 187–92
adult education 165
advertising of autobiographies 30
age of consent 37
ages of authors 111
Albrinck, Meg 156
amanuenses 65, 66
'ambivalent,' feeling 153
Anderson, Lynda 165
anthologies 176
apartheid policies 237–8, 246, 249–50, 252
apologies, memoirs as 23

appeal memoirs 23
Astor, Nancy 201
Atkinson, Blanche 73
Auntie Rita *see* Huggins, Rita
Australian writers *see* Huggins, Rita; Langford, Ruby; Morgan, Sally
autobiography
  definitions of 3, 9
  modern foundations of 1–5
  see also women's autobiography, history of
autonomous selfhood *see* selfhood

Bantu Education Act (1953) 237–8
BBC 175
Bentinck, Lord Charles 64
Berry, Paul 116
Besant, Annie
  childhood 79–80
  education 80
  and Frances Cobbe 73–4
  masculine pronoun, use of 59
  private life 94–5
  production of memoir 74–5
  public life 89–90
  religious beliefs 74–5, 83–5, 104–5
  sense of self 104–5
  working life 89
biographical publications 69, 113–14
Black African women 220, 221–2
  see also Emecheta, Buchi; Kuzwayo, Ellen; Magona, Sindiwe; Namhila, Ellen Ndeshi; Otieno, Wambui Waiyaki; El Saadawi, Nawal

Black motherhood 256
blackmail 62, 63
Blixen, Karen 219–20
Bloom, Ursula 121, 125, 128, 134–5, 146
Bostridge, Mark 116
Bowen, Marjorie 121, 125, 128, 139–40, 146
Bowen, Stella 133–4
Breashears, Caroline 23, 27, 28
British Empire 15
'British World' autobiographies 10–11, 219–60
　features of 219–23
　producing an autobiography 223–32
　sense of self 253–9
　shaping a life 232–53
Brittain, Vera 13, 110–11
　age of author 111
　education 130
　independence, struggle for 138–9
　justifications for autobiography 116–17
　marriage 144–5, 195–6
　openness of 111
　personal life 143–5
　production of memoir 115–16
　public life 151
　religious beliefs 130
　sense of self 155–6
　sexual knowledge 132–3
　success of 117
Brontë, Charlotte 77, 100, 101
　Jane Eyre 77, 100–1
brother-sister relationships 92–3
Broughton, Trev 70
Butler, Josephine 113
Byron, Lord George 64

Caitlin, George 144–5
Callil, Carmen 177
Campbell, Margaret *see* Bowen, Marjorie
Campion, Jane 174
Carlyle, Thomas 3–4
Cawley, Robert 172–3, 210
Chapman, Guy 197
Chapman, Maria Weston 71

Charke, Charlotte
　childhood 35–6, 37
　cross-dressing 32, 35–6, 52
　education 36
　father 25, 30, 31–2, 45, 46–7
　instalments, publishing of 31, 32
　justifications for autobiography 31
　life of struggle 46–8
　literary relationships 25
　marriage 40
　Narrative of Charlotte Charke 21
　poverty of 32–3
　reception of 26
　relationships of 23, 47
　selfhood, lack of sense of 51–2
　writing by 25
Charke, Richard 40
child psychiatry 77
childhood
　'British World' autobiographies 233–7
　eighteenth-century autobiographies 34–7
　nineteenth-century autobiographies 71, 75–81, 101
　twentieth-century autobiographies 112, 121–6, 179–87
children 148, 199–200, 214, 256
Churchill, Sue 33
Cibber, Colley 25, 30, 31–2, 45, 46–7
circumcision 242, 243
Clarke, Norma 20, 26, 28–9, 30, 31, 51
class *see* middle-class women; working-class women
Cobbe, Frances Power
　adolescence 80–1
　and Annie Besant 73–4
　autobiography 12
　cautious approach of 72–3
　childhood 79
　education 79
　finances 88–9
　justifications for autobiography 59
　and Mary Somerville 72
　posthumous publication 73
　private life 93–4
　production of memoir 72
　public life 89–90

religious beliefs 81, 82, 83
sense of self 102–4
The Theory of Intuitive Morals 88
travels 88
working life 61, 88, 89
Coffey, Ray 230
collaborations with authors
   'British World' autobiographies
      225, 226, 230–2
   eighteenth-century autobiographies
      28–9
   nineteenth-century autobiographies
      61–2, 65, 71, 72
   twentieth-century autobiographies
      174–6
Comte, August 102
confessions of criminals 26
Connell, Lisa 63
'consciousness-raising' 165
Cook, Daniel 22
Cookson, Catherine
   childhood 182–4, 187
   domestic service 200
   education 183, 184
   justifications for autobiography 165
   therapeutic value of writing 171–2
   writing group 165, 172
copyright 24, 63, 231
corporal punishment 235–6
Coullie, Julie 224–5, 256
courtesans 60, 62, 85–6
   see also Phillips, Constantia;
      Wilson, Harriette
coverture, laws of 42
Crimean War 68, 98–9
criminal penitents 26
Croft, Andy 120
cross-dressing 32, 35–6, 52
cruelty of parents 34, 35, 39, 71, 181,
   235–6
Crutchley, Leigh 175
Culley, Amy 22

Danahay, Martin 4–5
Davies, Peter 175
Daymond, Margaret 254
Dayus, Kathleen
   adolescence 190
   childhood 185–6

   children, separation from 200
   intermediaries, helped by 175–6
   justifications for autobiography 168
   mother, relationship with 187
   working life 202
'democratisation of literature' 164
deprivation 120, 124, 125
Dictionary of National Biography 33,
   54
discipline 235–6
discrimination against women 15, 220,
   222
   see also apartheid policies; racial
      discrimination
doctors 36
domestic labour 184, 187, 235, 239
domestic service 190–1, 200–2, 250, 251
domestic violence 244, 245
Dorr, Rheta Childe 113–14
Drabble, Margaret 264
Driver, Dorothy 223
Dublin 31

Eakin, John Paul 4
earnings of authors 30, 31, 32–3, 89,
   90
editors, role of 65, 69, 226, 230–2
education
   'British World' autobiographies
      237–41
   eighteenth-century autobiographies
      36
   nineteenth-century autobiographies
      78–9, 80, 96–7, 101–2
   twentieth-century, earlier
      autobiographies 112, 122,
      127–30, 151
   twentieth century, later
      autobiographies 181, 183,
      184–5, 186, 191–2
   see also adult education; literacy
Egyptian writers *see* El Saadawi,
   Nawal
eighteenth-century autobiographies
   11–12, 19–55
   features of 19–24
   production of 24–33
   selfhood 48–53
   shaping a life 33–48

INDEX

Eliot, George 6, 58
Emecheta, Buchi
  career 174
  childhood 234
  marriage 198–9
  therapeutic value of writing 168, 174
  working life 205–6
eminent women 58–9
employment *see* working women
enslaved people 60, 65–8, 147
exiles 226–7

family breakdown 125
family dynamics 179–80
family histories 69, 113
family memoirs 261
father-daughter relationships 185
fathers
  anthology of 176
  belittling by 123
  care of 103, 119
  cruelty of 39, 189
  deceased 87, 88, 137, 233
  extramarital relationships of 134–5
  illness of 237
  support of 131
  weakness of 34
  see also Cibber, Colley
Fawcett, Millicent Garrett 114, 147–8
Fawcett, Philippa 148
fears 171–2
female genital mutilation 242, 243
feminine norms 60, 89
feminism 155, 165, 213
feminist autobiographies 73, 112–15
feminist networks 225, 226
fiction, influence of *see* novels, influence of
fiction, relationship to memoir 263–4
fictional material 178–9
Fielding, Henry 25, 47
  Pasquin 47
films 174
financial independence 86
  see also working women
financial support, need for 42, 45, 61, 62
  see also earnings of authors
Finney, Brian 212

First World War 110–11, 115–17
Foakes, Grace 193
Frame, Janet
  adolescence 189
  career 173
  film about 174
  novel 173
  reception of 173
  sense of self 210–11
  sexuality 193–4
  therapeutic value of writing 168, 172–3
  working life 203–5

Gagnier, Regina 158
Gamble, Rose 175
Gates, Henry Louis Jr. 65
gender, issues of 32, 156, 213, 216
Gentleman's Magazine, The 32
Gerard, Christine 35
Gibson, Anna 100
Golden Age of Autobiography 57
Gooch, Elizabeth 25, 35
Great War *see* First World War
Grimes, Mr 38, 38 n.64, 42
group areas acts 246
Gusdorf, Georges 3, 4

Hampton, Susan 231
hardships *see* struggle, lives of
Harrison, Rosina 175, 187, 190–1, 201, 202
health 78
Holden, Philip 221
Huggins, Rita 236, 247
husbands *see* marriages
Huxley, Elspeth, *The Flame Trees of Thika* 219–20

identity *see* modern identity; selfhood
illegitimacy 182, 214, 246, 247
imperial world 219–21
imprisonment 223–4, 226
income of authors *see* earnings of authors
independence
  from colonialism 221
  women's struggle for 135–41

Indigenous Australian women 220, 228–9, 231
  see also Huggins, Rita; Langford, Ruby; Morgan, Sally
individualism 3–4
indulgence by parents 36, 37
infamy, descent into 41–8
Ingrassia, Catherine 27–8
initiation of adolescents 242
instalments, publishing of 30, 31, 32, 62
intermediaries 174–6
  see also collaborations with authors
intimate relationships *see* relationships
introspection 2–3
It Takes All Sorts (BBC radio) 175

Jameson, Anna 77
Jameson, Storm 14
  age of author 111
  childhood 180–1
  education 181
  justifications for autobiography 169
  marriages 196–8
  motherhood 199
  reception of 169–70
  sense of self 207–8
  university, experience of 191
  working life 203
Jelinek, Estelle 7
Jermy, Louise 120, 124, 131, 140
Joannou, Maroula 110
John, Angela 150, 151
Johnstone, Julia 75
journalists 61, 70, 88
justifications for autobiography
  'British World' autobiographies 223–5, 226, 228, 229
  eighteenth-century autobiographies 27, 31
  nineteenth-century autobiographies 62, 68
  twentieth-century autobiographies 116–17, 167–8

Kenney, Annie 13
  age of author 111
  personal life 142
  production of memoir 115
  public life 148–9
  religious beliefs 131
  self-effacement 157, 158
  working-class background 120
Kenya 219–20
Kenyan writers *see* Otieno, Wambui Waiyaki
Kuhn, Annette 178
Kuzwayo, Ellen 222
  adolescence 241–2
  childhood 233–4, 235
  education 238
  family life 246
  marriage 245–6
  production of memoir 223–6, 232
  religious beliefs 241–2
  sense of self 256–7
  violence in the community 252
  working life 251

La Touche, Mme. 28
Langford, Ruby
  adolescence 243–4
  childhood 236–7
  education 240–1
  family life 247–8
  production of memoir 229, 230–2
  sense of self 255–6
League of Nations 151–2
Leeson, Margaret 35, 39
Leighton, Roland 143–4
lesbian relationships 93–4
lesbianism 194–5
Lessing, Doris
  adolescence 188
  childhood 181–2
  justifications for autobiography 167–8
  marriages 199
  sense of self 208–10
  sexuality 194
  working life 205
literacy 35
literary influences 25–6
literary relationships 25, 41
literary style 64
literature as a profession 20
Lloyd, Helen 170
Lloyd, Mary 93–4

Lobban-Viravong, Heather 52
Loftus, Donna 5
loss, issue of 23
Lumley-Saunderson, Thomas, 3rd Earl of Scarborough 38 n.64
Lytton, Constance 114

MacDonald, Helen 264
Mackay, Carol 104
Magona, Sindiwe *218*, 222
   adolescence 241–2
   childhood 233, 234, 235
   education 238–9
   family life 246–7
   religious beliefs 241–2
   sense of self 258–9
   violence in the community 253
   working life 249–50
Mannin, Ethel 14
   age of author 111
   career 120–1
   childhood 125
   education 128–30
   personal life 145–6
   religious beliefs 130–1
   sexual knowledge 134
Mansbridge, Alison 226
Mantel, Hilary 263
marketing 63
marriages
   'British World' autobiographies 244–9
   eighteenth-century autobiographies 38, 39–41, 42–3, 45, 46, 49
   nineteenth-century autobiographies 90, 94–5
   twentieth-century, earlier autobiographies 137, 138, 140, 141–2, 144–5, 146
   twentieth-century, later autobiographies 192, 193, 194, 195–200
Martineau, Harriet 56
   adolescence 80
   and Charlotte Brontë 101
   childhood 71, 78–9, 101
   collaborations 71
   duty to write 58, 70
   education 78–9, 101–2

   engagement 91
   health 78
   Household Education 77
   importance of 12, 70
   private life 91–3
   publication of 70–1
   reception of 71
   religious beliefs 81–3, 102
   sense of self 99, 101–2
   working life 61, 70, 87–8
   writing processes 70, 71
Mascuch, Michael 26
masculine roles 36
Mashinini, Emma, production of memoir 226
Mason, Mary 7
Mass Observation 164
Mayhall, Laura 114
media *see* films; radio programmes
medical profession 36
memoir 9, 261–2
   see also autobiography; women's autobiography, history of
menstruation 189, 243
micro-histories 166
middle-class women
   childhood 122, 180
   education 79–80
   marriage 195
   sexual ignorance 134
   working lives 86–7, 202–3
Mill, Harriet Taylor 5
Mill, John Stuart 3–4, 5, 119
Miller, Carolyn 105
Mitchell, Sally 72–3
Mitchison, Naomi 14
   justifications for autobiography 168–9
   marriage 198
   private life 171
   sense of self 170–1
   sexual ignorance 193
   university, experience of 191–2
   working life 202–3
modern identity 3–4
Morgan, Sally 222–3
   childhood 237
   education 240
   production of memoir 228–9, 230

sense of self 254–5
working lives 251
mother-daughter relationships
  earlier autobiographies 125–6,
    137–8, 139–40
  later autobiographies 180–1, 181–4,
    187, 188, 190, 197, 198
motherhood 199–200, 214, 256
mothers 34, 35, 71, 79, 91–2
  see also single mothers; stepmothers
motivation of authors see justifications
    for autobiography
Muilman, Henry 29, 42–3, 44, 49
Murray, John 64, 72
Myers, Mitzi 83, 102

Namhila, Ellen Ndeshi 222
  childhood 234, 235–6
  education 239
  marriage 248–9
  production of memoir 226–7
Namibian writers see Namhila, Ellen
    Ndeshi
'national autobiographies' 221
necessarianism 82–3
Neeley, Kathryn 72
Nehru, Jawaharlal 221
New Woman novels 94
Newman, J. H. 3–4
Ni Ghriofa, Doireann 264
Nigerian writers see Emecheta, Buchi
nineteenth-century autobiographies
    3–5, 12–13, 57–105
  features of 57–61
  production of memoir 61–75
  selfhood 95–105
  shaping a life 75–95
Nord, Deborah 117, 118, 119, 143
novelists 14, 120–1, 163, 262–4
  see also Cookson, Catherine;
    Emecheta, Buchi; Frame, Janet;
    Jameson, Storm; Lessing,
    Doris; Mitchison, Naomi
novels
  and ideas of child psychiatry 77
  influence of 21, 25–6, 53, 57, 94,
    99–101, 152–3
nursemaids 123
Nussbaum, Felicity 22, 23, 52

Oakley, Ann 178–9, 185, 189–90, 192,
    212–13
O'Brien, Edna 263
Oliphant, Margaret 71
Olney, James 67
Oppenheimer, Harry 224
'ordinary' women 164
Otieno, Wambui Waiyaki 221
  adolescence 242
  childhood 235
  education 239–40
  marriage 228, 249
  production of memoir 227–8, 230,
    232
  working life 252
Ouditt, Sharon 176
outcasts 41–8
Owen, Ursula 176, 177

pacifism 151
Pankhurst, Christabel 148–9, 157
Pankhurst, Emmeline 113–14
  children 148
  public life 147, 148
paratexts in autobiographies 27–8, 66,
    72, 178–9
parents
  alternatives to 233, 235–6
  cruelty of 34, 35, 71, 181, 187, 197
  efforts of 79, 235
  indulgence of 36, 37
  influence of 91–2, 123
  see also Cibber, Colley; fathers;
    mother-daughter
    relationships; mothers
pastimes 261, 264
periods see menstruation
personal hygiene 189
personal lives 141–6
  see also marriages; private lives
personality see selfhood
Peterson, Linda 67, 69, 70
Pethick-Lawrence, Emmeline 115,
    122–3, 143
Phillips, Constantia *18*
  Apology of Constantia Phillips 21
  childhood 34
  collaborations 29
  earnings 30

financial support, need for 42
justifications for autobiography 27
literary influences 26
marriage 42–3, 44, 49
paratexts 27
production of memoir 24
publishing process 29–30
relationships of 23, 43–4
selfhood, lack of sense of 50
sexual initiation 38–9
translations 30
Phillips, Mark Salber 22
physical violence 124, 181, 235–6
Pilkington, Laetitia
adolescence 38
childhood 34–5
collaborations 28–9
earnings 31
fall from grace 21, 44–5
hardships of 45–6
and Jonathan Swift 41
justifications for autobiography 27
literary relationships 25, 41
marriage 40–1, 45, 46
Memoirs of Laetitia Pilkington 21
novels, influence of 26
poems 27–8
selfhood, lack of sense of 50–1
subscribers, sought by 30–1
writing by 24
Pilkington, Matthew 40–1, 44, 46
pirating of books 62–3
poems in autobiographies 27–8
political autobiographies 221–3
poverty *see* deprivation
Powell, Margaret
and the BBC 175
childhood 186, 187
domestic service 190, 191, 200–1, 202
education 186
pregnancy 240, 244, 246
Presley, Cora Ann 232
Prince, Mary
amanuensis, use of 65, 66
childhood 76
editing of story 65–6

The History of Mary Prince . . . 60
lawsuits 67
slave narrative 60, 65
status of autobiography 67
success of 66
Pringle, Thomas 65–6, 67
prisoners 223–4, 226
'private life' 3
private lives
nineteenth-century autobiographies 91–3, 93–4, 94–5
twentieth-century autobiographies 111, 141–6, 171
promotion 63
pronouns 59
propriety 6, 10, 32, 60
prostitutes 6, 21, 133
see also courtesans
psychiatry *see* child psychiatry
psychic dimension of class 183
psychoanalysis 125–6, 153, 167
psychology 77, 99–100, 153
see also family dynamics
puberty 242
public figures 58–9, 89–90
public life 109–10, 147–52
publishers 112, 165, 176–7
publishing, eighteenth century 24, 29–30
Purvis, June 113, 114

racial discrimination 250
see also apartheid policies
racism against women 15, 98
radio programmes 175
Ravenscroft, Alison 231
reasons for autobiographies *see* justifications for autobiography
reception of autobiographies
'British World' autobiographies 259–60
eighteenth-century autobiographies 12, 22, 26, 32
nineteenth-century autobiographies 68–9, 71
twentieth-century autobiographies 169–70, 173
see also success of autobiographies

Rehder, Robert 52
relationships
   eighteenth-century autobiographies 23, 43–4, 46–7
   nineteenth-century autobiographies 90–5
   twentieth-century autobiographies 112, 125, 141–6
   see also literary relationships; marriages; sexual activities
religious beliefs
   'British World' autobiographies 241–2
   nineteenth-century autobiographies
      of Annie Besant 74–5, 83–5, 104–5
      of Frances Cobb 83
      of Harriet Martineau 81–3, 102
   twentieth-century autobiographies 130–2
      of Beatrice Webb 127, 131–2
remuneration of authors see earnings of authors
residential laws 246
'revisionist autobiography' 178
Rhondda, Margaret Haig Thomas, Viscountess 128, 133, 142, 150–1
Richardson, Samuel, *Pamela* 21, 26
Rita, Auntie see Huggins, Rita
Robinson, Mary 24, 29
Rosenthal, Laura 22
Rousseau, Jean Jacques, *Confessions* 1–2
Rowse, Tim 255, 256
Rudd, John 176
Russell, Bertrand 196
Russell, Dora 191, 196

El Saadawi, Nawal 222, 243, 244–5, 249
Sage, Lorna 178, 179–80
Salih, Sarah 66
same-sex relationships 93–4
Sargeson, Frank 204
scandalous autobiographies 21–3, 60
Scarborough, Thomas Lumley-Saunderson, 3rd Earl of 38 n.64

schools 79, 127–8, 129
   see also education
scientists 72
Scott, Sir Walter 64
Seacole, Mary
   childhood 76, 80
   justifications for autobiography 68
   reception of 68–9
   sense of self 97–9
   The Wonderful Adventures of Mary Seacole 61
   working life 87
Second World War 164
seduction of women 20–1
selfhood 2–4, 7
   'British World' autobiographies 253–9
   eighteenth-century autobiographies 48–53
   nineteenth-century autobiographies 95–105
   twentieth-century, earlier autobiographies 118–19, 152–8
   twentieth century, later autobiographies 169–70, 178, 206–14, 216–17
serial publications 30, 31, 32, 62
Setzer, Sharon 64
sexual activities
   eighteenth-century autobiographies 21–2, 37–9
   nineteenth-century autobiographies 65, 66–7, 85–6
   twentieth-century autobiographies 145
sexual ignorance 94, 192, 193, 243–4
sexual knowledge 6, 13–14, 112, 132, 190, 240, 242
sexuality 132–5, 192–5
Sharp, Evelyn 128, 142, 149, 150
Sheridan, Dorothy 164
Shuttleworth, Sally 77, 99, 100
single mothers 246, 247
slave narratives 60, 65–8
   see also Prince, Mary
Smith, Sidonie 52
Smollett, Tobias, *Peregrine Pickle* 25, 28

Smyth, Ethel 1
Somerville, Mary
    collaborations 72
    Recollections of Mary Somerville 72
South Africa
    apartheid policies 237–8, 246, 249–50, 252
    education 237–8
    Soweto 225, 252
South African writers *see* Kuzwayo, Ellen; Magona, Sindiwe
Spacks, Patricia Meyer 53
Spedding, Patrick 30
Stage Licensing Act (1737) 47
Steedman, Carolyn
    childhood 183–4, 187
    on Kathleen Woodward 120, 126, 177
    sense of self 213–14
    stories, use of in autobiography 179, 183–4
    university, experience of 192
Stephen, Leslie 57
stepmothers 34, 124
Stockdale, John Joseph 62–3
Strachey, Ray 114
Strickland, Susan 66
struggle, lives of 41–8, 135–41, 174, 207
subscribers to autobiographies 30–1
success of autobiographies 30–1, 60, 63, 117
    see also reception of autobiographies
suffrage 110
suffragette autobiographies 13, 110, 112–15, 147–51, 157
Suffragette Fellowship 115
Suleri, Sara 223, 229
summary publications 32
Swanwick, Helena
    childhood 123
    education 127–8, 130
    independence, struggle for 137–8
    inner conflict 154
    marriage 138, 143
    public life 151–2
    religious beliefs 131

sense of self 155
sexual knowledge 132
Swift, Jonathan 25, 31, 41

Tartufe 43–4
teenagers 187–92
    see also adolescence
theatrical world 46–7
Theism 83, 85
Theosophy 74–5, 85, 104–5
therapeutic value of writing 167, 168, 171–2, 231, 256
Thomas, Margaret Haig, 2nd Viscountess Rhondda 128, 133, 142, 150–1
Thomas, Sue 66
Thompson, Linda 36
Titmuss, Richard 185
Tonna, Charlotte Elizabeth 76–7, 81, 90
trades 47–8
translations of autobiographies 30, 63
trauma and autobiography 220–1, 261
    see also imprisonment
travel writing 68
Tremain, Rose 262, 263
tribal initiation practices 242
tribal issues 228
Turley, Hans 32
twentieth century, earlier autobiographies 13–15, 109–60
    features of 109–12
    production of 112–21
    selfhood 118–19, 152–8
    shaping a life 121–52
twentieth century, later autobiographies 163–217
    features of 163–7
    production of 167–79
    selfhood 169–70, 178, 206–14, 216–17
    shaping a life 179–206
twenty-first-century autobiographies 261–5

Unitarianism 83
university 130, 191–2

Vane, Frances, Viscountess
    adolescence 38
    childhood 35, 37
    collaborations 28
    literary relationships 25
    marriages 39–40
    The Memoirs of a Lady of Quality, 21, 25, 28
Vaughan, Ruth 226
victims, status as 49
Victorian autobiographies 69–70
    see also nineteenth-century autobiographies
Vincent, David 119
violence 220–1, 252–3
    see also domestic violence; physical violence
Virago Press 165, 176–7

war diaries and memoirs 116
wars 220–1
    see also Crimean War; First World War; Second World War
Webb, Beatrice 13, *108*
    age of author 111
    childhood 122
    education 127
    First World War and 117
    independence, struggle for 135–7
    inner conflict 153–4, 155
    marriage 142–3
    process of writing 117–18
    religious beliefs 127, 131–2
    selfhood 118–19
Webb, Sidney 117, 142–3
Whitlock, Gillian 65, 256
'whore biographies' 62
    see also courtesans; prostitutes
Whyte, Samuel 32–3
Wilson, Elizabeth 177, 178, 194–5, 211–12
Wilson, Frances 86
Wilson, Harriette
    and Byron 64
    childhood, not described 75–6
    collaboration with Stockdale 62–3
    as courtesan 85–6
    education 96–7
    financial support, need for 61, 62

intimate life 90
    justifications for autobiography 62
    lawsuits 63
    literary style 64
    sense of self 96–7
    success of 60, 63
Winterson, Jeanette 263–4
Witwatersrand University 224
Wolpert, Elizabeth 225, 226
Women of Letters 20
women's autobiography, history of
    eighteenth century 19–24
    nineteenth century 57–61, 69–70, 72
    twentieth century, earlier 109–12, 118
    twentieth century, later 163–7, 177–9, 215–16
    twenty-first century 261–5
women's autobiography, introduction to
    approaches to 7–8
    changes in 8–9
    diversity of 8
    feminist readings of 6–7
    form of 6, 7
    history of 6, 10, 11–15
    'other voice' in 7, 8
    texts, selection of 11–12
Women's Press 165, 225, 226
women's rights 73, 113, 151–2
women's suffrage 110
Woodward, Kathleen
    childhood 124
    independence, struggle for 141
    introduction to *Jipping Street* 177
    mother-daughter relationship 126
    sense of self 158
    working-class background 119–20
Woolf, Virginia 1, 45, 111
working-class women
    adolescence 190
    childhood 180–1, 182–4, 185–7
    domestic service 200–2
    earlier autobiographies 119–20
    education 128
    intermediaries and 174–6
    later autobiographies 163

parental manipulation 139–41
poverty 124
psychic dimension of class 183
religious beliefs 131
sense of self 156–7, 158
sexual ignorance 193
sexuality 194
working women
   'British World' autobiographies 246–7, 249–53
   eighteenth-century autobiographies 24–5, 32, 37–8, 46–8
   nineteenth-century autobiographies 60–1, 68, 85–9
   twentieth-century, earlier autobiographies 110–11, 116, 120–1, 124–5
   twentieth-century, later autobiographies 184, 190–1, 200–6
   see also courtesans; domestic service; slave narratives
World War I *see* First World War
writers of colour *see* Emecheta, Buchi
writing, by women 20, 166–7, 229–30
writing groups 164–5, 172
writing processes 28, 63–4, 112, 167, 171–2